# Montréal & Québec City

## FOR

# DUMMIES®

### 3RD EDITION

## by Austin Macdonald

John Wiley & Sons Canada, Ltd.

**Montréal & Québec City For Dummies,® 3rd Edition**

Published by
**John Wiley & Sons Canada, Ltd.**
6045 Freemont Boulevard
Mississauga, Ontario, L5R 4J3
www.wiley.com

**Library and Archives Canada Cataloguing in Publication**

Macdonald, Austin

　　　Montréal & Québec City for dummies / Austin Macdonald. — 3rd ed.
Includes index.

ISBN 978-0-470-15338-3

　　　1. Montréal (Québec)—Guidebooks. 2. Québec (Québec)—Guidebooks.

I. Title. II. Title: Montréal and Québec City for dummies.
FC2947.18.M33 2008　　　　917.14'28045　　　　C2008-900899-5

Printed in Canada

1 2 3 4 5 TRI 12 11 10 09 08

Distributed in Canada by John Wiley & Sons Canada, Ltd.

For general information on John Wiley & Sons Canada, Ltd., including all books published by Wiley Publishing, Inc., please call our warehouse, Tel 1-800-567-4797. For reseller information, including discounts and premium sales, please call our sales department, Tel 416-646-7992. For press review copies, author interviews, or other publicity information, please contact our marketing department, Tel 416-646-4584, Fax 416-236-4448.

For authorization to photocopy items for corporate, personal, or educational use, please contact in writing The Canadian Copyright Licensing Agency (Access Copyright). For an Access Copyright license, visit www.accesscopyright.ca or call toll free 1-800-893-5777.

WILEY

# About the Author

**Austin Macdonald** (austin_macdonald@yahoo.com) first came to Montréal for school. For three summers, while studying English Literature at McGill University, he worked as a tour guide in both Montréal and Québec City. Since teaching English in Tokyo, counting down the millennium in Rio, and having a series of misadventures in the dot-com world, Austin has been working as a freelance writer concerned with urban affairs at large. His work has been published in magazines such as *Art and Antiques*, *Toronto Life*, and *Azure* and in newspapers, including *Globe and Mail*, the *National Post*, and the *Montréal Gazette*.

# Publisher's Acknowledgments

We're proud of this book; please send us your comments at canadapt@wiley.com. Some of the people who helped bring this book to market include

### Acquisitions, Editorial, and Media Development

**Executive Editor:** Robert Hickey

**Associate Editor:** Gene Shannon

**Copy Editor:** Kelli Howey

**Cartographer:** Mapping Specialists

**Front Cover Photo:**
© Richard Cummins/Lonely Planet Images. Description: A restaurant in Old Montréal.

**Back Cover Photo:** © Stuart Gregory/ Getty Images.

Description: Chateau Frontenac at dusk.

**Cartoons:** Rich Tennant (www.the5thwave.com)

### Composition

**Vice President Publishing Services:** Karen Bryan

**Publishing Services Manager:** Ian Koo

**Project Manager:** Elizabeth McCurdy

**Production Coordinator:** Lynsey Stanford

**Layout and Graphics:** Stacie Brooks, Carl Byers, Christine Williams

**Proofreaders:** Laura Albert, Cara Buitron, David Faust

**Indexer:** Claudia Bourbeau

---

### John Wiley & Sons Canada, Ltd.

**Bill Zerter,** Chief Operating Officer

**Jennifer Smith,** Vice-President and Publisher, Professional and Trade Division

### Publishing and Editorial for Consumer Dummies

**Diane Graves Steele,** Vice President and Publisher, Consumer Dummies

**Joyce Pepple,** Acquisitions Director, Consumer Dummies

**Kristin A. Cocks,** Product Development Director, Consumer Dummies

**Michael Spring,** Vice President and Publisher, Travel

**Kelly Regan,** Editorial Director, Travel

### Publishing for Technology Dummies

**Andy Cummings,** Vice President and Publisher, Dummies Technology/ General User

### Composition Services

**Gerry Fahey,** Vice President of Production Services

**Debbie Stailey,** Director of Composition Services

# Contents at a Glance

# Maps at a Glance

# Table of Contents

# Introduction

*E*uropean flair and French *joie de vivre* — you'll definitely find these elusive old-world qualities in Montréal and Québec City.

Visiting Montréal is like escaping into a little corner of Europe, except that you don't have to cross the Atlantic to get here. And Montréal doesn't feel European only because life and business is carried out mostly in French. Things really are different here. People eat later (and, may I add, better), they party differently (ditto), and life is infused with a touch of European style. Montréalers seem to keep one eye on Paris all the time.

Visiting Québec City is like slipping into the past without actually leaving the present. One of the oldest, most picturesque cities in North America, Québec City has preserved all its historic charm while hanging on to its vibrant and distinct culture.

To give you a better idea, the whole province of Québec consumes half the wine sold in all of Canada. Yet Québec is only about 20 percent of the country's total population. Although the rest of Canada's colonial roots are English, Protestant, and Anglo-Saxon, in Québec the French arrived first, making many people's roots Catholic and Latin. So life's bound to be a little different in many ways in this still-predominantly-French-speaking corner of the world.

Yet make no mistake. Both cities have their feet firmly planted in North America. Distinct as they are, Montréal and Québec City feel familiar, too: The road system looks similar, telephones work the same way, and people here smile at strangers. You'll feel a *je ne sais quoi* about both cities, but people here won't seem as foreign as the people you meet when traveling to another part of the world.

## About This Book

By no means is *Montréal & Québec City For Dummies,* 3rd Edition, an encyclopedia about the two cities. Although I've scoured both cities, this book highlights the *best* — not the *most* — of each. It's the insider information and street knowledge you need to know to make savvy decisions during your trip. I assume you have only so much time and need to cut to the chase. With that in mind, I've organized the chapters to answer your questions roughly in the order they pop up — from figuring out whether you really want to visit these cities to knowing when to go, planning a budget, deciding where to stay and eat, and figuring out what to see and do.

Of course, you may not have the same questions in the same order, so feel free to jump ahead and read the chapters in any order you want. Who am I to judge? In these pages, you find a fair bit more information about Montréal than Québec City, but that's not because I'm choosing favorites. Montréal is a much bigger city, with much more to see and do (and many more places to eat!). To give you the best of Montréal, I have to give you more. However, if you decide to skip Montréal, don't worry, because I cover all the bases in Québec City, too.

**Remember:** Travel information is a dicey game — things change — particularly prices. So, take heed; be sure to call ahead for confirmation, especially of such essential matters as your travel and lodging reservations. Once on-site, you have a little more leeway to improvise. Please keep in mind: the authors, editors, and publisher can't be held responsible for the experiences of readers while traveling. Your safety is important to us, however, so I encourage you to stay alert and be aware of your surroundings. Generally, keep a close eye on cameras, purses, and wallets — all favorite targets of thieves and pickpockets in cities worldwide.

# Conventions Used in This Book

*Montréal & Québec City For Dummies,* 3rd Edition, uses a few conventions to help you find information quickly.

All prices in this book are shown in Canadian dollars. At the time of this writing, the Canadian dollar was equivalent in value to the U.S. greenback. This may change by the time you read this and when you travel to these cities.

In the hotel sections, the prices I give are the *rack rates* (the official rates the hotel publicizes) for one night for a double room, during the high season of tourism: May to October. The price you end up paying may be significantly lower if you travel off season or with a package deal.

In the restaurant sections, I give you the price range of a main course at each establishment. In most cases, these are the prices of dinner entrees, but if a restaurant doesn't serve dinner, I give you the price of a lunch entree.

I also use dollar-sign symbols ($) in both the hotel and restaurant sections. These signs give you the price range of a night's stay at a hotel (nondiscounted, standard rates) or a restaurant meal (including tip). Check out the table that follows to decipher the dollar signs.

| Cost | Hotels | Restaurants |
|------|--------|-------------|
| $ | Less than C$100 | Less than C$20 |
| $$ | C$100–C$199 | C$20–C$39 |
| $$$ | C$200–C$299 | C$40–C$59 |
| $$$$ | C$300 or above | C$60 or above |

I also use abbreviations for credit cards, so that you can quickly see how you can pay for hotels and restaurants. They are:

**AE:** American Express

**DC:** Diner's Club

**DISC:** Discover

**MC:** MasterCard

**V:** Visa

In addition, I keep the addresses of hotels, restaurants, and attractions in French, because that's what you'll see on street signs — I hope this simplifies finding your way around. Here's the rundown of French street terminology:

| French Term | U.S. Equivalent |
|-------------|-----------------|
| *Rue* | Street |
| *Bd.* | Boulevard |
| *Av.* | Avenue |
| *Est* | East |
| *Ouest* | West |
| *Nord* | North |
| *Sud* | South |

You may sometimes see the odd street name starting with *place*. Some street names also start with *côte*, which means hill, so at least you know what to expect before you get there. (Don't worry, though, most hills are just gentle slopes.) Also, many streets are named for saints, whose given names are preceded by *Ste* (for female saints) or *St* (for male saints). *Vieux* means "old," as in *Vieux-Montréal* and *Vieux-Québec,* the older sections of the cities, which are loaded with history and character.

I also keep names of buildings and sites in French, except where they are very frequently referred to in English.

Otherwise, I translate French words and expressions into English as much as possible. However, some terms just don't translate very well, and when that happens, I leave the words in French and put them in italics. For a list of handy French expressions, see the Cheat Sheet at the front of this book.

For those hotels, restaurants, and attractions that are plotted on a map, a page reference is provided in the listing information. If a hotel, restaurant, or attraction is outside the city limits or in an out-of-the-way area, it may not be mapped.

## Foolish Assumptions

I make a few assumptions about you, dear reader. You probably fall into one or more of these categories:

- ✓ **You're a first-time visitor to Montréal or Québec City.** Or you stopped here briefly, say, on business, got a taste of it, and want to come back for more. I don't want to give you a comprehensive course on these cities. I simply show you how to enjoy them best with the least amount of planning and painstaking research possible.

- ✓ **You're busy.** Perhaps you're an experienced traveler, but you don't have a ton of time to spend planning a trip, or you don't have loads of time to spend in Montréal and Québec City after you get there. You want expert advice on how to maximize your time and enjoy a hassle-free trip.

- ✓ **You don't want to spend your entire trip reading a guidebook.** This book is a quick and easy read, focusing on the very best that Montréal and Québec City have to offer. It's also a reliable reference for a quick recommendation while on-the-fly, booting around town.

## How This Book Is Organized

*Montréal & Québec City For Dummies,* 3rd Edition, is both a planning guide to help you prepare for your trip and a travel guide that gives you all the information you need to have an interesting and fun stay that doesn't break the bank. As such, this book is organized into five parts.

### Part 1: Introducing Montréal and Québec City

Right out of the gate I introduce you to the very best of Montréal and Québec City. I describe the main attractions for each city, tell you what the weather is like, and give you ideas of what's going on throughout the year.

## Part II: Planning Your Trip to Montréal and Québec City

I tell you how much everything costs, give you tips on how to plan a budget, and help you decide whether to use cash, credit, traveler's checks, or ATMs. From the advice in this chapter, you'll be able to decide on the best way to travel to Montréal and Québec City. Finally, I give specialized advice for gay and lesbian travelers, people traveling with kids, travelers with disabilities, and senior citizens.

## Part III: Settling Into and Exploring Montréal

I start this part by explaining what to do when you arrive in Montréal and where to get the information you need to visit the city. Here is where you'll begin to familiarize yourself with the different Montréal neighborhoods. The chapters in this part also list the best hotels, restaurants, attractions, and shopping in the city. I then cover the best nightspots in Montréal and also describe the best daytrips, in case you want to get out of the city for an afternoon.

## Part IV: Settling Into and Exploring Québec City

Here, I describe the Québec City neighborhoods you want to spend time exploring. I also give you a list of my top hotel picks, recommend what to see and do, and direct you to the best food in town — whether you want fine French cuisine or a simple pizza. Finally, I suggest some sample itineraries that let you explore different themes in the city.

## Part V: The Part of Tens

One thing to never forget when you travel is your sense of humor. In this part, I tell you how to have fun in Montréal and Québec City. Some of my advice is practical. Some of it is whimsical — just an indirect way of poking fun at the cities and their inhabitants. You be the judge.

In the back of this book I've included an *appendix* — your Quick Concierge — with pages of handy information you may need once you've arrived, like phone numbers and addresses, emergency personnel, area hospitals and pharmacies, lists of local newspapers and magazines, protocol for sending mail or finding taxis, and more. Check out this section when searching for answers to the little questions that may come up as you travel. You can find Quick Concierge easily because it's printed on yellow paper.

# Icons Used in This Book

To help you find information as quickly and easily as possible, every *For Dummies* book includes a series of icons that serve as little road signs, alerting you to pleasures and dangers ahead — or just alerting you, period. In this book, I add an icon of my own to tell you what's really, truly, unique about this French-speaking corner of the continent.

 Keep an eye out for the Bargain Alert icon as you seek out money-saving tips and/or great deals.

 Best of the Best highlights the best the destination has to offer in all categories — hotels, restaurants, attractions, activities, shopping, and nightlife.

 Watch for the Heads Up icon to identify annoying or potentially dangerous situations such as tourist traps, unsafe neighborhoods, budgetary rip-offs, and other things to beware.

 Look to the Kid Friendly icon for attractions, hotels, restaurants, and activities that are particularly hospitable to children or people traveling with kids.

 Some of the sites, foods, and activities in Montréal and Québec City sum up what's unique about Québec. I don't want you to miss out on these or accidentally overlook them, so I flag them with this icon. *Vive la différence!*

 This icon alerts you to special, insider advice on everything from dealing with Québec's extreme weather to exchanging money and finding the best rate on accommodations.

## Where to Go from Here

Time to dig in and do some reading. You won't find any fixed rule about which chapters to read first. I've organized them in what I thought was a logical sequence, but you're free to wander in and out of them to your heart's content, in whatever order suits you. You may actually want to read about attractions and restaurants before you dig in to the nitty-gritty about planning a trip and buying air tickets — just to see what fun stuff is in store for you.

Don't worry, though. Regardless of the order in which you plan this trip, you'll be amply rewarded when you arrive. So start reading!

# Part I

# Introducing Montréal and Québec City

The 5th Wave    By Rich Tennant

"Here's something. It's a language school that will teach you to speak French for $500, or for $200 they'll just give you an accent."

## In this part . . .

This part will help you get a first taste of Montréal and Québec City. Dive right in and discover the best features of each city, learn about life in this French-speaking corner of North America, and find out what highlights you can expect over the course of a year. These are two wonderful destinations that will leave you with two distinct impressions of New France. Don't feel that one is a replacement for the other; ideally, try to experience both.

# Chapter 1

# Discovering the Best of Montréal and Québec City

*In This Chapter*

▶ Walking through the best neighborhoods

▶ Finding fantastic ways to spend your time in Québec

*M*ontréal is modern, fun, sexy, and sophisticated. It's a city with charisma, a place with flair. Even the people who live here think so. Is it the mix of French and North American cultures that is so appealing? Is it Montréal's tumultuous past as a battleground between English and French? Or is it just the great food and pulsing nights and the generally hedonistic ways of today's Montréalers? Actually, it's the combination of these and other qualities that give the city its unique beat.

In 2006, UNESCO named Montréal as a World Design City, one of three, part of a new network along with other creative capitals like Berlin and Buenos Aires. The honor is largely due to the striking examples of colonial, modern, and contemporary architecture juxtaposed against the skyline — from the neo-classical to the futuristic. Montréalers would like to think it's equally due to their collective tastes, attitudes, sensibilities, and swagger.

The economy of the world's second largest French-speaking city has seen a remarkable upturn over the last decade, so the city boasts more great restaurants, clubs, and attractions than ever. The city's festivals are getting bigger and more glamorous every year, attracting an amazing array of talent. The ever-multiplying stores and boutiques, from big names downtown to edgy boutiques on Vieux-Montréal side streets, mean that the shopping can be engrossing.

Tensions between English and French feel like ancient history now. And, best of all, this cultural and economic germination is really putting Montréalers in a good mood.

In 2008, Québec City celebrates its 400th anniversary, highlighting its status as one of the oldest cities in North America. It played a central role in the founding of French North America and is the last fortified city on the continent (think castle-like walls with turrets and arched gates). The celebrations should make it feel like a year-long carnival — *"le fun"* and *"le party,"* as the locals say.

Québec City's quaint cobblestone streets and impressive colonial architecture, with top-notch restaurants, beautiful vistas, and old-world charm, never go out of style. In fact, it's gaining popularity. In 2006, *Travel + Leisure* magazine ranked Québec City seventh in a top-ten list of North American cities, based on the results of its annual reader's poll. In 2007, it climbed to fifth. The city is quickly going from one of the best- to one of the worst-kept travel secrets around.

So there's never been a better time to visit, as Québec City matures from small town to North American city. Still, the net effect is *so* European — French, in fact. If while visiting you get swept up in the moment, you could easily forget which continent you are on.

And the city is in no danger of losing the title of North America's most romantic holiday destination. Just being in this fortified, cliff-top, port city is enough — although you can find plenty more to do than just soak up the view.

For a small city (600,000 people), it offers an impressive roster of cultural events, exhibitions, performances, festivals, and more. The booming economy through the province of Québec hasn't done its capital city any harm, either.

In the following pages I introduce you to the choicest parts of both cities.

## Montréal's Best Neighborhoods

**Vieux-Montréal** is a "must-see" for its yesteryear architecture and cobblestone streets. During the day, this bustling neighborhood is home to many businesses, boutiques, restaurants, and cafes. **Rue St-Paul** is the main shopping street. The establishments on **Place Jacques Cartier** have terraces that spill out onto the square, where there's always a busker shilling for the large crowds. Many gather and gaze in awe at the **Notre-Dame Basilica**. The **Old Port,** a boardwalk and green space along the riverfront, has many attractions and hosts special events throughout the year. By dark, Vieux-Montréal empties out somewhat, which makes it *very* romantic for the strolling couples whose steps echo down the streets. Increasingly, though, bars and lounges are setting up here, and it's in the early stages of becoming an exciting nightlife destination. From **Square Victoria** stroll down to the water on recently revamped **rue McGill.** The widened sidewalks now accommodate several clusters of street-side tables and chairs belonging to new bistros and cafes. Take the ferry to **Parc Jean Drapeau,** two islands in the St. Lawrence and site of the 1967 World Fair. The **Montréal Casino** is in the former French Pavilion.

**The Plateau** is Montréal's trendiest neighborhood and the epicenter of the city's pulse. Strut up **boulevard St-Laurent,** across **avenue Mont-Royal,** and down **avenue St-Denis** and you will have covered the Plateau's main commercial drags and seen some of what it's all about. You'll have difficulty passing yourself off as a local at first, but you, too, will immediately wish you were a *Plateauzard,* the name for the indigenous hipsters from this 'hood.

**Little Italy** is northeast of downtown, just beyond the Plateau neighborhood. The main attraction here is **Marché Jean Talon.** It's worth getting up early to catch all the morning hubbub of merchants setting up their stalls and haggling with shoppers over fresh produce and other local ingredients. (*Note:* See Chapter 10 for a brief discussion on the importance of *terroir,* locally grown specialty ingredients, on Montréal's restaurant scene.) The **Marché Atwater,** at the opposite end of the city, is not such a large-scale operation.

## Québec City's Best Neighborhoods

Québec City is much smaller than Montréal. In fact, at first glance, the whole seems happily contained in the **Haute-Ville** and **Basse-Ville,** the upper and lower parts of **Vieux-Québec.**

Step beyond the fortified walls to experience a more everyday version of Québec City, the province's capital. Exit the gate on **rue St-Jean.** Beyond, this street becomes a long commercial strip with many independent boutiques, cafes, and bars — fewer tourists and more locals going about their daily errands. Also outside the walls, **rue St-Louis** becomes **La Grande Allée,** which is Québec City's nightlife hub.

Several blocks farther in the same direction lies a cross-street, **avenue Cartier,** which is another charming district that's somewhat hidden from the tourists buzzing between sights. In the Basse-Ville, if you go past Place Royale you'll come to a narrow sliver of land between the cliff and the river — the three or four blocks in here are fun to troll. **Rue St-Paul** is Québec City's **"Antique Alley."** Farther along in the same direction, hidden away in the up-and-coming district of **St-Roch,** don't miss the shopping on **rue St-Joseph.** Once an undesirable part of town, this strip is now lined with destination boutiques, bustling bistros, and happening pubs.

## The Best Festivals and Events

The several days of festivities leading up to the **Canadian Grand Prix** in June are a screaming good time of high-octane excitement. Even if you have no interest in attending the race, the city shuts down several main drags such as **boulevard St. Laurent** and **rues Peel** and **Crescent.** The downtown is packed and everyone's parading about, posing for pictures with the fancy cars, excited by the onset of summer, and looking for a good time.

Shortly after, the entire city swings with the syncopated rhythms and soulful melodies of the **Montréal International Jazz Festival,** with more than 500 concerts taking place in just two weeks. It's considered the world's biggest and best (even Tony Bennett said so). Launched in 1980, its enduring popular success has to do with all the high-caliber, free programming on multiple stages in the closed streets surrounding **Place des Arts,** Montréal's performing arts complex.

Sundays during the summer **Piknic Électronik** is a daytime, outdoor dance party hosted by DJs spinning the latest electronica music, which attracts quite a crowd to a picturesque spot on **Île Ste. Hélèn.** Everyone gathers to dance and listen to music under a giant metallic, abstract statue that is several stories high. If that's not your bag, **Tam-tams** is a Sunday drum circle, gypsy market, and counter-culture gathering at the foot of the Mountain, in **Parc Mont-Royal.**

The **Winter Carnaval** is Québec City's signature event. Everyone's actively looking for ways to stay warm amid the ice and snow. Some revelers drink *caribou* (ca-REE-boo), a local booze concoction that dates back to the earliest settlers. There's also the **Festival d'été** (Summer Fest), featuring an eye-opening lineup of big-name contemporary musicians, bands, and other musical acts. Alt-rock and songsters play on stages spread around the city, in **Vieux-Québec** and in **St-Roch.**

See Chapter 3 for an expanded selection of the "best of" happenings on Montréal or Québec City's annual calendars.

# The Best Restaurants

Eating well will be a major theme of your trip to Québec. In the French tradition, food, drink, and merrymaking are major concerns of the people here.

**Au Pied de Cochon,** which opened in 2002, remains one of the most exciting destinations on Montréal's culinary landscape. **Toqué!, Bonanotte,** and **Moishe's** are top-dollar places serving the very best. However, Montréal's restaurant scene is so varied that there's plenty of feasting for any budget.

Bistros **L'Express, Café du Nouveau Monde,** and **Chez l'Épicier** are favorites among foodies for continental dishes with French flair.

Montréal's restaurant scene reflects the many ethnic communities that make up its population. Numerous restaurants specialize in different cuisines from around the globe. Some of the most popular are also great values, such as **La Maison du Kebab, Rôtisserie Italienne,** and **Pushap**

Sweets (Indian). **Schwartz's,** a Hebrew deli, is a must for the city's best "smoked meat" (Montréal's much-better version of corned beef or pastrami).

Also, don't miss stopping in at **L'Avenue, Le Cartet,** or **Le Reservoir** for snazzy brunches on weekends.

Québec City is heavy on French food, with lots of small bistros doing escargot, steak frites, crème brûlée, and other brasserie-type staples. **Café du Monde** and **L'Ardoise** are two notables among them. **L'Utopie, Largo,** and **Laurie-Raphaël** are some of the locals' favorite new restaurants that break with Old World tradition. Québec City's finest tables include **Le Paris-Brest, Le Saint-Amour,** and **Initiale.** A great spot for a casual meal is **Chez Victor,** which has the best burgers in town.

# The Best Attractions

The **Musée d'Archéologie et d'Histoire de Montréal** and the **Canadian Centre for Architecture** are two of the city's best museums. Both are quite unusual by regular museum standards, and they reveal lots about Montréal. Of course, the **Musée des Beaux-Arts de Montréal** is the spot for culture vultures to get their fine-arts fix. Many visitors can't resist the temptation of winning big money at the **Casino de Montréal.** Winter or summer, **Parc Mont-Royal** attracts the fitness- or leisure-conscious. Visitors to Montréal should hike up to the lookout atop the Mountain — it's not that high or that steep, and the views are worth it. The penguins at the **Biodome** are always a favorite with the kids.

In Québec City, locals call the **Château Frontenac** — atop the cliff overlooking the St. Lawrence River — **Québec's Eiffel Tower;** and indeed it is — everyone goes to see it. Behind this famous hotel is **La Citadel,** a fortress that defended this hotly contested port city over the course of its history. Weather permitting, you can witness the **Changing of the Guard,** a procession of expressionless redcoat soldiers in tall fur hats — oddly enough, just like the ones in England. Behind it lie the **Parc des Champs-de-Bataille** and the **Plains of Abraham,** where the decisive battle between the French and English for the fate of colonial New France took place. In the Basse-Ville at the bottom of the cliff is the **Musée de la Civilisation,** featuring engaging exhibits on the first settlers and the Native American people who were already here. Beyond the Plains of Abraham is the **Musée du Québec,** which, along with its permanent collection, hosts temporary exhibits of a surprisingly high caliber.

# The Best Nightlife

Montréal's just hitting its stride when the sun goes down. Kick off your evening with after-work drinks — called the *cinq à sept* in local lingo — at a brew pub, like **Le Reservoir,** or a martini lounge like **Jello Bar.** Step it up another notch or two after dinner by hitting such places as **Mile End** or **Newtown.** After midnight, if you're looking to dance, **Club 1234** qualifies as Montréal's most crowded dance floor of the moment. The **Society of Art and Technology** and **Casa del Popolo** provide other good options for a more alternative crowd.

Nights in Québec City aren't necessarily more sedate, just smaller in scale. Pubs and other intimate settings with lots of live music are what dominate the scene. The two exceptions are the megaclubs on the Grand Allée, **Chez Dagobert** and **Chez Maurice.** Many revelers spend their night hopping between the two. **Les Salons Edgar, Scanner Bistro Multimedia,** and **Boudoir** are three good alternatives in the St-Roch neighborhood just beyond the Basse-Ville.

# Chapter 2

# Digging Deeper into Montréal and Québec City

........................................................

........................................................

*I*n this chapter, I provide some background information. The aim of these easily digestible bites is to steady your footing, open your eyes, and prime your senses to discover the different possibilities that Montréal and Québec City offer.

## History 101: The Main Events

The cities of Montréal and Québec City boast fascinating histories. The following are some highlights from the annals of two of the oldest cities in North America.

### The French discovered Québec . . .

Looking for a quick passage to Asia, French explorer Jacques Cartier landed at the future site of Québec City in 1535. For some reason, he thought the ground was rich with diamonds. It wasn't, so he went back to France.

In 1608, another French explorer, Samuel de Champlain, founded a fur trading post in Québec, which attracted French settlers. The British captured the colony from France in 1759 and began to settle it with Irish, Scottish, and English immigrants and American Loyalists.

In the 19th century, when railroads began cutting into Québec's port business and economic prospects looked grim, the English-speaking population moved to Montréal, leaving Québec City almost entirely to French speakers.

### . . . and then Montréal

Jacques Cartier also discovered Montréal in 1535, but again, he left without making much of an impression. In 1641, the French explorer Paul de Chomedey Maisonneuve founded a mission on the site and set out to convert natives to Christianity. Then, of course, the French ceded Montréal to the English in 1760.

By the early 1800s, Montréal was the cultural and commercial capital of Canada, with a booming port business and a wealthy English population running the show, while the Catholic French-speaking majority did the grunt work for them.

### . . . and then Québeckers took over

In the 1960s, Québec's French-speaking majority decided to become their own bosses and shake off the influence of the Catholic Church in one shot. The period is known as the *Quiet Revolution*. Practically overnight, French-speaking Québeckers went from being mostly farmers and working poor dominated by the Catholic Church to being a modern, secular society.

## Parlez-Vous?

The question on most people's minds when they visit either city is: "Can I get by without French?" To be honest, you can have more fun if you master a few words of French, but you can get by just fine without it. Although once upon a time the English and the French were throwing rocks at each other in the streets of both cities, today, young Montréalers are often as comfortable speaking English as they are French — or Spanish or Italian, for that matter. In Québec City, the booming tourism industry has done its work in making English widely

## Savoring the language

Before taking your trip, why not take some time to brush up on your French? Québec City is almost entirely French-speaking, and in Montréal, some of the most interesting parts of the city are predominantly French. Although you don't need to speak French to get around either city, knowing when to drop the occasional civility, such as *bonjour* and *au revoir,* or *s'il vous plait* and *merçi,* endears you to the locals. They may answer you in English anyway, but they'll be flattered by your effort. (The words and expressions I provide on the Cheat Sheet at the front of this book can definitely help get you in — and out of any tight spots.)

used and understood. You can always expect warmth and cordiality from Québeckers, but especially if you make an effort to speak a few words in their native tongue.

## Soaking Up That European Flavor

That Québec and Montréal have so much European flair isn't surprising. These are two of the oldest cities in North America — and definitely among the best preserved. In both, you can stroll cobblestone streets and gaze at stone buildings and churches that date back to the 1700s. The relaxed pace, late hours, and abundance of cafes only add to the illusion that you're somewhere in Europe. For maximum old-world impact, visit the port areas of both cities. In Vieux-Québec, don't miss **Le Petit Champlain.** In Montréal, **rue Notre-Dame** or **rue St-Paul** transport you back in time.

## Following Your Stomach

Thanks to the ongoing French influence on local cuisine, Montréal and Québec City are both renowned for excellent restaurants and a refined approach to dining. And trust me, it's getting better every day. That said, Québeckers also eat their share of fast food, so you want to be selective about where you eat. Chapters 10 and 18 give you the lowdown on the best food for every budget in both cities.

Excellent eateries can be found everywhere, but in some neighborhoods you just can't get a bad meal. Québec's Old City houses many fine choices, such as the **Café du Monde.** Montréal's Old Port area is actually not the best place to eat, but **rue St-Denis** and **boulevard St-Laurent** offer impressive dining choices.

## Experiencing the Festival Frenzy

Other cities may have summer festivals, but Montréal is *famous* for its festivals. Unlike elsewhere, this city shuts down large portions of downtown for a string of festivals lasting practically all summer long. An intoxicating mix of English and French permeates these widely attended events. The fact that party-hearty Montréalers attend the festivals in droves, not to mention various states of intoxication, certainly doesn't hurt. There's definitely a *je ne sais quoi* about the dozens of summer events here, whether it's the **Montréal International Jazz Festival,** the **Just for Laughs Comedy Festival,** the **International Film Festival,** the **Nuits d'Afrique** African-music festival, or the **FrancoFolies** (the largest French-language music festival in the world).

See Chapter 3 for a calendar of the major festivals in Montréal and Québec City.

## Living It Up After Hours

Back in the 1920s, when the rest of North America was in the grips of Prohibition, Montréal was known as the "City of Sin" for its freewheeling, immoral ways. Among modern-day Canadians, the city is still revered for late bar closings (last call is at 3 a.m.), public affection (couples get very cozy on benches in public parks), and general lack of political correctness — all of which can create a carnival-like atmosphere after dark. If you want to let your hair down or stay out all night, Montréal offers endless opportunities for entertainment. You can roam the hopping club scenes, which are concentrated along **boulevard St-Laurent, rue Crescent,** and **rue St-Denis.**

## Checking Out the Many Faces of Montréal

France isn't the only culture you taste in Montréal — and I mean that literally. Dozens of other nationalities have marked out distinct corners of the city and filled them with great restaurants. In sheer numbers of immigrants, Montréal doesn't compare to multicultural havens such as Toronto and Vancouver, but Montréal's long-established ethnic neighborhoods have left a lasting mark, and they continue to play a vital role on the urban landscape.

Have a cappuccino at **Café Italia** in Little Italy, pick up some bagels on **rue St-Viateur** in the heart of Montréal's Orthodox Jewish neighborhood, or grab a souvlaki along **avenue du Parc,** with its concentration of Greek restaurants, and you'll see what I mean.

Many of these areas boast interesting architecture as well, such as the famous winding staircases of the Plateau and Little Italy; the winding cobblestone streets and graceful, stone buildings of Vieux-Montréal; and the beautiful churches, basilicas, and cathedrals throughout the city.

## Walking (and Skiing and Eating) in a Winter Wonderland

There's no denying winter in Montréal and Québec City, where temperatures can regularly dip to –5°F (–20°C) or lower for weeks on end. However, while many North Americans live in denial of their semi-Nordic surroundings, Québeckers embrace winter. By April, locals have had enough of snow, slush, and those speeding sidewalk plows that terrorize pedestrians. But from November to March, locals whisk away the winter blues by dressing properly — and plenty stylishly — and then skiing, snowboarding, skating, snowshoeing, and, let's be honest, eating and drinking to their heart's content.

Join the fun and dive right into the season by taking your trip during Québec City's **Winter Carnival** or Montréal's **Fête des Neiges** (Snow Festival), both in February. In either city, you're less than an hour from great skiing and snowboarding destinations such as **Mont Tremblant** or **Mont Ste-Anne.** If you really can't take the cold, you can always retreat to Montréal's **underground city,** where you never have to leave the safety of central heating to visit a number of museums, shopping centers, skyscraper lobbies, and major hotels.

# Eyeing Recommended Books and Movies

Complement your hard-nosed research about the nuts-and-bolts of your trip to Montréal and Québec City with some lighter fare. You'll gain a better picture of life in Québec from the following novels and films. I've limited most of my recommendations to English movies and books; however, it's a minority perspective. *Remember:* Most media in Québec are in French, so, if you took French immersion or if you like foreign films with subtitles, there's a vast world of titles to explore.

## Turning the pages

Montréalers Leonard Cohen and the late Mordecai Richler were both English-speaking Québec's literary lions of the 20th century. Cohen's *The Favourite Game* and *Beautiful Losers* are set in Montréal and emblematic of life in the 1960s and '70s. Richler's *The Apprenticeship of Duddy Kravitz* and *Barney's Version* reveal much about the different facets of Montréal that may not be apparent to the naked eye of a first-time visitor. *Barney's Version* won the Giller Prize in 1997, one of Canada's most prestigious book awards.

Though not a Montréal native, Hugh MacLennan' novel *Two Solitudes* won the 1945 Governor General's Award for Literature and coined a term that's still used to describe the collectively imagined abyss between the lives of English- and French-speaking cohabitants of Montréal and the province at large.

Though Québec's independence may seem like a distant issue today, during the most recent bout of separatist unrest in the early 1990s, which prompted a referendum in 1995, Richler penned a satirical essay entitled *Oh Canada! Oh Québec!,* — his commentary on the mounting political tension of the time. William Weintraub's novel *The Underdogs* speculates about life in Québec after separation.

*The Anglo Guide to Survival in Québec* by Josh Freed and Jon Kalina has become a cult classic among expats of all stripes wanting the lowdown on the hidden codes of *la belle province* —. Rife with humor, some of what it reveals would possibly take years to learn otherwise.

In 1983, reviewers heralded Ken Dryden's *The Game* as the best book on hockey and, perhaps, the greatest sports book ever. It can also be enjoyed by someone who has never seen the game. This memoir tells of day-to-day life on the Montréal Canadiens, Stanley Cup dynasty team of the '70s — at a time when hockey and *les glorieux* were everything in Québec. They won six league championships during Dryden's eight years playing. The book reveals what the entire era was like, beyond hockey, including his experiences as an Anglophone in French-speaking Québec.

## Screening films

Like Toronto and Vancouver, Montréal is a popular destination for Hollywood movie productions — which seems to ensure the presence of at least one A-list celebrity in town at any time. Montréal's varied architecture offers many different looks, making it a great place to shoot "on location." By and large, the scenes shot in Montréal are for movies set elsewhere. Montréal rarely gets to play itself. This is particularly true of Vieux-Montréal, which regularly stands in for European cities: today it's Paris, tomorrow Prague.

Nonetheless, several movies actually are set in Montréal. A young Richard Dreyfuss plays the lead in *The Apprenticeship of Duddy Kravitz* (1974), a coming-of-age story adapted from Mordecai Richler's novel. In 1989, Québécois director Denys Arcand received an Oscar nomination for *Jesus of Montréal,* which follows a troupe of actors through the consequences arising from their avant-garde update of a "Passion play" for a local parish. Another homegrown movie is *Eldorado* (1995), where streetscapes from Montréal's Plateau neighborhood are the backdrop for several days in the lives of an odd cast of characters during a summer heat wave. *Le Violon rouge* (1998), about the fate of a priceless violin that shows up in a Montréal auction-house, is written by Francois Girard and Don McKellar, two prominent Canadian filmmakers.

*The Score* (2001), with Robert De Niro and Edward Norton, is a heist flick with a brief cameo by Marlon Brando. Almost the entire movie takes place in Vieux-Montréal, along rue St-Paul, Est, in front of the Marché Bonsecours and near the Canada Customs House, on the western edge of this historic district. (They're trying to break in.) *Saved By the Belles* (2003) is about an infamous pair of nightlife divas who rescue and adopt a lost stranger and indoctrinate him into their particular brand of fun. It's a rollicking romp through some of the darker corners of Montréal's nightlife scene. *Mambo Italiano* (2003) is a comedy arising from the fuss caused by Angelo and Nino, two first-generation Italian-Canadians, who are a gay couple and must come out to their somewhat more traditional families.

Denys Arcand's *The Barbarian Invasions* (2003) won an Oscar for Best Foreign-Language Film. It's the sequel to Arcand's *The Decline of the American Empire* (1986), which also received an Oscar nomination (but, alas, didn't win).

*C.R.A.Z.Y.* (2005) is the latest home-grown film out of Québec to make a stir. It won the audience award at the festival in Venice and Best Canadian Feature Film at the Toronto International Film Festival in the fall of 2005.

Most recently, Montréal has been the setting for the Will Ferrell and Jon Heder comedy *Blades of Glory* (2007). In the movie, the world pairs skating championship competition takes place in a (fictional) skating rink near Montréal's Olympic Stadium.

# Chapter 3

# Deciding When to Go

● ● ● ● ● ● ● ● ● ● ● ● ● ● ● ● ● ● ● ● ● ● ● ● ● ● ● ● ● ● ● ● ● ● ● ● ● ●

## In This Chapter

▶ Choosing a steamy urban jungle or a winter wonderland
▶ Examining the four seasons of each city
▶ Scanning Montréal's and Québec City's cultural calendars
▶ Timing your trip with your favorite event

● ● ● ● ● ● ● ● ● ● ● ● ● ● ● ● ● ● ● ● ● ● ● ● ● ● ● ● ● ● ● ● ● ● ● ● ● ●

Montréal is always hopping, — no matter when you decide to visit; — but the weather is always an issue. During the year, Montréal's climate swerves between scorching summer heat waves and icy winter cold snaps. Between these extremes, spring and fall are as unpredictable as they are short.

Québec City is 250 km (155 miles) down the St. Lawrence River from Montréal and 1 degree of latitude to the north, so the winters tend to be a couple of degrees Fahrenheit colder. Snowfalls are heavier and more consistent than in Montréal. In fact, by the end of the winter, the accumulated snow in the streets can reach as high as the rooftops. Summers are a little cooler than those in Montréal, but they can still be surprisingly hot and humid. During summer evenings, a wind off the river can make you feel a bit chilly.

Be aware when making travel plans that weather extremes and unpredictability are the general rules. The heat — or cold — can hit when you least expect it. Bring a sweater, even in July.

## Revealing the Two Faces of Montréal and Québec City

Freezing temperatures, snowy conditions, and icy roads may intimidate some travelers, but for residents of Montréal and Québec City winter's harsh conditions are merely facts of life. We simply don more layers, tread carefully over icy patches, and spend more time indoors. As soon as we have enough snow and the temperatures are low enough, we swing into hardy outdoor pursuits, such as ice hockey, cross-country skiing, skating, snowboarding, snowshoeing, snowmobiling — and even ice fishing, which is incredibly popular in Québec.

Fortunately, all these activities can be done within an hour's drive of either Montréal or Québec City. If you're tempted by the idea of trekking into the wilderness in winter, just remember that daylight hours are extremely short from November until March.

Quiet, midnight snowfalls and pristine snowbanks never seem to lose their magic. Fresh snow turns Québec City, with its fortifications, cannons, French colonial architecture, and cliff-top setting next to the river, into a winter wonderland. For the first two weeks in February, the provincial capital celebrates its Nordic spirit with the **Québec City Winter Carnival,** the world's largest outdoor winter festival.

Come March, however, all that snow turns into salty, gray-brown slush that coats both cities and drives everyone nuts. Navigating through slush ponds is an arduous, nerve-jangling task, whether you're driving or walking, and the salt that city officials dump on the roads to thaw the ice stains pant legs and ruins shoes.

 When spring comes, it's short; this is partly because Montréalers interpret any warm weather as proof that summer has begun. At the first sign of a parasol on a terrace, locals hit the streets and start tearing off their clothing. Really.

From the grease, glitz, and green light of the **Formula 1 Canadian Grand Prix** in early June to the last curtain of the **Montréal World Film Festival** in September, outdoor events and festivals jam this city's summer schedule. By the end of June, Montréal is a steamy urban jungle, where throngs of locals and visitors flock to the streets for free outdoor concerts, stand-up comedy shows, open-air film screenings, and more. Summer in Montréal is one long party.

## Experiencing the Secret of the Seasons

Your tolerance for cold — or heat — is probably the first aspect to consider when planning your trip to Montréal and Québec City. In the following sections, I tell you what to expect from the seasons. Table 3-1 provides the average temperatures and precipitations for Montréal, and Table 3-2 provides the information for Québec City.

| Table 3-1 | | | | Montréal's Average Temperatures and Precipitation | | | | | | | | |
|---|---|---|---|---|---|---|---|---|---|---|---|---|
| | Jan | Feb | Mar | Apr | May | June | July | Aug | Sep | Oct | Nov | Dec |
| High (°F/°C) | 22/–5.4 | 25/–3.7 | 36/2.4 | 52/11 | 66/19 | 75/23.7 | 80/26.6 | 77/24.8 | 67/19.4 | 54/12.3 | 41/5.1 | 28/–2.3 |
| Low (°F/°C) | 54/–12.4 | 13/–10.6 | 23/–4.8 | 37/2.9 | 50/10 | 59/14.9 | 64/17.9 | 62/16.7 | 53/11.9 | 43/5.9 | 32/–0.2 | 48/–8.9 |
| Rainfall (in./cm) | 1.11/2.84 | 0.89/2.27 | 1.66/4.22 | 2.57/6.52 | 3.39/8.61 | 3.44/8.75 | 4.18/10.62 | 3.96/10.06 | 3.96/10.08 | 3.20/8.21 | 2.7/6.89 | 1.75/4.44 |

| Table 3-2 | | | | Québec City's Average Temperatures and Precipitation | | | | | | | | |
|---|---|---|---|---|---|---|---|---|---|---|---|---|
| | Jan | Feb | Mar | Apr | May | June | July | Aug | Sep | Oct | Nov | Dec |
| High (°F/°C) | 9/–12.8 | 12/–11.1 | 24/–4.6 | 38/3.3 | 52/11.2 | 62/16.5 | 67/19.2 | 64/17.9 | 55/12.5 | 43/6.2 | 32/–0.7 | 16/–9.1 |
| Low (°F/°C) | 64/–17.6 | 3/–16 | 15/–9.4 | 30.66/–1.3 | 42/5.3 | 51/10.6 | 56/13.4 | 54/12.4 | 45/7.2 | 35/1.7 | 24/–4.3 | 8/–13.4 |
| Rainfall (in./cm) | 3.53/8.98 | 2.78/7.06 | 3.55/9.03 | 3.19/8.12 | 4.18/10.61 | 4.5/11.42 | 5.03/12.78 | 4.59/11.67 | 4.94/12.55 | 4/10.17 | 4.02/10.02 | 4.11/10.44 |

## Spring

With the annual great thaw, excitement in both cities builds as snow and ice melt away:

- ✔ Days are longer, particularly during daylight saving time.

- ✔ You encounter less snow, sleet, and cold.

- ✔ After a barren winter, life returns to the streets.

The dicey weather of the short transition between winter and summer, however, comes with its drawbacks:

- ✔ You usually can't put away your coat, hat, and gloves until the middle or end of April.

- ✔ As temperatures warm and the snow melts, expect a bit of everything, weather-wise. Definitely be prepared for some rain.

✔ Enormous slush ponds form at every street corner. Be prepared by wearing waterproof footwear or risk spending some of your stay with cold, wet feet.

## Summer

After the heat of a summer day, when the sun goes down, the city's nightlife comes alive:

✔ Expect festivals galore. Both in Montréal and Québec City, the summer season brings many special events.

✔ People in the streets bask in the glorious weather.

✔ Eating and drinking moves outdoors. People dine on their balconies. Restaurants open their patios, and the parks are filled with picnicking families (a popular option for travelers, too, because drinking wine and beer in parks is perfectly legal, as long as you accompany your drink with a meal).

On the downside, the heat and the crowds can get unbearable, so you may want to seek refuge in your air-conditioned hotel room — if you can find one, that is. Here are some other drawbacks:

✔ The crowds of tourists and festival-goers, although loads of fun, can be enough to give you a mild fit of agoraphobia.

✔ The heat can be brutal — and it's not just the temperature. Montréal and Québec City can be unbearably humid in the summer.

✔ Booking a room, particularly during the major festivals, can be difficult.

✔ Rates at hotels and attractions are high.

✔ During the Construction Holidays, in the last two weeks of July, many Québeckers take their summer vacations. It's a major holiday; so, many out-of-town accommodations can be booked solid at this time. Québec City also gets a major influx of visitors from around the province during these two weeks.

## Fall

Brisk fall days are glorious, with the brilliantly colored leaves, harvest bounty at the markets, and temperatures that are typically ideal:

✔ The leaves change color.

✔ Temperatures are cooler and usually remain pleasantly warm until the end of September.

✔ You have an easier time finding accommodations.

✔ Restaurants keep their terraces open practically until the first frost, when people eventually make their way inside.

✔ The cultural calendar kicks up again with the start of the seasons at the theater, opera, ballet, symphony, and arts in general.

However, autumn can turn nasty as winter begins:

✔ Cold, unpredictable weather can set in as early as October. First you see frost, then the ground freezes, and then you get snow.

✔ Most of the outdoor festivals are over, and the winter activities haven't begun yet, so on overcast days the cities can feel a tad drab.

## Winter

Instead of seeing the snow and ice as impediments, your best bet is to regard them as opportunities for seasonal recreation and leisure. By braving the extreme conditions in the name of fun — or *le fun,* as locals are likely to say — you're taking part in Québec's Nordic spirit:

✔ It's sunny almost all the time, and the days can be really exhilarating, even if your hands and feet are numb, your glasses are fogged, and you have hat-head all the time.

✔ By the end of December, both cities usually offer enough snow and ice for all winter sports. Skaters at the artificially frozen rink in the **Bonsecours Basin** (Montréal's Old Port) are usually the first to hit the ice outdoors.

✔ Good food, not to mention drink, goes down that much better when you've worked up an appetite by braving the elements all day.

Lots of layers and defensive driving are the winter's watchwords:

✔ You need a hat, mittens, and a scarf — and not just as fashion accessories.

✔ Driving can be difficult. When it snows, roads become slippery or icy and visibility is poor.

# Viewing Montréal's Calendar of Events

Montréal is definitely a four-season town — although one of its seasons can be brutally cold — so you get plenty of reasons to celebrate all year 'round.

## January/February

In January, bundled-up kids celebrate the annual *Fête des Neiges* (literally, Snow Party). The festival takes place on Île Ste-Hélène and features ice skating, ice sculptures, tube slides, dogsleds, mitten-making workshops, and more. Most activities are free of charge. For more information, visit `www.fetedesneiges.com`. Three weekends in late January and early February.

The **Montréal High Lights Festival** (www.montrealhighlights.com) is an adult version of a snow party, combining multimedia light shows, a performing arts program, and guest appearances by world-renowned chefs at the trendier downtown eateries. Eleven days in late February and early March.

## March

The **International Festival of Films on Art** (www.artfifa.com) is the only festival of its kind in the Americas. The screenings happen at different venues around town; the programming also includes conferences and seminars on the topic. Ten days in mid-March.

When the sap in Québec's maple trees starts to drip, it's **Sugaring-Off** time; groups of friends and families flock to the countryside to visit sugar shacks, where maple farmers boil the sap and make syrup. The main event on these excursions is a traditional meal in a mess hall where fresh maple syrup is used as a topping for everything — gulp, even fried pork fat. Back in town, outdoor stands at markets and on sidewalks sell *tire* (pronounced *teer*), which is maple taffy that's made by ladling thick, hot, unrefined syrup from a steaming caldron onto a bed of snow. When the syrup cools, you wrap the gooey stuff on a Popsicle stick and watch salivating kids devour it. The fun starts in early March and lasts until mid-April.

Everyone in Montréal is Irish on St. Patrick's Day, despite historic tensions between Anglophones and the French. Beginning at noon, thousands of onlookers line rue Ste-Catherine for Montréal's **St. Patrick's Day Parade,** a procession of floats, marching bands, and folk dancing. After the parade, the crowds get a little rowdy and roam the streets in search of green beer. The parade is the oldest and longest-running one of its kind in Canada, since 1824. For more info (but not beer) visit www.montrealirishparade.com. Mid-March.

## April

For five days early in the month on an annual basis, **Blue Metropolis** (www.blue-met-bleu.com) is Montréal's international literary festival. From its quiet beginnings in 1999, it has since grown into a significant event on the cultural calendar. Early April.

## May

Bikes are popular here. *Féria du vélo de Montréal* (www.velo.qc.ca), or **Bike Fest,** is a weeklong event near the end of the month celebrating this two-wheeled, environmentally sound, and health-inducing form of transportation. In fact, this is a unique event in North America. One of the high points is the **Tour de l'Ile,** which draws more than 30,000 participants. The course, which changes annually, winds through a number of Montréal neighborhoods, making for a fun group or family outing.

In May, the *Festival TransAmériques* (www.fta.qc.ca) begins. This critically acclaimed biennial offers two weeks of French-language theater productions from the Americas and Europe in odd-numbered years. Plays tend toward the edgy, and many make their North American debut here. The programming lasts for ten days, from the end of May to the beginning of June.

If you're in Montréal this time of year, take advantage of **Museum Day,** when entry to select museums is free, as is a shuttle service running among them. For more, check out www.museesmontreal.org. Last Sunday in May.

Starting from late May, two weekly pagan Sunday rituals begin and run until mid-September. The longest running of the two is **Tam-Tams** in **Parc Mont Royal.** Held from around noon to sundown, this weekly drum-circle takes place under the Sir Georges-Étienne Cartier monument. The happening attracts representatives from a wide cross-section of counter-culture movements, from anarchists to vegans. Everyone's there for an afternoon of leisure on the grassy foothills of the Mountain, blanketed by the rumbling beat from the large congregation of percussionists and a handful of other musicians. It's been a Montréal institution for nearly two decades, and a social phenomenon well worth witnessing. More recently, on Île-Ste-Hélène in **Parc Jean-Drapeau,** an alternate to the Mountain's rhythmic cacophony has sprouted. **Piknic Électronik** (www.piknicelectronik.com), appeals to the DJ–dance floor set. It's best described as a family-oriented outdoor dance party, complete with DJ tent, speaker towers, and patches of turf carpeting with kiddie pools and sprinklers for cooling off. The dance floor, the focal point of the action, is in a dramatic setting. The milling crowds shuffle about in a rotunda under a giant, multi-storey abstract metal sculpture by Alexander Calder, which was built for the 1967 World Fair. There's also a stunning view of the Montréal skyline from across the waterway. It kicks up around 2 p.m. and lasts until 8 p.m.

## June

Start the month off at the *Mondial de la bière* (www.festivalmondial biere.qc.ca), or **World Beer Festival,** where visitors sample 250 liquid products, including beer, scotch, cider, and port, from around the world. It's one of the largest festivals of its kind on the continent. Though several electronic music events happen over the course of a year, **MUTEK** (www.mutek.ca) is Montréal's premier happening. It takes place early in June and draws acts from all over the world: new music producers brandishing their high-tech gear and making suitably far-out sounds. Some of the performances are simultaneously broadcast via the Web site.

The **Montréal Fringe Festival** (www.montrealfringe.ca) offers off-off-Broadway-type drama in venues up and down boulevard St-Laurent. Ten days in mid-June.

Late in the month, the **Formula 1 Grand Prix** (www.grandprix.ca) makes its only Canadian stop at *Circuit Gilles Villeneuve* on Île Notre-Dame. Even if you're not a race fan, taking in the action at the track, it's one of the most exhilarating weekends in Montréal. In the several days of festivities leading up to Sunday's race, motor oil and champagne mix freely on the main drags downtown.

The **Montréal International Jazz Festival** (www.montrealjazzfest.com) is the summer's main event. For two weeks, a boatload of international acts plays free outdoor shows and world-class headliners top the bills at ticketed venues. Each year, well over 1.5 million people swarm the downtown site of the festival, which takes place on the streets and in parks surrounding Place des Arts, Montréal's main performing arts center. Like clockwork, every year, you can count on the bands to strike up in the last week of June and carry on for a week into July.

At this time of year, after dark, it's always tough to choose between an evening at the Jazz Fest or catching the **Montréal International Fireworks Competition** (www.internationaldesfeuxloto-quebec.com). The riverfront in Vieux-Montréal is an ideal place to watch the pyrotechnics, which go off at 10 p.m. Wednesday and Saturday, mid-June to late July.

## *July*

In 2008, **Les FrancoFolies de Montréal** (www.francofolies.com) will celebrate its 20th anniversary. It's a festival that features a bevy of French-language musicians from across the planet. It takes place on the city's main festival site, which closes to car traffic and opens to hordes of music lovers and people watchers throughout the summer. End of July to the beginning of August.

A recent addition to the city's annual calendar is the **World Beach Volleyball Tour's Montréal Open** (www.worldbeachvolleyball.com). Along with a large, active, local fan base, it's also a wonderful spectator sport for the layperson. Men find the women's game riveting. And vice versa, I'm sure.

From mid-July to mid-August, **Theatre in the Parks** sees a local theater troupe give free outdoor shows in different neighborhoods around the island. They often stage an easily digestible, family oriented modern adaptation of a Shakespeare play or other theater classic. Visit Repercussion Theatre's Web site at www.repercussiontheatre.com for the where and when of it all.

Right after the Jazz Fest, the *Festival International Nuits d'Afrique* (www.festivalnuitsdafrique.com) showcases African and Caribbean musicians at paid venues downtown, and puts on free concerts in Place Émilie-Gamelin. *Nuits d'Afrique* is nearly two decades old, and by now many of the greatest names in world music have participated. Ten days in mid-July.

Gory B-movies and improbable sci-fi action are the hallmarks of the **FanTasia Film Festival** (www.fantasiafest.com). It's held at several venues downtown. The screenings start in mid-July; and, for about three weeks, these are some of the hottest tickets in town.

The **Just For Laughs Comedy Festival** (www.hahaha.com) is another roaring success with locals and visitors alike. This outdoor festival has launched the likes of Jim Carrey, Jerry Seinfeld, Ray Romano, and Tim Allen. It takes place on rue St-Denis south of rue Sherbrooke, where the scene turns into a veritable freak show, with clowns, street acts, and circus-school students all vying for the attention of passersby. Do your best not to end up as the victim of a gag on the festival's spin-off, candid-camera TV show. By all accounts, it's a hysterical two weeks in mid-July.

## August

The **Divers/Cité Festival** (www.diverscite.org) starts off the month with a weeklong celebration thrown by Montréal's gay community. It's an absolutely fabulous party that has attracted 800,000 people in past years.

Join the caber-toss at the **Montréal Highland Games** (www.montreal highlandgames.qc.ca), a sporting event that could best be described as the pole vault's distant, cross-dressing cousin. Men in kilts should not be vaulting over anything. Thankfully, here, it's the caber that goes over the bar atop the uprights. Also: bagpipes, drumming, and highland dancers over the course of a fun-filled Sunday, Celtic style; early in the month.

Tennis, anyone? Mid-month, Montréal hosts one-half of the **Tennis Masters Canada** (www.masters-series.com), sharing it with Toronto. Each year, the women's and men's tournaments alternate between the cities. The eight-day tournament is a warm-up for the U.S. Open, so many top-ranked players make a show here.

Park Maisonneuve, next to the Olympic Stadium, hosts *La Fête des enfants de Montréal* (www.fetedesenfants.ca) — a weekend festival for Montréal's kids in Parc Jean-Drapeau. Mid-August.

Children-at-heart, daredevils, and adrenaline junkies climb to the top of the Mountain and figure out the fastest way down in a variety of newfan-gled, action-sport disciplines such as street luge, speedboard, skate-board, and inline skating. It's the annual **Top Challenge** competition: see www.topchallenge.ca. Late August.

And, as if that's not fast-track enough, movie stars and paparazzi descend on the city for the **World Film Festival** (www.ffm-montreal.org). Screenings, premieres, and parties abound. "What, I'm not on the list? Do you *know* who I am?" Late August through beginning of September.

## *September/October*

Warmly anticipated by Montréalers, cooler weather brings the **Magic of Lanterns** (www.ville.montreal.qc.ca/jardin) to the Botanical Gardens, a dazzling annual display of more than 700 handcrafted lanterns of silk and bamboo from Shanghai. The show's theme changes annually; it lasts from the beginning of September until the end of October.

In odd-numbered years, it's *Mois de la photo* (www.moisdelaphoto. com), or **Image and Imagination,** and for a month the city stands still just long enough to play host to a variety of exhibits and events related to photography, including several outdoor galleries along major streets. Early September to early October.

Montréal's thick urban density makes the far-off footage from the **Montréal International Adventure Film Festival** (www.fifam.ca) nothing short of mind-shattering for entrenched urbanites. It'll make even the most maudlin denizen brim with courage. They'll want to zip up their polar-fleece, strap on the gear, and head for the hills — if only momentarily.

At the beginning of October, over the course of a weekend, Québec's arts community holds an open house of sorts, called *Les journées de la culture* (www.journeesdelaculture.qc.ca). Across the province, artists from every *métier* open the doors of their workshops, studios, cooperatives, and other creative spaces to the general public. The three days offer a variety of demonstrations, guided tours, and discussion forums. From architecture, to circus arts, to electronic art, to pluridisciplinary art — it's all-encompassing. Three days in early October.

Slated at the beginning of October, **Pop Montréal** (www.popmontreal. com) is a relative newcomer to the city's festival circuit. It's a weeklong bender staging a variety of alt-rock shows, reflective of the local live-music scene and focusing on innovative and independent artists both homegrown and from abroad. It's a thriving event and Montréal seems to have become a hotbed for producing this kind of breakout talent as of late, so there's lots of buzz. (Think Rufus Wainwright, the Sam Roberts Band, Arcade Fire, The Dears, and Wolf Parade — to name just a few.)

Also early in October, more than 12,000 people of all persuasions attend the **Black and Blue Festival's Main Event** (www.bbcm.org), an extravagant, mega–dance party with DJs and choreographed live performances making it one of the largest AIDS benefit events in the world. Everyone's there to dance into the wee hours of the morning for a good cause.

The **Montréal International Festival of New Cinema** (www.nouveau cinema.ca) pushes the frontiers of high-tech, digital art a little more each year, with its eclectic mix of provocative film and other media arts. Mid-October.

The **Botanical Gardens' Great Pumpkin Ball** is as close as Montréal gets to the Peanuts gang's *It's the Great Pumpkin, Charlie Brown.* Literally hundreds of decorated pumpkins are on display in the main greenhouse during most of October. It's actually a contest — a resident witch hosts the proceedings. Throughout October.

The *Grande Mascarade* (www.grandemascarade.com) is a Halloween-themed celebration that takes place on Place Jacques-Cartier and at the Marché Bonsecours in Vieux-Montréal. The historic part of the city is an ideal location for scaring up ghosts of yore with a costume ball. You don't have to be in costume to join the fun, but dressing up is encouraged. Several evenings leading up to Halloween.

### November/December

Get your game on in early November. The **Arcadia Festival** (www.festivalarcadia.com) is a festival dedicated the many facets of the gaming industry and the larger community — including a film zone screening game-inspired movies. Parents will love the academic zone, with booths from different educational institutions that teach related programs such as animation.

During the **Santa Claus Parade** (www.defileduperenoel.com), Montréalers bid *adieu* to the big guy just before he leaves for work at the North Pole. Yes, Santa spends his off season in Montréal. Kids line up to watch the procession down rue Ste-Catherine, shivering with excitement until the very last float. For information, call ☎ **514-937-7754.** Mid-November.

Montréal's documentary film festival, *Rencontres internationales du documentaire de Montréal* (www.ridm.qc.ca), features the work of local, Canadian, and international documentary filmmakers. Ten days in mid-November.

Just in time for the holiday season, the **Salon des métiers d'art du Québec** (www.salondesmetiersdart.com) is a crafts show with more than 450 artisan exhibitors displaying their unique creations. The three-week event, starting in early December, draws mainly local and some international designers and creators with decorative objects ranging from fashionable to eclectic.

## Checking Out Québec City's Calendar of Events

In 2008, much of *le fun* will be in the name of the 400th anniversary of Québec City's founding. So, along with the special events for the celebration, the annual happenings should be extra festive.

## January/February

A red-sashed snowman, known as the *Bonhomme du Carnaval,* leads the festivities at the **Carnaval de Québec** (www.carnaval.qc.ca). More than a million people brave the cold to join parades, concerts, and nightly winter balls in an ice palace. Many fortify themselves against the cold with *caribou,* a Québec specialty consisting of red wine and pure alcohol, which in colonial times contained actual caribou blood. Two weeks in late January and early February.

## March/April

In early March, **Crashed Ice** (www.redbull.ca), organized by an energy-drink maker, is a unique action sport taking full advantage of Québec City's steep cliff. Groups of four competitors, dressed in hockey equipment and ice skates, descend a narrow, half-mile, snaking course with big jumps. Best time wins.

Slurp up as much maple syrup as you can at the **cabanes à sucre (sugar shacks)** surrounding the city, from the beginning of March to mid-April (www.laroutedelerable.ca).

***Festival de la gastronomie de Québec/Coupe des nations*** (www.crq.ca) is a food-and-drink extravaganza and competition that showcases Québec's regional specialties. Three days in late April.

Over the course of five days at the end of March and at the beginning of April, the **Festival de cinéma des 3 Amériques** (www.fc3a.com), a pan-American film festival, screens more than 100 short and feature-length films in Saint-Roch, a neighborhood just outside the Old City.

## May

The ***Manifestation internationale d'art de Québec*** (www.manifdart. org), a biennial exhibition taking place in the odd years (the next one is in 2009), showcases the newest and the best contemporary and multidisciplinary artists in Québec City. First two weeks of May.

During the last half of May, the **Carrefour international de theatre** (www.carrefourtheatre.qc.ca) is a festival that stages nearly 100 contemporary theater performances from the world over.

## June

Mid-month, the Québec Air Show at the Jean Lesage Airport (www. fondationmauricetanguay.com) takes to the skies. It's grown into the largest air show in Canada and is among the top five in North America, occurring biannually in even-numbered years. Watch the Canadian Snowbirds go through their aerial maneuvers and acrobatics.

**St-Jean-Baptiste Day** (www.snqc.qc.ca), Québec's so-called national holiday, was named in honor of the province's patron saint. This holiday is taken very seriously in Québec City, which many Québeckers consider their "national" capital. June 24.

Daredevils ride iron horses at Mt. Ste-Anne, one of eastern Canada's highest peaks, during **Velirium** (www.velirium.com), a mountain biking festival and competition. Three weekends during the middle of the month.

## July

The *Festival d'été de Québec* (www.infofestival.com) is one of the world's largest French-speaking cultural events, featuring more than 600 performers from 22 countries. First two weeks of July.

*Les grands feux* (www.lesgrandsfeux.com), a fireworks display choreographed to music, starts at the end of the month. Wednesday and Saturday nights for three weeks from mid-July to early August, against the backdrop of the Montmorency waterfalls.

## August

In the middle of the month, the **New France Festival** (www.nouvelle france.qc.ca) reproduces colonial life of Québec City, as it was in the 17th and 18th centuries.

The biennial *Festival des Troubadours et Saltimbanques* (www.lefestival.info) is early in the month over a weekend. This medieval festival is a tip of the hat to the popular origins of street performance and public spectacle.

For five days in the middle of August, it's the **Québec City International Festival of Military Bands** (www.fimmq.com). This annual *tattoo* (military exhibition) gives marching bands a chance to perform somewhere other than parades and college football-game halftimes.

## September/October

*Envol et Macadam* (www.envoletmacadam.com) is a weekend at the beginning of September jam-packed with alt-rock, punk, techno, and hip-hop acts, including international headliners.

When Québec's colorful autumn leaves start to fall, visitors lift their spirits with inspirational music at the **Québec Festival of Devotional Music** (www.festivalmusiquesacree.ca), ten days at the end of October that feature internationally known gospel singers, Gregorian chanters, and a cappella groups.

# Part II
# Planning Your Trip to Montréal and Québec City

The 5th Wave                    By Rich Tennant

I'm not sure what he's yelling about. It's all in French. But I think you made a wrong turn.

# In this part . . .

Planning your trip in advance will help you hit the ground running, and save you from learning while on vacation when your time's most precious. This part focuses on the essential steps of setting a budget for your trip, figuring out how to get to Québec, and other important matters to consider before you leave. When you're in Montréal or Québec City, you want to be out and about on the town experiencing the street life, yakking with locals, shopping for gear, tasting different foods from around the world, and drinking it all in. It's a balancing act — of course, you'll have to refer to this book and your other material throughout — but the more you know beforehand the better equipped you'll be to enjoy these cities to their fullest.

# Chapter 4

# Managing Your Money

. . . . . . . . . . . . . . . . . . . . . . . . . . . . . . . . . . . . . . . . . . . .

## In This Chapter

▶ Gauging how you'll spend your money

▶ Avoiding hidden expenses and finding ways to cut costs

▶ Understanding the Canadian dollar, or "loonie"

▶ Considering different ways to carry cash and pay

▶ Dealing with a lost or stolen wallet

. . . . . . . . . . . . . . . . . . . . . . . . . . . . . . . . . . . . . . . . . . . .

*O*n the whole, the living is easy in Montréal and Québec City. Like their European cousins the French, Québeckers tend to consider eating at restaurants and going out more like a basic human right than a luxury. That attitude somehow keeps prices affordable. Plus, you can find plenty to do for free — strolling quaint streets, gazing at stunning architecture, gawking at beautiful people.

## Planning a Budget

Planning a budget is a little bit like performing a juggling act. You have six vacation pins: lodging, transportation, dining, attractions, shopping, and nightlife. You can't really afford to drop any of them (that is, unless you want to be truly spartan), but you may want to throw some pins higher than others. First, decide ahead of time what's most important to you: Staying in a fine hotel? Eating gourmet meals? Hitting the chicest shops? After you set your priorities, look for ways to cut costs in other areas. To get you started, the following sections show you what to expect — and expect to pay — from each category of basic travel expenses.

### Lodging

Like it or not, accommodations are your biggest expense. Before leaving on your trip, do your homework to find bargains and reserve rooms. Plan ahead and you may save enough to stay another night! (See Chapter 9 for details on getting the best hotel deals.)

The minimum you want to spend on accommodations per night is around C$100. Sure you can get better deals, but your comfort may be compromised.

## Transportation

Here's an area where you can save. You don't need a car unless you want to take day trips around Montréal and Québec City. Driving in either city can be a nightmare, and you don't need to put yourself through it. Québec's Old City is so small and compact you can walk everywhere. Montréal has a great **public transportation system,** with a subway that serves all major attractions — even the ones outside the city. A booklet of six tickets (valid for both buses and the subway) costs C$12, less than the price of a single taxi ride across downtown.

If you're bent on **renting a car,** check Chapter 7 for details on getting a good rental deal. When you're doing your calculations, remember that gas is expensive in Canada. At press time, the price of gas was hovering around the C$1 mark (per liter), or the equivalent of C$4/gallon. Nothing on the nightly news suggests prices will be dropping significantly any time this century.

Montréal and Québec City have an abundance of **taxis** that are easy to flag in case you're too tired to walk back to your hotel. Just find a busy street and raise your arm.

See Chapter 5 for ways to save on your trip to and from Montréal or Québec City. Booking your travel arrangements well in advance is one sure way to save money. Researching and comparing the prices of lots of different fare options, such as discount airlines, seat sales, courier fares, or flying standby, is another. Usually both factor into what you end up paying.

## Dining

Dining is probably not the place to trim the fat in your budget. Look at it this way: Eating out in Montréal and Québec City is an entertaining, potentially evening-long activity. Splurge at the dinner table, and you won't need to spend money on entertainment for the rest of the night. With a little planning, you won't need to bust the bank to satisfy your palate, either. I suggest eating a big breakfast and then cutting back on lunch, either by grabbing a sandwich at a cafe or picnicking in a park.

Prices at fast food restaurants are comparable to U.S. prices. You can get inexpensive lunches at many ethnic eateries — usually around C$10 per person. See Chapters 10 and 18 for recommendations. In the evening, most fine restaurants offer a *table d'hôte* (also called a *menu*) that's usually a good deal with prices ranging from C$20 to C$65 for a meal, not including drinks. For the higher-end places, expect to spend from C$30 to C$100 per person for a complete dinner, including drinks.

## Attractions

The adult admission price for most museums and attractions is between C$10 and C$12. Pricier attractions, such as La Ronde, set you back about

C$37 for adults and C$25 for kids under 12. Kids under 6 get in to most attractions for free. See Chapters 11 and 19 for prices in each city.

## Shopping

Shopping in Montréal and Québec City can be hazardous to your budget. With so much great stuff to buy — from clothes to art to home decorations — the abundance of merchandise may make you lose your perspective, not to mention your senses. I recommend you give yourself a shopping allowance before you leave home, either a daily one, a weekly one, or one that's for the entire trip (if you're disciplined and do your accounting regularly). If shopping isn't your thing, you can save big bucks in this department.

## Nightlife

Nightlife is another area where money can disappear before you know it. But you can indulge inexpensively. The cheapest time to visit a bar is during happy hour, or _cinq à sept,_ as it's called in Québec. (The expression "five to seven" refers to the early-evening hours, not the number of drinks you get for one price!) Many places offer after-work specials, such as two-for-one, and drinks usually range between C$5 and C$10.

Tickets for shows seem to start around C$10 and go up to C$100, or more for prime seats. The cabaret show (without dinner) at the Montréal Casino starts at C$43. Movie prices range from C$9 to C$13. For details on the prices of outings, see Chapters 15 and 21.

# Watching Out for Hidden Expenses

Planning a travel budget is like renovating a house. It always ends up costing more than you think. Both endeavors are laden with temptations. Trust me, if you're setting out to be a spartan traveler, Montréal and Québec City will test your willpower. To help you stick to your budget, keep in mind the tips in the following sections.

## Taking taxes into account

There's a price to easy living throughout Québec: **steep taxes on sales and services.** Whenever you see a price, except on alcoholic beverages, add 13 percent.

You can still live it up here with limited damage to your pocketbook. The secret? Make a travel budget and stick to it.

## Tipping

To tip or not to tip, and how much? These are the eternal questions when you find yourself in a strange land. In Québec, tipping waiters 15 percent is the norm. You can go higher or lower if you'd like to make a statement about the quality of the service. Taxi drivers usually expect 10 percent. For bellhops, C$1 or C$2 per bag does the trick. For hotel housekeeping, count C$1 per person per day. For valet parking, plan on C$1 or C$2.

In restaurants, remember that you're tipping on the total price *before* taxes, not the total on the bottom of the bill. There's an easy trick to calculate a tip around 15 percent. Just add up the two taxes, federal and provincial, that appear above the total on the bill — they equal 13 percent of the bill's subtotal, which is just a little bit less than how much you should tip.

## Cutting Costs — But Not the Fun

A little foresight and planning are all you need to cut down on your basic travel expenses. Follow these tips so that you can free up some extra funds for a shopping spree or a wild night on the town.

- **Go in the off season.** You get better deals when you travel at non-peak times between November and April. For winter trips, avoid the Christmas season, New Year's Eve, and the school March break.

- **Travel midweek.** If you can travel on a Tuesday, Wednesday, or Thursday, you may find cheaper flights to your destination. When you ask about airfares, see if you can get a cheaper rate by flying on a different day. For more tips on getting a good fare, see Chapter 5.

- **Check out package tours.** You may get airfare, hotel, ground transportation, and even some sightseeing for less just by making one call to a travel agent or packager. (See Chapter 5 for more on package tours.)

- **Reserve a room with a kitchen.** Doing a bit of cooking is an easy way to save on your food budget. Grab some basic food items — cereal, coffee, bread, and milk — at a *dépanneur* (corner store) near your hotel. Make some sandwiches before you leave in the morning so you can afford to splurge on some serious gastronomy in the evening.

- **Always ask for discount rates.** You may be eligible for deals and not know it. Membership in AAA, frequent-flier plans, trade unions, AARP, or other groups could qualify you for savings on car rentals, plane tickets, hotel rooms, and even meals. It never hurts to ask.

- **Bunk with your kids.** A room with two double beds usually doesn't cost more than one with a queen-size bed. Many hotels won't charge you extra if you put your little angels (usually under age 12) in the extra bed. If they do charge a surplus, it's still cheaper than renting another room. Fees for rollaway beds are usually C$10 to C$15 per day.

- **Try expensive restaurants at lunch rather than dinner.** Lunch tabs usually are a fraction of what dinner costs at top restaurants, and the menu often boasts many of the same specialties. Chapters 10 and 18 suggest a number of cheap eats — some of the best meals are at inexpensive ethnic joints.

✔ **Walk.** A good pair of walking shoes can save you plenty of money getting around. Montréal and Québec City were meant for walking — particularly the historic districts. Both are old cities, so car culture isn't as entrenched. Walking — combined with the Métro (subway), city buses, and the occasional taxi ride — is an unbeatable way to see either place.

✔ **Skip the souvenirs.** Your photographs and memories are probably way more valuable to you than any trinkets you pick up to commemorate the trip. Doing without the T-shirts, key chains, salt-and-pepper shakers, and moose antlers can save you money you'd rather spend elsewhere.

# Handling Money

Should you spend cash? Credit? Traveler's checks? This section explains the pros and cons of the various options.

You're the best judge of how much cash you feel comfortable carrying or what alternative form of currency is your favorite. That's not going to change much on your vacation. True, you'll probably be moving around more and incurring more expenses than you generally do (unless you happen to eat out every meal when you're at home). But, that aside, the only type of payment that won't be quite as available to you away from home is your personal checkbook.

## Understanding the loonie

The tails-side of the Canadian dollar coin has an image of a loon — a bird common to the Canadian north — therefore, it's called a "loonie." It seems natural that the two-dollar coin would be called a "toonie" — and it is. In Canada, coins come in denominations of $1 (loonie), $2 (toonie), and C1¢, C5¢, C10¢, and C25¢.

Canadian bills are all sorts of different colors, prompting many Americans to joke about them looking like Monopoly money — and, until recently, there was a lot of truth to that. Bills come in C$5 (blue), C$10 (purple), C$20 (green), C$50 (red), and C$100 (brown) denominations.

## Converting your greenbacks

As a currency, the Canadian dollar has generally lagged behind the U.S. dollar in terms of its value on the world market. However, as of late, the Canadian currency has caught up with the American; in fact, the loonie is at an all-time high against the greenback. This means that Canada is still a deal — but less so than before.

Currency exchange rates fluctuate based on different world events. Perhaps you're not tracking the flight of the loonie on a daily basis, but the Bank of Canada is. Their Web site (www.bankofcanada.ca) has a currency converter that will quickly tell you exactly how many Canadian dollars your money's worth.

The Canadian dollar was at par with the American dollar at the time of writing this guide, which may or may not be the case at the time of your departure. Don't fret if you can't score any Canadian dollars before you leave — there's an automated teller machine (ATM) at the airport.

## Using ATMs and carrying cash

The easiest and best way to get cash when you're away from home is from an ATM, sometimes referred to as a "bank machine," "cash machine," or "cashpoint." The Cirrus (☎ 800-424-7787; www.mastercard.com) and PLUS (☎ 800-843-7587; www.visa.com) networks span the globe — look at the back of your bank card to see which network you're on.

The major Canadian banks in Montréal and Québec City and the bank-card system they honor are:

- ✔ **Bank of Montréal:** Cirrus

- ✔ **Banque Nationale du Canada:** Cirrus

- ✔ **Caisse populaire Desjardins:** PLUS

- ✔ **CIBC:** PLUS

- ✔ **Royal Bank of Canada:** Cirrus and PLUS

- ✔ **Scotia Bank:** Cirrus

- ✔ **TD Canada Trust:** Cirrus and PLUS

Be sure you know your personal identification number (PIN) and your daily withdrawal limit before you leave home. You'll also want to keep in mind that many banks impose a fee every time your card is used at a different bank's ATM, and that fee can be higher for international transactions (up to C$5 or more) than for domestic ones (where they're rarely more than C$1.50). On top of these fees, the bank from which you withdraw cash may charge its own fee. With your bank, check the fees for withdrawals from foreign ATMs before you leave.

In many international destinations, ATMs offer the best exchange rates, even taking into account the extra withdrawal fees you may be charged. Avoid exchanging money at commercial exchange bureaus and hotels, which often have the highest transaction fees.

Is there a place on earth that doesn't accept or exchange U.S. dollars? If one exists, I've never seen it. But use them only if you're in a pinch. You get less bang for your buck when doing a cash exchange in a retail shop, because most establishments will ding tourists on the exchange rate, skewing the exchange rate by at least 10 percent for the convenience.

## Charging ahead with credit cards

Credit cards are a safe way to carry money. They also provide a convenient record of all your expenses and generally offer relatively good exchange rates. You can also withdraw cash advances from your credit cards at banks or ATMs, provided you know your PIN. If you've forgotten yours, or didn't know you had one, call the number on the back of your credit card and ask the bank to send it to you. It usually takes five to seven business days, though some banks will provide you the number over the phone if you tell them your mother's maiden name or some other personal information. If you do opt for a cash advance, remember that you're charged interest from the moment of the transaction, rather than only after your account's billing date.

Keep in mind that when you use your credit card abroad many banks now assess a 1 percent to 3 percent transaction fee on **all** charges you incur abroad (whether you're using the local currency or your native currency). But credit cards still may be the smart way to go when you factor in things like exorbitant ATM fees and higher traveler's check exchange rates and service fees.

Some credit-card companies recommend that you notify them of any impending trip abroad so they don't become suspicious when the card is used numerous times in a foreign location and end up blocking your card. Even if you don't call your credit-card company in advance, you can always call the card's toll-free emergency number if a charge is refused. But perhaps the most important tip is to carry more than one card with you on your trip. For any number of reasons, a card may not work, so having a backup is the smart way to go.

## Toting traveler's checks

These days, traveler's checks are less necessary because most cities have 24-hour ATMs that allow you to withdraw small amounts of cash as needed. However, keep in mind that you will likely be charged an ATM withdrawal fee if the bank is not your own; so if you're withdrawing money every day, you might be better off with traveler's checks.

You can buy traveler's checks at most banks. They are offered in denominations of $20, $50, $100, $500, and sometimes $1,000. Generally, you'll pay a service charge ranging from 1 percent to 4 percent. The most popular traveler's checks are offered by **American Express** (☎ **800-807-6233** or ☎ **800-221-7282** for card holders — this number accepts collect calls, offers service in several foreign languages, and exempts Amex gold and platinum cardholders from the 1 percent fee);

**Visa** (☎ 800-732-1322) — AAA members can obtain Visa checks for a $9.95 fee (for checks up to $1,500) at most AAA offices or by calling ☎ 866-339-3378; and **MasterCard** (☎ 800-223-9920).

If you choose to carry traveler's checks, be sure to keep a record of their serial numbers separate from your checks in the event they are stolen or lost. You'll get a refund faster if you know the numbers.

**American Express, Thomas Cook, Visa,** and **MasterCard** offer **foreign currency traveler's checks,** useful if you're traveling to one country or to the Euro zone; they're accepted at locations where dollar checks may not be.

Another option is the new prepaid traveler's check cards, reloadable cards that work much like debit cards but aren't linked to your checking account. The **American Express Travelers Cheque Card,** for example, requires a minimum deposit, sets a maximum balance, and has a one-time issuance fee of $14.95. You can withdraw money from an ATM (for a fee of $2.50 per transaction, not including bank fees), and the funds can be purchased in dollars, euros, or pounds. If you lose the card, your available funds will be refunded within 24 hours.

## Dealing with a Lost or Stolen Wallet

Be sure to tell all of your credit card companies the minute you discover your wallet has been lost or stolen, and file a report at the nearest police station. Your credit card company or insurer may require a police report number or record of the loss. Most credit card companies have an emergency toll-free number to call if your card is lost or stolen; they may be able to wire you a cash advance immediately or deliver an emergency credit card in a day or two. **Visa's** U.S. emergency number is ☎ 800-847-2911 or 410-581-9994. **American Express** cardholders and traveler's check holders should call ☎ 800-221-7282. **MasterCard** holders should call ☎ 800-307-7309 or 636-722-7111. For other credit cards, call the toll-free number directory at ☎ 800-555-1212.

See the appendix for the major credit-card companies' Canadian toll-free numbers.

If you need emergency cash over the weekend when most banks are closed, you can have money wired to you via **Western Union** (☎ 800-325-6000; www.westernunion.com).

Identity theft and fraud are potential complications of losing your wallet, especially if you've lost your driver's license along with your cash and credit cards. Notify the major credit-reporting bureaus immediately; placing a fraud alert on your records may protect you against liability for criminal activity. The three major U.S. credit-reporting agencies are **Equifax** (☎ **800-766-0008;** www.equifax.com), **Experian** (☎ **888-397-3742;** www.experian.com), and **TransUnion** (☎ **800-680-7289;** www.transunion.com). Finally, if you've lost all forms of photo ID, call your airline and explain the situation; they might allow you to board the plane if you have a copy of your passport or birth certificate and a copy of the police report you've filed.

## Chapter 5

# Getting to Montréal and Québec City

· · · · · · · · · · · · · · · · · · · · · · · · · · · · · · · · · · · · · · ·

*In This Chapter*

▶ Making your travel arrangements

▶ Getting the best airfare

▶ Traveling to Montréal and Québec City

▶ Choosing the best package deal

· · · · · · · · · · · · · · · · · · · · · · · · · · · · · · · · · · · · · · ·

**S**o you're ready to chill in Montréal and Québec City. Even if you've been to another part of Canada before, you're in for a big surprise; because it's an entirely different kind of place. Brush up on your French pronunciation and get ready to plunge into a distinctive culture. But first, you'll have to decide how to get to either of these great cities. Are you coming by land, sea, or air?

## Flying to Montréal or Québec City

If you're flying to Montréal, you'll arrive at Montréal's **Pierre Elliott Trudeau International Airport** (☎ 800-465-1213 or 514-394-7377; www.admtl.com), YUL in airline-speak, in the suburb of Dorval, a 20 to 30 minute drive from downtown.

A number of major airlines serve Québec City's **Jean-Lesage International Airport** (☎ 418-640-2700), or YQB, but most of the traffic passes through Montréal first.

### Finding out which airlines fly there

Below, are the airlines that fly into Montréal and Québec City. For the contact information of specific airlines mentioned, see the Quick Concierge at the back of the book. For how to make your way to downtown Montréal and Québec City from each airport, see Chapters 8 and 16, respectively.

✔ Montréal's **Trudeau** airport is 12¾ miles (20.4 km) from downtown. Getting from the airport to downtown takes about 30 minutes from door to door — if there's no traffic. Many North American airline carriers fly there nonstop from the United States: **Air Canada** (from Boston, Chicago, Denver, Fort Lauderdale, Las Vegas, Los Angeles, Miami, New York, Orlando, San Francisco, San Juan, Tampa, Washington), **American Airlines** (from Chicago, Dallas/Fort Worth, Miami, New York), **Continental** (from Cleveland and Newark), **Delta** (from Atlanta, Cincinnati, New York), **Northwest** (from Detroit, Minneapolis/St. Paul), **United** (from Chicago, Washington), **US Airways** (from Philadelphia), and **WestJet** (Fort Lauderdale, Orlando). Some international airlines also fly to Montréal nonstop, including **Air Algérie** (from Algiers), **Air Canada** (from Bridgetown, Cancun, Cayo Coco, Cayo Largo, Frankfurt, Holguin, London, Mexico City, Montego Bay, Nassau, Paris, Pointe-à-Pitre, Port-au-Prince, Providenciales, Puerto Plata, Punta Cana, Rome, Santa Clara, Varadero), **Air France** (from Paris), **British Airways** (from London), **Czech Airlines** (from Prague), **KLM** (from Amsterdam), **Lufthansa** (from Munich), **Mexicana** (from Mexico City), **Olympic Airlines** (from Athens), **Royal Jordanian** (from Amman), **Royal Maroc Airlines** (from Casablanca), **Swiss International Air Lines** (from Zürich), and **Transaero** (from Moscow).

✔ Québec City's **Jean Lesage Airport** is somewhat smaller. It's served nonstop by **Air Canada** (from Montréal, Ottawa, and Toronto), **Continental** (from New York), and **Northwest** (from Detroit). Throughout the year, charter companies such as Air Transat offer nonstop transatlantic flights from London and Paris.

## Getting the best deal on your airfare

Competition among the major U.S. airlines is unlike that of any other industry. Every airline offers virtually the same product (basically, a coach seat is a coach seat is a coach seat), yet prices can vary by hundreds of dollars.

Business travelers who need the flexibility to buy their tickets at the last minute and change their itineraries at a moment's notice — and who want to get home before the weekend — pay (or at least their companies pay) the premium rate, known as the *full fare*. But if you can book your ticket far in advance, stay over Saturday night, and are willing to travel midweek (Tues, Wed, or Thurs), you can qualify for the least expensive price — usually a fraction of the full fare. Obviously, planning ahead pays.

Search **the Internet** for cheap fares. The most popular online travel agencies are **Travelocity.com** (www.travelocity.co.uk); **Expedia.com** (www.expedia.co.uk and www.expedia.ca); and **Orbitz.com.** In the U.K., go to **Travelsupermarket** (☎ 0845-345-5708; www.travelsupermarket.com), a flight search engine that offers flight comparisons for the budget airlines whose seats often end up in bucket-shop sales. Other Web sites for booking airline tickets online include **Cheapflights.com, SmarterTravel.com, Priceline.com,** and **Opodo** (www.opodo.co.uk). Meta search sites (which find and then direct you to airline and hotel Web sites for booking) include **SideStep.com** and **Kayak.com** — the latter includes fares for such budget carriers as JetBlue and Spirit as well as the major airlines. **Lastminute.com** is a great source for last-minute flights and getaways. In addition, most **airlines** offer online-only fares that even their phone agents know nothing about.

Watch local newspapers for **promotional specials** or **fare wars,** when airlines lower prices on their most popular routes. Also keep an eye on price fluctuations and deals at Web sites such as **Airfarewatchdog.com** and **Farecast.com.**

**Consolidators,** also known as bucket shops, are wholesale brokers in the airline-ticket game. Consolidators buy deeply discounted tickets ("distressed" inventories of unsold seats) from airlines and sell them to online ticket agencies, travel agents, tour operators, corporations, and, to a lesser degree, the general public. Consolidators advertise in Sunday newspaper travel sections (often in small ads with tiny type), both in the U.S. and the U.K. They can be great sources for cheap international tickets.

On the down side, bucket shop tickets are often rigged with restrictions, such as stiff cancellation penalties (as high as 50 percent to 75 percent of the ticket price). And keep in mind that most of what you see advertised is of limited availability.

Several reliable consolidators are worldwide and available online. **STA Travel** (www.statravel.com) has been the world's leading consolidator for students since purchasing Council Travel, but their fares are competitive for travelers of all ages. **Flights.com** (☎ 800-TRAV-800) has excellent fares worldwide, particularly to Europe. They also have "local" Web sites in 12 countries. **FlyCheap** (☎ 800-FLY-CHEAP; www.1800flycheap. com) has especially good fares to sunny destinations. **Air Tickets Direct** (☎ 800-778-3447; www.airticketsdirect.com) is based in Montréal; they also book trips to places that U.S. travel agents won't touch, such as Cuba.

**Frequent-flier membership** doesn't cost a cent, but it does entitle you to better seats, faster response to phone inquiries, and prompter service if your luggage is stolen or your flight is canceled or delayed, or if you want to change your seat. And you don't have to fly to earn points; **frequent-flier credit cards** can earn you thousands of miles for doing your everyday shopping. With more than 70 mileage awards programs on the market, consumers have never had more options. Investigate the program details of your favorite airlines before you sink points into any one. Consider which airlines have hubs in the airport nearest you, and, of those carriers, which have the most advantageous alliances, given your most common routes. To play the frequent-flier game to your best advantage, consult the community bulletin boards on **FlyerTalk** (www.flyertalk.com) or go to Randy Petersen's **Inside Flyer** (www. insideflyer.com). Petersen and friends review all the programs in detail and post regular updates on changes in policies and trends.

# Driving to Montréal or Québec City

From the south, you'll approach Montréal on either Highway 10 or 15; at the border, these highways are 87 from New York and 89 from Vermont. When you hit the city limits, follow signs for downtown, or "Centre-ville." From both the east and west, you drive into Montréal on Highways 20 or 40. You're also looking for Centre-ville.

Unless you're crossing the border in Maine, where you'd eventually hit Highway 73 to Québec City, cars from the United States should drive to Montréal first, and then follow either Highway 20 or 40, east to Québec City.

# Arriving by Other Means

If flying isn't an option, or if you're in the mood to see some country-side panoramas, you can always take the train. It's slower, but it's more romantic than air travel and not terribly stressful. Take a book along (I recommend the one you're reading now), spend hours talking to perfect strangers, or stare out the window like a 6-year-old on a car trip with his parents. Montréal's **Central Station** is located at 895 rue de la Gauchetière Ouest (☎ 514-989-2626). Québec's **Gare du Palais** is located at 450 rue de la Gare-du-Palais (☎ 418-832-0784).

 **VIA Rail** (☎ 888-842-7245; www.viarail.ca), Canada's national pas-senger rail network, offers significant discounts if you book at least five days ahead of time. Since a limited number of discounted seats are avail-able per train, they can sell out before advance offers expire. If you know that you're taking the train, try to book early.

**Amtrak** (☎ 800-872-7245; www.amtrak.com) offers daily departures to Montréal from New York City, departing in the morning and arriving in the early evening.

Another option is traveling by bus. **Greyhound Lines, Inc.** (☎ 800-661-8747; www.greyhound.com) travels to Montréal from the United States and Ottawa. Another bus line operates the route from Toronto. Yet another company takes care of busing people to and from Québec City. Regardless, in Montréal, all buses arrive at the **Station Centrale,** 505 bd. de Maisonneuve (☎ 888-999-3977 or 514-842-2281), in the Quartier Latin neighborhood. In Québec City the bus station, the **Terminus Gare du Palais,** is located at 320 rue Abraham-Martin (☎ 418-525-3000).

Both Montréal and Québec City are increasingly popular ports for east-ern seaboard boat cruises. The two cities are usually on St. Lawrence River and Great Lakes itineraries. Conveniently, the historic districts of both, Vieux-Montréal and Vieux-Québec — both must-sees of any stopover — are on the water, adjacent to the ports.

In Montréal, cruise ships dock in the commercial port. Travelers disembark at the **Iberville Passenger Terminal.** It's a short cab ride into town. Check out the **Port of Montréal's** Web site (www.port-montreal.com) for more info, including a schedule of cruise vessels. Or, call ☎ 514-283-7011.

Cruise-ship visitors stopping in Québec City arrive at the **Port de Québec's** new terminal (☎ 418-648-3640; www.portquebec.ca). It's located beside the Basse-Ville, but I suggest taking a taxi uphill to the front of the Chateau Frontenac to start your visit. You can walk down on your way back.

## *Joining an Escorted Tour*

You may be one of the many people who love escorted tours. The tour company takes care of all the details and tells you what to expect at each leg of your journey. You know your costs up front, and, in the case of the tamer tours, you don't get many surprises. Escorted tours can take you to the maximum number of sights in the minimum amount of time with the least amount of hassle. Many escorted tours to Montréal and Québec City also include other Canadian cities, such as Toronto and Ottawa, or other regions, such as Eastern Canada.

If you decide to go with an escorted tour, I strongly recommend purchasing travel insurance, especially if the tour operator asks you to pay up front. But don't buy insurance from the tour operator! If the tour operator doesn't fulfill its obligation to provide you with the vacation you paid for, you have no reason to believe that the operator will fulfill its insurance obligations, either. Get travel insurance through an independent agency. (I tell you more about the ins and outs of travel insurance in Chapter 7.)

When choosing an escorted tour, along with finding out whether you have to put down a deposit and when final payment is due, ask a few simple questions before you buy:

- ✔ **What is the cancellation policy?** Can the tour company cancel the trip if it doesn't get enough people? How late can you cancel if you're unable to go? Do you get a refund if you cancel? What if the tour group cancels?

- ✔ **How jam-packed is the schedule?** Does the tour schedule try to fit 25 hours into a 24-hour day, or does it give you ample time to relax by the pool or shop? If getting up at 7 a.m. every day and not returning to your hotel until 6 or 7 at night sounds like a grind, certain escorted tours may not be for you.

- ✔ **How large is the group?** The smaller the group, the less time you spend waiting for people to get on and off the bus. Tour operators may be evasive about this, because they may not know the exact size of the group until everybody has made reservations, but they should be able to give you a rough estimate.

✔ **Is there a minimum group size?** Some tours have a minimum group size and may cancel the tour if it doesn't book enough people. If a quota exists, find out what it is and how close the tour company is to reaching it. Again, tour operators may be evasive in their answers, but the information may help you select a tour that's sure to happen.

✔ **What exactly is included?** Don't assume anything. You may have to pay to get yourself to and from the airport. A box lunch may be included in an excursion, but drinks may be extra. Beer may be included but not wine. How much flexibility do you have? Can you opt out of certain activities, or does the bus leave once a day, with no exceptions? Are all your meals planned in advance? Can you choose your entree at dinner, or does everybody get the same chicken cutlet?

# Choosing a Package Tour

For lots of destinations, package tours can be a smart way to go. In many cases, a package tour that includes airfare, hotel, and transportation to and from the airport costs less than the hotel alone on a tour you book yourself. That's because packages are sold in bulk to tour operators, who resell them to the public. It's kind of like buying your vacation at a buy-in-bulk store — except the tour operator is the one who buys the 1,000-count box of garbage bags and resells them ten at a time at a cost that undercuts the local supermarket.

Package tours can vary widely. Some offer a better class of hotels than others; others provide the same hotels for lower prices. Some book flights on scheduled airlines; others sell charters. In some packages, your choice of accommodations and travel days may be limited. Some let you choose between escorted vacations and independent vacations; others allow you to add on just a few excursions or escorted day trips (also at discounted prices) without booking an entirely escorted tour.

Travel packages are also listed in the travel section of your local Sunday newspaper. Or check ads in the national travel magazines such as *Arthur Frommer's Budget Travel Magazine, Travel & Leisure, National Geographic Traveler,* and *Condé Nast Traveler.*

Another good source of package deals is the airlines themselves. Most major airlines offer air/land packages, including **American Airlines Vacations** (☎ 800-321-2121; www.aavacations.com), **Delta Vacations** (☎ 800-654-6559; www.deltavacations.com), **Continental Airlines Vacations** (☎ 800-301-3800; www.covacations.com), and

United Vacations (☎ 888-854-3899; www.unitedvacations.com).
Several big **online travel agencies** — Expedia, Travelocity, Orbitz, and
Lastminute.com — also do a brisk business in packages. If you're unsure
about the pedigree of a smaller packager, check with the Better Business
Bureau in the city where the company is based, or go online at www.bbb.
org. If a packager won't tell you where it's based, don't fly with it.

## *Package deals to Montréal and Québec City*

Some of the following companies offer both package and escorted tours.
Normally, a travel agent books these packages, but you can call or visit
the company Web sites on your own, too. Remember that some agencies
have better reputations than others; your travel agent, if you have one,
can guide you. Transportation to and from airports is often included but
is sometimes optional.

- ✔ **Air Canada Vacations** (☎ 800-254-1000; www.aircanada
  vacations.com) is the largest carrier flying into Montréal. It offers
  lots of options for visiting both cities, separately or together, including escorted tours, independent packages, fly/drive tours, ski holidays, and more. This is a great place to start.

- ✔ **Collette Tours** (☎ 800-340-5158; www.collettetours.com) offers
  three-, four-, and five-day getaways to Québec City, Montréal, or
  both cities, including accommodations, dinner at local restaurants,
  and city tours. Longer city tours of Eastern Canada also offer stops
  in Montréal and Québec City.

- ✔ **Continental Airlines Vacations** (☎ 800-301-3800; www.co
  vacations.com) offers separate packages to Montréal and Québec
  City, with hotel and airfare included and car rental optional. This is
  a good option if you like fancy hotels, because its packages include
  accommodations in upscale hotels.

- ✔ **Gogo Worldwide Vacations** (☎ 800-299-2999 or 702-457-1615;
  www.gogowwv.com) offers two- or three-night stays in Montréal and
  Québec City and cruises that pass through one or both ports. The
  short-stay packages do not include airfare, but they offer a good
  choice of hotels. Most of the packages are targeted to specific
  tastes and preferences, including casino admission, sightseeing,
  and admission to historical and cultural attractions, depending on
  what you're into. This company accepts reservations from U.S. and
  Canadian travel agents only.

- ✔ **Yankee Holidays** (☎ 800-225-2550 or 978-922-4819; www.yankee-
  holidays.com) offers vacation packages of mainly the two-day/
  three-night variety to both cities. Packages are targeted toward specific interests and can include museum passes, show tickets, gourmet meals, sightseeing tours, and festival admissions. The activity
  options are more limited in Québec City. Airfare is not included.

# Chapter 6

# Catering to Special Travel Needs or Interests

*M*ontréal and Québec City are about as open-minded and welcoming as cities get. The fun factor is spread out across all groups, whether you're traveling with a family, you qualify for senior discounts, you travel with a disability, or you're a gay or lesbian traveler.

## Traveling with the Brood: Advice for Families

Montréal is a safe, clean, relatively inexpensive city full of fun things for kids to do. While Québec City is hardly Disney World, you can find plenty of activities and sights that interest kids, and the city is well organized to accommodate families.

If you have enough trouble getting your kids out of the house in the morning, dragging them thousands of miles away may seem like an insurmountable challenge. But family travel can be immensely rewarding, giving you new ways of seeing the world through smaller pairs of eyes.

To locate accommodations, restaurants, and attractions that are particularly kid-friendly, refer to the "Kid Friendly" icon throughout this guide.

Here are a few tips to keep in mind when you're planning your kid-friendly trip:

✔ **Find out what your kids want to do.** Look for kid-friendly activities before you travel, and let the kids get in on the action by having them check Web sites, read brochures, and, well, dream of adventures to come.

✔ **Surf the Web for ideas.** Check out the "Family" filter in the Events Calendar section of www.tourisme-montreal.org for lists of kids' activities. The Montréal-based site www.yikeskids.com has an "Ask the Experts" link, where you can ask a local expert about entertaining little ones. Québec City's tourism site, www.quebecregion.com, doesn't have a specific kids section, but ask your kids to let you know what appeals to them.

✔ **Play up the history.** From bayonets and epic battles to fancy frocks and horse-drawn carriages, Montréal and Québec City have plenty of historical aspects that set kids' imaginations on fire.

✔ **Locate kid-friendly establishments.** Throughout this book, I identify kid-friendly hotels, restaurants, and attractions with the Kid Friendly icon.

✔ **Visit tourism centers.** In Montréal, the **Infotouriste Centre** is downtown at 1000 Square-Dorchester (☎ **877-266-5687** or 514-873-2015). In Québec City, the **Bureau d'information touristique** is just outside the walls of the Old City at 835 av. Wilfrid-Laurier (☎ **418-649-2608**). Both centers distribute free **Official Tourist Guides** with special sections on activities for kids.

✔ **Have a Plan B.** As far as the weather goes, the only certainty is uncertainty. Abrupt rain cancellations can definitely send kids into a tailspin, so plan activities for rain, shine, heat, and cold. Plan indoor activities, like museums, on rainy days, for relief from the cold in winter, or when you need to avoid the noonday heat in summer. Outdoor activities, such as inline skating or amusement parks, are best in late afternoon or early evening.

✔ **Have a little talk about language before you leave.** Older kids may be miffed when they don't understand what people around them are saying. Explain that most people in Québec speak French, and teach them a few words. *Bonjour* and *au revoir* will probably do (or check out the Cheat Sheet at the front of this book). You can turn it into a game and pick up a few words yourself.

Traveling with kids can be a riot, but sometimes it actually turns into one. If you want to leave the kids behind for a day — in trustworthy hands, of course — some hotels offer babysitting services. Ask at the front desk. The **Montréal YMCA,** downtown on rue Stanley, offers educational day care for kids 18 months to 5 years (☎ **514-849-8393;** www.ymca.ca).

The books *Family Travel* (Lanier Publishing International) and *How to Take Great Trips with Your Kids* (The Harvard Common Press) are full of good general advice that can apply to travel anywhere. Another reliable tome with a worldwide focus is *Adventuring with Children* (Foghorn Press).

You can also check out *Family Travel Times,* published six times a year by Travel with Your Children, 40 Fifth Ave., 7th Floor, New York, NY 10011 (☎ **888-822-4FTT** or 212-477-5524; www.familytraveltimes.com). It includes a weekly call-in service for subscribers. Subscriptions are $40 a year. A free publication list and a sample issue are available upon request.

You can find good family-oriented vacation advice on the Internet from sites such as **Family Travel Forum** (www.familytravelforum.com), a comprehensive site that offers customized trip-planning; **Family Travel Network** (www.familytravelnetwork.com), an award-winning site that offers features, deals, and trips; **Traveling Internationally with Your Kids** (www.travelwithyourkids.com); and **Family Travel Files** (www.thefamilytravelfiles.com), which offers an online magazine and a directory of off-the-beaten-path tours and tour operators for families.

# *Making Age Work for You: Tips for Seniors*

Montréal and Québec City are both great cities for such refined pleasures as fine dining and visiting museums and galleries. And, of course, if you're not in the mood for culture you can always head to the Montréal Casino.

Mention the fact that you're a senior citizen when you make your travel reservations. Many hotels still offer discounts for seniors. In most cities, people over the age of 60 qualify for reduced admission to theaters, museums, and other attractions, as well as discounted fares on public transportation.

Several Canadian tour companies offer organized holidays for seniors. In Montréal, **Prométour Cultural Tours** is located in Vieux-Montréal (☎ 514-848-7292). In Québec City, **Groupe Voyages Québec** is located right in the thick of it on Grande Allée (☎ 800-463-1598 or 418-525-4585).

If you need help or advice finding senior services, contact the **Fédération de l'age d'or du Québec (Québec Golden Age Federation)** in Montréal (☎ 418-650-3552).

CARP — Canada's Association for the 50-plus set — offers exclusive savings for members on various travel expenses such as flights and hotel rooms. They have an exhaustive travel website plus experienced travel experts standing by on their phone lines (☎ 877-450-7587; www.carptravel.com).

Most attractions in the city offer senior discounts, as do public transportation and movie theaters. Members of **AARP** (formerly the American Association of Retired Persons), 601 E St. NW, Washington, DC 20049 (☎ 888-687-2277 or 202-434-2277; www.aarp.org), get discounts on hotels, airfares, and car rentals. AARP offers members a wide range of benefits, including *AARP: The Magazine* and a monthly newsletter. Anyone over 50 can join.

Many reliable agencies and organizations target the over-50 market. **Elderhostel** (☎ 877-426-8056; www.elderhostel.org) arranges study programs for those ages 55 and over (and a spouse or companion of any age) in the United States and in more than 80 countries around the world. Most Canadian courses last five to seven days and may include airfare, accommodation in university dormitories or modest inns, meals, and tuition. **ElderTreks** (☎ **800-741-7956;** www.eldertreks.com) offers small-group tours to off-the-beaten-path adventure-travel locations, restricted to travelers 50 and older.

Recommended publications offering travel resources and discounts for seniors include the quarterly magazine *Travel 50 & Beyond* (www.travel 50andbeyond.com); *Travel Unlimited: Uncommon Adventures for the Mature Traveler* (Avalon); *101 Tips for Mature Travelers,* available from Grand Circle Travel (☎ 800-221-2610 or 617-350-7500); and *Unbelievably Good Deals and Great Adventures That You Absolutely Can't Get Unless You're Over 50* by Joan Rattner Heilman (McGraw-Hill).

# Advice for Travelers with Disabilities

Canada is a world leader in promoting the rights of people with disabilities. If you or someone in your party is traveling with a disability, you can find loads of resources and services to make your trip as hassle-free and fun as possible.

## Worldwide resources

Check out *A World of Options,* a 658-page book with resources for disabled travelers. It is available from **Mobility International USA,** P.O. Box 19767, Eugene, OR 97440 (☎ **541-343-1284** voice and TTY; www.miusa.org).

Organizations that offer a vast range of resources and assistance to disabled travelers include **MossRehab** (☎ **800-CALL-MOSS;** www.moss resourcenet.org); the **American Foundation for the Blind (AFB)** (☎ **800-232-5463;** www.afb.org); and **SATH (Society for Accessible Travel & Hospitality)** (☎ **212-447-7284;** www.sath.org). **AirAmbulance Card.com** is now partnered with SATH and allows you to preselect top-notch hospitals in case of an emergency.

**Access-Able Travel Source** (☎ **303-232-2979;** www.access-able.com) offers a comprehensive database on travel agents from around the world who offer experience in accessible travel; destination-specific access information; and links to such resources as service animals, equipment rentals, and access guides.

Many travel agencies offer customized tours and itineraries for travelers with disabilities. Among them are **Flying Wheels Travel** (☎ **507-451-5005;** www.flyingwheelstravel.com); and **Accessible Journeys** (☎ **800-846-4537** or 610/521-0339; www.disabilitytravel.com).

**Flying with Disability** (www.flying-with-disability.org) is a comprehensive information source on airline travel. **Avis Rent a Car** (☎ **888-879-4273**) has an "Avis Access" program that offers services for customers with special travel needs. These include specially outfitted vehicles with swivel seats, spinner knobs, and hand controls; mobility scooter rentals; and accessible bus service. Be sure to reserve well in advance.

Also check out the quarterly magazine *Emerging Horizons* (www.emerginghorizons.com), available by subscription ($16.95 year U.S.; $21.95 outside the U.S).

The "Accessible Travel" link at **Mobility-Advisor.com** offers a variety of travel resources to disabled persons.

Vision-impaired travelers should contact the **American Foundation for the Blind,** 11 Penn Plaza, Suite 300, New York, NY 10001 (☎ **800-232-5463**).

**British travelers** should contact **Holiday Care** (☎ **0845-124-9971** (in U.K. only); www.holidaycare.org.uk) to access a wide range of travel information and resources for disabled and elderly people.

## Canadian resources

While visiting Montréal and Québec City, you may also seek support or information from these national sources:

- ✔ *Abilities Magazine* is Canada's best magazine on disability lifestyle issues. The magazine's Web site (www.enablelink.org) offers links to a wide range of services in Canada for persons with disabilities.

- ✔ **The Active Living Alliance for Canadians with a Disability** can direct you to resources and services in Canada (☎ **800-771-0663** or 613-244-0052).

## Local resources

The best resource for accessible travel in Québec is an organization called **Kéroul.** Check out its tourism guide, *Accessible Québec,* for lists of accessible attractions. The group also provides travel packages for travelers with disabilities and a database of accessible places in the province (☎ **514-252-3104;** www.keroul.qc.ca).

Québec's **Recreation Association for People with Disabilities** *(Association Québécoise pour le loisir des personnes handicappées)* also provides information on accessible leisure activities (☎ **514-252-3144;** www.aqlph.qc.ca).

Most large hotels in both cities have some accessible rooms, so call around. The **Hyatt Regency Montréal,** 1255 Jeanne-Mance (☎ **514-285-1450**), in downtown Montréal, provides information on its facilities for disabled travelers.

Also consider:

- ✔ **Access to Travel** (www.accesstotravel.gc.ca): This government organization provides information on wheelchair-accessible transport in Québec.

- ✔ **Montréal Association for the Blind** (☎ 514-489-8201).

- ✔ **Office for Persons with Disabilities** (Montréal: ☎ 888-873-3905; Québec City: ☎ 888-643-1599).

- ✔ **West Island Association for the Intellectually Handicapped** (☎ 514-694-7090).

- ✔ **Québec Society for Disabled Children** (☎ 877-937-6171).

## Support while traveling to either city

In this section, I include the organizations to call while traveling to and from Montréal and Québec City:

- ✔ **Air Canada** (☎ 888-247-2262) and **Air Transat** (☎ 877-872-6728) offer wheelchair-accessible service.

- ✔ **Greyhound** (☎ 800-661-8747) and **Orléans Express** (☎ 514-395-4000) offer wheelchair-accessible bus service between Montréal and Québec City.

- ✔ **Via Rail** offers wheelchair-accessible service on some of its routes, but you have to reserve in advance (☎ 888-842-7245).

## Support while traveling within cities

Montréal's transit commission has 456 low-floor, wheelchair-accessible buses on over 40 routes in the city (☎ 514-280-5100). Despite the good intentions of the public-transport system, however, the buses are not actually that accessible, especially during peak periods.

**Paratransit** in Montréal offers free wheelchair-accessible minivan service, but you have to apply for the right to use it (☎ 514-280-8211). You can get the application from its Web site at www.stm.info/English/t-adapte/a-index.htm. Apply two months in advance. For wheelchair-accessible taxis, call **Taxi Boisjoli** (☎ 514-255-2815).

In Québec City, **Paratransit** (☎ 418-687-2641) also offers free wheelchair-accessible minibus service, but, as in Montréal, you need to reserve in advance. Call several days before your departure to register for services. Note that these are public transportation services, and you may wait up to eight hours for your minibus.

# Out and About: Advice for Gay and Lesbian Travelers

Québeckers have an extremely tolerant attitude toward gay and lesbian travelers. This is a country where gays and lesbians can legally marry, after all. The gay community in Montréal is one of the largest in the world, and the city even has its own **Gay Chamber of Commerce** and a **Gay Village Merchants Association.** For a list of gaycentric activities, events, and accommodations, go to www.montrealplus.ca. In Québec City you find fewer services and resources for the gay and lesbian communities, but that's because it's a smaller city, not because people are uptight.

## General resources

**The International Gay and Lesbian Travel Association (IGLTA)** (☎ 800-448-8550 or 954-776-2626; www.traveliglta.com) is the trade association for the gay and lesbian travel industry, and offers an online directory of gay- and lesbian-friendly travel businesses and tour operators.

Many agencies offer tours and travel itineraries specifically for gay and lesbian travelers. Among them are **Above and Beyond Tours** (☎ 800-397-2681; www.abovebeyondtours.com), **Now, Voyager** (☎ 800-255-6951; www.nowvoyager.com), and **Olivia Cruises & Resorts** (☎ 800-631-6277 or 510-655-0364; www.olivia.com).

**Gay.com Travel** (**800-929-2268** or 415-644-8044; www.gay.com/travel or www.outandabout.com), is an excellent online successor to the popular *Out & About* print magazine. It provides regularly updated information about gay-owned, gay-oriented, and gay-friendly lodging, dining, sightseeing, nightlife, and shopping establishments in every important destination worldwide.

The Canadian Web site **GayTraveler.ca** offers ideas and advice for gay travel all over the world.

The following travel guides are available at many bookstores, or you can order them from any online bookseller: *Spartacus International Gay Guide, 35th Edition* (Bruno Gmünder Verlag; www.spartacusworld.com/gayguide); *Odysseus: The International Gay Travel Planner, 17th Edition* (www.odyusa.com); and the *Damron* guides (www.damron.com), with separate, annual books for gay men and lesbians.

## The Montréal scene

According to Tourism Québec, Montréal's gay tourism industry is the third biggest draw to the city, after the Grand Prix and the Jazz Festival. With its circuit of bars, clubs, restaurants, boutiques, antiques shops, discos, bathhouses, and more, there's plenty of action. Montréal's Gay Village runs along rue Ste-Catherine between rue Berri and rue Papineau, in gritty-but-vibrant south-central downtown.

### Places to stay

Gay Village offers plenty of gay-friendly hotels and inns. For lesbians, there's **Pension Vallières,** 6562 rue de Lorimier (☎ 514-729-9552), an all-women hotel. For men, there's the **Auberge Cosy,** 1274 rue Ste-Catherine Est (☎ 514-525-2151; www.aubergecosy.com), **Bed & Breakfast du Village,** 1281 rue Montcalm (☎ 888-228-8455 or 514-522-4771; www.bbv.qc.ca), or **Le Chasseur B&B,** 1567 rue St-André (☎ 514-521-2238; www.lechasseur.com).

### Places to eat

Gay Village also has no shortage of great restaurants. I recommend **Area,** 1429 rue Amherst (☎ 514-890-6691), for fine French cuisine. Check out **La Piazetta,** 1101 rue Ste-Catherine Est (☎ 514-526-2244), for good thin-crust pizza.

### Bars and clubs

The hot spots of the moment in the Gay Village are **Unity II,** 1171 rue Ste-Catherine Est (☎ 514-523-2777); **Sky Club Pub,** 1474 rue Ste-Catherine Est (☎ 514-529-6969); **Club Parking,** 1296 Amherst (☎ 514-282-1199); and **Stereo,** 858 rue Ste-Catherine Est (☎ 514-286-0300), which opens late and carries on until the next morning. You can also find dozens of clubs and bars just by walking around the Village at night.

### Special events

The big yearly events in the gay and lesbian community are Montréal's **Gay Pride Parade** (☎ 514-285-4011; www.diverscite.org), which takes place at the beginning of August; the gay and lesbian film festival, **Image+Nation** (www.image-nation.org), in September; and the **Black and Blue Festival** (www.bbcm.org), the world's largest gay and lesbian benefit event, in October.

## The Québec City scene

In Québec City, the gay community is centered on rue St-Jean, between rue Dufferin and rue St-Augustin, just outside the walls of the Old City. For accommodations, the most famous inn is **Le 253,** 253 rue de la Reine (☎ 418-647-0590). Other good options are **Le Coureur des Bois,** 15 rue Ste-Ursule (☎ 418-692-1117), and **Guest House 727,** 727 rue d'Aiguillon (☎ 418-523-7705).

# Chapter 7

# Taking Care of the Remaining Details

● ● ● ● ● ● ● ● ● ● ● ● ● ● ● ● ● ● ● ● ● ● ● ● ● ● ● ● ● ● ● ● ● ● ● ● ● ● ● ● ● ● ● ● ●

*In This Chapter*

▶ Gathering your documents

▶ Understanding the ins and outs of renting a car

▶ Figuring out what travel insurance you need

▶ Making advance reservations for meals and special events

▶ Mastering the art of packing

● ● ● ● ● ● ● ● ● ● ● ● ● ● ● ● ● ● ● ● ● ● ● ● ● ● ● ● ● ● ● ● ● ● ● ● ● ● ● ● ● ● ● ● ●

  **T**ime is especially precious when you're traveling, so you don't want to learn on the job. This chapter explains all the things you need to know *before* you leave.

## Getting a Passport

A valid passport is the only legal form of identification accepted around the world. You can't cross an international border without it. Getting a passport is easy, but the process takes some time. U.S. citizens can find an up-to-date, country-by-country listing of passport requirements around the world on the "Foreign Entry Requirement" Web page of the U.S. Department of State Web site (http://travel.state.gov).

### Applying for a U.S. passport

If you're applying for a first-time passport, follow these steps:

1.  Complete a **passport application** in person at a U.S. passport office; a federal, state, or probate court; or a major post office. To find your regional passport office, either check the **U.S. Department of State** Web site (http://travel.state.gov) or call the **National Passport Information Center** (☎ 877-487-2778) for automated information.

2.  Present a **certified birth certificate** as proof of citizenship. (Bringing along your driver's license, state or military ID, or social security card is also a good idea.)

# Dealing with a lost passport

Always pack a photocopy of the inside photo page of your passport separate from your wallet or purse. In the event your passport is lost or stolen, the photocopy can help speed up the replacement process. While traveling in a group, never let one person carry all the passports. If the passports are stolen, obtaining new ones can be much more difficult, because at least one person in the group needs to be able to prove his or her identity so the others can be identified.

If you're a U.S. citizen and you either lose your passport or have it stolen, go to the **Consulate General of the United States of America,** 1155 rue St-Alexandre, Montréal (☎ **514-398-9695;** http://montreal.usconsulate.gov). Australians need to contact the **Australian High Commission,** in Ottawa (☎ **888-990-8888** or 613-236-0841; www.ahc-ottawa.org). New Zealanders should contact the **New Zealand High Commission,** also in Ottawa (☎ **613-238-5991;** www.nzembassy.com/canada).

U.K. citizens should contact the **British Consulate-General,** 1000 rue de la Gauchetière Ouest, Suite 4200, Montréal (☎ **514-866-5863;** www.britainincanada.com). In Québec City, an **Honorary Consulate,** Le Complexe St-Amable, 1150 Claire-Fontaine, Suite 700 (☎ **418-521-3000;** www.britainincanada.com), provides a more limited array of services for British Nationals, but it is still the first call to make upon losing your passport in Québec City.

---

3. Submit **two identical passport-sized photos,** measuring 2 inches by 2 inches in size. You often find businesses that take these photos near a passport office. *Note:* You can't use a strip from a photo-vending machine because the pictures aren't identical.

4. Pay a **fee.** For people 16 and over, a passport is valid for ten years and costs $97. For those 15 and under, a passport is valid for five years and costs $82.

Allow plenty of time before your trip to apply for a passport; processing normally takes three weeks but can take longer during busy periods (especially spring).

If you have a passport in your current name that was issued within the past 15 years (and you were over age 16 when it was issued), you can renew the passport by mail for $67. Whether you're applying in person or by mail, you can download passport applications from the U.S. Department of State Web site (http://travel.state.gov). For general information, call the **National Passport Agency** (☎ **202-647-0518**). To find your regional passport office, either check the U.S. Department of State Web site or call the **National Passport Information Center**'s toll-free number (☎ **877-487-2778**) for automated information.

### *Applying for other passports*

The following list offers more information for citizens of Australia, Canada, New Zealand, and the United Kingdom.

- ✔ **Australians** can visit a local post office or passport office, call the **Australia Passport Information Service** (☎ **131-232**), or log on to `https://www.passports.gov.au/Web/Contact.aspx` for details on how and where to apply.

- ✔ **New Zealanders** can pick up a passport application at any New Zealand Passports Office or download it from their Web site. Contact the **Passports Office** at ☎ **0800-225-050** in New Zealand or 04-474-8100, or log on to `www.passports.govt.nz`.

- ✔ **United Kingdom** residents can pick up applications for a standard ten-year passport (it's 5 years for children under 16) at passport offices, major post offices, or a travel agency. For information, contact the **United Kingdom Passport Service** (☎ **0870-521-0410**; `www.ukpa.gov.uk`).

## *Renting a Car — Or, Understanding Why Not To*

 If you plan to spend most of your time visiting Montréal within city limits, a car is probably more trouble than it's worth. In Québec City, driving is even less advisable. And Vieux-Québec is so small that you can walk anywhere you want to go.

---

# Traveling with minors

Having plenty of documentation always is wise when traveling with children in today's world. Usually, to prevent international child abduction, governments in some countries require documented evidence of your relationship with your children and permission for their travel from any parent or legal guardian who isn't present.

Having such documentation in hand, even if not required, facilitates entries and exits. All children must have their own passports. To obtain a passport, the child must be present — that is, in person — at the center issuing the passport.

Both parents must be present as well if the child is younger than 14. If one or both parents cannot be present, then a notarized statement from the absent parent is required.

In the United States, for more information about passport requirements for your children, call the **National Passport Information Center** (☎ **877-487-2778**) Monday to Friday 8 a.m. to 8 p.m. eastern standard time.

---

Parking in either city can be tough. Although you find lots of metered parking in downtown areas, competition for those spaces is fierce. In Montréal's residential neighborhoods, a system of reserved parking zones still has many locals baffled; you get the added handicap of trying to figure out the signs in French. To get out of the downtown core of Montréal, take the subway (known as the **Métro**) or any number of bus lines. Ask for a public transportation map at your hotel or at the ticket booth of any Métro station. You can also easily flag taxis in both cities.

Still want to drive? Well, the truth is, finding your way around Montréal is easy in a car, and renting one is a snap (see the appendix for agencies in both cities). Just remember that traffic signs are in French. Some other peculiarities to keep in mind are:

- ✔ It's legal to turn right on a red light everywhere in Québec except in Montréal.

- ✔ At many lights in both cities, the greens start out as green pointing arrows. For their duration, you can travel through the intersection only in the directions they are pointing.

- ✔ Gas is more expensive in Canada than the United States. You'll pay around C$50 to fill the tank of a midsize car.

Car rental rates vary even more than airline fares. The price depends on the size of the car, the length of time you keep it, where and when you pick it up and drop it off, where you take it, and a host of other factors. Asking a few key questions may save you hundreds of dollars.

- ✔ Weekend rates may be lower than weekday rates. If you're keeping the car five or more days, a weekly rate may be cheaper than the daily rate. Ask if the rate is the same for pickup Friday morning as it is Thursday night.

- ✔ Some companies may assess a drop-off charge if you don't return the car to the same rental location; others, notably National, don't.

- ✔ Check whether the rate is cheaper if you pick up the car at a location in town rather than at the airport.

- ✔ Find out whether age is an issue. Many car rental companies add on a fee for drivers younger than 25, while some don't rent to them at all.

- ✔ If you see an advertised price in your local newspaper, be sure to ask for that specific rate; otherwise, you may be charged the standard (higher) rate. Don't forget to mention membership in AAA, CAA, AARP, CARP, and trade unions. These memberships usually entitle you to discounts ranging from 5 percent to 30 percent.

- ✔ Check your frequent-flier accounts. Not only are your favorite (or at least most-used) airlines likely to have sent you discount coupons, but most car rentals add at least 500 miles to your account.

✔ As with other aspects of planning your trip, using the Internet can make comparison shopping for a car rental much easier. You can check rates at most of the major agencies' Web sites. Plus, all the major travel sites — **Travelocity.com** (or www.travelocity.ca), **Expedia.com** (or www.expedia.ca), **Orbitz** (www.orbitz.com), and **Smarter Living** (www.smarterliving.com), for example — have search engines that can dig up discounted car-rental rates. Just enter the car size you want, the pickup and return dates, and location, and the server returns a price. You can even make the reservation through any of these sites.

In addition to the standard rental prices, other optional charges apply to most car rentals (and some not-so-optional charges, such as taxes). The *collision damage waiver* (CDW), which, if purchased, releases you from having to pay for damage to the car in a collision, is covered by many credit card companies. Check with your credit card company before you go so you can avoid paying this hefty fee (as much as C$20 a day).

The car rental companies also offer additional *liability insurance* (if you harm others in an accident), *personal accident insurance* (if you harm yourself or your passengers), and *personal effects insurance* (if your luggage is stolen from your car). Your insurance policy on your car at home probably covers most of these unlikely occurrences. However, if your own insurance doesn't cover you for rentals or if you don't have auto insurance, definitely consider the additional coverage (ask your car rental agent for more information). Unless you're toting around the Hope diamond — and you don't want to leave that in your car trunk anyway — you can probably skip the personal effects insurance, but driving around without liability or personal accident coverage is never a good idea. Even if you're a good driver other people may not be, and liability claims can be complicated.

Some companies also offer *refueling packages,* in which you pay for your initial full tank of gas up front, and can return the car with an empty gas tank. The prices can be competitive with local gas prices, but you don't get credit for any gas remaining in the tank. If you reject this option, you pay only for the gas you use, but you have to return the car with a full tank or face charges of C$3 to C$4 a gallon for any shortfall. If you usually run late and a fueling stop may make you miss your plane, you're a perfect candidate for the fuel-purchase option.

Taxes on purchases are steep in Québec. The Goods and Services Tax (on your bill, in French, this shows up as the TPS) is 5 percent. The provincial sales tax (TVQ) is 7.5 percent. Québec squeezes an extra bit of provincial sales tax out of each purchase by calculating the TVQ on the total of the original price *plus* the TPS. I'm not sure how they get away with it, but no one seems to complain.

# Playing It Safe with Travel and Medical Insurance

The cost of travel insurance varies widely, depending on the cost and length of your trip, your age and health, and the type of trip you're taking, but expect to pay between 5 percent and 8 percent of the cost of the vacation itself. You can get estimates from various providers through **InsureMyTrip.com.** Enter your trip cost and dates, your age, and other information, for prices from more than a dozen companies.

**U.K. citizens** and their families who make more than one trip abroad per year may find an annual travel insurance policy works out cheaper. Check **Moneysupermarket.com,** which compares prices across a wide range of providers for single- and multitrip policies.

Most big travel agents offer their own insurance and will probably try to sell you their package when you book a holiday. Think before you sign. **Britain's Consumers' Association** recommends you insist on seeing the policy and reading the fine print before buying travel insurance. **The Association of British Insurers** (☎ 020-7600-3333; www.abi.org.uk) gives advice by phone and publishes *Holiday Insurance,* a free guide to policy provisions and prices. You might also shop around for better deals: Try **Columbus Direct** (☎ 0870-033- 9988; www.columbusdirect.net).

## Trip-cancellation insurance

Trip-cancellation insurance helps you get your money back if you have to back out of a trip, if you have to go home early, or if your travel supplier goes bankrupt. Allowed reasons for cancellation can range from sickness to natural disasters to the Department of State declaring your destination unsafe for travel.

The latest news in trip-cancellation insurance is the availability of **expanded hurricane coverage** and the **"any-reason"** cancellation coverage — which costs more but covers cancellations made for any reason. You won't get back 100 percent of your prepaid trip cost, but you'll be refunded a substantial portion. **TravelSafe** (☎ 888-885-7233; www.travelsafe.com) offers both types of coverage. Expedia also offers any-reason cancellation coverage for its air–hotel packages.

For details, contact one of the following recommended insurers: **Access America** (☎ 866-807-3982; www.accessamerica.com); **Travel Guard International** (☎ 800-826-4919; www.travelguard.com); **Travel Insured International** (☎ 800-243-3174; www.travelinsured.com); and **Travelex Insurance Services** (☎ 888-457-4602; www.travelex-insurance.com).

## Medical insurance

For travel overseas, most U.S. health plans (including Medicare and Medicaid) do not provide coverage, and the ones that do often require you to pay for services up front and reimburse you only after you return home.

As a safety net, you may want to buy travel medical insurance, particularly if you're traveling to a remote or high-risk area where emergency evacuation might be necessary. If you require additional medical insurance, try **MEDEX Assistance** (☎ **410-453-6300;** www.medexassist. com) or **Travel Assistance International** (☎ **800-821-2828;** www.travel assistance.com; for general information on services, call the company's **Worldwide Assistance Services, Inc.,** at ☎ **800-777-8710**).

## Lost-luggage insurance

On international flights (including U.S. portions of international trips), baggage coverage is limited to approximately $9.07 per pound, up to approximately $635 per checked bag. If you plan to check items more valuable than what's covered by the standard liability, see if your homeowner's policy covers your valuables, get baggage insurance as part of your comprehensive travel-insurance package, or buy Travel Guard's "BagTrak" product.

If your luggage is lost, immediately file a lost-luggage claim at the airport, detailing the luggage contents. For most airlines, you must report delayed, damaged, or lost baggage within 4 hours of arrival. The airlines are required to deliver luggage, once found, directly to your house or destination free of charge.

# Staying Healthy When You Travel

Getting sick will ruin your vacation, so I *strongly* advise against it (of course, last time I checked, the bugs weren't listening to me any more than they probably listen to you).

For domestic trips, most reliable health-care plans provide coverage if you get sick away from home. For travel abroad, you may have to pay all medical costs up front and be reimbursed later. For information on purchasing additional medical insurance for your trip, see the previous section.

Talk to your doctor before leaving on a trip if you have a serious and/or chronic illness. For conditions such as epilepsy, diabetes, or heart problems, wear a **MedicAlert identification tag** (☎ **888-633-4298;** www.medic alert.org), which immediately alerts doctors to your condition and gives them access to your records through MedicAlert's 24-hour hotline.

Contact the **International Association for Medical Assistance to Travelers (IAMAT)** (☎ 716-754-4883 or, in Canada, 416-652-0137; www.iamat.org) for tips on travel and health concerns in the countries you're visiting, and lists of local, English-speaking doctors. The United States **Centers for Disease Control and Prevention** (☎ 800-311-3435; www.cdc.gov) provides up-to-date information on health hazards by region or country and offers tips on food safety. **TripPrep.com,** sponsored by a consortium of travel medicine practitioners, may also offer helpful advice on traveling abroad. You can find listings of reliable clinics overseas at the **International Society of Travel Medicine** (www.istm.org).

## Staying Connected by Cellphone or E-Mail

Just because your cellphone works at home, doesn't mean it will work elsewhere on the continent — due to North America's fragmented cellphone system. Canadian cellphone networks support the following standards: GSM, TDMA, and CDMA.

If you're not from North America, you'll be appalled at the poor reach of our **GSM (Global System for Mobiles) wireless network,** which is used by much of the rest of the world. Your phone will probably work in most major cities; it definitely won't work in many rural areas and you may or may not be able to send SMS (text messaging) home.

In Canada, Microcell and some Rogers customers are GSM. GSM phones function with a removable plastic SIM card, encoded with your phone number and account information.

If your cellphone is on a GSM system, and you have a world-capable multiband phone such as many Sony Ericsson, Motorola, or Samsung models, you can make and receive calls across civilized areas on much

---

## Avoiding "economy class syndrome"

**Deep vein thrombosis,** or as it's known in the world of flying, "economy-class syndrome," is a blood clot that develops in a deep vein. It's a potentially deadly condition that can be caused by sitting in cramped conditions — such as an airplane cabin — for too long. During a flight (especially a long-haul flight), get up, walk around, and stretch your legs every 60 to 90 minutes to keep your blood flowing. Other preventive measures include frequent flexing of the legs while sitting, drinking lots of water, and avoiding alcohol and sleeping pills. If you have a history of deep vein thrombosis, heart disease, or other condition that puts you at high risk, some experts recommend wearing compression stockings or taking anticoagulants when you fly; always ask your physician about the best course for you. Symptoms of deep vein thrombosis include leg pain or swelling, or even shortness of breath.

of the globe, from Andorra to Uganda. Just call your wireless operator and ask for international roaming to be activated on your account. Unfortunately, per-minute charges can be high.

For many, **renting a phone** is a good idea. While you can rent a phone from any number of overseas sites, including kiosks at airports and at car-rental agencies, I suggest renting the phone before you leave home. North Americans can rent one before leaving home from **InTouch USA** (☎ 800-872-7626; www.intouchglobal.com) or **RoadPost** (☎ 888-290-1606 or 905-272-5665; www.roadpost.com). InTouch will also, for free, advise you on whether your existing phone will work overseas; simply call ☎ 703-222-7161 between 9 a.m. and 4 p.m. EST, or go to http://intouchglobal.com/travel.htm.

**Buying a phone** can be economically attractive, as many nations have cheap prepaid phone systems. Once you arrive at your destination, stop by a local cellphone shop and get the cheapest package; you'll probably pay less than C$100 for a phone and a starter calling card. Local calls may be as low as C10¢ per minute, and in many countries incoming calls are free.

# Accessing the Internet Away from Home

Travelers have any number of ways to check their e-mail and access the Internet on the road. Of course, using your own laptop — or even a PDA (personal digital assistant) or electronic organizer with a modem — gives you the most flexibility. But even if you don't have a computer, you can still find ways to access your e-mail and even your office computer.

## Without your own computer

It's hard nowadays to find a city that *doesn't* have a few cybercafes. Although there's no definitive directory for cybercafes — these are independent businesses, after all — three places to start looking are at www.ilesansfil.org, www.cybercaptive.com, and www.cybercafe.com.

Aside from formal cybercafes, most **youth hostels** nowadays have at least one computer you can get to the Internet on. And most **public libraries** across the world offer Internet access free or for a small charge. Avoid **hotel business centers** unless you're willing to pay exorbitant rates.

Most major airports have **Internet kiosks** that provide basic Web access for a per-minute fee that's usually higher than cybercafe prices. Check out copy shops such as **Kinko's** (FedEx Kinko's), which offer computer stations with fully loaded software (as well as Wi-Fi).

## With your own computer

More and more hotels, resorts, airports, cafes, and retailers are going **Wi-Fi** (wireless fidelity), becoming "hotspots" that offer free high-speed

Wi-Fi access or charge a small fee for usage. Most laptops sold today have built-in wireless capability. To find public Wi-Fi hotspots at your destination, go to **Jiwire.com;** its hotspot finder holds the world's largest directory of public wireless hotspots.

For dial-up access, most business-class hotels throughout the world offer dataports for laptop modems, and some offer free high-speed Internet access.

Wherever you go, bring a **connection kit** of the right power and phone adapters, a spare phone cord, and a spare Ethernet network cable — or find out whether your hotel supplies them to guests.

## Keeping Up with Airline Security

With the federalization of airport security, security procedures at U.S. airports are more stable and consistent than ever. You can check the average wait times at your airport by going to the TSA **Security Checkpoint Wait Times** site (waittime.tsa.dhs.gov). Generally, you'll be fine if you arrive at the airport **1 hour** before a domestic flight and **2 hours** before an international flight; if you show up late, tell an airline employee and she'll probably whisk you to the front of the line.

Bring a **current, government-issued photo ID** such as a driver's license or passport. Keep your ID at the ready to show at check-in, the security checkpoint, and sometimes even the gate. (Children under 18 do not need government-issued photo IDs for domestic flights, but they do for international flights to most countries.)

Know what you can carry on and what you can't. For the latest updates on items you are prohibited to bring in carry-on luggage, go to www.tsa.gov/travelers/airtravel.

Beat the ticket-counter lines by using the self-service electronic ticket kiosks at the airport or even printing out your boarding pass at home from the airline Web site. Using curbside check-in is also a smart way to avoid lines.

Help speed up security before you're screened. Remove jackets, shoes, belt buckles, heavy jewelry, and watches and place them either in your carry-on luggage or the security bins provided. Place keys, coins, cellphones, and pagers in a security bin. If you have metallic body parts, carry a note from your doctor. Liquid items must be less than 3.4 oz., and all must fit together in a quart-size Ziploc baggie; if you need more than that, place them in your checked baggage.

Use a TSA-approved lock for your checked luggage. Look for Travel Sentry certified locks at luggage or travel shops and Brookstone stores (or online at www.brookstone.com).

# Making Reservations in Advance

If you're counting on attending any of the big shows at festivals — particularly the **Jazz Festival** or the **Just For Laughs Festival** — purchase your tickets in advance. In the summer, try to book your room at least several weeks in advance — on the weekend of Montréal's Gay Pride Parade (early August), for example, there isn't a room to be had in town. The following sections give you some tips for advance planning.

## Surfing ahead of time

The Web is the best and cheapest way to find out what's going on in Montréal and Québec City, make reservations, and buy tickets before you leave home. Here are my favorite sources for Montréal.

- ✔ **Events:** To find out what's going on in Montréal, visit the **Montréal Plus** Web site (www.montreal-plus.com) or **Tourism Montréal** (www.tourism-montreal.org).

- ✔ **Sports:** Get schedules and reserve tickets for the Montréal Alouettes, Canadiens, or Impact through the **Admission Network** (www.admission.com).

- ✔ **Entertainment:** The best sources are the sites of Montréal's weekly cultural magazines, the Montréal *Mirror* (www.montrealmirror. com) and *Hour* (www.hour.ca); and Montréal's English-language daily paper, *The Gazette* (www.montrealgazette.com).

And for Québec City:

- ✔ **Culture:** *Voir* (www.voir.ca) is a free weekly cultural magazine, with a Québec City edition. The site covers special events and concerts, as well as film and dining.

- ✔ **A little bit of everything:** **Québec Plus** (www.quebecplus.ca), has directories of entertainment, accommodations, shopping, dining, and nightlife, bolstered with profiles and seasonal features. **Bonjour Québec** (www.bonjourquebec.com), operated by the province's Ministry of Tourism, contains pages on the entire province but has a section devoted to Québec City and the surrounding area. Québec City's official site, www.quebecregion.com, is run by the Québec City and Area Tourism and Convention Bureau.

## Reserving a table for dinner

Québeckers eat late. In the summer, restaurants in Montréal and Québec City fill up at 9 p.m. and serve until 11 p.m. or later. If you want to be in the thick of the eating action, don't make dinner reservations before 7:30 p.m. On the flip side, if you want to get a table at a popular restaurant at the last minute, tables are almost always available at 6 p.m. or earlier.

Weekends are the only times you have trouble making same-day reservations at most restaurants. In Chapters 10 and 18, I tell you which restaurants require reservations. If all my suggestions are booked, don't despair! Ask for alternatives at the front desk of your hotel. Neither city suffers from a shortage of culinary choices.

# Getting a Few Packing Tips

Think you can visit Montréal and Québec City in a sweat suit and sneakers? Think again. Both cities are slightly more stylish and formal than the North American norm; you really won't feel comfortable walking around in a jogging suit. Make sure you have at least a decent pair of slacks, a nice shirt, and clean shoes.

After you set your style standards, think practically. The weather is always unpredictable, so make sure you have at least one warm sweater, plus sunscreen, a sun hat, and an umbrella. For winter, bring a warm coat, mitts, hats, gloves, and boots — sorry, there's no way around it.

Travel lightly. I know I just told you to be stylish and prepare for rain or shine, but don't break your back over it. One large, preferably wheeled, suitcase and a carryon bag is the way to go.

## What not to bring

You probably don't need formalwear, so don't bog down your bags with fancy suits or satin pumps. For women, one dressy outfit will do — preferably a knit for ease of packing. For men, one jacket and tie combo will suffice. The best idea is always to have something versatile.

## What to bring

Your airline can tell you how much luggage you can bring. Usually you are allowed to check two pieces and carry one small bag with you, but many charter airlines allow only one checked piece of luggage and a carry-on bag. Airlines have become fairly strict about baggage limitations in the last couple of years, so if you plan to take a lot with you call the airline for specific weight and size limitations. You don't want any unpleasant surprises at check-in.

Your carry-on bag should contain whatever you can't afford to lose, and whatever you need to get by for a day in case your luggage gets lost (if they lose your bag, most airlines locate it quickly). Return tickets, vital documents, prescriptions, toiletries, an extra pair of underwear, something to read, a small bottle of water, and a light sweater or jacket does the trick.

Don't pack any sharp objects (scissors, tweezers, and so on longer than 4 inches in length) in your carryon bag. These items are strictly prohibited. Pack them in your checked luggage, or leave them at home.

In addition, think about the following when packing:

- **Leave your new shoes at home.** Even if your old ones are a little scuffed, you'll be far happier walking around in them instead of nursing bruises and blisters.

- **Find a color scheme.** When packing, choose colors that complement each other. Black, white, gray, and navy work wonders, as do beige and brown. Remember, most of the people who see you while traveling will probably never see you again.

- **Stick to knits.** They don't wrinkle. Leave your linen shirts at home. They're not worth it.

- **Bring along a little laundry soap.** A small bottle of laundry detergent weighs a lot less than those three extra shirts you were going to bring along just in case you dribble truffle juice down your collar. Do a little hand washing in the hotel sink.

- **Save up small bottles.** Pour into them only as much shampoo or shower gel as you need for your stay. You won't believe how much space and weight you save. Pharmacies also sell miniature travel versions of everything from toothpaste to hand cream.

- **Find an itsy-bitsy, teeny-weeny, yellow polka-dot . . . umbrella.** These days they make umbrellas that practically fit into your fist. An umbrella is a must for any trip to Montréal or Québec City; a compact version takes some weight off your shoulders.

# Part III
# Settling Into and Exploring Montréal

The 5th Wave · By Rich Tennant

"Montréal is wonderful. We spent the morning at Vieux Port, the afternoon at Vieux Mont-Royal, and right now we're at Vieux hotel room."

## In this part . . .

Now comes the fun part. Here's where I tell you about Montréal and guide you through its highlights, its best hotels and restaurants, and its hottest attractions. We'll talk shopping and nightlife, and you can follow one of my itineraries for visiting the city on foot. In case you want to swap urban landscapes for mountains, lakes, rivers, and wildlife, I offer a few recommended day-trips around Montréal.

# Chapter 8

# Arriving and Getting Oriented in Montréal

- - - - - - - - - - - - - - - - - - - - - - - - - - - - - - - - - - - - -

*In This Chapter*

▶ Finding your way into town

▶ Discovering Montréal's neighborhoods

▶ Knowing where to find tourist information

▶ Getting around on foot, via public transport, by bicycle, or in a car

- - - - - - - - - - - - - - - - - - - - - - - - - - - - - - - - - - - - -

**M**ontréal is a slender yet pot-bellied island with a mountain in the middle. Well, sort of. Mont Royal is a 761-foot-high hill, topped by a crucifix, that everyone calls "the Mountain." It looms large over several Montréal neighborhoods. And unless you're near the water, like in Vieux-Montréal, it's not obvious that you're on an island in the mighty St. Lawrence River. Suburban Montréalers who creep over the bridges and snake through the tunnels on their daily commutes never forget it, though. This chapter explains how to get to Montréal and how to get around after you arrive.

## Navigating Your Way through Passport Control and Customs

Canadians are such welcoming folks. We're well-known for being particularly nice, saying "sorry" all the time, and, generally, not wanting to offend. Our Customs officials, thankfully, are sterner individuals, charged with protecting our borders. The drill here, as at any border crossing, is to answer the officer's questions: no more, no less. If you think about it, this usually brief exchange just before beginning your vacation is like the opposite of a job interview, but you should treat it seriously just the same.

Customs officers usually ask where you're from, how long you plan to stay, and, maybe, whether you have anything to declare. Your answer to this last question is "no," unless you're importing goods or an incredibly large sum of cash. Just answer politely and don't take the interrogation personally.

## *Greater Montréal*

JARRY

Jean-Talon

De Castelnau

arc

adie

Fabre

Beaubien

Belanger

Beaubien

Rosemont

Christophe-Colon

de Lorimer

Papineau

bd. Rosemont

Charlemagne

bd. Pie-IX

JARDINS
BOTANIQUE

Masson

bd. St-Joseph

Biodome

Olympic
Complex

Viau

Pie-IX

Sherbrooke

Joliette

Outremont

St-Laurent
St-Urban
du Parc

St-Denis

Laurier

Frontenac

du Mont-Royal

Prefontaine

Ste-Catherine

MILE-
END

PLATEAU MONT-ROYAL

Mont-Royal

Rachel

Ontario

Ste-Catherine

Mont-Royal
Cemetery

PARC
LAFONTAINE

du Parc
la Fontaine

Duluth

GAY VILLAGE

Frontenac

Saint Lawrence River

PARC
ONT-ROYAL

des Pins
Dr.-Penfield

LE

uy-Concordia

ter

Antoine

Prince Arthur

Sherbrooke

Saint-Laurent

Place-des-Arts

McGill

Peel

Berri-UQAM

QUARTIER
LATIN

Papineau

Beaudry

bd. de Maisonneuve

Port
Ste-Hélène

La Ronde

CHINATOWN

Champ-de-Mars

Pont
Jacques-Cartier

Longueuil

Peel

Gare
Centrale

Place-d'Armes

ÎLE-
STE-HÉLÈNE

Gare
Windsor

Square-Victoria

Bonaventure

Lucien-L'Allier

Georges-Vanier

VIEUX-
MONTRÉAL

Pont de la
Concorde

Jean-Drapeau

el-Groulx

VIEUX-
PORT

Casino de
Montréal

Charlevoix

Wellington

ÎLE
NOTRE-DAME

LaSalle

Pont Victoria

Aut. Bonaventure

Saint Lawrence River

ÎLE DES SŒURS

Pont Champlain

| 0 | 150 Mi |
| 0 | 150 Km |

QUÉBEC

Québec

Ottawa

Toronto

**Montréal**

New York

See Chapter 7 for how to go about getting a passport.

While the reverse is no longer true, U.S. citizens and permanent residents don't require passports or visas to enter Canada. Americans can provide proof of citizenship and a government-issued photo ID (a citizenship or naturalization card, or a birth certificate with a valid photo identification, such as a driver's license). If you're not a U.S. citizen, but are a permanent resident of the United States, bring your green card and a photo ID.

All other foreign travelers visiting Canada need at least a passport — and maybe a visa. Before you go, find out what you need to enter Canada by visiting the **Canada Border Services Agency** Web site at www.cbsa.gc.ca.

See Chapter 12 for Customs regulations regarding how much loot you can take home.

# Making Your Way to Your Hotel

After you make it through Customs (see the preceding section), you're almost there. Now you have to drop your bags where you'll be staying. A good, hot shower can be worth several hours of sleep for weary travelers. Changing your socks is the next best thing. (Don't believe me? Try it.)

Depending on how you traveled to Montréal, these are the different options for finding your way downtown to your hotel room. After you're settled, your visit can begin.

## If you arrive by plane

You will arrive at Montréal's recently renovated and renamed **Pierre Elliott Trudeau International Airport** (☎ **800-465-1213** or 514-394-7377; www.admtl.com), formerly known as Dorval. After clearing Customs and claiming your checked baggage, you'll emerge in the public part of the Arrivals hall on the ground floor of the airport's only terminal.

At this point you may wish to exchange some money. The currency exchange counter in the Arrivals hall is open between 11:00 a.m. and 1:30 a.m. You can also withdraw Canadian cash from the 24-hour ATM located on this level.

Although it's often overlooked because people landing in Montréal typically rush downtown, there's a travelers' information counter in the Arrivals hall, which is open from 3:00 p.m. to 9:00 p.m. This is a useful place to obtain some initial guidance from a helpful, knowledgeable local. If you have yet to tie up some loose ends, they can help finalize your plans and confirm reservations or find last-minute alternatives. Either way, it may be one of your first encounters with a Montréaler. If the kiosk is closed, there is a phone that provides a direct line to the airport's general information desk, which is open around-the-clock.

All of the ground transportation happens curbside, in front of the Arrivals hall. From here, plenty of ways to travel downtown can be found.

## Getting to your hotel by taxi

**Taxis and limousines** are available from a dispatcher immediately upon exiting the Arrivals level of the terminal. Airport limousines are not the stretch brand favored by Paris Hilton and Co., but black, tinted-window, leather-interior sedans of the type used for whisking around international dignitaries.

The cabs charge a flat rate of C\$35 for fares to anywhere in downtown Montréal. If you're going elsewhere from the airport the trip is on the meter, with a minimum charge of C\$15. The limos charge a C\$50 flat fee for downtown.

If you didn't exchange any of your foreign money and didn't withdraw from the ATM, you could arrange to pay the fare by credit card at the taxi and limo dispatcher's booth. Some cab drivers will accept American dollars, but clear this up beforehand rather than after getting into the taxi and zooming off.

## Getting to your hotel by shuttle

The **Aérobus** (☎ 514-842-2281; www.laerobus.qc.ca) is a **shuttle bus** that runs frequently between the airport and downtown. This is the best value for getting downtown as quickly and hassle-free as possible. The one-way adult fare is C\$14, or C\$25 return. For seniors, the fares are C\$13 for a single and C\$22 return. Children between 5 and 12 years old pay C\$11.

The trip takes about 45 minutes. The shuttle from the airport departs every 25 minutes starting at 7 a.m. and ending at 2 a.m. (The return shuttle service from downtown to the airport is just as frequent but runs between 4 a.m. and 11 p.m.) The coach service from the airport isn't door to door, however. It takes visitors to Montréal's bus station, **Station Central,** in the Quartier Latin, adjacent to the Berri-UQAM Métro stop. From there, a free minivan shuttle takes travelers to any hotel.

## Getting to your hotel by public transportation

For a mere C\$2.75 in pocket change you can get downtown by Montréal's **public transportation system,** on the **STM** (☎ 514-786-4636; www.stm.info), but it's a bit of a schlep, requiring two buses and a subway (Métro) ride. To me, it's worth the extra bucks for the shuttle, especially if you have lots of luggage. If you arrive with only carryon bags, however, you can save some money going this route.

If you have time beforehand, check the STM's website, which has extensive schedules and maps for the bus and subway systems. It's always a good idea to know where you're going. However, if you're not exactly sure, you can rely on the bus drivers and the attendants in the Métro station ticket booths for general directions.

Catch city-bound bus No. 204 on the concrete island across the first lanes of traffic on the lower level in front of the terminal. It takes you on a short ride to Dorval Station, where you transfer to a second bus, No. 211, which goes directly to the Lionel-Groulx Métro (Orange Line). Hold on to your transfer stub — which the first driver extends in exchange for your fare — because you'll need it to get on the second bus and then onto the subway.

### Getting to your hotel by rental car

I discourage **renting a car,** mainly because Montréal is such a great walking city and because its traffic, one-way streets, and scarce parking are maddening. However, at Trudeau airport, the car rental agencies are located on the ground floor of the short- and long-term parking lot, located in front of the terminal, near the international arrivals. After you have your keys in hand, you can drive into town.

From Trudeau Airport, follow the signs for Autoroute 20 Est (Highway 20 East). You encounter many sharp turns exiting the airport, so be careful. Eventually, you come to a light and a traffic circle going through an overpass. Follow it around, counterclockwise, and get on the highway ramp on the other side — going eastbound. Follow the signs for Montréal, and **Centre-Ville,** and this highway takes you right into the heart of the city.

For tips on getting the best car-rental rates and information on car-rental insurance options, see Chapter 7. For names and contact information for car-rental agencies, see the appendix.

## If you arrive by car

**From the Canada–U.S. border,** allow an hour to get to Montréal. Depending on where you crossed, you approach Montréal's South Shore on either Autoroute 15 or Autoroute 10. To get to Montréal proper, you must traverse the river onto the island via one of the bridges; look for the Pont Jacques-Cartier or Pont Champlain, which are the two main ones.

**From Ontario,** you're about an hour away, depending on traffic, after you cross into the province of Québec going east along the Trans-Canada Highway. To remind you that you're no longer in Ontario, an extravagant, three-dimensional, illuminated sign-cum-monument stands on the border. You'll find an *Infotouriste Centre* at the first rest area, but you can always wait until you get to town. Eventually, the highway splits, so take Autoroute 20 and follow it straight into downtown (or *Centre-ville,* in French). At one point, Autoroute 20 breaks down into a slower road with a series of traffic lights and strip malls on either side. Do not despair — the highway starts again after a mile or two.

**From Québec City,** travel west along Autoroute 20 or 40; either takes you through Montréal. Autoroute 40 runs along the top of the island, and Autoroute 20 along the bottom.

## If you arrive by train

In these ultrafast times, rail travel has an undeniable romance. All passenger trains bound for Montréal rumble into the downtown *Gare Centrale*, 895 rue de la Gauchetière Ouest. **Via Rail (☎ 888-842-7245** or 514-989-2627; www.viarail.ca) is responsible for passenger train travel in Canada.

After you disembark and claim your luggage, you have several options. The Gare Centrale connects to the Bonaventure Métro station through a twisting network of store-lined corridors, part of the city's fabled "underground city." Follow the signs for the Métro. The subway system's logo is an eye-catching blue circle with a downward pointing arrow. Closer at hand, you'll find a taxi stand on the same level as the main hall. In addition, several excellent, though pricey, hotels are within walking distance. The Infotouriste Centre, a good place to begin your visit, is at the north end of nearby Square Dorchester. See the "Finding Information after You Arrive" section for hours.

 If you've ever wanted to know the words to Canada's national anthem, check out the inscription along the bottom of the bas-relief sculpture on the upper walls around Gare Centrale's main hall.

# Traveling between Montréal and Québec City

You have several options to get to Québec City from Montréal's main airport or from downtown.

## By rental car

To get to Québec City — a two- to three-hour haul eastbound — drivers can take either Autoroute 20 or Autoroute 40. Both end up in Québec City. The 20 goes along the south of the St. Lawrence River; the 40 goes along the north shore, past Trois Rivières.

For tips on getting the best rental deals, see Chapter 7. For telephone numbers of rental companies, see the appendix.

## By bus

**Autocars Orléans Express (☎ 514-842-2281;** www.orleansexpress.com) is the bus company that serves the Montréal–Québec City corridor.

From the airport, four daily bus departures to Québec City (11 a.m. and 2, 5, and 9:30 p.m.) occur via Montréal. If you're more than an hour away from one of these times, you may as well head to the downtown bus

station. There, with any luck, you'll be able to catch an earlier bus to
Québec City.

Express buses leave every hour on the hour to Québec City from
Montréal's **Central Bus Station,** located at 505 bd. de Maisonneuve Est.
The trip takes about three to four hours. Adult one-way tickets cost
C$50, and round-trip tickets cost C$77. See the section "Getting to your
hotel by shuttle" earlier in this chapter for details on the best way to get
from Trudeau Airport to Montréal's Central Bus Station.

### By train

Trains leave four times a day from Montréal's **Central Station,** 895 rue
de la Gauchetière Ouest (☎ 514-989-2626), to Québec City's **Gare du
Palais,** 450 rue Gare-du-Palais (☎ 418-692-3940). The regular fare costs
C$76. The trip takes a little over three hours.

See Chapter 16 for more information on arriving in Québec City.

# Figuring Out Montréal's Neighborhoods

Although a map comes in handy, Montréal's central neighborhoods are
so different from each other that you can orient yourself just by looking
around. You can walk them all in a single day, if you're an athlete. If
you're a normal person, take your time. Depending on your interests,
you can walk through each neighborhood in a matter of minutes, spend
an afternoon visiting, or take the entire day exploring its different parts.

### Vieux-Montréal

This is the oldest part of the city and the crown jewel of Montréal's
neighborhoods. Travelers flock here to soak up the European flavor
from the well-preserved remains of the French and English colonial periods. Just exploring the neighborhood's nooks and crannies is a treat.
Walk down an interesting-looking street and then another; find a secret
courtyard, fountain, or square; ride in a horse-drawn carriage; or stop
for drinks in the heart of it all, at an outdoor terrace along Place
Jacques-Cartier.

While Vieux-Montréal has always been "old," in recent years it has
shaped up into one of Montréal's most exciting neighborhoods. Residents
have rediscovered it, and returned to this neighborhood. They've bought
newly built condominiums or recently converted lofts. Tourists and
nine-to-five office workers used to have the sole run of the place — it
was desolate after dark — but not anymore. Now a wide variety of new
restaurants, stores, and nightspots are sprouting up at an incredible
rate. In many ways, Vieux-Montréal will play a large and central role in
the future of the city.

## Downtown

Rue Ste-Catherine is the downtown's main commercial artery. It is crowded all day long with businesspeople, tourists, shoppers, and all varieties of Montréal street creatures. In the morning, office types wielding aluminum mugs of caffeine dodge delivery trucks. After lunch, the shoppers are out in full force, hitting the street's boutiques, department stores, and shops. The foot traffic is especially heavy after work as the two crowds mingle. By dark, the mobs thin, leaving behind couples rushing to catch a movie or packs of friends carrying on into the night.

There's plenty more to downtown than the bright lights of rue Ste-Catherine. If you're a culture vulture, you can get your fix at the *Centre Canadien de L'architecture* (**Canadian Center for Architecture**), the *Musée des Beaux Arts* (**Fine Arts Museum**), the **McCord Museum,** and **McGill University**'s gated campus.

## Chinatown

Dim sum, dragon-beard candy, bubble tea, exotic fruits, herbal remedies, and curio shops — Montréal's Chinatown reveals many treasures to the adventurous traveler. The red, imperial arches along boulevard St-Laurent mark the neighborhood's northern and southern borders. Halfway in between and to the west, you can stroll along rue de la Gauchetière, which is closed to cars and has a greater concentration of Chinese shops and restaurants.

## Quartier Latin

Rue St-Denis, south of rue Sherbrooke, spills into Montréal's lively Latin Quarter. Serviced by the city's largest Métro station, Berri-UQAM, and squeezed between downtown, the Plateau, the Gay Village, and Chinatown, this neighborhood's central location makes it a crossroads of sorts. It's home to the recently completed *Grande Bibliothèque du Québec,* a feat of modern architecture. By evening, this neighborhood fills with friends looking for a spot to rendezvous over drinks. During the warmer months, the same friends are hanging out on the numerous terraces that run the length of the street. The **Bar St-Sulpice** is a choice destination for such occasions, with its huge beer garden that's extremely popular among university students.

## Gay Village

Happily, Montréal is an extremely gay-positive city. The stretch of rue Ste-Catherine, east of rue Amherst and as far east as avenue Papineau, is the epicenter of Montréal's vibrant and colorful gay community. Gay couples wander along the restaurant- and boutique-lined street hand-in-hand, and life goes on in a perfectly banal way.

## Plateau

For a long time, this has been Montréal's trendiest neighborhood. In the early '90s, the low rents of this formerly working-class neighborhood attracted artists and other creative types, and hip boutiques, restaurants, bars, and cafes soon followed. Now the very people who made the Plateau what it is are fighting tooth and nail to keep their rent-controlled apartments, as the Plateau's absentee landlords look to cash in with the condo crowd.

Despite the recent gentrification, everyone here still has their look and plenty of swagger. It's a great neighborhood for people-watching, shopping, and eating. The main streets with all the action include avenue Mont-Royal, boulevard St-Laurent, and rue St-Denis.

## Mile End/Outremont

Mainly a residential area, a mix of artists, writers, students, young couples, and immigrant families — predominantly Greek, Orthodox Jew, and Italian — inhabit this idyllic neighborhood. The shops along rue St-Viateur reflect the community's varied tastes and backgrounds. For several blocks, between avenue du Parc and boulevard St-Laurent, rue St-Viateur is full of appealing, yet quaint, health-food stores, cafes, restaurants, booksellers, gourmet shops, and the like. **Café Olympico** is the neighborhood hangout, with some of the best coffee in town.

Mile End is also bagel country. Montréal's bagels are even better than those in New York City; some say that they're the best in the world! Thinner and chewier than their Big Apple cousins and the inner circle tends to be much bigger, making it sometimes difficult to schmear with your favorite topping. **St-Viateur Bagel** and **Fairmount Bagel,** a block south on rue Fairmount, are the city's two most famous factories, churning out the bagels 24/7, and Montréalers keep up a perennial debate as to which bagel is best.

One block north on rue Bernard you find a similar scene, but everything becomes decidedly more upscale west of avenue du Parc, which is the neighborhood of **Outremont.** Although open only seasonally, **Bilboquet,** at the westernmost point on this commercial strip, serves up scoops of homemade ice cream in a wide variety of interesting flavors — including maple taffy, or *tire* (pronounced *teer*), available for only a few fleeting days in the spring. It's worth the trek for any flavor, really.

And, several blocks to the south, Avenue Laurier is another popular shopping street for the Outremont set. Several popular cafes, bistros, and upscale boutiques are well worth exploring.

## Little Italy

Boulevard St-Laurent north, way north, is the heart of Montréal's Italian community. This is where to go to catch up on European soccer league scores, challenge elderly men to bocce ball games in **Parc Martel,** or sip cappuccino and munch on biscotti at a sidewalk cafe. The loyal patrons of the '50s-style **Café Italia** claim that the coffee here is the best in Montréal.

At the strip's northern end, and a couple of blocks east of the intersection of boulevard St-Laurent and avenue Jean Talon, the immense **Marché Jean Talon (Jean Talon Market)** is at the geographical center of the city. It's packed on weekends. Formerly filled with new Canadians foraging for deals on produce, the crowd these days consists also of culinary highbrows searching for *terroir* items — quality local ingredients — and frugal gourmets of all stripes shopping for produce, cheeses, meats, and specialty items from Québec's bountiful regions, like ostrich meat from Salaberry de Valleyfield.

# Finding Information after You Arrive

Québec's Ministry of Tourism runs Montréal's **Infotouriste Centre,** 1001 Square Dorchester (www.bonjourquebec.com), a block south of rue Ste-Catherine, between rue Peel and rue Metcalf, and at the north end of Square Dorchester. It's the city's main resource for travel information on Montréal and the surrounding regions, and it's chock-full of free flyers and booklets.

It's a great place to start. Visitors can gather extensive information to plan their trip and book accommodations anywhere in Québec. There's a currency exchange counter, travel agency, sightseeing-tour operators, and a provincial parks representative. The keen and knowledgeable staff can answer almost any query you can muster. During the high tourist season, from mid-June through the beginning of September, the center is open daily from 8:30 a.m. to 7:30 p.m. After Labour Day until the end of May, it operates daily from 9 a.m. to 6 p.m. You can also reach the center by phone (☎ **877-266-5687** or 514-873-2015), should you need some roadside assistance while out and about. With different hours from the actual information center, lines are open June through August, Monday to Friday 8 a.m. to 10 p.m. (except for Wed, when they don't open until 10 a.m.), and from early September through May Monday through Friday 9 a.m. to 7 p.m. (except for Wed, when they don't open until 10 a.m.). On weekends all year, you can reach the center from 9 a.m. to 5 p.m.

The **Tourist Information Centre of Vieux-Montréal** (www.tourisme-montreal.org) is at 174 rue Notre-Dame Est, at the northwest corner of Place Jacques-Cartier, an immense sloping square in honor of the city's founder. This is an excellent resource with a helpful staff, maps, and brochures. In this part of town their hours are somewhat different. During the high tourist season from early June to early September they are open every day from 9 a.m. to 7 p.m. Otherwise, their hours are between 9 a.m. and 5 p.m. During the winter from mid-October to mid-April they close Mondays and Tuesdays, and the opening hours during the rest of the week remain 9 a.m. to 5 p.m. The office is closed for the lunch hour, from noon to 1 p.m.

Directory Assistance is free from Bell pay phones. If you're looking to find a local number, dial ☎ **411,** just like in the United States. Doing so from a hotel room isn't such a hot idea. The usual charge from a land line is C$1.75, but it's common practice for hotels to add on a hefty premium for connecting you to directory assistance. Online directory assistance, if you have access to the Internet, is www.canada411.ca.

# Getting Around Montréal

However you choose to get around Montréal, keep in mind that it's a large city with all the modern conveniences and headaches caused by the sheer volume of people on the move. In other words, getting around the city has its ups and downs.

On the plus side:

- ✔ The city's central neighborhoods are compact and well served by bike paths and an extensive public transport system that includes four subway lines and a network of buses.
- ✔ Taxis are plentiful and reasonably priced.

On the minus side:

- ✔ Driving in the city can be a hassle, because of an inordinate number of narrow, one-way streets. Chances are you'll spend some of your time in a taxi stuck behind a garbage or recycling truck, with only Montréal's mediocre English-language radio programming to help you pass the time.
- ✔ Parking, construction, and rush hours are the same nightmares you get in any big city.

## By foot

Walking is one of the best ways to travel in Montréal (see Chapter 13 for suggested walking itineraries). With the occasional support of public transportation and taxis, you can get everywhere you need to go on foot. Along the way, you experience much more of what Montréal has to offer. Even in the cold weather, a couple layers of clothing and a brisk pace go a long way toward combating the elements. So, don gloves, a warm hat, and a scarf, and be on your way!

Compared to most of the continent, where suburban attitudes are the rule, Montréal *feels* urban. Montréal's spirit is on the sidewalks of the neighborhoods, not in malls in the outlying areas. The sights and smells of the rapidly changing streetscapes are a feast for the senses.

The city's streets are inordinately safe by North American standards. Although a modicum of street smarts is a must, there's no mood of fear and imminent danger on Montréal's streets. In fact, it's quite the contrary. The general population of stylish pedestrians is laid back, friendly, and usually glad to offer directions.

## By public transportation (Métro and bus)

Completed for Expo '67, Montréal's Métro stations were built with a futuristic vision that has yet to materialize above ground. Today, the look is retro, maybe a little kitschy. Even the orange interiors of some trains are reminiscent of something out of Stanley Kubrick's film *2001: A Space Odyssey.*

Run by the *Sociéte de Transport de Montréal,* or **STM** (☎ **514-786-4636;** www.stm.info), the Métro has 68 stops. The lines extend to the farthest reaches of the city. The downtown core is serviced by the Green and Orange lines, between Lionel-Groulx in the west and Berri-UQAM in the east. The trains run from 5:30 a.m. until about 12:30 a.m. See the Cheat Sheet in the front of this book for a tear-out map.

 Ask the ticket collector at any Métro station for a free map of the Island of Montréal's entire transit system, which includes all the bus routes. (The map is very handy, even if you never board public transport during your stay.)

Near the ticket booths, schedules and routes of individual buses departing from that station are available. Most bus stops around the city have a departure schedule. The buses on some of the city's major arteries run 24 hours a day; other schedules vary. During the day, the service is regular — both above and below ground — so you won't need to plan around it, but just in case you can also get transit schedules by calling the STM or visiting its Web site. (See Chapter 6 for information on public transportation for the disabled.)

A single fare is good for one transfer, or *correspondence,* between the Métro and the buses. The rule is that you have to take a transfer at your point of origin, not ask for one later.

In the Métro stations, silver mechanized dispensers just beyond the turnstiles spit out transfers at the press of a button. Bus drivers automatically extend one to you when you pay the fare, and they're valid for an hour and a half.

Should you forget to grab one before getting on the subway, you can get it on your way out, and bus drivers usually accept them. If drivers question you, tell them you're a tourist and new at this and they'll probably let you on. You must also produce a valid transfer when switching between buses.

 The STM charges C$2.75 for a single ride, but if you plan to use public transit several times while in Montréal buying in bulk may prove more economical. A strip of six tickets costs C$12, a single-day pass is C$9, a three-day pass is C$17, and a weekly pass (from Mon–Sun) runs you

C$19. Monthly passes are also available for C$65. You can buy any of these at a Métro station's ticket booth and at some *dépanneurs* (convenience stores) and drugstores throughout the city.

## By bicycle

Montréal is North America's bicycling capital. Despite the harsh winter climate that sends most cyclists into hibernation for four months, *Bicycling Magazine* rated Montréal tops in North America for its cycling infrastructure and culture.

A bike is great way to get around Montréal when the weather's not too nasty, although doing battle in traffic with aggressive drivers can be a hair-raising experience. Luckily, the city has an extensive network of bike paths, 250 miles in all, which provides a less harrowing ride through much of the city, including stretches through parks and along the waterfront.

You can rent a bicycle at several places in Montréal. The best are:

- **Cycle Pop et Pop Tours,** 1000 rue Rachel Est (☎ **514-526-2525;** www.cyclepop.ca)

- **La Cordée Plein-Air,** 2159 rue Ste-Catherine Est (☎ **800-567-1106** or 514-524-1106; www.lacordee.com)

- **Montréal on Wheels,** 27 rue de la Commune Est (☎ **514-866-0633;** www.caroulemontreal.com)

Just recently, the Plateau's municipal officials launched the city's first summer bike-share program, named **Bécik Vert,** or green bike (www.mont-royal.net). From mid-June to early September, using the program merely requires that you entrust it with a photo ID while you borrow one of its 20 bikes. Two bike-share outlets exist: the main one is at the **Av. Mt-Royal information kiosk**, at 470 av. du Mont-Royal Est, in Place Gérald-Godin, just in front of the entrance to the Mont-Royal Métro.

## By car

If there were no cars in the streets, Montréal would be an easy city to navigate. Unfortunately, the driving culture here is somewhat distinct from the rest of Canada. Drivers don't ask; they take. For example, in other cities, drivers request a lane change by using their turn signals. Montréalers don't really wait for an answer, they just signal and squeeze right in, often simultaneously — that is, if they bother to signal at all.

There's more. You can't turn right on a red light in Montréal (a fine rule when you consider that many drivers here are still learning to associate red lights with full stops). A green arrow means you can turn only in that direction; a solid green means you can go in any direction. Advanced (flashing) green lights can occur either at the beginning or at the end of a green light's phase. On a flashing green, the oncoming traffic has a red light, pedestrians are supposed to stay put, and drivers with the light can turn right and left at will.

And then there are the turning signs. Rather than say where you can't go at an intersection, Québec's traffic signs tell drivers where they *can* go. Most intersections have a white sign with a green circle around a set of black arrows. These black arrows indicate the directions a car can legally turn at that intersection. A sign with an arrow pointing straight ahead and an arrow pointing to the right means you *can't* turn left. Go figure. If you don't see a sign with green arrows, you can turn in any direction.

### Filling up

In Canada, car owners buy their gasoline or diesel fuel by the liter, which is roughly equivalent to a quart. Canadian gas prices are somewhat more expensive than in the United States but are still considerably cheaper than European fuel. Multiply the per-liter price by four for an approximate gallon comparison.

### Parking tips for the brazen

Like any big city, parking in Montréal is a hassle. Deciphering the parking signs is probably the most difficult part. You need not only a keen eye but also a firm grasp of the days of the week in French. (Beginning with Monday, it's *lundi, mardi, mercredi, jeudi, vendredi, samedi,* and *dimanche.*) Most of the time, these words appear in their abbreviated form on the signs, which is just the first three letters of each. You also need to familiarize yourself with 24-hour (military) clock times.

One plus to driving is that Montréal has lots of metered parking downtown and in the commercial areas of the city. You can also find free parking in the residential neighborhoods just north of rue Sherbrooke — though, to be honest, you may spend half the evening looking for a spot.

Montréal residents with parking permits add to the confusion, hogging much of the residential curbsides. Arrows delimit the extent of their permit parking zones. If you see two empty spots in a row, chances are you're staring at a restricted zone.

The downtown area has plenty of parking lots. They hit you up for C$12 to C$15 per day — not bad compared to other large cities, but it still hurts.

## By taxi

Montréal taxis don't sport bold color schemes or patterns like cabs in other cities. A white light mounted on its roof is the only indication that a vehicle is a taxicab. When the light is on, the cab is available. Getting around in one of them is a reasonable proposition as long as you don't get snarled in traffic. At that point, your ride can begin to get expensive.

The meter starts at C$3.15 and climbs at a rate of roughly C$2.50 per mile of driving or C55¢ per minute of waiting in traffic. Trips across the downtown core usually range between C$5 and C$15. The city's chauffeurs are a mixed bag — from career cabbies, who can tell you that boulevard René-Levesque used to be called rue Dorchester, to recently arrived immigrants, sometimes sitting on their PhDs in chemistry. Hailing a cab is easy. Just stick out your hand, and cabs swarm you like gadflies. Late at night, the more enterprising chauffeurs sometimes honk gently at pedestrians to remind you of their presence.

If you aren't near a main artery or don't feel like waiting for a taxi to pass, you can call for one. The two big local cab companies are **Taxi Co-op** (☎ 514-725-9885), and **Taxi Diamond** (☎ 514-273-6331).

# Chapter 9

# Checking In at Montréal's Best Hotels

*W*ith more than 25,000 rooms, Montréal has the highest proportion of hotel rooms per capita in North America. Options run the full gamut, giving you loads of choices for your stay. You can opt for the cinder-block austerity of a college dorm room, the opulent luxury of a penthouse suite, and anything in between. However, booking a room on short notice can be a problem, especially during weekends or any time during the high tourist season of May to September. To get the room you want, plan ahead. Making your reservations well in advance can save you money, too.

## Getting to Know Your Options

Prices for double rooms at the most lavish hotels begin around C$250 a night. That may sound steep, but compared to elsewhere in the world it's a steal. So Montréal may be the place to splurge on lap-of-luxury accommodations if that's what you're into. If that's not what you want, Montréal offers loads of affordable options, too.

### Boutique hotels

Step into a world of design-forward surroundings and attentive care. Because boutique hotels usually offer fewer than 100 rooms, you receive the conscientious hospitality that has long since disappeared from the hustle and bustle of larger hotel operations. The good feng shui and the Zen-like service make you feel like you've stumbled into a futuristic utopia.

### Luxury hotels

The classic elegance and grandeur of these hotels make them the pinnacle of luxury accommodations. The committed staff in dapper uniforms buzz about seeing to the guests' every desire (well, almost). The rooms are top-notch, and the amenities usually include a pool, a spa, and a gym.

### Chain hotels

A familiar name can be comforting when you're away from home. International hotel chains, such as Hilton, Holiday Inn, Marriott, Novotel, and Sheraton, offer guests a similar product the world over, so you know more or less what to expect. Most of these large, somewhat anonymous hotels are downtown and cater to business travelers and convention-goers. The rooms are well kept, and the décor is usually subdued and inoffensive.

### Independent hotels

The rooms and services can vary greatly among independently owned and operated establishments. They tend to be smaller, offer more personalized service, and exude greater amounts of local character and flair than large chain hotels.

### Bed-and-breakfasts

Bed-and-breakfasts (B&Bs) can be anything from one to a half-dozen rooms in a private house. The home usually has a separate bathroom for guests, but you may have to share it if other guests are at the B&B. In-room bathrooms are available at some B&Bs but usually at a premium. As the name indicates, the deal includes breakfast — either continental or full. The proprietors are usually welcoming, helpful types, brimming with interesting perspectives and insider recommendations. Although they don't offer the amenities of a large hotel, staying in these places can sometimes be a surprisingly inexpensive way to travel.

In Montréal, several agencies broker the available rooms at the bed-and-breakfasts in the city.

- ✔ **Bienvenue B&B** (☎ **800-363-9635** or 514-844-5897)
- ✔ **Downtown Montréal B&B Network** (☎ **800-267-5180**)
- ✔ **Montréal Oasis** (☎ **514-935-2312**)

## Finding the Best Room at the Best Rate

The timing of your trip dictates how much you end up spending on accommodations. Hotel room prices are higher during the tourist season, which is from early May through September. During the summer, Montréal hosts a variety of festivals and special events, and rooms can be scarce during the festival season. Check what's going on during your stay, and then book well in advance if you plan to arrive during a major event. (See Chapter 3 for Montréal's festival and events schedule.) During the rest of the year, expect to pay between 10 percent and 15 percent less than during the summer peak.

## Finding the best rate

The *rack rate* is the maximum rate that a hotel charges for a room. It's the rate you get if you walk in off the street and ask for a room for the night. Hotels are happy to charge you the rack rate, but you almost always can do better. Perhaps the best way to avoid paying the rack rate is surprisingly simple: Just ask for a cheaper or discounted rate. You may be pleasantly surprised.

In all but the smallest accommodations, the rate you pay for a room depends on many factors — chief among them is how you make your reservation. A travel agent may be able to negotiate a better price with certain hotels than you can get by yourself. (That's because the hotel often gives the agent a discount in exchange for steering his or her business toward the hotel.)

 Reserving a room through the hotel's toll-free number may also result in a lower rate than calling the hotel directly. On the other hand, the central reservations number may not know about discount rates at specific locations. For example, local franchises may offer a special group rate for a wedding or family reunion, but they may neglect to tell their central booking line. Your best bet is to call both the local number and the toll-free number and see which one gives you a better deal. If the telephone operator tries to steer you to the reservations call center, trump her move by asking to speak with the front desk.

If you're staying only for a couple days in the middle of the week, be sure to ask for the midweek rate.

Room rates (even rack rates) change with the season, as occupancy rates rise and fall. But even within a given season room prices are subject to change without notice, so the rates quoted in this book may be different from the actual rate you receive when you make your reservation. Be sure to mention memberships (AAA, CAA, AARP, CARP, unions, professional associations, and so on). You never know when an affiliation may be worth a few dollars off your room rate.

In order to make a meaningful price comparison between room rates, always ask whether the quoted price includes sales tax. If it doesn't, count on paying 13 percent more at checkout. Ask about any other hidden charges that you may encounter during your stay, like parking.

## Surfing the Web for hotel deals

Gleaning impressions from the Internet can be helpful when you're choosing accommodations. Through the pictures on a hotel's Web site, you can get a feel for its lobby, facilities, rooms, and neighborhood location — invaluable information.

Shopping online for hotels is generally done one of two ways: by booking through the hotel's own Web site or through an independent booking agency. These Internet hotel agencies have multiplied in mind-boggling numbers of late, competing for the business of millions of consumers surfing for accommodations around the world. This competitiveness can be a boon to consumers who have the patience and time to shop and compare the online sites for good deals — but shop they must, for prices can vary considerably from site to site. And keep in mind that hotels at the top of a site's listing may be there for no other reason than that they paid money to get the placement.

However, you can use the Web in other ways to hunt for discounted rooms. Of the "big three" travel booking sites, **Expedia.com** (or www.expedia.ca) offers a long list of special deals and "virtual tours" or photos of available rooms so you can see what you're paying for (a feature that helps counter claims that the best rooms are often held back from bargain-booking Web sites). **Travelocity.com** (or www.travelocity.ca) posts unvarnished customer reviews and ranks its properties according to the AAA rating system. Also reliable are **Hotels.com** and **Quikbook.com.** An excellent free program, **TravelAxe** (www.travelaxe.net), can help you search multiple hotel sites at once — even ones you may never have heard of — and conveniently lists the total price of the room, including taxes and any service charges. Another booking site, **Travelweb** (www.travelweb.com), is partly owned by the hotels it represents (including the Hilton, Hyatt, and Starwood chains) and is, therefore, plugged directly into the hotels' reservations systems. *Remember:* When shopping for accommodation online it's a good idea to **get a confirmation number** and **make a printout** of any online booking transaction. Perhaps call before of your departure to confirm your reservation as well.

**HotelChatter.com** is a daily webzine offering smart coverage and critiques of hotels worldwide. Go to **TripAdvisor.com** or **HotelShark.com** for helpful independent consumer reviews of hotels and resort properties.

In the opaque Web site category, **Priceline** and **Hotwire** are even better for hotels than for airfares. With both, you're allowed to pick the neighborhood and quality level of your hotel before offering up your money. Priceline seems much better at getting five-star accommodations for three-star prices, rather than anything at the bottom of the scale. Be sure to go to the **BiddingForTravel** Web site (www.biddingfortravel.com) before bidding on a hotel room on Priceline; it features a fairly up-to-date list of hotels that Priceline uses in major cities. For both Priceline and Hotwire, you pay up front and the fee is nonrefundable. *Note:* Some hotels don't provide loyalty-program credits or points or other frequent-stay amenities when you book a room through opaque online services.

## Reserving the best room

To ensure you get peace and quiet in your room, request one on an upper floor, away from the hotel's meeting areas, dining rooms, and other noisy amenities like the pool. Also ask that your room be away from any scheduled renovations. In addition, more and more hotels distinguish between smoking and nonsmoking rooms. If you feel adamant about getting one room or the other, be sure to tell every person handling your reservation about your preference.

Corner rooms are often big and bright, and sometimes one is available at the same rate as a standard room. If you're traveling as a family or small group, consider asking about a suite, which may sleep as many people but usually costs less than two separate rooms. If you're not happy with your room, tell the front-desk staff immediately. Most hotels will exchange your room if another is unoccupied.

## Arriving without a Reservation

If you're trundling around at dusk with no place to stay, call Tourism Québec's **Infotouriste Centre** (☎ 877-266-5687) or stop in. The center is open daily from 8:30 a.m. to 7:30 p.m. during the high tourist season. In the low season its hours are daily 9 a.m. to 6 p.m. The office is downtown at 1001 Square Dorchester, near the corner of rue Peel and rue Ste-Catherine. Look for the blue-and-white question-mark sign. The staff there can get you situated for one night or for the duration of your stay.

Tourism Québec's member hotels set aside rooms for a proprietary database spanning every price range and star rating. Friendly bilingual representatives tell you whether any are available in places that may otherwise claim to be sold out. They can also book B&Bs, condos, chalets, and university dormitories. The latter are available only during the summer season.

## Montréal's Best Hotels from A to Z

Each hotel listing includes $ symbols, indicating the price range of the hotel's rack rates (based on double occupancy) for one night. Table 9-1 shows what to expect in each price category.

| Table 9-1 | Key to Hotel Dollar Signs | |
|---|---|---|
| *Dollar Sign(s)* | *Price Range* | *What to Expect* |
| $ | Less than C$100 | Simple and inexpensive, these accommodations should offer all the basics: a room with a lock, a firm bed, and clean towels and sheets. A light continental breakfast may be included. Hotels offering rooms at these prices probably don't have an extensive catalog of services to cater to your every whim, but the front-desk clerks are usually delighted to point you in the right direction for whatever you want. |

*(continued)*

## Downtown Montréal Accommodations

Auberge de La Fontaine **15**
Best Western Hotel Europa **9**
Crowne Plaza **14**
Fairmont The Queen Elizabeth **11**
Hilton Montréal Bonaventure **12**
Hotel de la Montagne **6**

Hôtel Le Germain **5**
Hotel Omni Mont-Royal **4**
Hôtel Opus **13**
Loews Hotel Vogue **7**
Meridien Versailles Montréa

Montréal Marriott Château Champlain  **10**
Novotel Montréal Centre  **8**
Ritz-Carlton Montréal  **2**
Sofitel Montréal  **3**

## Vieux-Montréal Accommodations

Métro **M**
Information *i*
Church ✝

Auberge Bonaparte **8**
Auberge du Vieux Port **12**
Auberge Les Passants du Sans Soucy **9**
Delta Centre-Ville **2**
Hôtel Gault **6**
Hôtel Le St.-James **3**
Hôtel Nelligan **11**
Hôtel Place D'Armes **5**
Hôtel St. Paul **7**
Hôtel XIXe Siècle **4**
Le Saint-Sulpice Hôtel Montréal **10**
W Montréal **1**

## Table 9-1 *(continued)*

| Dollar Sign(s) | Price Range | What to Expect |
|---|---|---|
| $$ | C$100–C$199 | Many of the rates offered by the chain hotels fall into this price range, as do the rates of the fancier independents. You can already expect the amenities to be better, like bathrooms with hair dryers, coffeemakers with complimentary coffee, and Internet access. Some hotels in this category may have kitchens that provide late-night room service or a breakfast cart. Some even have swimming pools. |
| $$$ | C$200–C$299 | Along with the upper end of the chain hotels, boutique hotels and luxury hotels begin competing in this price bracket, with fine bed linens, feathery pillows, fluffy towels, and bathtubs built for two. The first-class hotels seem to differentiate themselves by striving for regal scale and elegance, while boutique hotels are strikingly modern. Expect high-speed Internet access in your room. |
| $$$$ | C$300 or above | At this price, you should want for nothing in terms of your stay. Expect a great view, an in-room hot tub, a CD player, thick terry-cloth bathrobes, and even flowers. Highly deferential, personalized service is included, as well. |

Rack rates merely provide a rough guideline, so don't be afraid to investigate an interesting choice even if it seems pricey. Most of the time a better rate is available, so make sure to ask.

### *Auberge Bonaparte*
$$–$$$  **Vieux-Montréal**

Located in Vieux-Montréal, this gem of a hotel has 30 rooms on five floors decked out in early-19th-century antiques, while the bathrooms are modern and shaped out of marble slabs. Hardwood floors, exposed brick walls, large windows, and views of the Basilique Notre-Dame (ask for a room at the back) are some of the charming features that visitors can look forward to when they step inside this centuries-old building. The rooms here are neither fancy nor modern, like the bigger hotels. No, the brand power at work here is the simplicity and elegance of old-world refinement. For breakfast they serve delicious, fresh croissants in the main-floor dining room, which is also a popular spot for lunch and dinner among locals.

*447 rue St-François-Xavier.* ☎ **514-844-1448.** *Fax: 514-844-0272.* www.bonaparte. ca. *Parking: C$15. Rack rates: C$145–C$215. AE, DC, MC, V. Métro: Place-d'Armes.*

### Auberge de La Fontaine
**$$** **The Plateau**

Staying at this inn on Montréal's third-largest park lets you be a temporary resident of the übertrendy Plateau neighborhood. Two attached, renovated town houses contain 21 rooms. An elaborate and healthy continental breakfast is served in the lobby, which has large windows for gazing at lovely La Fontaine Park, across the street. Two suites with hot tubs that overlook the park are extremely popular among guests. Stroll along nearby avenue Mont-Royal and rue St-Denis to your heart's content.

*1301 rue Rachel Est.* ☎ ***800-597-0597*** *or 514-597-0166. Fax: 514-597-0496.* www. aubergedelafontaine.com. *Parking: Three free spaces behind the hotel. Rack rates: C$170–C$193. Rates include continental breakfast. AE, DC, DISC, MC, V. Métro: Sherbrooke, Mont-Royal.*

### Auberge du Vieux-Port
**$$$** **Vieux-Montréal**

This 27-room hotel in a late-19th-century building in Vieux-Montréal was once a warehouse and general store. Consequently, the rooms have a decidedly period-loft feel: stone and brick walls; high ceilings with huge, wooden pillars and beams; hardwood floors; and wrought-iron beds. The rate includes a breakfast and evening cocktail, the latter allowing hotel guests a rare opportunity to socialize. The streets surrounding the hotel are continually streaming with daytime tourists or nighttime revelers, which can be noisy for light sleepers. Many of the rooms look out over the St. Lawrence River and Old Port area. If yours doesn't, the rooftop terrace provides an eye-popping panorama. The pricey in-house restaurant serves market cuisine featuring *terroir* ingredients and an extensive wine list.

*97 rue de la Commune Ouest.* ☎ ***888-660-7678*** *or 514-876-0081. Fax: 514-876-8923.* www.aubergeduvieuxport.com. *Parking: Valet C$21. Rack rates: C$200–C$290. Rates include breakfast. AE, DC, DISC, MC, V. Métro: Champ-de-Mars.*

### Auberge Les Passants du Sans Soucy
**$$–$$$** **Vieux-Montréal**

An extremely personable and engaging staff, wonderful breakfasts, and a unique setting will make your stay at this small inn a memorable part of your visit to Montréal. Book early, particularly during high season. With just nine rooms, landing one on short notice is nearly impossible. The would-be lobby is actually a street-front art gallery. The rooms are in a 19th-century warehouse building, so they're somewhat raw and rustic: stone walls and bare wooden beams. The fireplaces have been updated from logs to gas-burning hearths. The breakfasts feature fluffy omelets, French toast, croissants, and other baked goods. Copious quantities of fresh fruit and a variety of juices accompany these morning feasts.

*171 rue St-Paul Ouest.* ☎ ***514-842-2634.*** *Fax: 514-842-2912.* www.lesanssoucy. com. *Parking: C$13. Rack rates: C$155–C$215. AE, DC, MC, V. Métro: Champ-de-Mars.*

### Best Western Hotel Europa
**$$ Downtown**

Although the lobby resembles the far-off land of Atlantis, the Europa provides the familiar comforts of the Best Western hotel brand. Located just south of rue Ste-Catherine, the Europa has 180 rooms, on six floors. Each room contains a king-size, queen-size, or two double beds; contemporary, European wood furnishings finish the room. The white bathrooms have no frills but seem particularly clean. You find plenty of English-language service in this part of the city.

*1240 rue Drummond.* ☎ *800-361-3000 or 514-866-6492. Fax: 514-908-2879.* www. europahotelmtl.com. *Parking: C$20. Rack rates: C$149–C$179. AE, MC, DC, V. Métro: Peel.*

### Crowne Plaza
**$$ The Plateau**

Well located near the Plateau, Quartier Latin, and the Gay Village, this 24-story converted apartment building has spacious rooms and excellent views and is a good foothold for exploring the trendy neighborhoods east of boulevard St-Laurent. It is also adjacent to the Sherbrooke Métro station. Painted vines climb along the low archways of the marble-floored lobby. Stark landscape murals, plants, and flower arrangements give it a winter garden feel. The rooms are quite large and include a sitting area and a large desk but come with a standard-size bathroom.

*505 rue Sherbrooke Est.* ☎ *800-477-3365 or 514-842-8581. Fax: 514-842-8910.* www. cpmontreal.com. *Parking: C$16 or valet C$19. Rack rates: C$160–C$210. AE, DC, DISC, MC, V. Métro: Sherbrooke.*

### Delta Centre-Ville
**$$–$$$ Downtown**

This 28-story glass tower is part of a Canadian chain of corporate hotels and is of no relation to the airline. Its spacious rooms offer great skyline and river views and all the amenities that today's weary business travelers demand. When it opened in 1977, this hotel was state-of-the-art. Today, the Delta still has the city's only revolving restaurant on its top floor, amusingly named *Tour de Ville.*

*777 rue Université.* ☎ *800-268-1133 or 514-879-1370. Fax: 514-879-1761.* www.delta hotels.com. *Parking: C$20. Rack rates: C$189–C$249. AE, DC, DISC, MC, V. Métro: Square-Victoria, Bonaventure.*

### Fairmont The Queen Elizabeth
**$$$ Downtown**

Built atop the Gare Centrale, the Queen E is the grande dame of Montréal's hotels. It's also where John and Yoko did their nude rendition of "Give Peace a Chance" in 1969, while they were on their honeymoon. Now a

Fairmont property, the Queen has made the *Condé Nast Traveler*'s Gold List in past years. The hotel's Beaver Club restaurant is one of the best places for fine Continental cuisine in Montréal. You'll find several grades of accommodation, but even the so-called moderate rooms are pretty lavish. The downtown location is convenient, but there's lots of traffic on the surrounding streets.

*900 bd. René-Levesque Ouest.* ☎ *800-441-1212 or 514-861-3511. Fax: 514-954-2256.* www.fairmont.com. *Parking: Valet C$26. Rack rates: C$229–C$299. AE, DC, DISC, MC, V. Métro: Bonaventure.*

### Hilton Montréal Bonaventure
**$$$ Downtown**

A serene penthouse perched above Place Bonaventure — 17 floors up — this two-story Hilton comprises a perimeter of modular, concrete-walled rooms that surround an immense, landscaped parkland inspired by the Canadian wilderness. The emphasis here is on quiet. All the hotel's services are in a central hub away from the rooms, which are spacious and come with bathrooms finished in marble. The hotel makes children feel at home by giving them a welcoming gift and stocking the concierge desk with games to loan.

*900 rue de la Gauchetière Ouest.* ☎ *800-267-2575 or 514-878-2332. Fax: 514-878-1442.* www.hilton.com. *Parking: C$17 or valet C$24. Rack rates: C$220–C$280. AE, DC, DISC, MC, V. Métro: Bonaventure.*

### Hôtel de la Montagne
**$$–$$$ Downtown**

Elegance, location, and particularly large rooms are what recommend this hotel, a former 20-story apartment building. With 135 rooms in all, each floor offers a choice of nine different units, all of which have modern bathrooms with separate tub and shower. All rooms have balconies facing east or west and provide great views of downtown. The back of the hotel fronts rue Crescent, a vibrant nightlife strip. If you're a particularly light sleeper, you may want to request a room on the other side, away from the action.

*1430 rue de la Montagne.* ☎ *800-361-6262 or 514-288-5656. Fax: 514-288-9658.* www.hoteldelamontagne.com. *Parking: Valet C$15. Rack rates: C$185–C$250. Rates include breakfast on weekends. AE, DC, DISC, MC, V. Métro: Peel.*

### Hôtel Gault
**$$–$$$$ Vieux-Montréal**

The immense rooms of this 30-room boutique hotel feel like loft apartments. The floors are of polished concrete, and the rooms are furnished with mobile, custom cabinetry made from white oak. Rooms include a wooden trellis at the door for increased privacy. Some rooms have secret terraces and ornate 19th-century wrought-iron detailing in the windows. Most impressive are the bathrooms, with large tubs and heated floors. The furniture in the lobby, with a bar, seating area, and reading room, are all reproductions of design classics such as Harry Bertoia chairs and Artemide lamps.

*449 rue Ste-Hélène.* ☎ *866-904-1616 or 514-904-1616. Fax: 514-904-1717.* www. hotelgault.com. *Parking: Valet C$20. Rack rates: C$209–C$589. Rates include breakfast. AE, MC, V. Métro: Square-Victoria.*

### Hôtel Le Germain
$$$ Downtown

According to the concierge, "Art Deco minimalism with a touch of Zen" is what awaits you at this 99-room boutique hotel. Outside, the color scheme is dark and earthy, but inside it's clean and contemporary. The smaller scale of this hotel operation allows the staff to be meticulous in its service and upkeep. Fresh flowers, a sumptuous seating area, and a wood-burning fireplace greet guests in the subdued lobby. Perhaps the most intriguing detail is that each bathroom has a glass wall. The architects envisioned it as a way of allowing natural light into the bathroom. The set up's ideal for those with an exhibitionist streak, the more demure can draw a Venetian blind.

*2050 rue Mansfield.* ☎ *877-333-2050 or 514-849-2050. Fax: 514-849-1437.* www. hotelgermain.com. *Parking: Valet C$23. Rack rates: C$255–C$300. Rates include breakfast. AE, DC, MC, V. Métro: McGill.*

### Hôtel Le St-James
$$$$ Vieux-Montréal

The last time the Rolling Stones were on tour in Montréal, they booked this entire hotel. The 61 units, many of them suites, are among the most deluxe and expensive accommodations in Montréal, with huge marble bathrooms and working fireplaces. The lobby and guest rooms are ornate and decorated with art and antiques. At night, the building's Second Empire facade lights up and looks spectacular. Its Vieux-Montréal location is away from much of the tourist melee and slightly closer to downtown than other hotels in this neighborhood.

*355 rue St-James.* ☎ *866-841-3111 or 514-841-3111. Fax: 514-841-1232.* www.hotel lestjames.com. *Parking: Valet C$30. Rack rates: C$400–C$475. AE, DC, DISC, MC, V. Métro: Place-d'Armes.*

### Hôtel Nelligan
$$$ Vieux-Montréal

This 63-room boutique hotel was named after Québec poet Emile Nelligan, whose verses are sprinkled on its interior walls. Located in two historic buildings on rue St-Paul, one of Vieux-Montréal's main strips, Hôtel Nelligan is filled with galleries, cafes, and boutiques. Originally built in 1850, the premises have exposed stone and brick walls that create a warm and welcoming aura. Guest rooms feature dark woods and leather furnishings along with high ceilings, fireplaces, and hot tubs. Nightly wine-and-cheese gatherings welcome hotel guests in the lobby's central atrium, which is also a popular restaurant and bar.

*106 rue St-Paul Ouest. ☎ 877-788-2040 or 514-788-2040. Fax: 514-788-2041.* www.hotelnelligan.com. *Parking: Valet C$24. Rack rates: C$235–C$300. Rates include breakfast and evening cocktail. AE, DC, DISC, MC, V. Métro: Place-d'Armes.*

### Hotel Omni Mont-Royal
$$$–$$$$   **Downtown**

For a central downtown location, the Omni can't be beat. You can walk just about anywhere, and the Peel Métro station is close at hand. Be sure to ask for a room facing Mont-Royal for an excellent view. Plus, the rooftop pool is heated year-round. However, for the money, some guests feel that Montréal's Omni leaves something to be desired, with standard-size rooms that have a somewhat tired feeling, particularly in the '80s vintage bathrooms.

*1050 rue Sherbrooke Ouest. ☎ 800-843-6664 or 514-284-1110. Fax: 514-845-3025.* www.omnihotels.com. *Parking: Valet C$26. Rack rates: C$200–C$330. AE, DC, DISC, MC, V. Métro: Peel.*

### Hôtel Opus
$$$–$$$$   **The Plateau**

At the foot of all the action on boulevard St-Laurent, just steps away from avenue St. Denis and not far from the festivals, this 146-room boutique hotel is an ideal *pied-à-terre* for a fabulous weekend on the town. The calm atmosphere at the Opus seems just right for rejuvenating a hung-over rock star. The interior's textures are rich and its lines are dramatic. The rooms feature luxurious, well-appointed white beds. The ceilings are of exposed concrete. The hotel's designers painted the rooms in a handful of bold colors. The different schemes aim to appeal to different personality types. Despite the muted tones, elsewhere, the rooms are warm and inviting. Part of the hotel occupies a heritage building, the first-ever residential construction in North America to be made out of poured concrete.

*10 rue Sherbrooke Ouest. ☎ 866-744-6346 or 514-843-6000. Fax: 514-843-6810.* www.hotelgodin.com. *Parking: Valet C$24. Rack rates: C$275–C$375. AE, DC, MC, V. Métro: Sherbrooke, St-Laurent.*

### Hôtel Place d'Armes
$$$–$$$$   **Vieux-Montréal**

This 44-room boutique hotel, located near the Basilique Notre-Dame and the Montréal Convention Centre, has a rooftop terrace overlooking the varied patinas of the copper rooftops of Vieux-Montréal. The architects harnessed the beauty of the facade and carried it over into the design of the interior. The result is a welcoming environment that's cozy, contemporary, and comfortable. Brick walls and wood furnishings add to the warmth. Many of the black-and-white marble tiled bathrooms have a hot tub built for two.

*701 côte de la place-d'Armes.* ☎ *888-450-1887 or 514-842-1887. Fax: 514-842-6469.* www.hotelplacedarmes.com. *Parking: Valet C$21. Rack rates: C$225–C$335. Rates include breakfast and an evening cocktail. AE, DC, DISC, MC, V. Métro: Place-d'Armes.*

### Hôtel St-Paul
**$$$–$$$$   Vieux-Montréal**

Located on the recently renovated Rue McGill in Vieux-Montréal, soon to be a bustling-high street, the imposing Second Empire exterior disguises the ultra-modern inside of this 120-room boutique hotel. The lighting is almost theatrical — definitely moody — from the mysterious hearth hovering in alabaster in the lobby to the knee-level, colored floodlights in the halls. The dark, 100-year-old wooden floors of the rooms are warm and welcoming. The rooms are sparsely furnished — intentionally, of course. Along with other custom pieces, a television screen in each room displays the room-service menu, which changes on a daily basis.

*355 rue McGill.* ☎ *514-380-2222 or 866-380-2202. Fax: 514-380-2200.* www.hotel stpaul.com. *Parking: Valet C$19. Rack rates: C$260–C$410. Rates include breakfast. AE, DC, MC, V. Métro: Square-Victoria.*

### Hôtel XIXᵉ Siècle
**$$$–$$$$   Vieux-Montréal**

A Victorian reading room with extremely high ceilings — resembling a set on *Masterpiece Theatre* — sets a tone of intimate grandeur in this Vieux-Montréal boutique hotel in a renovated, 19th-century, neoclassical bank building. The 59 rooms are of the same scale and thoughtfully decorated in French Second Empire style. The large and luxurious bathrooms have black-and-white tiled floors, large marble countertops, and deep tubs. Rates include a lavish continental breakfast, featuring a selection of breads, jams, juices, yogurts, and so on, served in the main floor dining room.

*262 rue St-Jacques Ouest.* ☎ *877-553-0019 or 514-985-0019. Fax: 514-985-0059.* www.hotelxixsiecle.com. *Parking: Valet C$20. Rack rates: C$195–C$320. AE, DC, DISC MC, V. Métro: Place-d'Armes.*

*1201 bd. René-Levesque Ouest.* ☎ *888-627-7102 or 514-878-2000. Fax: 514-878-3958.* www.sheraton.com/lecentre. *Parking: C$19 or valet C$26. Rack rates: C$200–C$300. AE, DC, DISC, MC, V. Métro: Peel.*

### Le Saint-Sulpice Hôtel Montréal
**$$$$   Vieux-Montréal**

Near Basilique Notre-Dame in the heart of Vieux-Montréal, this spacious and classy 108-suite hotel is splendid and lavish without being gaudy. Each condo-style suite, between 550 and 1,500 sq. ft. (51 and 139 sq. m), has a full kitchen, a living room with leather seating, and French doors that open to a courtyard or the streets of Vieux-Montréal. Many have their own fireplaces. The bathrooms are well lit, stocked with high-end toiletries, and have large showers. The staff are helpful, energetic, and well trained in the art of pampering.

*414 rue St-Sulpice.* ☎ *877-785-7423 or 514-288-1000. Fax: 514-288-0077.* www. lesaintsulpice.com. *Parking: Valet C$25. Rack rates: C$310–C$390. Rates include American buffet breakfast. AE, DC, DISC, MC, V. Métro: Place-d'Armes.*

### Loews Hotel Vogue
**$$$–$$$$ Downtown**

Loews, a luxury hotel brand, owns distinct properties in cities across North America. In Montréal, it's the 142-room Hotel Vogue, right downtown and a block away from rue Crescent. For some guests, the large marble bathrooms, featuring a two-person hot tub and a television, are absolutely to die for. However, you may be disappointed if you're expecting a room with a view. The black-and-white marble lobby is elegant, though.

*1425 rue de la Montagne.* ☎ *800-465-6654 or 514-285-5555. Fax: 514-849-8903.* www.loewshotels.com/vogue. *Parking: Valet C$30. Rack rates: C$259–C$400. AE, DC, DISC, MC, V. Métro: Peel.*

### Meridien Versailles Montréal
**$$–$$$ Downtown**

A fancy name for a fancy hotel, the Versailles walks the walk with its understated elegance. Located in the western part of the downtown core, this 106-room hotel is at the end of a long stretch of antiques shops, art galleries, and designer boutiques on rue Sherbrooke. The lobby is small and cozy, just a front desk and a seating area. The rooms are large and tastefully finished in neutral tones and lush textures.

*1808 rue Sherbrooke Ouest.* ☎ *800-543-4300 or 514-933-8111. Fax: 514-933-7102.* www.versailleshotels.com. *Parking: Valet C$23. Rack rates: C$190–C$385. AE, DC, DISC, MC, V. Métro: Guy-Concordia.*

### Montréal Marriott Chateau Champlain
**$$$ Downtown**

This 36-floor high-rise, halfway down the hill between downtown and Vieux-Montréal, offers standard-size rooms but with all the amenities and services of a first-class hotel. The north-facing view is the best, with a close-up of the other buildings in the downtown core. Inspired by glorious Windsor Station next door, the Moorish-style, semicircular, floor-to-ceiling windows are particularly remarkable.

*1 place du Canada.* ☎ *800-200-5909 or 514-878-9000. Fax: 514-878-6761.* www.mariott hotels.com/yulcc. *Parking: C$18 or valet C$24. Rack rates: C$230–C$300. Rates include breakfast on weekends. AE, DC, DISC, MC, V. Métro: Bonaventure.*

### Novotel Montréal Centre
**$$–$$$**   **Downtown**

You detect subtle differences in this hotel's approach to hospitality from the minute you enter the lobby until you depart. For example, rather than a long front counter, guests check in at individual islands. The service is considerate but expedient. The rooms have a modern feel with clean lines, warm tones, and accents of primary colors. It's just steps away from shopping on rue Ste-Catherine and the restaurants and bars of rue Crescent.

*1180 rue de la Montagne.* ☎ **800-668-6835** *or 514-861-6000. Fax: 514-861-2295.* www.novotelmontreal.com. *Parking: C$15.50. Rack rates: C$169–C$259. AE, DISC, MC, V. Métro: Lucien-L'Allier or Peel.*

### Ritz-Carlton Montréal
**$$$–$$$$**   **Downtown**

Opened in 1912 and recently refurbished, Montréal's Ritz-Carlton, the only Ritz in Canada, remains a bastion of elegance — the crown jewel of downtown's Golden Square Mile that's filled with art galleries, swank boutiques, and antiques shops. The quality of service is high; the staff seem to remember each guest's name. Surprisingly, it is not the most expensive hotel in town — although it is definitely the grandest. High tea is served daily, and in the summer you can sit in the garden. The rooms and suites are spacious with large closets, chandeliers, and marble bathrooms. Some have working fireplaces. Liz Taylor married Richard Burton here, many moons, and perhaps even more husbands, ago.

*1228 rue Sherbrooke Ouest.* ☎ **800-363-0366** *or 514-842-4212. Fax: 514-842-3383.* www.ritzmontreal.com. *Parking: Valet C$30. Rack rates: C$200–C$325. AE, DC MC, V. Métro: Peel.*

### Sofitel Montréal
**$$–$$$$**   **Downtown**

This 258-room hotel offers its guests modern European elegance and refinement on a grand scale in a part of downtown known as the Golden Square Mile. Owned by a French hotel group, the Sofitel is a well-known brand throughout Europe. The hotel is allegedly designed on the principles of the *art de vivre* — something like a French version of feng shui. Despite its minimalist and understated décor, the luminous lobby's 18-foot ceilings make it an imposing space. The floor-to-ceiling windows in the rooms are only half as high and offer spectacular views of the downtown core. The rooms, with soft tones of taupe and rust, have original artwork on the walls and teak furniture. Large bathrooms of ocher marble and black granite countertops feature a glass-walled shower and a deep tub.

*1155 rue Sherbrooke Ouest.* ☎ **877-285-9001** *or 514-285-9000. Fax: 514-289-1155.* www.sofitel.com. *Parking: Valet C$26. Rack rates: C$195–C$425. AE, DC, DISC, MC, V. Métro: Peel.*

## *W Montréal*
**$$$–$$$$** **Vieux-Montréal**

Canada's first W opened in the converted Bank of Canada Building on Victoria Square on the western fringe of Vieux-Montréal. Overnight, the building went from a drab financial institution to an institution of cool. A W, to some extent, sanctifies a city as being a world capital of global culture. You have to want the W experience, because it is somewhat over the top by regular hotel standards. You never escape the feeling of being in a nightclub, be it the futuristic lounge areas, house music in the elevators with green lighting, or the actual throb of bass from the wildly popular bar below. Ask for a park-facing, upper-floor room for the most peace and quiet. There's so much eye candy and mood lighting here that it's hard to imagine ever shutting your eyes. The rooms are predominantly in black and white and have electric-blue accents throughout, from the glowing night tables to a sheet of blue-tinted glass which is all that separates the bathroom and shower from the rest.

*901 Victoria Square.* ☎ **514-395-3100.** *Fax: 514-395-3150.* www.whotels.com. *Parking: Valet C$39. Rack rates: C$250–C$390. AE, DC, DISC, MC, V. Métro: Square-Victoria.*

# Chapter 10

# Dining and Snacking in Montréal

- - - - - - - - - - - - - - - - - - - - - - - - - - - - - - - - - -

### In This Chapter
▶ Understanding the ins and outs of dining in Montréal
▶ Finding Montréal's top dining spots
▶ Locating the best snacks and light meals

- - - - - - - - - - - - - - - - - - - - - - - - - - - - - - - - - -

*Y*our options are staggering when dining in Montréal, one of the world's great restaurant cities and a food-lover's paradise. Montréalers eat out often, so the city is brimming with contenders hoping to be the next "it" restaurant with the "in" crowd. But don't be intimidated. Eating in Montréal doesn't have to be an ordeal. Many restaurants offer tasty and diverse options at a good price, and the city has an endless variety of ethnic eats. In fact, Montréalers looking to score a quick bite are likely to choose a *shish-taouk* (Lebanese souvlaki), a *samosa* (meat or veggie Indian pastry), or sushi over a burger and fries. Don't fret: You can find burgers and fries, too.

In this chapter, I attempt to simplify your choices by offering a representative selection of Montréal's best places to eat, including fine dining, trendy spots, and some neighborhood gems. After that, I tell you where to find the best picnic food, BYOB restaurants, coffee, and more.

## Getting the Dish on the Local Scene

Montréal's real specialty, of course, is French food. Although the better French restaurants tend to be a little on the expensive side, I think they're worth every penny. If you leave Montréal without eating at least one great French meal, you'll miss out on one of the best things about the city.

### Your terroir is my local ingredient
Many of Montréal's best restaurants offer some variation of French or contemporary continental cuisine. What's particularly new and exciting is the trend toward *terroir*, the French word describing high-quality, locally produced, seasonal ingredients. (Actually, the trend started in

France in the late '90s.) Menus of finer restaurants are peppered with names of specialty ingredients from Québec's bountiful rural regions. Thankfully, most of the best kitchens go beyond such obvious Canadian staples as salmon and maple syrup, and some offer items you've probably never heard of before.

## The brunch bunch

Does anyone in Montréal have the makings of a sensible breakfast in their fridge anymore? Not if you judge by the action in the Plateau neighborhood. On weekends, Montréalers flock here looking for somewhere to land a late-morning or midday brunch. Lines are common at the better places, and new spots specializing in all-day breakfasts are popping up at an amazing rate. Brunch patrons are a mixed bag, a potentially volatile combination of chipper morning people and groups of extremely hungover friends. Everyone's happy, though, as waiters arrive with elaborate breakfasts on oversized plates accompanied by fresh juice and hot coffee. See "Big breakfast bonanza" later in this chapter for locations.

## Tasty tapas for fast friends

*Tapas* refers to the small plates Spaniards use to cover the carafes of wine so that flies don't get into the drink. Bars there serve them topped with bite-sized appetizers to accompany the alcohol, rounding out the experience some and allowing patrons to linger longer. They're ideal for sharing among busy friends with competing schedules, who can just manage to meet for drinks. They provide sustenance without having to sit down for a formal meal. In Spain, it's a specific culinary tradition with such dishes as garlic shrimp, chorizo and dates, seared scallops, frittata, and ham Serrano. Several places in Montréal carry on in this vein, while other *tapas* joints cast a wider net, offering starters from around the globe. So the term has been diluted some. Basically, if you see a *tapas* menu, it means there's food available to go with your drinks and you can expect, hopefully, something above and beyond the traditional pub grub of nachos, chicken wings, pies, and so on.

## Super-fun supper clubs

This recent restaurant category blurs the lines between dinner, party, and celebrity. You sit down at a table for dinner and when you get up the restaurant has transformed into a full-on nightclub, with a picky doorman and an expensive cover — which helps keep the riff-raff out. When the second part of the night has begun, the only way to secure a table is to buy a bottle of liquor. Then, out comes a tray with cranberry and orange juice as mixers, a bucket of ice, and a stack of glasses. You get to play Mr. Magnanimity and host your own little party, making drinks as strong as you like and giving them to whomever you like. Much mingling ensues. You don't have to buy a bottle to go to these raucous dens, but if you don't you have to line up at the busy bars. The food portion of the evening usually features contemporary and daring dishes served by leggy waitresses culled from local modeling agencies.

# Trimming the Fat from Your Budget

Eating is not particularly expensive in Montréal, especially when you consider how good the food generally is. Still, you can find a few ways to cut corners on your food budget without sacrificing too much.

- ✔ **Pack a picnic.** This obviously isn't an option in midwinter, but during the summer months it makes sense. With plenty of parks across the city where you can find a shady corner to have a light meal, even if you splurge on some fancy cheese or pâté you'll still save.

- ✔ **Enjoy a French breakfast.** An economical breakfast, which is typically French and easy enough to reconstruct in Montréal, is a croissant or two and a bowl of café au lait. Jam and dipping are optional. See my picks for the best croissants in the "Coffee and pastries" section later in this chapter.

- ✔ **Eat your big meal at lunch.** Lunch menus are considerably cheaper than their equivalent at dinner. Check the lunch *table d'hôte*, a fixed menu including a starter and dessert, which is often a very good deal.

- ✔ **Check your memberships.** You may be eligible for discounts of 10 percent to 15 percent off your restaurant bill if you're a member of clubs such as AAA. Always ask.

- ✔ **Eat in your own kitchen.** If your hotel room has a kitchenette, you can store some milk, bread, and a few staples. Eat in for breakfast, pack a picnic lunch, and save your dining dollars for the evening.

- ✔ **Bring your own wine.** Montréal has many BYOB restaurants. Taste-wise, you may have difficulty deciding on a wine when you have yet to look at the menu. But budget-wise, you'll come out ahead.

# Homing In on Dining Etiquette

Here are a few do's and don'ts for dining out.

- ✔ **Dressing:** In Montréal, people look put together when they go out to eat, but they don't really dress up. For both men and women, a nice pair of pants or even jeans (*nice* jeans) and a decent top make you feel comfortable almost anywhere.

- ✔ **Deciphering the menu:** Don't worry about language barriers between you and your plate. In most restaurants, the menu is available in English. When it's not, waiters are used to translating. Just take note of one common trap to spare you from some confusion: an *entrée* in French actually means a starter. A main course, therefore, is not an entree but a *plat principal*.

✔ **Dining hours:** Montréalers typically eat later than other North Americans. Many restaurants don't fill up until 10 p.m., especially on weekends. That's good news if you're an early eater and want a table at a popular restaurant: you can almost always find something available around 6:30 p.m. or so. The restaurant may be dead, but the food will taste the same as it does at 10 p.m.

✔ **Cigarettes:** Smoking in restaurants and bars became illegal in Québec as of May 31, 2006. Now people craving a cigarette have to go outside.

✔ **Cellphones:** As a matter of common courtesy, annoying ring tones, no matter how soft, should be off during dinner at a restaurant. If you absolutely need to be reached, put your phone on vibrate. When the time comes, excuse yourself from the table and scout out an appropriate location to have your conversation. Outside with the smokers is a safe bet. Otherwise, afford yourself the time to enjoy the food and company — uninterrupted.

✔ **Reservations:** Reservations guarantee you a table at a particular time. If your schedule's tight or you're dead set on a meal at a certain spot, by all means, call in advance so they'll have a table waiting for you. Reserving is also a good practice when it's a large group, a special occasion, or on Thursday through Saturday, the busiest nights of the week. However, except for the poshest of places, you usually don't need to reserve in advance to get a table. So, just walk in. Actually, this is an excellent tactic for getting a table at a restaurant where you couldn't get a reservation over the phone. If you're no more than two people, you can usually snag something by just showing up. If you do try this, have a Plan B in case things don't work out.

✔ **Tipping:** The standard is 15 percent, and you can give more or less depending on your appreciation of the service. A good way to come up with this amount is to add up the two sales taxes (the TVQ and TPS) and round up. The taxes equal 13 percent of what you ordered.

# Montréal's Best Restaurants from A to Z

To simplify your choices, I give you two ways to evaluate how expensive each place is. The first way is a dollar-sign rating. This represents the price of one complete meal (appetizer, main course, and dessert) including tip; the dollar signs correspond with the price ranges in Table 10-1.

| Table 10-1 | Key to Restaurant Dollar Signs |
|---|---|
| *Dollar Sign(s)* | *Price Range* |
| $ | Less than C$20 |
| $$ | C$20–C$39 |
| $$$ | C$40–C$59 |
| $$$$ | C$60 or above |

In my reviews, I also include the price range of a main course, from lowest to highest. That price does not include drinks, taxes, or tip. It just gives you an idea of what the prices on the menu will actually be.

### Au Pied de Cochon
$$$–$$$$    **Plateau    FRENCH CONTEMPORARY**

In 2002, *enRoute,* Air Canada's in-flight magazine, named Au Pied de Cochon one of the ten best new restaurants in Canada. Chef-owner Martin Picard is the man behind the inspired and upscale French cooking. But a word to the wise: Delicate and decorative nouvelle cuisine this is not. Instead, the kitchen's forte is hearty, almost peasantlike comfort food, prepared with the finest ingredients and the greatest of care. Come hungry. As the name suggests, the restaurant specializes in pork and even serves pigs' feet. You also find a choice of excellent venison, lamb, and duck plates. *Foie gras* (goose liver) is a bit of a fetish item on the menu, appearing in several new and unusual places, like in a foie gras burger and foie gras *poutine.* (See the "Eating like a local" section later in this chapter for more info about this local delicacy.)

*536 av. Duluth Est (near rue St-Hubert).* ☎ ***514-281-1114.*** *Reservations recommended. Main course: C$15–C$50. AE, DC, DISC, MC, V. Open: Dinner Tues–Sun. Wheelchair accessible. Métro: Sherbrooke.*

### Beaver Club
$$$$    **Downtown    FRENCH**

Don't be put off by the dated, old-money feel of the Fairmont The Queen Elizabeth's restaurant, which actually was an exclusive men's club dating back to the 18th century. Beaver Club, a restaurant since 1959, ranks among the top ten hotel restaurants in the world. The menu offers an absolutely delectable range of classic French dishes, many made with Canadian ingredients, including Québec veal, lobster, caviar, foie gras, and more. The French sommelier is a great fan of Canadian wines and will gladly find a way for you to taste as many as possible. Service is warm,

## *Downtown and Vieux-Montréal Dining and Snacking*

0          1/4 mi
0          0.25 km

PARC MONT-ROYAL

MONT-ROYAL

av. des Pins

St-Sulpice

av. des Pins

av. Docteur-Penfield

rue McTavish

ch. de la Côte-des-Neiges

rue Simpson
rue Redpath
rue du Musée
rue de la Montagne
rue Drummond
rue Stanley
rue Peel

McG
Unive

av. Atwater

rue Sherbrooke

rue Lincoln

GUY-CONCORDIA

Chomedey

rue du Fort

St-Marc

St-Mathieu

rue Crescent

rue Bishop

rue Mackay

rue Ste-Catherine

rue Guy

bd. de Maisonneuve

PEEL

CENTREVILLE

bd. René-Lévesque

rue Drummond
rue Stanley
rue Peel
rue Metcalfe
rue Mansfield

PLACE BONAVENTURE

Belm

autoroute Ville-Marie

rue St-Antoine

rue Argyle

LUCIEN-L'ALLIER

GEORGES-VANIER

rue de la Montagne

rue Lucien-L'Allier

rue de la Gauche

BONAVENTURE

Gare Windsor

rue St-Antoine

rue Georges-Vanier

rue des Seigneurs

rue St-Jacques

rue St-Jacques

rue Notre-Dame

rue Notre-Dame

rue Guy

PARC JARRY

MONT-ROYAL

PLATEAU MONT-ROYAL

PARC MONT-ROYAL

AREA OF DETAIL

VIEUX-MONTRÉAL

ÎLE DES SOEURS
Saint Lawrence River

Métro
Infotouriste Office
Underground City

Al-Taib **10**
Amélio's **29**
Atwater Market **6**
Au Pain Doré **17, 34**
Beaver Club **19**
Café du Nouveau Monde **28**
Chez L'Épicier **35**
Cluny **21**
Cosmos Snack Bar **3**

congenial, and beyond reproach. Prices are surprisingly reasonable, considering the level of artistry you experience.

*In Fairmont The Queen Elizabeth, 900 bd. René-Levesque Ouest. ☎ 514-861-3511. Reservations strongly recommended. Main course: C$45–C$50. AE, DC, DISC, MC, V. Open: Lunch Mon–Fri, dinner Tues–Sat. Wheelchair accessible. Métro: Bonaventure.*

### Buona Notte
**$$$–$$$$    Plateau    SUPPER CLUB**

This snazzy, contemporary Italian restaurant is a fixture on boulevard St-Laurent and a popular destination for A-list celebrities like Bono and Jim Carrey. Check out the wall of signed plates at the back of the restaurant for proof of their passing through. Buona Notte has been one of the city's trendiest spots practically since it opened in 1992, thanks at least in part to the exceptionally statuesque waitresses that saunter about the quasi-industrial space. But the place doesn't get by on good looks alone: The kitchen is meticulous about its cuisine, serving fresh takes on classic Italian ingredients. Along with delicate starters and fresh pasta dishes, the menu offers main courses of meats and fish. The restaurant's wine cellar, stocked exclusively with Italian wines, has won coveted awards from *Wine Spectator* magazine.

*3518 bd. St-Laurent (north of rue Milton). ☎ 514-848-0644. Reservations recommended. Main course: C$16–C$48. AE, DC, MC, V. Open: Lunch Mon–Sat, dinner daily. Métro: St-Laurent or Sherbrooke.*

### Café du Nouveau Monde
**$$$    Quartier Latin    FRENCH BISTRO**

Mingle among Québec's cultural elite in a restaurant reminiscent of a Parisian *grand café*. It's attached to the province's premier French-language theater and the main-floor dining room bleeds into the lobby. There can be a crush of people at the bar before and after a show, so the traffic keeps things lively. Busy waiters bustle about attending to the clientele's various demands, yet stopping long enough to provide considerate advice about the menu. Upstairs is a more sedate and intimate dining room with a heavier menu. The same kitchen cooks for both, and the menus have several items in common; however, the downstairs one includes panini, club sandwiches, and the like, whereas upstairs the selections tend toward braised meats and duck. Both have an excellent wine list with several selections by the glass. The eye-catching, undulating, green roof housing the downstairs cafe, on the corner of rues Ste-Catherine and St-Urbain, has large, floor-to-ceiling windows that open onto the street. During the warmer months, when the festival season is in full swing, it's an ideal perch for people-watching. Closed, the windows' yellow stain adds warmth to the interior.

*84 rue Ste-Catherine Ouest (corner rue St-Urbain). ☎ 514-866-8669. Reservations recommended. Main course: C$14–C$20. AE, DC, MC, V. Open: Lunch and dinner daily. Métro: Place-des-Arts.*

*Plateau and Mile End Dining*

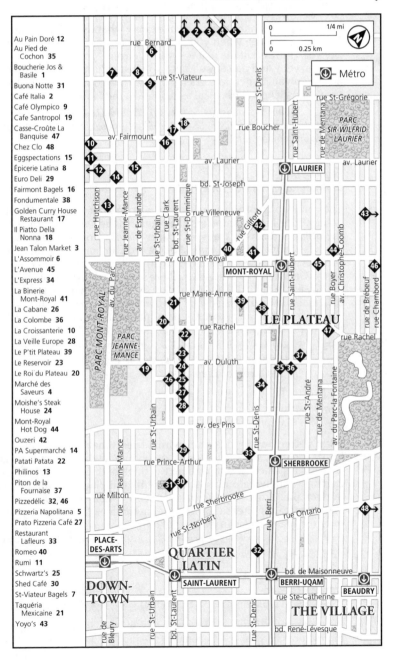

Au Pain Doré **12**
Au Pied de
  Cochon **35**
Boucherie Jos &
  Basile **1**
Buona Notte **31**
Café Italia **2**
Café Olympico **9**
Cafe Santropol **19**
Casse-Croûte La
  Banquise **47**
Chez Clo **48**
Eggspectations **15**
Épicerie Latina **8**
Euro Deli **29**
Fairmont Bagels **16**
Fondumentale **38**
Golden Curry House
  Restaurant **17**
Il Piatto Della
  Nonna **18**
Jean Talon Market **3**
L'Assommoir **6**
L'Avenue **45**
L'Express **34**
La Binerie
  Mont-Royal **41**
La Cabane **26**
La Colombe **36**
La Croissanterie **10**
La Veille Europe **28**
Le P'tit Plateau **39**
Le Reservoir **23**
Le Roi du Plateau **20**
Marché des
  Saveurs **4**
Moishe's Steak
  House **24**
Mont-Royal
  Hot Dog **44**
Ouzeri **42**
PA Supermarché **14**
Patati Patata **22**
Philinos **13**
Piton de la
  Fournaise **37**
Pizzedélic **32, 46**
Pizzeria Napolitana **5**
Prato Pizzeria Café **27**
Restaurant
  Lafleurs **33**
Romeo **40**
Rumi **11**
Schwartz's **25**
Shed Café **30**
St-Viateur Bagels **7**
Taquéria
  Mexicaine **21**
Yoyo's **43**

### Chez L'Épicier
**$$$$** **Vieux-Montréal** **FRENCH CONTEMPORARY**

At first sight it's hard to figure out exactly what this establishment is. The first thing you see when you walk in are rows of jams and preserves on shelves. However, if the name — which means "grocery store" — suggests the everyday and banal, wait until you taste. Plates are inventive and fun, like the oh-so-French foie gras glazed with tandoori sauce or the dessert club sandwiches. Whimsical as it sounds, the food is top-notch.

*311 rue St-Paul Est (near rue St-Claude).* ☎ *514-878-2232. Reservations recommended. Main course: C$25–C$40. AE, MC, V. Open: Lunch Mon–Fri, dinner daily. Métro: Champ-de-Mars.*

### Euro Deli
**$** **Plateau** **ITALIAN AMERICAN**

The campy approach of this cafeteria-style pizza and pasta spot attracts boulevard St-Laurent hipsters at all hours of the day. No one seems to mind the bright-red plastic trays and paper plates, probably because the fresh pasta is so amazing. In terms of being seen on boulevard St-Laurent in the summer, nothing is quite cooler than sipping an espresso on Euro Deli's stoop. Open later on weekends, there's often a mad rush of revelers chowing down late-night. During the day, it's perfect for a quick lunch. The pesto tortellini, the Caesar salad, and the plain cheese pizza are all good choices. Otherwise, you can select a type of pasta and sauce from a list or get a slice of pizza or *panzerotti* (pizza pockets) on display.

*3619 bd. St-Laurent (north of rue Prince-Arthur).* ☎ *514-843-7853. Reservations not accepted. Main course: C$7.50–C$12. Cash only. Open: Breakfast, lunch, and dinner daily. Métro: St-Laurent or Sherbrooke.*

### Fondumentale
**$$–$$$** **Plateau** **FONDUE**

What better way to kick back with a friend than by dunking morsels of bread, meat, or veggies into a pot of fondue? If you crave fondue and a fun time, this is where it's at, right in the thick of the action on stylish rue St-Denis. Fondumentale's laid-back, slightly rumpled atmosphere makes it a perfect place to let your hair down. Fondue is not fine dining, but Fondumentale's cheese, broth, and oil fondues have kept locals coming back for years. Make an evening of it.

*4325 rue St-Denis.* ☎ *514-499-1446. Reservations essential. Main course: C$17–C$28. AE, DISC, MC, V. Open: Dinner daily. Métro: Mont-Royal.*

### Garde Manger
**$$$–$$$$** **Vieux-Montréal** **SEAFOOD**

It's an unassuming spot, tucked away off rue St-Paul, but this intimate dining room and bar has become all the rage for both its first-rate maritime cuisine and the electric atmosphere. The latter probably has something to do with the music: '80s hits blare and the clientele of young- to mid-career professionals out for a good time shamelessly enjoy it. The chalkboard menu changes regularly but features several steadfast favorites such as the calamari, tuna tartar, and steak frites. The kitchen's serious about the food but the presentation is decidedly low-brow: plastic baskets with checkered wax paper and frying pans placed on paint can lids, a nod to the crab-shack and clam-bake traditions of Canada's Atlantic coast. If you're up to the task, the dessert menu features a deep-fried Mars bar or homemade pecan pie.

*408 St-François-Xavier (just north of rue St-Paul).* ☎ **514-678-5044.** *Reservations essential. Main course: C$15–C$25 Open: Dinner Tues–Sun. Métro: Square-Victoria or Place-des-Armes.*

### Golden Curry House Restaurant
**$–$$  Plateau  INDIAN**

Locals call this place the Golden Closet, but that's exaggerating a little. It's actually a narrow hallway packed with tables. In spite of the severe space restrictions this place is almost always packed. I can't say with absolute certainty that this is the best Indian food you'll find in Montréal, but popular opinion ranks it highly; the locale is great, and the prices are very reasonable, so it's hard to knock. The menu is classic Indian fare: nan bread; samosas; beef, lamb, and chicken curry; tandoori chicken; agaloo peas; and more. Wash it down with a pint of Double Diamond or Newcastle. Waiters are polite and do their job well with, literally, very little breathing room, so don't complain if service is on the perfunctory side.

*5210 bd. St-Laurent.* ☎ **514-270-2561.** *Reservations recommended on weekends. Main course: C$6–C$15. AE, DC, MC, V. Open: Lunch Mon–Sat, dinner daily. Métro: Laurier.*

### Il Piatto Della Nonna
**$$–$$$  Mile End  ITALIAN**

It sure is fun to find truly traditional Italian cooking in the Mile End, a neighborhood where most traditions are giving way to the yuppie tastes that are taking over the neighborhood. Il Piatto Della Nonna is a family-run establishment that offers fresh, homemade pasta and hearty dishes like grilled Italian sausage, chicken legs stuffed with cheese and bread crumbs, and veal shank. This is a good place to fill up if you're on a budget. The menu, which changes regularly, is a *table d'hôte* (appetizer, main course, dessert, and coffee) posted on a chalkboard. Service is warm and informal (the owner's little girl lends a hand to the waitstaff every now and again). The coffee and biscotti are excellent.

*5171 bd. St-Laurent.* ☎ **514-843-6069.** *Reservations recommended on weekends. Table d'hôte: C$15–C$30. MC, V. Open: Lunch Mon–Fri, dinner daily. Métro: Laurier.*

## Isakaya
$$$   Downtown   JAPANESE (SUSHI)

First things first: Isakaya has the best sushi in town. That said, *isakaya* is the generic word for Japan's informal eateries, so, true to form, this restaurant features a wide variety of what amounts to Japanese pub-fare favorites. Of course, these popular Japanese dishes are much more delicate than their Western counterparts, and they're healthier, too. Start with an order of *edamame,* steamed and salted pods of baby soybeans, which go well with beer. *Gyoza* (browned dumplings of pork and cabbage) and *yakitori* (barbecued skewers of chicken) are also good starters. If you really want to wow your date with your sushi savoir faire, ask for a spot at the bar. Gently lean in toward the sushi chef and ask for "a selection of what he thinks is best" — some sashimi, some nigiri, and some maki rolls. A delightful parade of sushi will follow.

*3469 av. du Parc (south of rue Milton).* ☎ *514-845-8226. Reservations recommended. Main course: C$14–C$23. AE, DC, MC, V. Open: Lunch Tues–Fri, dinner Tues–Sun. Wheelchair accessible. Métro: Place des Arts.*

## L'Assommoir
$$–$$$   Mile End   TAPAS

This 125-seat tapas lounge brims with lively chatter and mingling by fashionably dressed 20- and 30-somethings. The menu features delectable *seviche,* grilled items, and other small platters meant for sharing over drinks. The wood-paneled front room is narrow, with a long bar opposite a row of high tables and stools. Through a stuccoed archway, a dining room at the back has long tables and two large banquettes. The close quarters and communal dining arrangements make for a convivial atmosphere. The kitchen's open late, until midnight on weekdays and 1:30 a.m. on the weekend, so there's no real dinner hour; instead, the feeling of an extended cocktail hour pervades.

*112 av. Bernard Ouest (corner of rue St-Urbain).* ☎ *514-272-0777. Reservations recommended. Main course: C$15–C$25. AE, DC, DISC, MC, V. Open: Dinner daily. Métro: Outremont.*

## La Croissanterie
$–$$$   Outremont   FRENCH

There's always a bit of action at La Croissanterie. People flow in and out as they please — for a late-morning coffee and croissant, a light midday meal, a late-night snack of French onion soup, or a glass of wine any time of the day. That's probably what makes it so charming — that, and the breezy, quiet, expansive outdoor terrace, which is a jewel in the hot summer months. If you're not feeling up to a full-force French feast, but you still have a hankering for something Gallic, not too pricey, and a place you can rest your hind quarters for a while without remorse, La Croissanterie is your destination. Soups and sandwiches are served all day long, and such dishes as filet mignon, chicken breast, and fish are available in the evening.

*5200 rue Hutchison.* ☎ *514-278-6567. Reservations not accepted. Main course: C$14–C$19. AE, DC, DISC, MC, V. Open: Lunch and dinner daily. Métro: Laurier.*

### La Maison du Kebab
**$  St-Henri  PERSIAN**

Perhaps surprisingly, Persia has a great barbecue tradition. The kebabs that give the place its name are brochettes of meat or chicken cooked over the white-hot embers of an open charcoal fire. Filet mignon and chicken legs (with bones) are also popular choices on the menu. Come on Thursdays, when this family-run establishment serves up a braised lamb's leg special that sells out fast. All of the main dishes come with a choice of soup or salad starter, a heaping portion of saffron-seasoned rice, and all the traditional trimmings: fresh pita, onion, radishes, and parsley. The idea, to be as authentic as possible, is to assemble bite-sized tacos with the meat or to use the pita wedges as a sort of spoon. This place is one of the best dining values around and you'll be hard pressed to finish what you've ordered. The only drawback is that they don't have a liquor license.

*820 av. Atwater (corner of St-Antoine).* ☎ *514-933-0933. Reservations not accepted. Main course: C$9–C$19. No credit cards. Open: Lunch and dinner daily. Métro: Lionel-Groulx.*

### Le Roi du Plateau
**$$  Plateau  PORTUGUESE GRILL**

Le Roi du Plateau has a reputation for the best chicken among the Portuguese grills that dot the several blocks on either side of "The Main" (boulevard St-Laurent) between avenue Duluth and rue Marianne. They'll baste your half chicken with a spicy sauce that adds zest but no real heat. The house specialty is grilled meat, all forms of it, braised over the embers of a charcoal fire, from squid and sardines to steak and lamb. On a busy evening, families and boisterous groups of friends who flock here create a loud din over carafes of red wine. Snapshots adorn the wood-paneled walls, and ledges are adorned with trinkets and souvenirs from Portugal.

*51 rue Rachel Ouest (at the corner of rue Clark).* ☎ *514-844-8393. Reservations required. Main course: C$10–C$25. V. Open: Dinner Mon–Sat. Métro: Sherbrooke or Mont-Royal.*

### L'Express
**$$–$$$$  Plateau  FRENCH BISTRO**

You may have heard the term *brasserie* floating around to describe a category of French cuisine and wondered whether it's a food or a place. The answer: It's both. L'Express, a Montréal landmark since 1979, is brasserie in the purest form — or at least in the purest North American form. A bustling restaurant-bar complete with black-and-white tiled floors and a zinc bar, L'Express serves steak frites, duck confit, and other French comfort food with a jar of pickles and basket of baguettes on the table. The white table-cloths and tie-wearing waiters may trick you into thinking that formality is de rigueur here, but don't be fooled. Brasseries are high-quality but casual eating. Whether you want to linger over a leisurely meal or wolf down a swift lunch, the waiters will figure it out and cater to you accordingly. Just don't expect them to spend hours talking to you. They're busy!

*3927 rue St-Denis.* ☎ *514-845-5333. Reservations recommended. Main course: C$14–C$22. AE, MC, V. Open: Lunch and dinner daily. Wheelchair accessible. Métro: Sherbrooke.*

### L'Orchidée de Chine
$$$–$$$$  **Downtown  CHINESE**

Located in central downtown, this four-floor restaurant with a pared-down décor may feel a bit cold at first, but the food will definitely warm you up. Don't come here looking for inexpensive, buffet-style Chinese food. L'Orchidée de Chine has been one of Montréal's most popular Chinese restaurants for years because of the sophistication and refinement of its fare. The uniform sea of soy sauce that plagues so much Chinese food is not to be seen here. Sauces are light and subtle. Don't miss the juicy five-flavored spare ribs and perfectly crispy fried spinach.

*2017 rue Peel.* ☎ *514-287-1878. Reservations essential. Main course: C$14–C$22. AE, DC, MC, V. Open: Lunch Mon–Fri, dinner Mon–Sat. Métro: Peel.*

### Moishe's Steak House
$$$–$$$$  **Plateau  STEAK**

A revered restaurant that has been in business for 65 years, Moishe's is Montréal's steak mecca, hands-down. A recent face-lift has given the establishment a modern allure, but it is still very much a remnant of the days when "The Main" (boulevard St-Laurent) was the heart of Montréal's Jewish community. The Lighter brothers, who inherited this place from their father, consider the quest for quality meat a high art. Their steaks come exclusively from corn-fed beasts raised on a hand-picked ranch in Colorado, and the best cuts will melt in your mouth. Accompanying potatoes and vegetables are also top-notch, and the walls are stocked with bottles of fine wine. Career waiters are knowledgeable and friendly, glad to entertain even the most obscure questions. Come with an appetite.

*3961 bd. St-Laurent.* ☎ *514-845-3509. Reservations recommended. Main course: C$28–C$52. AE, DC, MC, V. Open: Lunch Mon–Fri, dinner daily. Métro: Sherbrooke.*

### Ouzeri
$$  **Plateau  CONTEMPORARY GREEK**

Exposed brick walls and storeroom shelves stocked with bottles of wine and vats of olive oil give Ouzeri a warm, yet stripped-down feel with a designer edge. A bit of a scene for Montréal's work-hard, play-hard crowd, this is where urbanites in their late 20s and 30s stop in for a late dinner. It's a great place for Greek tapas, the restaurant's specialty. Service is friendly and expedient as the waiters rush about the main dinning room. Two other spaces, one upstairs, the other down, are more intimate and less noisy.

*4690 rue St-Denis (at the corner of rue Gilford).* ☎ *514-845-1336. Reservations recommended. Main course: C$6–C$18. AE, DC, MC, V. Open: Lunch and dinner daily. Wheelchair accessible. Métro: Laurier.*

### Patati Patata
**$–$$    Plateau    DINER**

*Quirky* is the word for this little fish-and-chips and burger joint on boulevard St-Laurent. The 20-something owners converted a minuscule old 12-chair diner into a minuscule new 12-chair diner. They whip up tasty, fresh fast food behind the counter while you watch — breading the fish, tossing the salad, and frying the burgers before your eyes. The entertainment value is great, but the food is even better. Don't skip the skinny fries, even if you're on a diet. Homemade brownies also hit the spot.

*4177 bd. St-Laurent (at corner of rue Rachel).* ☎ *514-844-0216. Reservations not accepted. Main course: C$5–C$8. No credit cards. Open: Breakfast, lunch, and dinner daily. Métro: Mont-Royal or Sherbrooke.*

### Philinos
**$$–$$$    Plateau    GREEK**

Avenue du Parc, just north of Parc Mont-Royal, is Montréal's traditional Greek neighborhood, and oodles of souvlaki joints and fish restaurants line this busy avenue and the smaller side streets nearby. Philinos stands out for its solid, satisfying food and inviting atmosphere. It's usually full of Greek customers, which is always a good sign. You can order from a selection of tapas-style appetizers, such as *szatiki,* or go for generous plates of kebabs. Don't miss the divine dessert of thick yogurt drizzled with honey.

*4806 av. du Parc.* ☎ *514-271-9099. Reservations recommended. Main course: C$16–C$40. AE, DC, DISC, MC, V. Open: Lunch and dinner daily. Wheelchair accessible. Métro: Laurier.*

### Rosalie
**$$$$    Downtown    SUPPER CLUB**

During the summer, the long narrow terrace with immense, black canvas parasols in the front is a major draw for the suits from downtown office buildings. They arrive for after-work drinks, and then linger for a big-ticket dinner. It's usually money well spent, as Dave McMillan, the restaurant's executive chef, devises contemporary yet refined dishes. Appetizers include a foie gras (goose liver) sundae and salmon tartare with mixed greens. The main courses feature a variety of meats, such as pork, fish, duck, sweetbreads, and rabbit, and come in robust and flavorful sauces. The restaurant's contemporary yet serene interior can best be summed up as retro-Scandinavian, with lots of wood, chrome, and black leather seats and banquettes. The pleasant sommelier can help you choose from the extensive wine list.

*1232 rue de la Montagne (south of rue Ste-Catherine).* ☎ *514-392-1970. Reservations recommended. Main course: C$20–C$35. AE, DC, DISC, MC, V. Open: Lunch Mon–Fri, dinner daily. Wheelchair accessible. Métro: Peel.*

### Rôtisserie Italienne
**$–$$  Downtown  ITALIAN**

Don't let the counter service, bright lighting, and lackluster dinning room faze you — the pasta dishes are irreproachable. Excellent Italian fare at a great value is the trade-off for the odd setting. There's a disproportionate amount of oblivious, lovey-dovey couples doing their own version of the spaghetti scene from Disney's *Lady and the Tramp*. Perhaps the fresh pasta and house wine here have a quickening effect on the evening. A wall of signed hockey sticks is testament that it's also a mecca of sorts for out-of-town hockey players. They flock to this eatery looking to load up on carbs and protein before the big game. The pizzas have thin, crunchy crusts and come in individual-sized pans. The convivial cooks dressed in white behind the counter beckon you to approach. The menu is at the front, above the refrigerated display. Don't forget to consider the daily special, scrawled on a whiteboard; it's often what everyone's eating. They'll call your name when your order's ready. In the meantime, find a seat or engage the willing staff in pleasantries.

*1933 rue Ste-Catherine Ouest (corner of rue Towers).* ☎ *514-935-4436. Reservations not accepted. Main course: C$6–C$13.25. No credit cards. Open: Lunch and dinner Mon–Fri. Métro: Guy-Concordia.*

### Rumi
**$$–$$$  Outremont  MIDDLE EASTERN**

For atmosphere, this Middle Eastern cafe–style restaurant is hard to beat. The interior is warm, spacious, and comfortable, decorated with Arabian trimmings. The sidewalk terrace, spanning half a block on the corner of two quiet streets, is one of the most relaxing in the city. A haven of peace, Rumi is a good place to put an end to a busy day. Tapas-style portions of Middle Eastern standards include hummus and marinated red peppers, as well as more substantial plates such as veal kebabs and seasonal fish. In the summer, arrive before 7 p.m. if you want a spot on the terrace, or you can call to reserve a table.

*5198 rue Hutchinson (at the corner of rue Fairmont).* ☎ *514-490-1999. Reservations recommend. Main course: C$19–C$29. AE, MC, V. Open: Lunch and dinner Tues–Sun. Métro: Laurier.*

### Schwartz's
**$–$$    Plateau    SMOKED MEAT**

This cramped deli, staffed mainly by surly seniors, is a fixture on boulevard St-Laurent and positively the best place to sample Montréal's famous smoked meat. While you'll find little else on the menu, order these juicy slices of beef brisket, cured, smoked, or spiced, then heaped on rye bread and served with mustard. The sandwiches or plates come in lean, medium, or fatty varieties. The medium-fatty is my favorite. French fries, pickles, roasted red peppers, and coleslaw sides are available separately. Tradition dictates a black cherry soda to wash it all down. Most days bring a long line outside, but it's definitely worth the wait.

*3895 bd. St-Laurent.* ☎ *514-842-4813. Reservations not accepted. Main course: C$8–C$18. No credit cards. Open: Lunch and dinner daily. Métro: Sherbrooke.*

### Taquéria Mexicaine
**$    Plateau    MEXICAN**

Taquéria Mex offers the usual selection of tacos, burritos, quesadillas, and more — all in beef, chicken, and vegetarian versions, with a choice of salad, rice, or chips. The ingredients are fresh. The salad is never wilted and is always accompanied by perfectly ripe avocados. The fresh tomatoes even taste good year-round. We're not sure how they do it, actually, but we've never been disappointed. Kids will find familiar fare here, like tacos and tortilla chips. This place is hard to beat if you want a satisfying meal for *poco pesos.*

*4306 bd. St-Laurent.* ☎ *514-982-9462. Reservations not accepted. Main course: C$9–C$15. MC, V. Open: Lunch and dinner daily. Métro: Mont-Royal or Sherbrooke.*

### Toqué!
**$$$$    Downtown    FRENCH CONTEMPORARY**

If you're willing to lay down some big money for a serious gastronomic experience, don't miss this high-end French restaurant, considered one of the best in the province. Québec celebrity chef Normand Laprise uses as many fresh local ingredients as possible to make dishes like veal, scallops, red snapper, risotto, guinea hen, and delectable French desserts. The food is wildly imaginative, but it's dished out in small portions. The atmosphere is chic and intimate, and the same can be said about the crowd. Don't worry about dressing up, but most of all, don't be intimidated by the snobby-looking waiters. Many are chefs-in-training, along with decent types who know a lot about their vocation. They magically lose their attitude if you ask a straightforward question. Reserve a week ahead to get a table on the weekend, and don't plan anything else for the evening.

*900 place Jean-Paul Riopelle.* ☎ *514-499-2084.* www.restaurant-toque.com. *Reservations recommended. Main course: C$32–C$45. AE, DC, MC, V. Open: Lunch Tues–Fri, dinner Tues–Sat. Métro: Place-d'Armes.*

### Trattoria Trestevere
**$$–$$$ Downtown ITALIAN**

This inconspicuous locale, on southern Crescent below rue Ste-Catherine, serves some of the city's best Italian food. It has a strong base of regular clientele, happy to be back for another authentic meal. Middle-aged, career waiters welcome guests and make them feel at home with warm and knowing smiles. The service is discreet and reassuring — the waitstaff feels like a band of Italian uncles you never had. The semi-basement has stucco walls and Roman arches, and the whole scene is vaguely reminiscent of a wine cellar or grotto. If you've never felt strongly about gnocchi, a pasta dumpling made from potatoes, you can make up your mind after trying it here. It's mind-boggling. You can have it with any of the sauces on the menu. In fact, you can also mix and match the sauces with any of the fresh, homemade pastas. Ask your waiter what's best if you can't make up your mind. The pastas are velvety and melt in your mouth — al dente, not overcooked. However, pasta and sauces aren't the only thing on the menu. As you gaze over the other choices of old-world, Italian classics, rest assured you'll get a true rendition of whatever you're craving.

*1237 rue Crescent (south of rue Ste-Catherine).* ☎ *514-866-3226. Reservations recommended. Main course: C$14–C$35. AE, DC, MC, V. Open: Lunch Mon–Fri and dinner Mon–Sat. Métro: Peel, Guy-Concordia, Lucien-L'Allier.*

# Dining and Snacking On the Go

In Montréal, fast food doesn't equal tasteless — not even close. If you don't want to go out for fine dining every night, don't despair. Montréal's food festival carries on in every corner of the city's dining experience, from pizza and picnicking to *poutine*.

## Pizza and burgers

Almost everything you eat in Montréal has a distinct local twist, including these fast food staples. Like the French, many Montréalers prefer pizzas with very thin crusts. If you want to try one, hit a **Pizzadélic,** with various locations around town: 1250 av. Mont-Royal Est (☎ 514-522-2286) and 1641 rue St-Denis (☎ 514-499-1444). Also a sit-down place, **Romeo,** 285 av. Mont-Royal Est (☎ 514-987-6636), with a see-and-be-seen clientele grabbing a quick nosh before heading out to the bars. They serve small pizzas with gourmet toppings in interesting combinations.

An Italian butcher cum gourmet shop cum pizza parlor a block away from the Marché Jean-Talon is one of this town's best kept pizza secrets: **Boucherie Jos & Basile,** 6995 av. Casgrain (☎ 514-274-6358). Also nearby in Little Italy, **Pizzeria Napolitana,** 189 rue Dante (☎ 514-276-8226), offers an astounding number of varieties and an authentic setting. Perhaps more central, **Prato Pizzeria Café,** 3891 bd. St-Laurent (☎ 514-285-1616), also makes a great thin-crust pie in a casual, brick-walled dining room right on "The Main" (boulevard St-Laurent).

Amélio's, 201 rue Milton (☎ 514-845-8396), is downtown in the heart of the McGill University's student ghetto and has been a favorite for several generations. An Arab bakery, **Al-Taib,** 2125 rue Guy (☎ 514-931-1999), holds the title of best pizza in the west end of downtown. It's open 24 hours and broadcasts a live satellite feed of Al-Jazeera.

The tastiest delivery pizza in the city comes from **Tasty Food Pizza,** 6660 bd. Décarie (☎ 514-739-9333), as its name suggests.

Montréal isn't a big burger town, but if you get a craving you'll appreciate that a few places seem to have perfected the genre. Downtown, try **La Paryse,** 302 rue Ontario Est (☎ 514-842-2040). On boulevard St-Laurent, there's **Shed Café,** 3515 bd. St-Laurent (☎ 514-842-0220), and **La Cabane,** 3872 bd. St-Laurent (☎ 514-843-7283). **Hurley's Irish Pub,** 1225 rue Crescent (☎ 514-861-4111), has garnered quite a reputation for its fine burgers. Feel like bison? Try a bison burger at **Mckibbins Irish Pub,** 1426 rue Bishop (☎ 514-288-1580).

## The best bagels

A war rages on over who bakes the best bagels: New York or Montréal. (I don't have to tell you whose side I'm on.) But even inside Montréal, there's a civil war of sorts between bagel lovers who love one of two major bagel bakeries in Montréal. Don't show your colors to locals until you know which side they're on.

**St-Viateur Bagels,** 263 rue St-Viateur Ouest (☎ 514-267-8044), is my favorite. Bagels come piping hot out of a wood-burning oven, drawing a faithful following from all corners of the city. From the fridges beside the counter, you can buy cream cheese, smoked salmon, and other toppings.

**Fairmont Bagels,** technically the Bagel Factory, 74 rue Fairmount Ouest (☎ 514-272-0667), offers several variations on its famous sesame-seed bagel. Here, you can try bagels with raisins and cinnamon or even olives and sun-dried tomatoes, plus a variety of toppings.

## Sandwich, anyone?

Montréalers love good bread — in particular, long, thin, crusty baguettes — and that's good news for anyone looking for a sandwich. Whether you grab one on the run or settle into a cafe for a bite, this section gives you some options.

**Le Cartet Boutique Alimentaire,** 106 rue McGill (☎ 514-871-8887) is a mega-mall for your stomach, disguised as a hip gourmet shop and bustling lunch counter. The walls are chock-full of upmarket, gourmet grocery items, like spring water from Japan. It's a foodie's delight. The sandwiches are made fresh and go quickly, with all the Vieux-Montréal office workers cramming in a quick bite. The kitchen also makes rather elaborate main courses. The choices are scrawled on a blackboard above the kitchen. There's always pasta, a meat, a fish — but what they are changes on a regular basis.

**Cluny,** 257 rue Prince (☎ 514-866-1213), tucked away in an up-and-coming warehouse district adjacent to Vieux-Montréal, this daytime cafe shares its locale with an artists' cooperative in a former foundry. Sandwiches, antipasto, and a more substantial daily special are what the "in" crowd of new media professionals comes for.

**Les Gourmets Pressés,** 406 St Jacques (☎ 514-842-5525), located in the heart of the banking district, is a small lunch counter serving a light yet creative menu of sandwiches, soups, and salads. There's seating at the front, but it can be scarce during lunch hours.

**Olive and Gourmando,** 351 rue St-Paul Ouest (☎ 514-285-1000), has some of the best sandwiches in town. Choose from the six choices on the chalkboard, familiar combos with gourmet ingredients like portobello mushrooms. The bread is always fresh because they make it on-site, along with a dazzling array of other sweet and savory baked goods like brownies and focaccia. It used to be a well-kept secret among locals, but the word is definitely out. You may have to wait for a table, but it's worthwhile.

**Titanic,** 445 rue St-Pierre (☎ 514-849-0894), in Vieux-Montréal, is also a popular lunch spot. Sandwich-wise, it serves rather exotic combinations of ingredients on delicious crusty bread. Homemade soups, daily specials, and heaping antipasto plates are all delicious.

**Au Pain Doré,** one of Montréal's major bakery chains, has locations throughout the city. Each sells very respectable prewrapped sandwiches — classics such as ham and cheese or smoked salmon. This is a good place to stop if you need to grab something on the run. Popular downtown locations include 556 rue Ste-Catherine Est (☎ 514-282-2220) and 1415 rue Peel (☎ 514-843-3151). In the Plateau, head to 1145 av. Laurier Ouest (☎ 514-276-0947).

Ditto **Première Moisson,** which also has several outlets throughout the city. Some stores have cafes with many choices of sandwiches and salads and other market-inspired, ready-to-eat lunchables. One is in the promenade of the Gare Centrale, the downtown train station, at 895 rue de la Gauchetière Ouest (☎ 514-393-6540). Another is at 1490 rue Sherbrooke Ouest (☎ 514-931-6540), near the Montréal Museum of Fine Art.

## Big breakfast bonanza

Montréalers are extremely fond of working off their morning blues (or hangover) over a plate of eggs and bacon. Join a citywide ritual and load up at one of the following renowned breakfast joints. You can have it fancy, surrounding yourself with stylish locals and fruit smoothies, or go in for a classic, greasy-spoon formula.

**Le Cartet** (see the preceding section) and **Le Reservoir,** 9 rue Duluth Est (☎ 514-849-7779), deserve special mention here. They've upped the ante in terms of what to expect. Although the brunch places first distinguished themselves by serving copious quantities of fresh fruit — and have largely stuck to that formula — Reservoir and Cartet have turned this weekend ritual into a gastronomic adventure of carefully matched flavors and creative presentations.

**L'Avenue,** 922 av. Mont-Royal Est (☎ 514-523-8780), located in the heart of the hip Plateau neighborhood, has been extremely popular for years. Trendy denizens line up for the breakfasts; to beat them, aim to arrive before 11 a.m.

**Mont-Royal Hot Dog,** 1001 av. Mont-Royal Est (☎ 514-523-3670), is one of the few remnants of this neighborhood's working-class past. Breakfasts are generous and cheap, the gum-smacking waitresses give you exactly what you want, and you don't have to listen to any jazz while you're eating.

**Eggspectations,** 98 av. Laurier Ouest (☎ 514-278-6411) and 1313 bd. de Maisonneuve Ouest (☎ 514-842-3447), as well as other locations around the city, is a chain that serves eggs any which way, all day long. It's on the fancier side of the greasy-spoon scale, and so are the prices.

**Cosmos Snack Bar,** 5843 rue Sherbrooke Ouest (☎ 514-486-3814), is a tiny breakfast and lunch counter that seats six, run by a Greek family. Sit at the counter and join the locals in idle chatter. You'll feel like you're sitting in on a sitcom set in a greasy spoon. Breakfast here gets you through a lumberjack's day.

**Chez Clo,** 3199 rue Ontario Est (☎ 514-522-5348), is a Montréal landmark, serving authentic Québec-style breakfast and lunch at absurdly low prices.

## *Picnicking and markets*

The best place to picnic in Montréal, by far, is **Parc Mont-Royal** (see Chapter 11 for details). Prime spots are the slope in front of **Beaver Lake,** or the slope facing avenue du Parc. To pick up some bread, cheese, pâté, or cold cuts, visit nearby **PA Supermarché,** 5029 av. du Parc; **La Veille Europe,** 3855 bd. St-Laurent; or **Épicerie Latina,** 185 rue St-Viateur Ouest.

Montréal's two major outdoor markets are also great places to pick up some light fare and explore among the locals. Both are conveniently located next to Métro stops. To get to the **Atwater Market** in the west end of downtown, get off either the orange or green line at Lionel-Groulx station. To get to the **Jean-Talon Market** in Little Italy, go to Jean-Talon station, at the intersection of the blue and orange lines.

These are great places to taste locally grown Québec *terroir* products. Both markets begin carrying local produce by mid-June and are usually going strong well into October. At the Jean-Talon Market, don't miss the **Marché des Saveurs,** 280 place du Marché-du-Nord — one of the best specialty food stores in the city, which carries Québec wines, cheese, maple syrup products, and more.

As an added bonus, municipal authorities remain convinced that drinking wine in a park with a meal poses no greater danger to public morality than drinking wine at a sidewalk restaurant. As long as you're eating a meal, drinking wine and beer in parks is legal.

## Eating like a local

Like the French, Québeckers love fine cuisine. But in the dietary staples here — notably *steamies* (steamed hot dogs), *bines* (baked beans), and *poutine* (fries served with gravy and cheese curds) — Québeckers distinguish themselves as a totally separate gastronomic race. These regional favorites are true fuel. Loaded with fat and dripping with grease, this is the kind of food that sticks to your stomach and keeps you warm on winter nights, although, come to think of it, people eat it all year round.

Give local delicacies a try, ideally on a very empty stomach. The legendary **La Binerie Mont-Royal,** 367 av. du Mont-Royal Est (☎ 514-285-9078), is Québec's spiritual home of baked beans. **Casse-Croûte La Banquise,** 994 rue Rachel Est (☎ 514-525-2415), is reputed to make the best *poutine* in Montréal, and has more varieties than you can shake a stick at. **Restaurant Lafleurs,** 3620 rue St-Denis (☎ 514-848-1804), also makes a noteworthy *poutine.* At **Chez Clo,** 3199 rue Ontario Est (☎ 514-522-5348), you can move up the *habitant* (Québec native) food chain a little and eat Québec specialties like pea soup, meat ball *ragoût* (stew), or *tourtière* (meat pie).

## The vegetarian scene

Most Montréal restaurants are enlightened enough to offer at least one vegetarian option on their menus. But most of the time, the vegetarian choice seems like an afterthought. Luckily, some restaurants around town cater exclusively to Montréal's vegetarians, who are no longer considered just patchouli-scented, placard-bearing, long-haired social activists.

Right in the heart of the Quartier Latin, **Le Commensal,** 1720 rue St-Denis (☎ 514-845-2627), was the first venue of what's now a vegetarian chain with several restaurants around the city. Its downtown location, 1204 av. McGill-College (☎ 514-871-1480), is extremely popular at lunch with the business crowd. Food is sold by weight, and both spots offer three different buffets at three different rates: hot, cold, and dessert. An average meal costs about C$20.

**Cafe Santropol,** 3990 rue St-Urbain (☎ 514-842-3110), occupies the first floor of a house at the corner of avenue Duluth. The restaurant has a wonderful back garden with rocks, trees, and a babbling fountain, making it an urban oasis on a hot summer day. Inside, it's a cozy place to warm up over a bowl of vegetarian chili after walking up the Mountain on a blustery fall day. Sandwiches of thick sliced bread, stuffed with fresh and original flavor combinations (cream cheese is a staple) are the main attraction. A couple of sandwiches include meat, so you can bring your carnivore friends, but the rest of the menu is all vegetarian.

**Pushap Sweets,** 5195 rue Paré (☎ 514-737-4527), is nirvana for vegetarians and Indian-food lovers, and it's not a bad deal either. Excellent samosas make good starters. Delicious and affordable *thalis* are what everyone's eating — combo platters that vary from day to day, usually featuring two different curries and served with a choice of flatbreads. Pushap also makes traditional Indian baked goods, which are very sweet.

**Spirite Lounge,** 1205 rue Ontario Est (☎ 514-522-5353), is an outlandish dining experience by any standard. Located in a sort of no-man's-land between the Quartier Latin and the Gay Village, its walls are covered with crumpled aluminum foil. This is deep-vegetarianism with a fascist bent. At the beginning, a waiter brandishing a riding crop lays down the exact rules. No menu, but a meal is three courses, each consisting of a dizzying list of ingredients, organic whenever possible. Choose your portion size wisely, because if you don't finish your main course or starter, you don't get dessert . . . plus you have to pay a fine of C\$2. The restaurant matches the fine and gives it to charity. If you don't finish your dessert, you're banned from the restaurant for life. If you use your cellphone, you're thrown out on your other ear.

## BYOB

One thing that makes Montréal's dining landscape unique in Canada is the availability — abundance, even — of restaurants that don't serve alcohol but allow you to Bring Your Own Bottle (BYOB) of wine to accompany your meals. This arrangement is ideal. It allows you to save substantially on alcohol or afford a better bottle of wine than you would normally order. I recommend striving to do both.

Unfortunately, in an attempt to compensate for nonexistent liquor sales, the majority of Montréal's BYOB restaurants, particularly those concentrated along the pedestrian part of rue Prince-Arthur, try to turn tables quickly. Quality and care can suffer, and the wham-bam approach to service can ruin your appetite as you begin to feel you're part of a giant, feeding herd. L'Academie, spanning three floors on the corner of rue St-Denis and avenue Duluth, packed most nights, is the worst offender in this regard.

However, a select few BYOBs are owned by artful restaurateurs, rather than proprietors blinded by their bottom lines. These are the hidden gems of Montréal's restaurant scene. Because they are usually small and extremely popular, you may need to reserve a couple of days in advance in order to get a table. Walking in on a weekend night is a gamble, but you may get lucky if you're looking only for a table for two. At these places, you can expect to pay between C$20 and C$30 per person, before tip and taxes, for a three-course meal.

Somewhat far-flung, **Yoyo's,** 4720 rue Marquette (☎ 514-524-4187), is located in the northeastern reaches of the Plateau, on an otherwise mainly residential street. It is considered one of the best BYOBs in town. The most serious gastronomes among the clientele bring magnums of cherished vintages from their own cellars for decanting, because they are confident that the kitchen will come through with food to match.

**O'Thym,** 112 bd. de Maisonneuve Est (☎ 514-525-3443), is a recent addition to the city's BYOB scene, located between the Quartier Latin and the Gay Village. The kitchen turns out excellent *table d'hôte* of fish, game, and more traditional dishes with interesting combinations of vegetable accompaniments. The décor is minimalist and the high ceilings give the dining room an airy feel. The oblique montage of wall photos is odd enough to serve as a good conversation starter.

Named after an active volcano, **Piton de la Fournaise,** 835 av. Duluth Est (☎ 514-526-3936), is the only restaurant in town that serves Creole cuisine from Reunion Island, a former French colony in the Indian Ocean. The flavorful dishes are a combination of French, African, and Indian influences. They are heavily seasoned, but not necessarily spicy. Bring a light red, slightly chilled wine.

**La Colombe,** 554 av. Duluth Est (☎ 514-849-8844), is a French BYOB that incorporates North African influences. Fish first, and then meat, are the specialties here. Of the four main courses, two are usually fish, although the menu items change daily based on what the chef finds on his morning shop at the market.

Reserve a table for the second of the two seatings (at 7 p.m.) at **Le P'tit Plateau,** 330 rue Marie-Anne Est (☎ 514-282-6342). The first seating, at 5:30 p.m., can feel a tad rushed. But no matter — when you dine here, the classic French is first rate. The chalkboard menu changes regularly but usually features beef, pork, fish, and game.

## Coffee and pastries

Montréalers who are serious about their coffee regularly trek to the northeastern reaches of the city to get their fix. In Mile End, **Café Olympico,** 124 rue St-Viateur Ouest, (☎ 514-495-0746), at the corner of rue Waverly and rue St-Viateur, is a neighborhood hangout for young couples, artsy types, grad students, and a supporting cast of colorful characters. A fair number of regulars hang out here, and everyone acts as though they're nonchalantly in-the-know.

Further up boulevard St-Laurent, in Little Italy, **Café Italia,** 6840 bd. St-Laurent (☎ **514-495-0059**), is also reputed for its coffee. Here, too, the café au lait comes in a glass. You can also order a cappuccino or an espresso. The remnant 1950s décor and the elderly Italian men give the place an old-world feel.

In up-and-coming St-Henri, **Lili and Oli,** 2515 rue Notre-Dame (☎ **514-932-8961**), is a recent contender on the coffee scene, making espresso, cappuccino, and café au lait that rivals the best in the city. It's right around the corner from the Atwater Market and amidst all the shops of Montréal's "Antique Alley" along rue Notre-Dame. It can be a welcome pit stop during a day of shopping for local food specialties and décor items. Coffee connoisseurs will find this a rewarding destination. Downtown, near rue Crescent, the Montréal Museum of Fine Art, and Concordia University's downtown campus, **Nocochi,** 2156 rue Mackay (☎ **514-989-7514**), makes a curious selection of delicate Middle Eastern pastries, cookies, and treats.

If you're trippin' about how French everything is, you may have a hankering for a croissant to top it off. The best in the city are baked at the **Duc de Lorraine Patisserie Francaise,** 5002 chemin Cote-des-Neiges (☎ **514-731-4128**). They're good enough to give a Frenchman pause.

# Chapter 11

# Discovering Montréal's Best Attractions

**In This Chapter**

▶ Checking out Montréal's best sights and activities
▶ Satisfying families, museum-goers, sports enthusiasts, and more
▶ Choosing a guided tour

*I*n this chapter, I give you Montréal's top sights and activities and tell you how to see them yourself or with the help of a guided tour. I also fill you in on some attractions that are perfect for families, sports fans, and others.

## Montréal's Top Sights from A to Z

Wondering what to do while in Montréal? Read through my suggestions in this section and choose the attractions that interest you most. You probably won't have enough time to see them all, so don't run yourself ragged trying.

### Basilique Notre-Dame (Notre-Dame Basilica)
**Vieux-Montréal**

Basilique Notre-Dame is a new-world version of Paris's Notre Dame Cathedral, a grandiose church overlooking a broad *place,* or square, in the heart of the historic city. Okay, so the style is Gothic Revival, not Gothic, and it was built in the 19th century, not the 12th. But still, this Catholic church is a feast for the eyes, from the intricately carved altar to the gilded ornamentation throughout. The effect is so moving that the basilica's Protestant architect, James O'Donnell, actually converted to Catholicism when it was completed. You can explore on your own or take a guided tour (available in English) at various times, starting at 9 a.m. Sound and light shows were recently introduced, with two performances nightly Tuesday through Saturday.

*110 rue Notre-Dame Ouest (on Place-d'Armes).* ☎ *514-842-2925.* www.basili quenddm.org. *Admission: Free for praying; otherwise, adults C$4, students C$2.*

*Open: Mon–Fri 8 a.m.–4:30 p.m., Sat 12:30–4:30 p.m., Sun 12:30–4:00 p.m. Light show: Adults C$10, seniors C$9, children 7–17 C$5, children 6 and under free. Light show open: Tues–Fri 6:30 p.m. and Thurs, Fri 8:30 p.m., Sat 7 p.m. and 8:30 p.m. Métro: Place-d'Armes or Champ-de-Mars.*

### Belgo Building
**Downtown**

This downtown building is now one of the most significant art spaces on the local Montréal scene. The several stories of hardwood-floored hallways are lined with doors to studios, gallery spaces, and showrooms belonging to some of the city's best contemporary artists and designers. Some of the notables are Galerie René Blouin (no. 501), Therese Dion Art Contemporain (no. 527), Optica (no. 508), Pierre-Francois Ouellette Art Contemporain (no. 216), Galerie Lilian Rodriguez (405), and Galerie Trois Points (no. 520). A particular favorite, Sharon Ramsay, has a gallery (no. 528) featuring oil paintings of wet cityscapes from streets in Old Montréal and elsewhere in the city. Spend an afternoon wandering around the different gallery spaces and showrooms on the different floors.

*372 rue Ste-Catherine Ouest. Admission: Free. Open: Tues–Sat noon to 6 p.m., though some artists' hours vary. Métro: Place-des-Arts.*

### Biodôme de Montréal (Montréal Biodome)
**East Montréal**

Built to fill the velodrome from the 1976 Olympics, Montréal's Biodôme is like a zoo and an indoor nature walk combined. You start at the penguin pool, a universal favorite among kids and grownups. Then you follow the trail through four different ecosystems: a Laurentian forest, the St. Lawrence marine system, a tropical rain forest, and a polar environment, each complete with its own plants and animals. You spend your visit largely in temperate surroundings, but you may want to bring a pullover for the Polar World segment. Kids go nuts here. Allow one hour.

*4777 av. Pierre-de-Coubertin (next to Stade Olympique). ☎ **514-868-3000.** www. biodome.qc.ca. Admission: Adults C$16, seniors and students C$12, children 5–17 C$8, children under 5, free. Open: Daily 9 a.m.–5 p.m. (until 6 p.m. in summer). Métro: Viau.*

### Boulevard St-Laurent
**Plateau**

"The Main," as it is known to English Montréalers, is the city's oldest north–south artery. It extends up from Vieux-Montréal through Chinatown and beyond Little Italy and the Jean Talon Market to the farthest reaches of the island. It also divides the city's street addresses between Est and Ouest. Boulevard St-Laurent has many interesting parts. The most colorful and liveliest stretch runs between rue Sherbrooke and avenue Mont-Royal, where the foot traffic is heavy all day and well into the night; a multitude of cafes, boutiques, delis, restaurants, and shops are frequented

## *Downtown Montréal Attractions*

Belgo Building **9**
Boulevard St-Laurent **11**
Centre Canadien d'Architecture **4**
Christ Church Cathédral **8**
CinéRobothèque **12**
Grande Bibliothèque **13**
Musée d'Art Contemporain de Montréal **10**

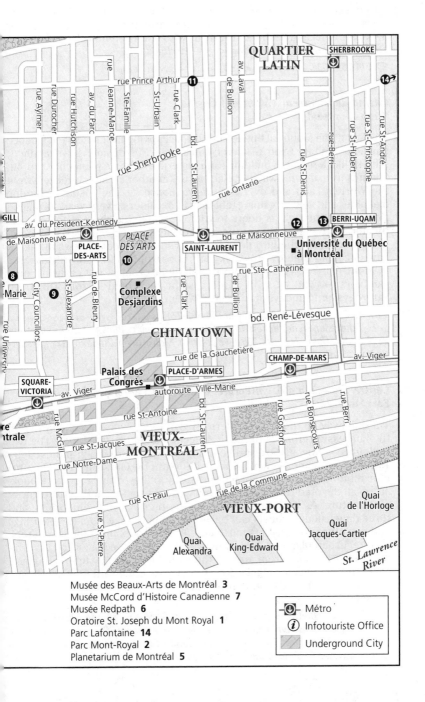

Musée des Beaux-Arts de Montréal **3**
Musée McCord d'Histoire Canadienne **7**
Musée Redpath **6**
Oratoire St. Joseph du Mont Royal **1**
Parc Lafontaine **14**
Parc Mont-Royal **2**
Planetarium de Montréal **5**

- Métro
(*i*) Infotouriste Office
Underground City

by a cosmopolitan clientele. By night, boulevard St-Laurent is one of the city's booming nightlife strips. It's a major destination and quite a scene for debonair dons and flesh-bearing divas who cram behind velvet ropes and crowd burly bouncers looking to get into *the* spot.

☎ *514-286-0334.* www.boulevardsaintlaurent.com.

### Casino de Montréal (Montréal Casino)
**Vieux-Montréal**

The Casino de Montréal opened in 1993, occupying the French and Québec pavilions built for Expo '67 on the banks of Île Notre-Dame. Lit up at night, it looks like a remnant building from Superman's home planet of Krypton. Minutes from downtown, past Habitat '67 (another architectural gem from the World's Fair) and over *Pont de la Concorde,* the casino's chiming machines and velvety gaming tables span five floors. Every year, six million guests pass through its doors to gamble, to catch a show at the cabaret theater, or to dine at one of the four restaurants. One of them, Nuances, nestled away on the fifth floor and offering spectacular views of the St. Lawrence and the downtown skyline, is one of two five-star restaurants in Montréal. You can also join the all-night cronies and early-morning gamblers — who must be quite a sight to behold — for brunch on Saturdays and Sundays starting at 9:30 a.m.

*1 av. du Casino.* ☎ *800-665-2274* or 514-392-2746. www.casino-de-montreal. com. *Admission: Free; tickets to matinee and evening shows at Le Cabaret are C$22–C$106. Open: 24 hours, 365 days per year. Métro: Jean-Drapeau; take the shuttle from there.*

### Centre Canadien d'Architecture (Canadian Center for Architecture)
**East Montréal**

Tucked away on the southwestern edge of the downtown neighborhood, the impressive grounds of the CCA occupy an entire city block. The two buildings — one austere and contemporary, the other a grandiose late-19th-century home — combine to make up the 130,000 sq. ft. (12,077 sq. m) of exhibition galleries, a library and study center, a theater, and a bookstore, all devoted to the understanding, appreciation, and betterment of architecture. As museum-going goes, the photography, blueprints, and three-dimensional models can be a refreshing change from the paintings and sculptures of most art museums. The CCA's exhibits focus on architecture, urban planning, and landscape design. While CCA attracts architecture enthusiasts from around the globe, it is usually interesting and accessible enough for regular folk, too. Across boulevard René-Levesque, to the south, the CCA Garden is a unique sculpture garden — ideal at sunset.

*1920 rue Baile (between rue du Fort and rue St-Marc).* ☎ *514-939-7026.* www. cca.qc.ca. *Admission: Adults C$10, seniors C$7, students C$5, children ages 6–12 C$3. Free on Thurs after 5 p.m. Open: Wed–Sun 10 a.m.–5 p.m. (until 9 p.m. on Thurs). Métro: Atwater, Georges-Vanier, or Guy-Concordia.*

*Vieux-Montréal Attractions*

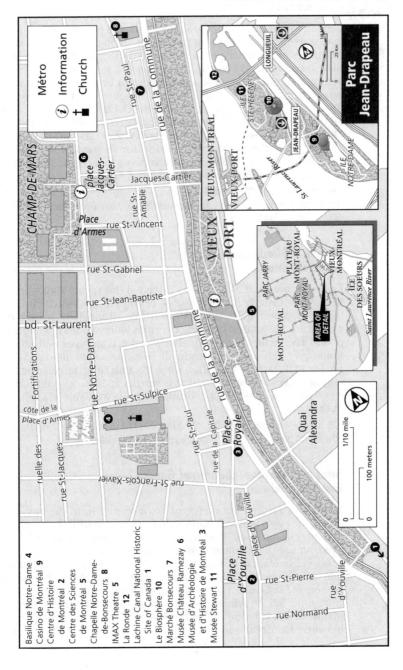

**Legend:**
- *i* Métro
- *i* Information
- ✝ 🏛 Church

CHAMP-DE-MARS

place Jacques-Cartier

Jacques-Cartier

Place d'Armes

rue St-Amable

rue St-Vincent

rue St-Gabriel

rue St-Jean-Baptiste

bd. St-Laurent

Fortifications

rue Notre-Dame

côte de la place d'Armes

rue St-Sulpice

ruelle des

rue St-Jacques

rue St-François-Xavier

rue St-Paul

rue de la Capitale

Place-Royale

rue de la Commune

VIEUX-PORT

Quai Alexandra

Place d'Youville

place d'Youville

rue St-Pierre

rue d'Youville

rue Normand

rue St-Paul

rue de la Commune

**Parc Jean-Drapeau** (inset)
- LONGUEUIL
- ÎLE STE-HÉLÈNE
- JEAN-DRAPEAU
- ÎLE NOTRE-DAME
- VIEUX-MONTRÉAL
- VIEUX-PORT
- St Laurent River
- .25 Km

**Area of Detail** (inset)
- PARC JARRY
- PLATEAU MONT-ROYAL
- PARC MONT-ROYAL
- MONT-ROYAL
- VIEUX MONTRÉAL
- ÎLE DES SOEURS
- Saint Laurence River

0 — 1/10 mile
0 — 100 meters

**Index:**

Basilique Notre-Dame **4**
Casino de Montréal **9**
Centre d'Histoire de Montréal **2**
Centre des Sciences de Montréal **5**
Chapelle Notre-Dame-de-Bonsecours **8**
IMAX Theatre **5**
La Ronde **12**
Lachine Canal National Historic Site of Canada **1**
Le Biosphère **10**
Marché Bonsecours **7**
Musée Château Ramezay **6**
Musée d'Archéologie et d'Histoire de Montréal **3**
Musée Stewart **11**

## CinéRobothèque
**Quartier Latin**

Canada's renowned National Film Board has a public screening space that makes use of a robotic arm to choose among the library's many documentaries and animation shorts — nearly 10,000 titles in all. Visitors get their own personal console consisting of a large screen for viewing the films and a touch-screen at arm's length for browsing the catalog. Double screening units are available as well. Selections include Chris Landreth's *Ryan* (2004), which received a nod at the Oscars. *The Sweater,* another animation short, breathes life into the children's story by Roch Carrier and illustrates how deeply hockey fandom runs in this part of the country — in particular the province's passion for *le tricolore* or the Montréal Canadiens. The CinéRobothèque also has a theater that holds screenings of the releases and festival programming.

*1564 rue St-Denis.* ☎ *514-496-6887.* www.nfb.ca/cinerobotheque. *Admission: Adults C$3 per hour, students and seniors C$2 per hour. Open: Tues–Sun noon to 9 p.m. Métro: Berri-UQAM.*

## Grande Bibliothèque
**Quartier Latin**

Eighteen thousand Montréalers attended the spring 2005 opening of the brand-new *Grande Bibliothèque* — or Big Library — which is similar to those being built in Paris and Mexico City. Although it's heralded by some as a futuristic cultural institution, critics worry about it being a white elephant. The facility houses Québec's national archives and other publications, over four million items in all. Some items are on loan, while others are for in-library consultation only. It's a striking, large-scale contemporary architectural structure that is worth experiencing and taking in even if you're not a bookish type. Group tours are available in English throughout the day.

*475 bd. de Maisonneuve Est.* ☎ *514-873-1100. Admission: Free. Open: Tues–Fri 10 a.m.–10 p.m. Sat–Sun 10 a.m.–5p.m. Métro: Berri-UQAM.*

## Jardins Botanique (Botanical Garden)
**East Montréal**

Montréal's Jardins Botanique offers a respite from the concrete jungle within the city's limits. By combining a visit here with the nearby Biodôme and Insectarium (see "Finding More Cool Things to See and Do"), you can make nature the theme of this daylong urban excursion. Spread over 178 acres (72 hectares) just north of the Stade Olympique, the gardens contain more than 22,000 plant species and offer a different treat for every season. In May, expect acres of fragrant lilac trees. Roses bloom from mid-June until fall. In winter, ten greenhouses shelter bonsai and tropical plants. In the fall, don't miss the Magic of Lanterns, a cooperative effort between Montréal and Shanghai that's the biggest of its type outside

## East Montréal Attractions

China. During this lantern exhibit, the gardens are particularly pretty at sunset. Picnics permitted.

*4101 rue Sherbrooke Est (opposite Stade Olympique).* ☎ **514-872-1400.** www.ville.montreal.qc.ca/jardin. *Admission: May–Oct adults C$16, seniors and students C$12, children 5–17 C$8, children 2–4 C$4; Nov–Apr adults C$14, seniors and students C$10, children 5–17 C$6, children 2–4 C$2. Open: 9 a.m.–5 p.m. year-round; May–Sept closed at 6 p.m.; and Sept–Oct closed at 9 p.m. Métro: Pie-IX.*

### Lachine Canal National Historic Site of Canada
**Vieux-Montréal**

If the founding of North America had to do with trading routes to Asia, this is an important stop in the settlement of the continent. *La chine* is French for China, which is where early French explorers thought they had landed. They were thwarted by this impressive stretch of rapids, stranded, and forced to found a settlement — what became Montréal. Later on the city built a 14.5-m-long series of canals and locks for raising and lowering ships around the dangerous and turbulent rapids between the St. Lawrence River and the Great Lakes. The canal served as an important trading route and was invaluable in Montréal's economic development. Today it is a waterfront path and green space, landscaped for leisure with a bike path running along the length of the canal. Several companies offer rafting trips through the rapids. **Lachine Rapids Tours (☎ 514-284-9607)** has 90-minute jet boat trips leaving from Vieux-Montréal. Call for prices, schedule, and location.

*Locks begin at the western end of the Old Port (rue McGill and rue de la Commune).* **☎ 514-283-6054**. www.pc.gc.ca/lhn-nhs/qc/canallachine. *Admission: Free. Open: Sunrise to 11 p.m. Métro: Square-Victoria.*

### La Ronde
**Vieux-Montréal**

Located on the former grounds of Expo '67, this amusement park is the pinnacle of a Montréal kid's summer fun. Six Flags recently bought La Ronde, and then renovated the grounds to the tune of C$90 million — and it shows. It's clean, slick, and packed with 35 rides. If you have a sturdy stomach, give Le Monstre, a classic wooden roller coaster, a try. Or venture onto Le Cobra, a stand-up roller coaster that reaches speeds of 60 mph and will definitely bring your last meal to mind. There's only one catch: La Ronde is packed in the summer, especially on weekends. According to my ten-year-old source, who waited for an hour to get onto Le Monstre, the lines can almost take the fun out of the entire experience. Luckily, though, waits are short for kiddy rides such as the Tchou Tchou Train. If you need to take a break between rides, try the rock-climbing wall or carnival booths galore.

*22 MacDonald Way (on Île Ste-Hélène).* **☎ 514-397-2000**. www.laronde.com. *Admission: 12 and over C$37, ages 3–11 $25; parking C$13. Open: Mid-May, Sat–Sun only; June–Aug and Labor Day weekend 7 days; Labor Day until end of Oct Sat–Sun only. Hours vary. Métro: Jean-Drapeau or Papineau, then bus 169.*

### Marché Bonsecours (Bonsecours Market)
**Vieux-Montréal**

You'll be sorely disappointed if you come expecting the vibrant market that closed in 1963. Today, the inside of the market building is a slick mall selling up-market tourist trinkets, mainly Québec jewelry, native crafts, and contemporary shelf furnishings. Yet the Marché Bonsecours is an impressive neoclassical building in its own right, with many columns and a silver dome. It remains an important Vieux-Montréal landmark and one of the top ten heritage buildings in Canada. Since its completion in 1847, it also served (alternately) as a meeting place of Montréal's hob-nobbing, men-only Beaver Club; as a theater where a young Charles Dickens performed as part of a touring troupe; as City Hall; and, briefly, as the Parliament of United Canada.

*350 rue St-Paul Est (at the bottom of rue Gosford).* ☎ *514-872-7730.* www. marchebonsecours.qc.ca. *Open: Daily 10 a.m.–6 p.m., until 9 p.m. on some nights. Métro: Champ-de-Mars.*

### Musée d'Archéologie et d'Histoire de Montréal (Montréal Museum of Archeology and History)
**Vieux-Montréal**

If you visit just one museum while in Montréal, this is my choice. And because it's a great introduction to Montréal's history, for the benefit of the rest of your stay visit this superb and unusual museum first. Officially opened on the city's 350th anniversary in 1992, this museum is located in the **Point-à-Callière building,** an uber-modern construction by Montréal architect Dan Hanganu. It was built on the site of the original 1642 French settlement — what would become today's Montréal. After a brief multimedia presentation, a self-guided tour takes visitors underground to discover literal layers of artifacts from the centuries of civilization and the partially excavated ruins of the city's first buildings, canal system, and cemetery. Along the way, five historical figures engage the willing in virtual conversation. A cafe on the third floor is popular for lunch among office workers in Vieux-Montréal.

*350 place Royale (at rue de la Commune).* ☎ *514-872-9150.* www.pacmusee.qc.ca. *Admission: Families C\$27, adults C\$13, seniors C\$8.50, students C\$7, children ages 6–12 C\$5. Open: Sept–June Tues–Fri 10 a.m.–5 p.m., Sat–Sun 11 a.m.–5 p.m.; July–Aug Mon–Fri 10 a.m.–6 p.m., Sat–Sun 11 a.m.–6 p.m. Métro: Square-Victoria.*

### Musée d'Art Contemporain de Montréal (Montréal Museum of Contemporary Art)
**Downtown**

Everything about this new museum is light and airy, as if it were custom-designed for daydreamers and escapists. Situated just off the sprawling plaza of **Place-des-Arts,** it's a great place to take a breather from the bustle of downtown. About 60 percent of the museum's permanent collection comprises works by contemporary Québec painters. You'll also find works from international painters such as Jean Dubuffet, Max Ernst, Jean Arp, Larry Poons, and Antoni Tàpies, as well as photographers Robert Mapplethorpe and Ansel Adams. The museum is a little light on explanations, but it does offer a few of the guiding principles of the major schools of modern art.

*185 rue Ste-Catherine Ouest.* ☎ **514-847-6226.** www.macm.org. *Admission: Families C$16, adults C$8, seniors C$6, students C$4, children under 12 free; general public free on Wed 6–9 p.m. Open: Tues–Sun 11 a.m.–6 p.m., until 9 p.m. Wed. Métro: Place-des-Arts.*

### Musée des Beaux-Arts de Montréal (Montréal Museum of Fine Arts)
**Downtown**

Since Toronto took over as Canada's business center 20 years ago, Montréal has been repositioning itself as the nation's cultural and artistic capital. Hence, the role and profile of the Montréal Museum of Fine Arts (MMFA) continues to grow. The permanent exhibit features an excellent survey of modern and contemporary Canadian art, including works by the Group of Seven and Emily Carr. It also displays paintings and sculptures by a number of the art world's international heavyweights, like El Greco, Renoir, Monet, Picasso, and Cézanne. In 1991, the completion of a modern-looking wing directly across the street from the original neoclassical building tripled the exhibition floor space. Throughout the year, the MMFA hosts temporary exhibits of an international caliber.

*1380 rue Sherbrooke Ouest (at rue Crescent).* ☎ **800-899-6873** *or 514-285-2000.* www.mmfa.qc.ca. *Admission: Entrance to the permanent collection is by donation; tickets for temporary exhibits vary but are half-price Wed 5:30–9 p.m. Open: Tues–Sun 10 a.m.–5 p.m., Wed–Fri until 9 p.m. Métro: Guy-Concordia.*

### Musée McCord d'Histoire Canadienne (McCord Museum of Canadian History)
**Downtown**

In the mood for some local history? This is the place to discover the past of Canada, Québec, and Montréal. The displays of clothing and artifacts may feel a little hokey by today's slick museum standards, but the collections are intelligently planned and well presented. Moderate history buffs will leave the museum with a concrete idea of how Québec's native population lived and how early settlers survived in hostile conditions with few comforts. Actually, you may leave wondering what kind of crazed, ice- and snow-loving souls decided to come here in the first place. Texts are in English and French. There's a cafe by the entrance and a great gift shop with books and work from local artisans, including jewelry, scarves, and other souvenir-friendly items.

*690 Sherbrooke Ouest (at rue Victoria).* ☎ **514-398-7100.** www.mccord-museum.qc.ca. *Admission: Families C$22, adults C$12, seniors C$9, students C$6, children ages 6–12 C$4, children 5 and under free. Open: Tues–Fri 10 a.m.–6 p.m., Sat–Sun 10 a.m.–5 p.m.; during the summer open daily. Métro: McGill.*

## Parc Jean-Drapeau
### Vieux-Montréal

Let the expansive green spaces and varied leisure activities offered by these two islands in the St. Lawrence River take you away from the stop and go of the downtown. Directly south of Vieux-Montréal and minutes away by ferry, Métro, or bridge, **Île Notre-Dame** and **Île Ste-Hélène** make up the park, recently renamed after the mayor who built them. Mayor Drapeau's city workers constructed Île Notre-Dame entirely out of the landfill excavated from the tunnels for the Métro. They also enlarged Île Ste-Hélène. The two islands were the site for Expo the '67, widely considered the best World's Fair of the last century. Now, the parklands of the islands have some of the city's main attractions, such as Casino de Montréal, the Biosphère, and La Ronde, but they are also a haven for swimming, canoeing, sailing, cycling, inline skating, picnicking, and strolling through the landscaped gardens. In the winter, for three successive weekends in February Île Ste-Hélène is the site for Montréal's winter carnival, the *Fête des Neiges.*

*Île Ste-Hélène and Île Notre-Dame.* ☎ *514-872-6120.* www.parcjeandrapeau. com. *Métro: Jean-Drapeau.*

## Parc Mont-Royal
### Plateau

Montréalers from all walks of life agree that Parc Mont-Royal is a gem. Built 125 years ago, the park is the brainchild of Frederick Law Olmsted, who also designed New York's Central Park. If you follow the wide trail that starts at the monument, you circle around the Mountain all the way to the top. It's an easy walk, and you won't feel like you're climbing — although there's not much to see except trees and other walkers until you get to the top. From there, the lookout onto the city and the river is spectacular. There's a chalet where you can rest and buy refreshments. Keep following the trail until you reach Montréal's famous cross, a huge, lit cross on the top of the mountain that's visible from the east side of the city. The entire walk takes about two hours. Although not particularly dangerous the park is not lit, so plan to be out before sunset. Watch out for the odd mountain biker who springs out of the woods onto the trail.

*Access from av. du Parc.* ☎ *514-843-8240.* www.lemontroyal.qc.ca. *Métro: Mont-Royal or Place-des-Arts, then take bus 80 and get off at the Monument Sir George-Étienne Cartier.*

## Stade Olympique (Olympic Stadium)
### East Montréal

Known locally as the Big O, the facilities of the 1976 Olympics are considered a feat of architectural prowess, an enormous concrete debt, or perhaps both, depending on which local you ask. Built by French architect Roger Taillibert, the gigantic, 60,000-to-80,000-capacity, white dome-shaped stadium topped by a sloping Eiffel-like, concrete tower is an impressive structure. In fact, it's the world's tallest inclined tower. Take that, Pisa! And no matter what your tastes, it's worth seeing up close. Okay, so the retracting roof has never worked and parts of the sloping tower ceded to the combined forces of time and gravity. The grounds of the complex still give you a distinct back-to-the-future experience, and the view of the city from the tower is incredible. The tour gives some highlights of the '76 Games and explains the municipal drama of preparing for the Montréal Olympics.

*4141 rue Pierre-de-Coubertin.* ☎ *514-252-8687.* www.rio.gouv.qc.ca. *Admission: Stadium Tour adults C$8, seniors and students C$7.25, children ages 5–17 C$6.25; tower adults C$14, seniors and students C$11, children 5–17 C$6.50. Open: Daily June–Aug 9 a.m.–7 p.m. and Sept–May 9 a.m.–5 p.m. Stadium tours depart regularly from 10 a.m. June–Aug, departures 11 a.m., noon, 1:30, 2:30, 3:30 p.m. Sept–May. Métro: Pie-IX or Viau.*

### The Underground City
**Downtown**

Eighteen miles of underground corridors, passageways, galleries, and atria full of shops, boutiques, food courts, an indoor ice rink, Métro stations, and movie theaters comprise Montréal's *ville souterraine,* the largest network of its kind in the world. It all began innocently enough in 1962 with the completion of the Ville-Marie skyscraper, which boasted as much retail space underground as the total square footage of its 47 stories of office space above. Other downtown buildings soon followed suit, converting their lower levels into retail malls. Over time, they began to connect haphazardly. **The Infotouriste Centre** has a good map of what's not much more than a maze of stores. It's handy as a scenic alternate route or as a hideout from any harsh weather, because it's always warm in the winter and cool in the summer. Ideal conditions — a shopper's paradise.

*Between rue Peel and bd. St-Laurent and bd. de Maisonneuve and rue St. Antoine.* ☎ *514-398-9438.* www.destinationcentreville.com.

### Vieux-Montréal

Settled in the 17th century, much of Vieux-Montréal's magic is due to its European flair, unique in North America. You feel eons away from the rest of the city's 21st-century hubbub. Today, Vieux-Montréal is at once a port, a waterfront park, and a financial district, chock-full of cafes, boutiques, art galleries, and hotels. After you've explored **rue St-Paul, Place Jacques-Cartier,** and **rue des Artistes,** head down to the waterfront. This narrow parkland stretches down several piers along the St. Lawrence River, and eventually gives way to a network of bike paths. One leads to the Formula 1 track on nearby **Île Ste-Hélène.** Inline skates and bikes are available for rent from several shops along rue de la Commune and the boardwalk.

www.tourisme-montreal.org, www.oldportofmontreal.com, old.montreal.qc.ca. *Métro: Champ-de-Mars, Place-d'Armes, or Square-Victoria.*

# Finding More Cool Things to See and Do

If the preceding section of top sights isn't enough to keep you busy, don't fret. There's plenty more to see and do in Montréal. The following sections give you some ideas for how to entertain kids and ways to get outside, plus museums, churches, and sports teams.

## Kid-pleasers

In this section, you find some all-time favorite Montréal attractions guaranteed to amuse the younger set.

### Le Biosphère (The Biosphere)
**Parc Jean-Drapeau**

Located in the former American pavilion of Expo '67, this interactive nature museum is much more focused on ecology than the Biodôme. With exhibits on the Great Lakes and St. Lawrence River ecosystem, this museum explains the effects of pollution and other environmental issues.

*160 chemin Tour-de-l'Île (on Île Ste-Hélène).* ☎ **514-283-5000.** biosphere.ec. gc.ca. *Admission: Adults C$9, seniors and students C$7.50, free for youth and children. Open: Daily June–Oct 10 a.m.–6 p.m.; Nov–May Tues–Sat Noon to 6 p.m. Métro: Jean-Drapeau.*

### Centre des Sciences de Montréal (Montréal Science Centre)
**Vieux-Montréal**

Who said learning isn't fun? Not the kids who go to the Montréal Science Centre. First of all, a trip to a museum where you can actually touch everything is way far-out. Room after room of interactive displays will keep them engaged and running between exhibits. Each zone contains experiments and games about a particular theme or is geared to a particular age group.

*2 rue de la Commune Ouest (in the Old Port).* ☎ **877-496-4724** or *514-496-4724.* www.centredessciencesdemontreal.com. *Admission: Families C$38, adults C$12, seniors and students 13–17 C$11, children C$9. Open: Mon–Fri 9 a.m.–4 p.m., Sat–Sun 10 a.m.–5 p.m. Métro: Champ-de-Mars.*

### IMAX Theatre
**Vieux-Montréal**

Kids get giddy watching hikers scale Mount Everest, divers explore coral reefs in Mexico, or cameras swoop through the Grand Canyon on a seven-story screen.

*2 rue de la Commune Ouest (behind the Science Centre).* ☎ **877-496-4724** or *514-496-4724.* www.centredessciencesdemontreal.com. *Admission: Families C$38, adults C$12, seniors and students 13–17 C$11, children C$9. Open: daily with screenings from 10 a.m.–9 p.m. Métro: Champ-de-Mars.*

### Insectarium de Montréal (Montréal Insectarium)
**East Montréal**

If you go to the Jardins Botanique, the Insectarium is included in the admission. See more than 3,000 varieties of bugs, from butterflies to beetles and maggots. In November and December — delight of delights — you can even indulge in an insect tasting!

*4581 rue Sherbrooke Est (at Jardins Botanique).* ☎ **514-872-1400.** ville.montreal. qc.ca/insectarium. *Admission: May–Oct adults C$16, seniors and students C$12, children 5–17 C$8, free for children under 5; Nov–Apr adults C$14, seniors and students C$10, children 5–17 C$6.25, free for children under 5. Open: Summer daily 9 a.m.–6 p.m., Sept–Oct 9 a.m.–9 p.m., Nov–May 9 a.m.–5 p.m. Métro: Pie-IX or Viau.*

### Planetarium de Montréal (Montréal Planetarium)
**Downtown**

For junior astronomers or any stargazers, this domed center explains it all: how the stars change with the seasons, space travel, the collisions of stars, and more. Shows alternate between English and French. The planetarium also hosts laser-light shows set to classic rock: Laser Beatles and Laser Pink Floyd.

*1000 rue St-Jacques (corner of rue Peel).* ☎ **514-872-4530.** www.planetarium. montreal.qc.ca. *Admission: Adults C$7.75, seniors and students C$6, children under 18 C$4. Open: July–Aug Mon noon to 5 p.m. Tues–Thurs 9:30 a.m.–5 p.m. Sept–June Tues–Fri 9:30 a.m.–5 p.m. Fri 9:30 a.m.–9:30 p.m. The English programming varies, call for the current schedule. Métro: Bonaventure.*

## Best city parks

If people-watching or just plain hanging out is on your agenda, don't miss these green spaces.

### Parc Lafontaine
**Plateau**

Lovers loll about the shaded, grassy slopes of this park, while ducks and paddle-boaters swirl about its large kidney-shaped pond. Parc Lafontaine is a very European-style park, as idyllic as it sounds. A great spot for a picnic or even a nap. Throughout the summer, the open-air theater, **Théâtre de Verdure,** presents many free music concerts and modern-dance performances in the evenings from the end of June through August.

*Between rue Sherbrooke and rue Rachel, on av. Parc-Lafontaine. Métro: Sherbrooke.*

### Parc Maisonneuve
**East Montréal**

Near the Stade Olympique, this former golf course is now one of the most popular and vibrant parks in Montréal, so score a point for the good guys. It's always buzzing with action, from inline skating, cycling, and Ultimate

Frisbee to cultural festivals and the annual celebrations of Québec's national holiday — St-Jean-Baptiste Day on June 24. The remains of the golf course's 19th hole now serve as the park's restaurant and facilities. *4601 rue Sherbrooke Est. Métro: Pie-XI or Viau.*

## Museums

Museum-wise, Montréal has much more than just art. Get your fill of natural history, local history, or even some humorous history while you're at it. (*Note:* Many of the museums and galleries are closed on Mon.)

Look into scoring a Montréal Museum Pass, which works in 25 of the city's gated attractions. It's valid for two days, over a three-day span (meaning you can skip a day and do something else). The pass costs C$39 and includes a pass for the subway and buses. You can buy them at the participating museums, the Infotouriste office on Dorchester Square, or at many hotels.

### Centre d'Histoire de Montréal (Montréal History Center)
**Vieux-Montréal**

Find out about Montréal's First Nations residents and the early European settlers, who started arriving in the 17th century. The museum tells about famous historical figures and gives you a pretty good idea of what everyday life was like over the past four centuries. *335 place d'Youville (at rue St-Pierre).* ☎ *514-872-3207.* www.ville.montreal. qc.ca/chm. *Admission: Adults C$4.50, seniors, students, and children C$3. Open: Tues–Sun 10 a.m.–5 p.m. Métro: Square-Victoria.*

### Musée Château Ramezay (Château Ramezay Museum)
**Vieux-Montréal**

Built in 1703, this medium-sized flagstone house with gated grounds is an anomaly smack in the middle of the otherwise chock-a-block historic district. Back then it was the palatial residence of Québec's governor, the king's representative in the New World. In 1775, Benjamin Franklin crossed the threshold of this building, but he was unsuccessful in convincing locals to fight the British in the American Revolution. (During his visit, he helped found the *Montréal Gazette,* which is still Montréal's oldest paper and the only English daily.) The chateau's exhibits reveal the early days of colonial life through art, costumes, popular artifacts, and coins. During the summer months don't miss the French garden at the back; it is one of only three in Montréal, and the only one accessible to the public. *280 rue Notre-Dame Est (across the street from City Hall, at the top of place Jacques-Cartier).* ☎ *514-861-3708.* www.chateauramezay.qc.ca. *Admission: Families C$16, adults C$8, seniors C$6, students C$5, children C$4. Open: Daily June–Sept 10 a.m.–6 p.m.; Tues–Sun Nov–May 10 a.m.–4:30 p.m. Métro: Champ-de-Mars.*

### Musée Redpath (Redpath Museum)
Downtown

This small natural-science museum may seem quirky by today's slick standards, with its old-school museology style, but it happens to have Canada's second largest collection of artifacts from ancient Egypt. If fossils and geological fragments are your cup of tea, check it out.

*859 rue Sherbrooke Ouest (on the campus of McGill University).* ☎ *514-398-4086.* www.mcgill.ca/redpath. *Admission: Free. Open: July–Aug Mon–Thurs 9 a.m.–5 p.m., Sun 1–5 p.m. Métro: McGill.*

### Musée Stewart (Stewart Museum)
Vieux-Montréal

The year is 1758, and costumed interpreters go about the daily chores of the era at this military and maritime museum in Montréal's last standing fort — making bread, repairing weapons, telling stories, and recruiting. Built after the War of 1812 between the Americans and the British, this fortification even has a moat. The permanent collection features artifacts from the colonial period, including soldiers' uniforms, rifles, cannons, early navigation instruments, portraits of historic figures, and household fineries brought over in cross-Atlantic trade. It's a fascinating look at 300 years of North American and European history. During the summer months (June–Aug) a garrison of soldiers parade around the grounds and reenact various military drills at various times throughout the day.

*Vieux Fort, chemin Tour de l'Île (Île Ste-Hélène).* ☎ *514-861-6701.* www.stewart-museum.org. *Admission: Families C$20, adults C$10, seniors and students C$7, free for children under 7. Open: Daily June–Sept 10 a.m.–5 p.m.; Wed–Mon Oct–May 10 a.m.–5 p.m. Métro: Jean-Drapeau.*

## Churches

Montréal's religious heyday is long gone, but luckily many of the city's glorious church buildings remain. Here are a few of the best.

### Chapelle Notre-Dame-de-Bonsecours
Vieux-Montréal

Originally built in the 17th century, this church is known as the Sailor's Church, thanks to its proximity to Montréal's port. Enjoy excellent views of the harbor and the Old City from the church's tower.

*400 rue St-Paul Est (near the Bonsecours Market).* ☎ *514-282-8670.* www.marguerite-bourgeoys.com. *Admission: Free for praying and attending mass; otherwise, families C$12, adults C$6, seniors and students C$4. Open: Tues–Sun; May–Oct 10 a.m.–5:30 p.m.; Nov to mid-Jan and Mar–Apr Tues–Sun 11 a.m.–3:30 p.m.; mid-Jan to Feb closed. Sun mass in English Mar to mid-Jan 10:30 a.m. Métro: Champ-de-Mars.*

### Christ Church Cathedral
**Downtown**

Located on one of the busiest, most commercial streets in the city, this graceful 19th-century Gothic-style cathedral has an elegant interior that's worth exploring. Local musicians give concerts here year-round.

*635 rue Ste-Catherine Est.* ☎ **514-843-6577.** www.montreal.anglican.org/cathedral. *Open: Daily 8 a.m.–6 p.m. Sunday services 8 a.m., 10 a.m., and 4 p.m. Métro: McGill.*

### Oratoire St. Joseph du Mont Royal (St. Joseph's Oratory)
**Outremont**

Located on the far side of the Mountain, dividing the neighborhoods of Outremont and Westmount, the green, copper dome of this oratory and basilica pierces the Montréal skyline. It's worth the trip for the devout — many pilgrims climb the hundreds of steps on their knees. What lies inside is the crypt of Brother André, a local monk said to have healing powers. Pope John Paul II's blessing elevated him to a status just under sainthood in the Catholic realm.

*3800 chemin Queen Mary (corner of av. Côte des Neiges).* ☎ **514-733-8211.** www.saint-joseph.org. *Open: Daily 10 a.m.–5:30 p.m. Métro: Côte des Neiges.*

## Spectator sports

Hey, sports fans! Montréal is a great sports town and currently home to professional hockey, football, and soccer teams. Montréal is, first and foremost, a hockey town, and the Montréal Canadiens are the most storied team in the history of the game. Since 1929, the Canadiens have won a record 24 Stanley Cup Championships while playing in the National Hockey League.

### Canadiens (hockey)

The relationship between the team and its city runs deep and is infinitely complex. The red, white, and blue jerseys are part of Montréal's cultural fiber.

Every season, from mid-September to the beginning of April, the Canadiens play about half of their 82-game schedule downtown at the **Bell Centre,** also called the New Forum or the Phone Booth. The original Montréal Forum, at the corner of rue Atwater and rue Ste-Catherine, is now a movie megaplex.

If you're in town for a Canadiens home game, definitely check it out. Buying a ticket on game day isn't easy, though; try buying them in person at the **Bell Centre Ticket Office,** 1260 rue de la Gauchetière Ouest, or phone the **Admission Ticket Line** at ☎ **800-361-4595** or 514-790-1245. You can get also your seats on the Web at either www.admission.com or www.canadiens.com. If the game is sold out, on most nights you'll find people outside the Bell Centre with extra tickets, and some may be willing to negotiate a price.

### Alouettes (football)

**Canadian football** is like the football played in the United States, but the field is longer and wider. Also, on offense, teams only have three tries to advance ten yards for a first down. Games tend to be high-scoring affairs. The season, including exhibition games and playoffs, runs from early June to mid-November.

The Montréal Alouettes are considered serious annual contenders for the Grey Cup Championship, so their tickets are hot. The Alouettes' home field is at the top of rue University, halfway up Mont-Royal. Watching the Als and their *gentille* cheerleaders can be a pleasant outing on a Saturday afternoon in the late summer or fall. Tickets are at the **Alouettes' Ticket Office,** on the second floor of 1260 rue University. You can also purchase tickets by phone (☎ **800-361-4595** or 514-790-1245) or on the Web at www.admission.com.

### Impact (soccer)

The new kids on the sports block, the Montréal Impact (☎ **514-328-3668;** www.montrealimpact.com), started in 1992 by a local cheese company, are already perennial contenders in the American Professional Soccer League (APSL). Soccer, not hockey, is currently Canada's fastest-growing sport in the amateur ranks, which translates into capacity crowds. In 2008 the Impact will debut at the 13,500 seat Saputo Stadium, located on the grounds of the Olympic Park (Métro: Pie-IX) for the Impact season, from late April to early September.

Buy tickets by phone (☎ **800-361-4595** or 514-790-1245) or on the Web at www.admission.com.

## Seeing Montréal by Guided Tour

Will a guided tour give you a better excursion than going it alone? It depends on what you want. If you want specialized explanations of neighborhoods or themes, or you want to see sights that are difficult to access on your own, a guided tour is hard to beat. Someone else takes care of the planning and answers your questions, to boot. If meeting and talking to locals is your thing, you can take a pass on the guided tours.

No matter how good it sounds on paper, call ahead to find out if the tour is right for you. Ask how long the tour lasts, what you'll see, how much it costs, what's included (and not), how many people will be on it, whether the tour is in English, and what if anything you should bring along. Call a day ahead to reserve a spot.

## *Walking it*

Montréal is a great city for walking because it's full of interesting neighborhoods with their own architecture, history, and flavor. Most of the walking tours available in Montréal focus on particular neighborhoods. These are the most popular ones.

- ✔ **Guidatour** (☎ **514-844-4021;** www.guidatour.qc.ca) offers daily tours of Vieux-Montréal in the summer. Tours depart from Basilique Notre-Dame at 11 a.m. and 1:30 p.m. Tickets are adults C$17, seniors and students C$14, and children ages 6 to 12 C$7.50. Tickets are available 15 minutes before departure, but try to buy them earlier. The two-and-a-half-hour tour is available in English.

- ✔ **Visites de Montréal** (☎ **514-933-6674;** www.visitesdemontreal. com) offers walking tours of Vieux-Montréal, including the Basilique Notre-Dame, for groups of up to 20 people. Reserve one week ahead of time. Prices vary for the two-hour tour.

- ✔ **Heritage Montréal** (☎ **514-286-2662;** www.heritagemontreal. org) offers architectural tours of various Montréal neighborhoods on foot or bicycle from June to September. Popular tours include the Plateau neighborhood, downtown churches, the Mile End neighborhood, and a tour of Montréal's Métro system.

## *Riding it*

Feel like a break from the walking? Want to sit back and let someone else run the show for a while? Because Montréal is such a great walking city, I don't recommend bus tours. However, bus tours do have their merits, especially if you have trouble walking long distances. Here are your options:

- ✔ **Gray Line** (☎ **514-934-1222;** www.grayline.com) operates 11 different sightseeing tours, departing from the tourism office on Square Dorchester. The basic city tour lasts about an hour and a half and costs C$32 for adults and children; children under 5 are free. Call for information on more specialized trips.

- ✔ **Impérial Autocar** (☎ **514-871-4733;** www.autocarimperial.com) offers narrated trips on open-top double-decker buses. Tours last six hours. Tickets are adults C$35, students C$32, and children ages 5 to 12 C$28. Buses depart from Square Dorchester. On some tours, you can get on and off the buses as you please.

- ✔ **Amphi-Bus** (☎ **514-849-5181,** www.montreal-amphibus-tour. com) offers tours of Vieux-Montréal with a twist: At the end of the tour, the bus waddles into the harbor. Reservations required. The basic one-hour tour costs adults C$30, seniors and students C$23, children 12 to 18 C$21, children 2 to 12 C$17.

## Boating it

Nothing beats the view of the city from the waters of the St. Lawrence. These companies offer short tours and longer dinner cruises:

✔ **Le Bateau-Mouche** (☎ **800-361-9952;** www.bateau-mouche.com) offers 90-minute excursions in air-conditioned, glass-enclosed barges (like the ones on the Seine in Paris) leaving the Jacques-Cartier Pier mid-May through mid-October daily at 10 a.m., noon, 2 p.m., and 4 p.m. Tours cost adults $25, seniors and students C$23, children 6 to 17 C$11; free for children under 5. Call for information on dinner cruises.

✔ **Croisières du Port de Montréal/AML Cruises** (☎ **800-667-3131** or 514-842-3871; www.croisieresaml.com) offers Montréal harbor cruises from May to October daily, departing from the Clock Tower Pier (at the foot of rue Berri). This company also cruises from Montréal to Québec City. Call for departure times and rates. Fares are adults C$30 to $46, seniors and students C$28 to $43, children 12 and under C$17 to C$25. The higher prices are for dinner cruises.

## Hoofing it

You can also tour around Vieux-Montréal or Parc Mont-Royal in a horse-drawn carriage, known as a *calèche*. No need to reserve. You see them along **rue de la Commune** in the Old Port, and they line up at **Place-d'Armes** (corner rue Notre-Dame and rue St-Sulpice). Count on spending C$45 per half hour or $75 per hour. Carriages take four or five people, and drivers usually explain historic and architectural sights along the way. In winter, horse-drawn sled-carriages are also available.

# Chapter 12

# Shopping the Montréal Stores

· · · · · · · · · · · · · · · · · · · · · · · · · · · · · · · · · · · ·

## In This Chapter

▶ Getting to know Montréal's shopping scene
▶ Checking out the best neighborhoods
▶ Locating the big names and big centers

· · · · · · · · · · · · · · · · · · · · · · · · · · · · · · · · · · · ·

**C**all it the French connection. If you're looking to adorn yourself, unearth unique treasures, or bring home something special for friends and family, Montréal is something of a shopper's horn of plenty. From the thriving fashion industry, vibrant gallery scene, and numerous shopping malls to the underground city, Montréal has your shopping needs covered.

## Surveying the Scene

Shopping hours in Montréal are similar to those in the rest of Canada. Stores generally open at 9:30 or 10 a.m. and close at 5 or 6 p.m., Monday through Wednesday. On Thursdays and Fridays, most stores stay open until 9 p.m. On Saturdays, the hours swing back to 9 or 10 a.m. to 5 or 6 p.m. Most stores are also open on Sundays: Hours vary, but you can usually count on finding stores open from noon to 5 p.m.

These are the standard hours for stores in commercial areas. In such neighborhoods as Westmount along rue Sherbrooke Ouest, which have many small boutiques, the hours can vary from one store to another, and owners of small shops sometimes close without warning to take a coffee break.

In Montréal, you can find pretty much any major brand-name item available anywhere else in North America. But you can also find a lot of items you probably can't find elsewhere. If you're looking for something unique, note that the following are Montréal's areas of strength:

✔ **Clothes:** The city's fashion industry gets better practically every season, and you can often buy clothing directly from the designers themselves. **Rue St-Denis** (between rue Sherbrooke and avenue Mont-Royal) are full of boutiques of local designers, with unique, quality fashion at reasonable prices. **Boulevard St-Laurent** specializes in extremely cool clothes for a youthful clientele, while **downtown** has a great mix of homegrown clothing chains for men and women, plus big-name shops of major designers. More and more new designers are also setting up shop in Vieux-Montréal.

✔ **Antiques:** French-speaking Québeckers don't actually care much for the old, rustic look, which means that tons of antiques and vintage pieces are available to you at good prices. (Antiques dealers from New York flock to the city to skim off the best of them.) **Rue Notre-Dame,** way west, is Montréal's "Antiques Alley," with dozens of shops to pick through, whether you're looking for furniture, home accessories, or memorabilia. There's also a clutch of antique shops on **Rue Amherst,** near the Gay Village.

✔ **Art:** Several high-quality fine-arts schools supply Montréal with what seems like a never-ending source of new talent. In addition, established painters sell their work in the city's traditional gallery strip on **rue Sherbrooke** around **rue Crescent.** The **Plateau** neighborhood has many smaller galleries featuring younger, more affordable artists. **Vieux-Montréal** has several galleries, as well as an artists' cooperative, featuring drawings, lithographs, etchings, and more.

✔ **Home décor:** If you like knickknacks and cool home accessories, you'll be in heaven. Boutiques specializing in household decorations can be found all over the city, including downtown, but especially on **rue St-Denis** and **avenue Laurier.**

✔ **Specialty foods and liquor:** The last decade in Québec has seen a surge of interest in local culinary specialties — from maple syrup and blueberry liqueurs to fine chocolates and Québec cheeses. The **Jean-Talon** and **Atwater markets** are good places to pick up local delicacies, as is **avenue Laurier.** Look to get your hands on some local unpasteurized cheese. Although wine and spirits are sold by a provincial liquor board, their offerings are anything but standard issue. The **Société des alcools du Québec (SAQ)** (look for the maroon and blue signage) offers an impressive selection of wines from France and other wine-producing nations. Québec's climate doesn't grow good grapes, but there's an increasing number of producers of iced ciders, Québec's knee-jerk reaction to the neighboring province of Ontario's recent success with icewine.

✔ **Books:** Not one other place in North America comes close to offering the quantity and variety of books in French that Montréal does. And the selection in English is good, too. Montréal has even managed to hold on to several independent English-language booksellers. Most of the English scene is **downtown,** while French bookstores are practically everywhere.

✔ **Music:** What I say about books is also true of music in Montréal. Compared to New York or even Toronto, Montréal can hardly be called CD city, but after Paris this is probably one of the best places in the world to sample French-language music. Several large chains, mostly **downtown,** pretty much dominate the market.

Sounds great, but how much stuff can you bring home?

If you spend more than two days in Canada, you're entitled to bring back US$800 worth of goods duty-free. Included in that price, you're allowed to take home 33.8 fluid ounces of alcohol and 200 cigarettes. You may bring back tinned goods, but no fresh foods. For more info on what you can and cannot take back to the United States, visit the **Customs and Border Protection** Web site at www.cbp.gov.

If you're a citizen of Australia, the United Kingdom, or New Zealand, check out the regulations on what you can bring back by contacting:

✔ **Australian Customs Service:** ☎ 02-9213-2000, www.customs.gov.au

✔ **HM Revenue & Customs (UK):** ☎ 0181-910-3744, www.hmrc.gov.uk

✔ **New Zealand Customs Service:** ☎ 09-4-359-6655, www.customs.govt.nz

Hold on to your receipts in case you have to prove your case at the border. Actually, hold on to your receipts so you can keep track of your spending and count up the cost of your loot *before* you get to the border. Customs agents aren't known to provide calculators to frenzied travelers.

If you bring more than US$800 in goods back to the United States with you, don't worry — no one is going to throw you in jail. You just have to pay a small tax on your purchases. And if you stay less than 48 hours in Canada, your duty-free limit drops to US$200 per person.

Taxes, taxes. They're rather steep in the Great White North. Don't forget that 13 percent will be tacked on to most of your purchases. For more information on taxes, see Chapter 4.

## *Checking Out the Big Names*

Department stores have taken a beating over the last decade, but downtown Montréal still has several venerable old stores that sell goods the old-fashioned way:

✔ **Harry Rosen,** 1445 rue Peel (☎ 514-284-3315), is a department store specializing in stylish, designer menswear for those who believe it's the clothes that make the man.

✔ **Holt Renfrew,** 1300 rue Sherbrooke Ouest (☎ 514-842-5111), is a luxury clothing store for the well-heeled and label-conscious.

✔ **La Baie,** 585 rue Ste-Catherine Ouest (☎ 514-281-4422), also known as the Hudson's Bay Company, is a three-centuries-old Canadian institution. The Montréal store sells everything from cosmetics to clothing to kitchen appliances, and it's a great place to pick up crystal, china, and bedding.

✔ **La Maison Simons,** 977 rue Ste-Catherine Ouest (☎ 514-282-1840), originally a Québec City chain of department stores, is the new kid in town. Great for clothes, coats, and accessories. In particular, look for their young and urban in-house clothing lines for men and women.

✔ **Ogilvy,** 1307 rue Ste-Catherine Ouest (☎ 514-842-7711), is an upscale department store for Montréal's establishment that feels like a collection of rather fancy boutiques.

# Discovering the Best Shopping Neighborhoods

Montréal is a great shopping city, but like all cities of plenty, you need to know where to go to get the goods. The following sections show you the prime stomping grounds of the city's consumer culture.

## Downtown

You can always go . . . downtown. The noise and the hurry can help your worries. And so can a little retail therapy at the shops, boutiques, and department stores along Montréal's main shopping drags.

### Rue Ste-Catherine

Montréal's downtown area is definitely not the most charming or quaint part of the city; parts of rue Ste-Catherine are actually pretty crass. Still, although it's not really a neighborhood for strolling among unique boutiques, it's *the* place to find the city's big department stores (see the "Checking Out the Big Names" section earlier in this chapter). It's where you find most of the shopping centers, movie theaters, and large bookstores. You also get a great concentration of chain stores of all sorts, although most are Canadian.

The downtown core is also home to Montréal's famous **underground city,** with over 1,500 boutiques. The 18-mile underground complex links up many of the major hotels, major shopping complexes, and most of the downtown Métro stations. You're likely to happen upon underground city shops as you pop in and out of it via a shopping center, Métro station, or hotel. The underground city is full of chain stores and cheap outlets for everything from shoes to electronics. Very few Montréalers actually shop in the underground city, because better stores exist above ground.

Unless the weather is particularly vicious (making the underground city particularly attractive), your best bet for downtown is shopping on **rue**

*Underground City*

**Ste-Catherine,** between rue Guy on the west and avenue du Parc on the east. The shopping complexes you'll find there are:

- ✔ **Centre Eaton,** 705 rue Ste-Catherine Ouest (☎ 514-288-3708; Métro: McGill): Eaton's used to be Canada's main mid- to high-end department store. It went out of business several years ago, but this five-floor shopping complex with 175 shops, cinemas, and eateries has retained the name.

- ✔ **Cours Mont-Royal,** 1455 rue Peel (☎ 514-842-7777; Métro: Peel): The shops in this center are a little more chic, and the entire effect is slightly more elegant than at the Centre Eaton. It's the place to go if you're looking for items from upmarket fashion labels.

- ✔ **Les Ailes de la Mode,** 677 rue Ste-Catherine Ouest (☎ 514-282-4537; Métro: McGill): Montréal's newest shopping complex is also the sleekest and the priciest. When it opened in 2002, it was hyped as a "new concept in shopping." Unfortunately, most shoppers report that they just can't find their way around the place.

- ✔ **Les Promenades de la Cathédrale,** at the corner of avenue University and rue Ste-Catherine (☎ 514-849-9925; Métro: McGill). Located right next to the Centre Eaton, this shopping center is virtually indistinguishable from it.

- ✔ **Place Montreal Trust,** 1500 av. McGill College (☎ 514-843-8000; Métro: McGill): Contains several noteworthy stores above ground and below, such as **Zara** and **Winners.**

Also along rue Ste-Catherine are some Montréal shops worth mentioning on their own. For contemporary Canadiana — leather, shoes, bags, clothes, and accessories — check out the sporty classic **Roots,** 1035 rue Ste-Catherine Ouest (☎ 514-845-7995). **Birks,** 1240, rue du Square-Phillips (☎ 514-397-2511), is a Canadian luxury jewelry brand started in 1879. It's still housed in their flagship store, an impressive and imposing building.

In terms of urban fashion, **Mannix** (☎ 514-284-3936), at 373 rue Ste-Catherine Ouest, is an apropos boutique that stocks all the latest lifestyle sneakers: Puma, Gola, Asics, and whatever other kicks are hot.

**Browns** (☎ 514-987-1206), 1191 rue Ste-Catherine Ouest, is another shoe store and Canadian chain, this time selling up-market footwear. Prada flip-flops anyone? However, good discounts and bargains usually are to be found, which turns the place into a mild feeding frenzy.

Just north of rue Ste-Catherine, between **rue Metcalf** and **rue Peel,** is the shopping center **Cours Mont-Royal,** housing **3 Monkeys** (☎ 514-284-1333), a store that has a unique collection of silk-screened T-shirts featuring prominent Montréal landmarks. (They make great souvenirs, fashionable rather than tacky.)

Lastly, the **Style Exchange** (☎ 514-282-6500) has a big outlet here. They have designer jeans and other fashionable, in-demand items. It's one of the best places to find an outfit's crucial, missing piece for a night out on the town.

Across the street is **Urban Outfitters,** 1250 rue Ste-Catherine Ouest (☎ 514-874-0063), purveyors of youth culture, including lewd coffee table books, gimmicky décor items that make great gifts, and retro clothing that are to-die-for essentials among high school- and college-aged shoppers. **Boutique Mens,** 1321 rue Ste-Catherine Ouest (☎ 514-843-8877), as the name suggests, carries only men's clothing. It's an excellent haberdasher with a selection of hip casual-wear from top designers.

**Chapters Bookstore,** 1171 rue Ste-Catherine Ouest (☎ 514-849-8825), is Canada's largest chain bookstore. The Montréal store is four floors high and includes an Internet cafe. A few blocks west, **Indigo,** 1500 av. McGill-College (☎ 514-281-5549), is part of the same chain and has a huge selection of books and a comfortable cafe. If you prefer a more intimate environment, check out the independent bookseller **Paragraphe Bookstore,** 2220 av. McGill-College (☎ 514-845-5811). For the best selection of French books, check out one of the **Renault Bray** stores, at 4380 rue St-Denis (☎ 514-844-1781) or at 5117 av. du Parc (☎ 514-276-7651).

For CDs, visit **HMV,** 1020 rue Ste-Catherine Ouest (☎ 514-875-0765). For a better selection of French CDs, try the big **Archambault** store near Place des Arts at 500 rue Ste-Catherine Est (☎ 514-849-6201).

## Rue Crescent

If you head west along rue Ste-Catherine, away from the department stores and malls, you soon hit **rue Crescent,** which has a handful of chic shops and upscale stores, including art galleries, antiques stores, and clothes stores. **Shan Boutique,** 2150 rue Crescent (☎ 514-787-7426), is where to go for designer bathing suits. **Aqua Skye,** 2035 rue Crescent (☎ 514-985-9950), is fun for fashionable jewelry. And **Formes Femme Enceinte,** 2185 rue Crescent (☎ 514-843-6996), is a locally designed line of maternity wear that will flatter forms of expectant mothers. **Matt Baily** (☎ 514-845-8878), 1427 rue Crescent, a watch merchant, carries the latest brands of must-have timepieces. **Olam,** 1374 rue Ste-Catherine Ouest (☎ 514-875-9696), is every pretty girl's favorite shop, with the latest designs of locals, such as Myco Anna, as well as such international names as Miss Sixty, Killah, and Muchacha.

This neighborhood is a nice one in which to stroll about after visiting the Montréal Museum of Fine Art, and you can also find plenty of cafes and bars to choose from.

**Betsey Johnson,** 1382 Rue Ste-Catherine Ouest (☎ 514-392-9786), has pretty dresses for formal occasions. She's the designer whose name is on every Westmount debutante's lips during prom season. She also carries cute cardigans and chiffon blouses.

**Les Modes Néon,** 1388 rue Ste-Catherine Ouest (☎ 514-393-1977), seems to stock plenty of affordable urban fashion. They are perhaps one of the sole bastions against skyrocketing designer jeans prices. They also have Blundstones, Australian boots all the rage among film industry types.

On the corner of **rue Bishop, Rudsak Collection (☎ 514-399-9925),** 1400 rue Ste-Catherine Ouest, is the shop of a successful local designer who makes streamlined leather garments, small leather goods, and accessories.

**Influence U (☎ 514-931-3283),** 1476 rue Ste-Catherine Ouest, and **Homogene Jeans (☎ 514-935-6800),** 1486 rue Ste-Catherine Ouest, are two shops side-by-side, both popular among Montréal's fashionistas, stocking mainstream, high-end brands such as Diesel, Energie, G-star, Miss Sixty, and Juicy Couture.

Continuing west along rue Ste-Catherine, look for more fun stores on both sides. **Fly Boutique,** 1970 rue Ste-Catherine Ouest (☎ 514-846-3324), is the strip's last outpost of cool, just before rue du Fort. Hipsters will find that it's worth the trek west for the store's many urban styles.

## Mile End/Outremont (avenue Laurier)

This upscale shopping street, the playground of Montréal's well-heeled Outremont residents, was hit hard by the recession that gripped the city in the early 1990s, but it's making a remarkable comeback at the moment. East and west of avenue Parc, you find great gourmet food stores, home décor shops, and clothing boutiques. **Gourmet Laurier,** 1042 av. Laurier Ouest (☎ 514-274-5601), is a foodie's dream: chocolate, cheese, caviar, foie gras, fancy oils, and other imported condiments.

**Lyla (☎ 514-271-0763),** at 400 av. Laurier Ouest, is a choice establishment for women's seductive undergarments imported from Europe. The store also stocks women's swim and sportswear. **Casa (☎ 514-279-7999),** 1101 av. Laurier Ouest, is one of several stores selling home décor items. Many of these shops on av. Laurier offer wedding registries, just to give you the gist.

**Michel Brisson (☎ 514-270-1012),** 1012 av. Laurier Ouest, is a shop with just menswear, including lines such as Valentino, Calvin Klein, Comme des Garçons, Etro, Blue Blood, Ernest Sewn, and Diesel. **La Boite Noire (☎ 514-277-6979),** 380 av. Laurier Ouest, is the best place to go in town for renting or buying obscure and cult movies. **Rodin (☎ 514-272-2343),** 281 Laurier Ouest, is a clothing store along avenue Laurier for posh babies and toddlers.

## The Plateau

You've no doubt noticed that Montréalers are a particularly fashionable bunch — this is where they come to perfect their look. Although you find more familiar offerings at the big stores downtown, the Plateau is the best place to go native.

### Boulevard St-Laurent

South of rue Sherbrooke, boulevard St-Laurent is home to Montréal's small, slightly run-down Chinatown. Walk north on boulevard St-Laurent, cross rue Sherbrooke, and St-Laurent turns into one of the hippest streets in the city — chock-full of trendy hair studios; even trendier clothes stores; and fashionable lounges, bars, and restaurants that recruit their wait staffs from local modeling agencies. For cosmetics, check out the St-Laurent store of the Canadian blockbuster makeup company **MAC Cosmetics,** 3487 bd. St-Laurent (☎ **514-287-9297**). **Boutique Scandale,** 3639 bd. St-Laurent (☎ **514-842-4707**), always has eye-catching outfits in its windows; if you step inside, you'll see that this boutique keeps its promise with an eclectic yet irresistible selection of clothes.

Head north on St-Laurent, and your shopping opportunities diversify (and food options abound) until just before avenue Mont-Royal. There, you find yourself smack in the middle of Montréal's up-and-coming furniture and interior-design neighborhood, including popular stores such as **Montauk,** 4404 bd. St-Laurent (☎ **514-845-8285**), and **Biltmore,** 5685 bd. St-Laurent (☎ **514-844-3000**). Farther north, you find antiques, frame stores, clothing stores, galleries, and more.

For used CDs, vintage clothes, and more clothes designers, head east on **avenue Mont-Royal** from boulevard St-Laurent. This former working-class neighborhood is reaching the peak of a decade-long colonization process led by students and young professionals. The result is tons of interesting little boutiques and shops.

### Rue St-Denis

The stretch between rue Sherbrooke and avenue Mont-Royal is the spiritual home of Montréal's bourgeoisie and the location of several higher-end, more established Montréal fashion designers. Rue St-Denis is a great shopping street featuring elegant clothing and unique home accessories. Alas, the last few years have been a little hard on the area, with stores coming and going a little faster than normal. It remains a lovely street to stroll, with many inviting cafes.

Check out the big **Mexx** store at the corner of rue Rachel, 4190 rue St-Denis (☎ **514-843-6399**). Farther north, don't miss the increasingly popular **Boutique Do,** 4439 rue St-Denis (☎ **514-844-0041**), with reasonably priced, local designs for women. **Révenge,** 3852 rue St-Denis (☎ **514-843-4379**), is another great store with local designs. **Artéfact,** 4117 rue St-Denis (☎ **514-842-2780**), has lovely and unusual suits and dresses by Québec designers.

For home décor and gourmet kitchenware, check out **Arthur Quentin,** 3960 rue St-Denis (☎ **514-843-7513**).

## St-Henri (rue Notre-Dame)

Although it looks a little downtrodden at first sight, the western strip of **rue Notre-Dame,** between rue Guy and avenue Atwater, is Montréal's Antiques Alley, with dozens of shops selling collectible furniture and memorabilia.

Check out **Lucie Favreau Antiques,** 1904 rue Notre-Dame Ouest (☎ 514-989-5117), for crazy collectibles; **Les Antiquités Grand Central,** 2448 rue Notre-Dame Ouest (☎ 514-935-1467), for more-elegant pieces; and **Lussier Antiques,** 3645 rue Notre-Dame Ouest (☎ 514-938-2224), for bargains on lamps, chests, and fixtures. **Retro Ville,** 2652 rue Notre-Dame Ouest (☎ 514-939-2007), is a real trip back into the not-so-distant past focusing on household and popular culture items from the last half of the 20th century. At avenue Atwater, just to the south, is the **Atwater Market,** with farmers, butchers, fishmongers, and gourmet shops.

Farther north on av. Atwater, at the corner of rue St-Antoine, look into the showroom of **Harricana,** 3000 rue St-Antoine Ouest (☎ 877-894-9919), which makes warm things for winter out of secondhand fur. *Note:* As of a couple of seasons ago, to everyone's collective surprise, fur made a big comeback on catwalks showing their winter collections.

## Vieux-Montréal (rue St-Paul)

Until several years ago, Vieux-Montréal was not considered much of a shopping area, unless you were in the market for cheesy tourist souvenirs. Large cash injections over the last decade changed all that, and **rue St-Paul** in particular has profited from the renaissance. This is *the* street to scout for arts and crafts. Check out **La Guilde Graphique,** 9 rue St-Paul Ouest (☎ 514-844-3438), where more than 200 artists display their work, or visit the craftspeople's collective **L'Empreinte,** 272 rue St-Paul Ouest (☎ 514-861-4427).

For modern-art galleries, try **Gallery 2000,** 45 rue St-Paul Ouest (☎ 844-1812); **Galerie Parchemine,** across the street at 40 rue St-Paul Ouest (☎ 514-845-3368); or **Galerie St-Dizier,** 20 rue St-Paul Ouest (☎ 514-845-8411).

Yes, it's a historical site but the main floor of the **Marché Bonsecours,** 385 de la Commune Est, is also an artisans' market with several merchants selling jewelry, fashion, reproduction, and contemporary Canadiana furniture, ceramics, and blown and tinted glass.

**Boutique Reborn,** 231 rue St-Paul Ouest (☎ 514-499-8549), a long, narrow space with an inconspicuous storefront, is easy to miss. Shoppers will be rewarded, however, by finding exclusive fashion items from here and abroad.

For sometimes far-out fashions, **Ed Exclusivité,** 387 rue St-Paul Ouest (☎ 514-843-0693), imports its clothing from lesser-known, harder-to-find European designers. It also carries avant garde furniture shaped like oversized river rocks. The larger cushions make for comfy, zen couches, while the smaller shapes are ottomans.

## Westmount (rue Sherbrooke Ouest)

Rue Sherbrooke Ouest around avenue Greene is very much the traditional English area of the city. You can find the usual selection of upscale clothing, shoes, and home furnishings. Over the last few years, perhaps because more and more French-speakers are moving into the neighborhood, stores in this district have taken on a more European flavor. In particular, don't miss **L'Occitane,** a popular French cosmetics chain full of luxurious soaps, moisturizers, and perfumes from Provence, at 4972 rue Sherbrooke Ouest (☎ **514-482-8188**).

**Lululemon Athletica,** 1394 av. Greene on the corner of Sherbrooke (☎ **514-937-5151**), sells Canadian-designed, übertrendy yoga gear, made of high-tech fabrics that breathe and wick away sweat. **Scarpa,** 4901 rue Sherbrooke Ouest (☎ **514-484-0440**), is the best place for shoes in the city; there's another location at 4257 rue St-Denis (☎ **514-282-6363**). **James,** 4910 rue Sherbrooke Ouest (☎ **514-369-0700**), is a boutique selling trendy looks by famous labels.

# Chapter 13

# Following an Itinerary: Five Great Options

## In This Chapter

▶ Seeing the best of Montréal no matter how much time you have
▶ Discovering what makes Montréal a city like no other

The Montréal experience is greater than the sum of its architecture, shopping, entertainment, dining, and attractions. Something quintessentially Montréal is happening in the city's streets all the time, whether you're along commercial strips, in landscaped parks, on outdoor terraces, or among the festival crowds. You can feel the city's attitude and could spend your whole holiday trying to put it into words — that's Montréal's *je ne sais quoi*.

What is it? Residents and visitors alike spend many an hour contemplating that question. (Answer: It's many things.) If you're in a car, though, chances are Montréal's ephemeral nature will pass you by. If you're on foot and still don't know what I mean, go for a drink on the back patio of **Bar St-Sulpice** on rue St-Denis on a busy summer night. Experience, wonder, discuss.

What follows are five suggested itineraries that will let you experience the city like a Montréaler. They're less about getting around among various attractions, and more about exploring neighborhoods and indulging in experiences and rituals that are favorites here.

## Montréal in Three Days

Three days is an ideal block of time for an excellent introduction to Montréal, say, over a holiday long weekend. Sleep could become a real issue, depending on how late you're willing to stay up. Or, you can take it slow and have a relaxing time not doing anything in particular, wandering through Montréal's street scenes, which can be entertainment enough; there's always something to behold.

The following is a medium-paced itinerary with suggestions for stringing together several of the attractions and other worthwhile destinations mentioned in this guide.

## Day 1

If you're just in for 24 hours, here's what to do. The idea is to get a quick taste of some quintessential experiences. It's **Vieux-Montréal** in the morning; start at Métro Square-Victoria (the exits open onto avenue McGill). Wind your way south and east, willy-nilly, through the streets, until you hit the rue de la Commune and the waterfront. Don't go too far east or you'll have to backtrack. As a more direct alternative, you can also walk straight down McGill and turn left when you hit the end. You're looking for the **Musée d'Archéologie et d'Histoire de Montréal,** located on the same site as the first European settlement. If you arrive before the museum opens, find a coffee shop with fresh baked goods and café au lait. If you've already located the museum, nearby **Olive and Gourmando,** at the corner of rues St-Paul and St-Pierre, is just the spot.

You can sip your coffee over a copy of one of the local papers — *The Montréal Gazette* (English) or *La Presse* (French). It's not just a good way to catch up on local affairs — the "Arts and Life" sections (or equivalent sections) often have a calendar of events that lists what's going that same day. The free-press weeklies, the *Mirror* and the *Hour* in English and *Ici* and *Voir* in French, cover the city's cultural calendar from Thursday to Wednesday. Even in the French papers, it's pretty easy to decipher the what, when, and where of an event.

Or, you can head back out into the street with your coffee and croissant and watch the neighborhood waking up. Above the storefronts Vieux-Montréal is filled with office spaces, so the streets will already be bustling with people rushing to work.

After visiting the museum, reward yourself with some shopping by taking a stroll along **rue St-Paul,** Vieux-Montréal's busiest street, jammed with galleries, restaurants, boutique hotels, and more. It runs just behind the **Old Customs House** on **Place Royale.** Walking north from de la Commune, turn right (west) on St-Paul and continue for about 5 blocks until you hit **Place Jacques-Cartier.** This sloped square, bearing the name of the explorer who first made landfall here, is the main gathering point for people in the neighborhood. Touristy restaurants with terraces and maître d's posted out front line both sides. Continue past Place Jacques-Cartier until you hit **Marché Bonsecours,** which has been everything from a market and a city hall to Canada's legislature. In its current role, it's an upscale mall selling Québec-designed decorative arts, Native Canadian crafts, jewelry, and other potential souvenirs. Time permitting, after this shopping run you can head to the waterfront and witness the mighty currents of the St. Lawrence from the boardwalk or atop a clock tower at the end of a pier in the **Old Port.**

Make your way back to Place Jacques-Cartier and head for the street at the top **(rue Notre-Dame).** In front and just to the right is Montréal's **Hôtel-de-Ville,** or City Hall. In 1967, French president Charles de Gaulle fanned the flames of Québec separatism by shouting, "Vive le Québec libre!" from the balcony, which roughly translates into, "Long live a free Québec!" Across the street from city hall on the same side as Place Jacques-Cartier is **Château Ramsey,** a museum about the colonial history of New France. During the summer and early fall, it's worth a stroll in the French garden at the back. If you don't feel like entering the museum, you can access the garden free from behind the museum, just off Place Jacques-Cartier.

Back on rue Notre-Dame, turn left and walk several blocks until you reach the **Basilique Notre-Dame.** This is where Céline Dion's wedding was. If you're enchanted with Vieux-Montréal and would like to come back around sunset, take note of the horse-drawn carriages parked in front of the church, which you can hire to take an extended tour at a romantic pace.

Now it's time for lunch. See Chapter 10 for my recommendations: **Le Cartet, Olive et Gourmando,** and **Cluny** are good choices at this point, but they're back near rue McGill where you started your day. You can continue along rue Notre-Dame to get there, or wander willy-nilly once again. Or, if you're feeling adventurous, from the basilica head north into **Montréal's Chinatown,** along boulevard St-Laurent between rue Viger and avenue Réne Lévesque. In the center of the action there's a pedestrian mall on **rue de la Gauchetière,** which is a good strip to explore.

After lunch, it's time for some shopping. Surface at the Mont-Royal Métro station. Turn left on avenue Mont-Royal and go to rue St-Denis. An ambitious but rewarding retail circuit would be a left turn down St-Denis; head right when you hit Carré St-Louis, a small square with a fountain in the middle; cross the square; take rue Prince-Arthur, a pedestrian mall, and turn right on boulevard St-Laurent; and carry on until avenue Mont-Royal, where you make a right. Soon you'll wind up back in front of the Métro station where you started. This lap will take you past some of the city's best boutiques and along several hot stretches of the Plateau neighborhood. Take a look at a map beforehand to gauge how far this really is. Of course, you can bail at any point, depending on what you see and how long you take in the stores. This is your afternoon activity.

Return to your accommodations, drop your loot, freshen up for dinner, and it's out the door for a predinner glass of wine. If it's summer, find a terrace — the action will be liveliest there. See Chapter 15 for some of my recommendations. In terms of picking a neighborhood for a drink, check out the **Quartier Latin** — it offers a multitude of choices and will leave you in a good position for a variety of dinner destinations. Or perhaps you scouted something on your walk around town and would rather go there.

After dinner, it's time to step out into the night. If you're looking for some live music, check out the schedules at Montréal's larger venues, **Metropolis, Club Soda,** and **Le Cabaret.** See Chapter 15 for details and a slew of other nightlife recommendations.

## Day 2

Start by following the "Brunch, Tam-tams, and Beyond" itinerary later in this chapter. Grab breakfast, or brunch, at **Café Souvenir** on rue Bernard or wait until rue St-Viateur and grab a coffee at **Café Olympico** and a bagel at **St-Viateur Bagels.** If it's not a Sunday or during warm weather, Tam-tams, a weekly drum circle and catch-all pagan gathering in Parc Mont-Royal, won't be happening. So your last stop for this first segment is avenue Laurier and the several blocks of charming shops and boutiques on either side of avenue du Parc.

Jump in a cab or hop on a bus and head downtown; bus 80 runs along avenue du Parc. If you hailed a cab, tell the driver that you're off to the **Canadian Centre for Architecture.** By bus, grab a transfer and get off at the Place-des-Arts Métro. Duck underground. Take the subway (direction Angrignon to Guy-Concordia); the CCA is a short walk from there.

By now it's lunch. You're downtown and starving. A great choice nearby is **Rotisserie Italienne.** Or, a strip of popular pan-Asian, stir-fry places runs along rue Ste-Catherine just north of the CCA. One of the more notable choices is **Bangkok II,** which has the best pad thai.

After lunch, stroll east along rue Ste-Catherine, in the same direction as the car traffic, until rue Crescent. Turn left and walk up this busy strip. Crescent above and below Ste-Catherine is a hopping nightlife district, but by day the boutiques and galleries, north of boulevard Maisonneuve, are of greater interest. At the top of the street, on your left, is **Musée des Beaux-Arts de Montréal.** The permanent collection is free, but the museum requests a donation. They charge admission to see the temporary exhibitions, which usually feature international-caliber artists.

When you emerge from the museum, take a walk east along rue Sherbrooke. In 2 blocks on the same side, there's an Art Deco building housing **Holt Renfrew,** Canada's answer to Bloomingdale's. You can either stop here for some chic shopping or continue along several more blocks and visit the gated campus of **McGill University.** The university bookstore is on rue McTavish, one block before the main gates to the campus.

Walk through the gates and the building you see in the middle, at the top of the road, is the Arts Building — the oldest of the bunch. This central quadrangle is usually filled with collegiate activity; sports or campus events on the playing field; and students going to class, sitting outside, or loitering in front of the library. The **Musée Redpath,** a natural history museum, is to the left, beyond the soccer field. If it's still earlier than 5 p.m., it's a fun, free visit to round out this portion of the day.

When you're done on campus, exit by the Milton Gates, which are to the right of the Arts Building. Walking east along avenue Milton to **boulevard St-Laurent** you're passing through the "McGill Ghetto" (don't worry, it's perfectly safe — it's named this way because so many McGill students live around here). It's several blocks through mainly residential streets. Halfway, you'll cross avenue du Park. Hungry, now? **Isakaya,** the best sushi in town, is a couple doors down from Milton. Otherwise, carry on just a little bit farther to the glitz and glamour of "The Main."

You can spend the rest of the evening on boulevard St-Laurent shopping for the remaining business hours, having dinner, and going out after. Don't worry: It will all become perfectly clear when you get there. The action is dense, the hip quotient off-the-chart, so you can freestyle your evening from here. If you're too tired and just want to sit down, or you're looking for something more sedate, catch a film at **Excentris,** a rep cinema with extra-comfy seats. If you're looking for more specific recommendations, see Chapter 10 for dining, Chapter 12 for shopping, and Chapter 15 for your nightlife options around here. Instead of reading through the entries, start by looking at the maps, seeing what's nearby, and then going from there.

## Day 3

Start your day by hopping on the Métro's green line (direction Honoré-Beaugrand) and get off at PIE-IX. You'll spend the first part of today touring around the Olympic Village of the 1976 Summer Games. The **Stade Olympique,** once home to Major League Baseball's Montréal Expos, was built by French architect Roger Tallibert at a cost of over C$1 billon, which Montréal taxpayers just finished paying off in 2006. The "Big O," as it is known among sports fans (or the "Big Owe" among its critics), has a tower that is the world's tallest leaning structure. (Take that, people of Pisa!) It was designed as a crane to retract the stadium's roof but the idea never really worked. There's an observatory with great views of the city's skyline at the top and you can tour the stadium, which remains a daring architectural feat.

The **Biodome de Montréal,** in an adjacent building, amounts to an indoor zoo. You can walk through different ecosystems. The penguins are everyone's favorite.

Depending on what you want to do for lunch you can either grab a snack from the concessions on-site or head downtown for something more meal-oriented. From Olympic Stadium in the east end you're not really close to anything, so find something in Chapter 10 that sounds appealing and head there.

A reason to stay in the vicinity of the Olympic Stadium would be a visit to the **Jardins Botanique,** a peaceful green space with more than 22,000 species of plants. On the grounds of the Botanical Gardens is the **Insectarium,** which can be "cool" or "gross" depending on which kid you ask. Every second year they have "insect tastings," which allows overly curious visitors to eat specially prepared insects. Dishes in the past years included Atta ants in a tortilla, roasted crickets served on a cucumber canapé, and bruschetta with olive tapenade and bamboo worms (I'm not kidding).

After lunch, a choice: two more museums or a hike up "the Mountain" in **Parc Mont-Royal.** The hike is an alternate outdoor activity, say, if you didn't already go to the Botanical Gardens. The two museums to round out your three days of attractions are the **Musée McCord d'Histoire Canadienne** (Métro McGill) and the **Musée d'Art Contemporain** (Métro Place-des-Arts), both downtown and within a short walk of each other.

To get to the top of the Mountain, start at the **Monument Sir George-Étienne Cartier** (for its exact location see the directions and map in the "Brunch, Tam-tams, and Beyond" itinerary later in this chapter) and follow the gravel paths to the top. You'll eventually reach the summit, with a lookout and a chalet.

# Montréal in Five Days

So you've fallen in love and decided to postpone your return, at least for a couple of days. Or, for whatever reason, you just have more time. Here are another two days' worth of suggested ways to go about seeing the best of Montréal.

Remember, many of these activities are interchangeable on different days. Mix-and-match the mornings and afternoons that suit you best. Or, return to your favorite places several times.

## Day 4

By now you should have your bearings, and can begin to explore farther into the city or circle back for a double-take, looking for things you missed or want to see again. You may have certain morning rituals, a favorite place for coffee or a bakery where you like to start your day.

Today, when you're ready to go, head to **Marché Jean-Talon** (Métro: Jean-Talon) for a morning stroll through the busy aisles lined by chatty merchants behind bountiful stalls of fruits and vegetables. Don't miss the cheese shops and gourmet boutiques in the surrounding buildings and streets. It's a hive of activity and a feast for the senses.

When you're done exploring the different corners of the market, take a walk, south, down boulevard St-Laurent. This is the main strip of the **Little Italy** neighborhood, between rues Jean-Talon and Beaubien. There's a high concentration of cafes, gourmet shops, fashion boutiques, and stores selling imported shoes, all with an Italian flair.

Around lunch, some good options are **Boucherie Jos & Basile** and **Pizzeria Napolitana,** or stop in for an espresso at **Café Italia.**

This afternoon, perhaps consider one of the options you missed on Day 3: the McCord museum, the Montréal Museum of Contemporary Art, or a hike up the Mountain. If you choose the latter, be sure to stock a backpack with goods from the Jean-Talon market for a spontaneous, midafternoon picnic.

If you're looking for a kid-friendly activity, head to **Vieux-Montréal** for the **IMAX Theatre** and the **Centre des Sciences de Montréal.**

Any of these afternoon activities will leave you well placed to make your way to Chinatown for dinner. **Kung Kee** on rue de la Gauchetière is a great bet. Also look for the stall, on the south side, just east of rue Clark, selling "Dragon Beard" candy. Bubble tea is a neighborhood curiosity: it's tea, hot or cold, flavored and served with tapioca beads in the bottom (which are the "bubbles"). **L2 Lounge,** 71A rue de la Gauchetière Est, is an Internet cafe and youth hangout, and it's where to go for this sweet delicacy.

After dinner, how about a night of big money and high stakes at the **Casino de Montréal?** It's on the Île Notre-Dame, so a cab is probably your best bet at this point in the evening. The casino is open 24 hours, so you can also go after the bars close, depending on your habits. From Chinatown, head north to the boulevard St-Laurent and rue Prince Arthur hub for frenzied nightlife action or south to Vieux-Montréal.

If gambling's not your thing, but you're still a sporting type, you may want to catch a game with one of Montréal's professional sports teams. The **Montréal Canadiens** are by far the most popular, so tickets are the most difficult to come by (on short notice there is always a handful of enterprising individuals reselling tickets outside the Bell Centre in the hours leading up to an event). The **Montréal Alouettes** (football) and **Impact** (soccer) also have legions of fans. Join in cheering on the home team or support the visiting team at your own risk.

## Day 5

So it's your last day in town? Time to get down to the essentials. What quintessential experiences are you missing: Have you been to **Schwartz's** for a smoked meat sandwich? **Café Olympico** for a café au lait? Have you tried the bagels from **St-Viateur Bakery?** Did you stroll the cobblestoned streets of **Vieux-Montréal?** The boardwalk of the **Vieux-Port?** If it's a

Sunday, you must drop by **Tam-tams** in **Parc Mont-Royal.** Whatever festival is going on during your stay, did you catch any of the free programming? Shopping on **rue St-Denis?** Have you sat on one of the crowded outdoor terraces for the always-busy *cinq à sept,* the after-work cocktail hours? Did you hit **Jello Bar** or **Salon Daome** on a Thursday night? Did you splurge at a supper club? If you're missing any of these, please add them to your to-do list.

If you feel your Montréal experience is complete, head for the hills on a day trip to the outlying regions, the **Laurentians** or **Eastern Townships.** In the winter, these are both popular destinations for skiers and snowboarders alike; in the summer, mountain-bikers and hikers abound. Many of the ski hills are within an hour's drive of Montréal. Coach buses from the **Station Centrale** also offer round-trips to the most popular ones.

Nearby **Ottawa** and **Québec City** are also two good options for day trips. Both are significantly smaller than Montréal, so you can cover a lot of ground, seeing the major attractions in a single day. For art lovers, Ottawa's **National Gallery of Canada** alone is often worth the trip. Francophiles who want to get deeper into the French-speaking part of the province can opt for Québec City.

# Connecting with Your French Roots

The term "two solitudes" describes coexisting universes of English and French in the province of Québec — and the abyss between them. Despite anyone's best efforts toward bilingualism in Montréal, two separate camps remain. They are not exclusive clubs, but they remain distinct for their differing senses of humor and ways of living the city life.

Assuming you're more comfortable in English than in French, you're going to experience the city as an *Anglophone* (English speaker). But keep in mind, there's an entire *Francophone* (French-speaking) world out there, with its own politicians, city officials, celebrities, rock stars, hockey players, biker gangs, talk radio, newspaper tabloids, sitcoms, music videos, and workplace humor.

You can visit Montréal and remain blissfully unaware of the French around you, partly because everyone in the service and tourism industries speaks very passable, if not impeccable, English. There's also plenty of English spoken around town, and most menus are bilingual. But, at any one time, the majority of the Montréalers surrounding you (over 60 percent) are French speaking and lead somewhat different lives from the English minority.

After Paris, Montréal is the second-largest French-speaking city in the world, so it stands to reason that there's plenty going on in French as well. This itinerary is a gentle introduction to Montréal's French side,

## Connecting with Your French Roots

1 Le Quai des Brumes
2 Bily Kun
3 Restaurant Lafleurs
4 Carré St-Louis
5 Bar St-Sulpice
6 Les Deux Pierrots

guiding you on a stroll among the many shoppers and denizens on the Plateau's main commercial streets. No real destinations exist along the way, just suggested landmarks to guide your journey.

If you're a true *Francophile* (lover of all things French) and want to dabble further in this part of the city's cultural calendar, try to decipher the listings in either of the two free French weeklies, *Voir* and *Ici,* which come out on Thursdays. Their English counterparts, the *Mirror* and the *Hour,* also list some of the Francophone community's events, but they are not as thorough.

Most of this itinerary runs along the orange line of the Métro, between Mont-Royal and Champ-de-Mars stations. You can use it at your discretion to get between the most interesting parts of the different segments I describe. You can walk this entire route quickly, in about two hours, or stretch it out into an afternoon and evening.

Starting at the Mont-Royal Métro station, turn right and walk along the central artery of the trendy Plateau neighborhood, once a hotbed for bohemian artists and now a hot real-estate market and shopping district.

Avenue Mont-Royal is packed with every kind of merchant imaginable. Small, locally owned businesses rule the blocks. Used-book and -CD stores, designer-clothing boutiques, small grocers, health-food shops, salons, outdoor-sports outfitters, bakeries, restaurants, cafes, and bars all cater to the locals, who justifiably feel that they are in the center of it all. Meander until you've had your fill and then return in the direction of the Métro.

Continue past the Mont-Royal Métro station and pause on the corner of rue St-Denis. If you're into vintage clothing, you may want to make a detour at this point by continuing straight on avenue Mont-Royal, past rue St-Denis. For several blocks up a slight grade, shops on both sides of the street sell retro clothing and some of their own designs.

Depending on the hour, this may also be time for refreshment. Both bars I recommend here are typically French Montréal but completely different. The first spot represents a somewhat dated mentality in Montréal, while the second is all about Montréal today. **Le Quai des Brumes,** located around the corner on the left at 4481 rue St-Denis (☎ **514-499-0467**), is a smoky and dark place festering with anti-Federalist sentiment and known as a hangout for staunch, but graying, separatists. Do try to start a conversation, but I suggest not opening with a line about the late former Canadian Prime Minister Pierre Trudeau. **Bily Kun,** 354 av. Mont-Royal Est (☎ **514-845-5392**), is a block to the west. It's populated with good-looking but casual 20- and 30-somethings, engaged in animated chatter over microbrewery beer and light snacks. Ostrich-head trophies high on the walls overlook the scene.

Back on rue St-Denis, you're faced with a similar scene to where this walk started on Mont-Royal, but the storefronts are glitzier, the foot traffic heavier, and the pace faster. It goes on at this rate for 4 long city blocks.

At the bottom of this strip there's a break in the action, but soon, on your right, you see the illuminated yellow sign of **Restaurant Lafleurs,** 3620 rue St-Denis (☎ **514-848-1804**) — *the* place to sample *poutine,* a local delicacy of French fries, cheese curds, and gravy. Lafleurs is the benchmark for all *poutine.*

*Poutine,* while delicious, is best consumed in small quantities. Finishing a small *poutine* at Lafleurs is a feat in itself. Sharing is probably a good idea. Do not order the *familiale* size — ever, under any circumstances.

If the weather is pleasant, you may as well ask for your *poutine* to go and enjoy it in nearby **Carré St-Louis,** where 19th-century town houses surround and enhance an already beautiful square with a multilayered, birdbath fountain as its core. Benign loafers of all kinds hang out on the benches and on the ledge of the fountain.

Continue south on rue St-Denis. After crossing rue Sherbrooke, you descend into the Quartier Latin. I suggest you plan your arrival for the early evening, after the shops close on upper St-Denis. That's when the night starts to get going in the streets below, surrounding the Université de Québec à Montréal (UQAM). The neighborhood's central location makes it a favorite destination for locals heading out for libations. It is jammed with choices, but the **Bar St-Sulpice,** 1680 rue St-Denis (☎ 514-844-9458), is the most popular place to meet up for pitchers of beer or sangria, particularly in the summer when the bar opens its immense back patio.

At this point, you may want to take the Métro at the Berri-UQAM station. The entrance is just a bit farther down rue St-Denis on the same side, just across boulevard Maisonneuve. You take it for only one stop, to Champ-de-Mars, but the walk isn't scenic — actually, it's a bit of a hike, and it goes through something of a no-man's land. Plus, you may be feeling a tad sluggish after all that *poutine.* If you still want to walk, keep going straight down St-Denis for several blocks until you come to rue Notre-Dame, and turn right.

Out of the Champ-de-Mars Métro station, follow the arrows to Vieux-Montréal, walk up the hill to rue Notre-Dame, and turn right.

On the right, you pass City Hall, and on the left is Place Jacques-Cartier, which bustles in the summer with street performers and bands of tourists. Cross the square diagonally and aim for 2 blocks down, at rue St-Paul. A couple of doors farther west, you hit your final destination. By now it should be late at night, and **Les Deux Pierrots,** 104 rue St-Paul Est (☎ 514-861-1270), is in full swing. This is a traditional *boîte à chansons,* where legions of French Montréalers gather to sing and clap along to Québec folk favorites. The songs won't be familiar, but they're catchy nonetheless. You'll be tapping your feet in no time, but it may take you considerably longer to learn the lyrics.

## *The English Establishment*

The historic conflict between the French and English in Québec was not only about two separate languages, religions, and identities, but

## The English Establishment

PARC MONT-ROYAL

-⊙- Métro

1 The Illuminated Crowd
2 McGill University
3 Musée Redpath
4 Montréal Amateur Athletic Association
5 Seagram House

also about two social classes. After 1759, when the English took over Montréal and the city began to industrialize, an increasing divide grew between the blue-collar French and the white-collar English. By the 1800s and early into the next century, much of Canada's wealth was concentrated in the **Golden Square Mile,** what's now the western part of Montréal's downtown.

Canada's post-industrial economy has gone a long way toward leveling the playing field, but the stately, 19th-century, gray stone town houses of the Golden Square Mile have thankfully stood the test of time and can be seen among the city's modern office buildings.

Begin at the **corner of avenue McGill-College and rue Ste-Catherine** (Métro: McGill), one of the downtown's major intersections. McGill-College is usually the recipient of the city's best landscaping efforts, including outdoor photo exhibits in the summer and millions of white Christmas lights during the winter.

Walk north up the slight grade on avenue McGill-College; at the top you see huge wrought-iron gates. Along the way, on the right-hand side of the street, you pass a sculpture that looks like it's made out of butter. The numerous near life-size figures stand together making up *The Illuminated Crowd,* a 1979 sculpture by Raymond Mason.

At the top of the street, you're at the main entrance to **McGill University,** a gated campus and a serene and scenic retreat, right in the downtown core. You're welcome to go in and walk around. Go up the central drive, which comes to a fork after the playing field. Hang a left. The building on your right is the **Musée Redpath.** Admission is free.

From the museum, continue traveling in the same direction (west) through a smaller set of gates. Turn left, down rue McTavish, and walk past the university's student union and bookstore.

At rue Sherbrooke, turn right. Then take a left at the first light, onto rue Peel. The red-brick building that dominates the right-hand side of the block is the **Montréal Amateur Athletic Association.** Now a posh sports club, it's a holdover of the era of English-speaking private men's clubs.

Almost at the end of the next block is the **Seagram House,** a 1929 castle-like structure and former headquarters of the Bronfman family, who built a liquor empire during Prohibition.

# *Brunch, Tam-tams, and Beyond*

Summer Sundays are still sacred in Montréal but are no longer a strictly Catholic affair. The day's main events are **brunch** (whenever) and **Tam-tams,** an all-afternoon drum-circle with dancers and a hippie crafts market at the Monument Sir George-Étienne Cartier at the foot of Mont-Royal.

## Brunch, Tam-tams, and Beyond

1 Théâtre Rialto
2 Restaurant Senzala
3 Café Souvenir
4 St-Viateur Bagels
5 Epicerie Latina
6 Café Olympico
7 Pâtisserie De Gascogne
8 Toi Moi et Café
9 Monument Sir George Etienne Cartier

Weekend brunch spots do brisk business on Saturday and Sunday. Most places serve breakfast specials until late in the afternoon, so there's absolutely no rush to get out of bed. And no one does. You see plenty of mussy-haired, rosy-cheeked couples grinning sleepily at each other and their menus.

This itinerary begins on **rue Bernard** in **Mile End**. From downtown, hop on bus 80 at Place-des-Arts Métro, heading north up avenue du Parc. After brunching at one of the hidden spots I recommend, you crisscross avenue du Parc several times as you explore its cross streets, while working your way south. You end up amid the masses in Parc Mont-Royal. The city blocks in between are particularly long in this part of town, but the route is really not that far. At any point, you can catch bus 80 going south to get between the different stops I suggest.

Ideally, attempt this itinerary on a sunny Sunday, beginning by late morning or in the early afternoon, before scoring breakfast. You can even follow this route on a Saturday or on weekends during the winter, but no one will be beating drums at the last stop.

Start by taking bus 80 up avenue du Parc to rue Bernard. You'll be in front of the **Théâtre Rialto,** 5723 av. du Parc, with its striking Art Nouveau facade and marquee. Take your pick of excellent brunch choices along rue Bernard: You can turn right and go a block to the east to the Brazilian **Restaurant Senzala,** 177 rue Bernard Ouest (☎ 514-274-1464), for a tropical brunch. I like the Tropicana: poached eggs in avocado or mango halves topped with tomato sauce and melted cheese, served with fried plantains and grilled fruit. Or, from the starting point in front of the Rialto, turn left and go west to **Café Souvenir,** 1261 rue Bernard Ouest (☎ 514-948-5259), which is several blocks down. Its menu is clever: Within each item are more choices, allowing you to customize, to a certain extent, what will appear on your breakfast plate. It's a small, neighborhood spot that also harks of faraway destinations, because dioramas of European capitals adorn the walls. During the summer, the seating spills out onto a sidewalk terrace.

After your *n*th refill of coffee, make your way back to the intersection of rue Bernard and avenue du Parc. Turn south on avenue du Parc and walk toward downtown.

At the next intersection, avenue St-Viateur, around the corner to the left is **St-Viateur Bagels,** 263 av. St-Viateur Ouest (☎ 514-276-8044). Although food may be the farthest thing from your imagination after a big brunch, tasting one of this bakery's famous bagels, fresh out of the oven, is a must — at least, I strongly suggest it. If you just can't do another bite, pick some up for a light picnic that you'll unveil at Tam-tams, the last stop along your route.

You can also find lots of small shops farther along avenue St-Viateur, on both sides of the street. At the next corner, **Epicerie Latina,** 185 av. St-Viateur Ouest (☎ **514-273-6561**), is a gourmet grocery store, specializing in Italian ingredients. The market has produce as well as butcher and cheese counters. If you're even slightly curious about any of their cheeses, the grocer slices you off a sample taste.

At this point, you may already be saturated with coffee and seeking a bathroom, instead of looking for more. But if you can stand another cup, the coffee at **Café Olympico,** 185 av. St-Viateur Ouest (☎ **514-273-6561**), is as good as it gets in Montréal. The scene is worth taking in, if only for a moment.

Now, turn back and walk a block toward avenue du Parc. Turn left, going south along **avenue de l'Esplanade.** The town houses on this street are some of the prettiest and most typical in the neighborhood. When you reach the next street, **avenue Fairmount,** jog to your right, by turning first to the right, and then immediately to the left, continuing down rue Jeanne-Mance until **avenue Laurier.**

This street to the east and west of avenue du Parc is an upscale shopping district, with clothing boutiques, cafes, restaurants, and magazine and video stores, mainly at the service of the sedate and upscale clientele who putter in from the überaffluent neighborhood of Outremont. It's where they go when they don't want to fight the traffic and riff-raff downtown.

If you're coming all the way from rue Bernard, you can window-shop along avenue Laurier to your heart's content. You can also locate several brunch options around here, offering an abridged version of this itinerary. You'll be right beside **Pâtisserie De Gascogne,** 237 av. Laurier Ouest (☎ **514-490-0235**), a French bakery with bread, pastries, a coffee bar, and seating. Across the street, **Toi, Moi et Café,** 244 av. Laurier Ouest (☎ **514-369-1150**), roasts its own coffees and serves a brunch menu that's consistently good.

 When you're ready to leave avenue Laurier, head south along avenue du Parc, once again. After 3 blocks, you come to avenue Mont-Royal ("the Mountain") on your right. A bit farther, beyond the lights, you come to the Sunday ritual of **Tam-tams,** which has grown to such an extent that tour buses now stop to gawk.

Beginning at 2 p.m., drummers and percussionists from all over Montréal converge on the **Monument Sir George-Étienne Cartier,** on avenue du Parc at the foot of the Mountain — you're in Parc Mont-Royal. After they begin, their beats roll up the Mountain's slopes and drone on for the rest of the afternoon. A crowd of dancers forms in front of them, and the entire thing gathers momentum. People keep coming from every direction armed with blankets, Frisbees, dogs — the works — and they set up camp on the grassy hills surrounding the monument, which are all within earshot of the incessant drums. It is a veritable circus and everyone gets in on the act, including children. Out on the fringes, there's even a group of Dungeons and Dragons kids whacking each other with foam-and-duct-tape swords.

# Chapter 14

# Going Beyond Montréal: Three Day-trips

. . . . . . . . . . . . . . . . . . . . . . . . . . . . . . . . . . . . . . . . . .

## In This Chapter

▶ Stretching your legs beyond the city limits
▶ Visiting Ottawa, the nation's capital
▶ Day-tripping into rural Québec

. . . . . . . . . . . . . . . . . . . . . . . . . . . . . . . . . . . . . . . . . .

"*P*aris is Paris, but it's not France," goes the French expression. The same holds true for Montréal, which is not quite representative of the rest of the province of Québec. Montréal is Babylon by comparison. Beyond the bright lights of the big city, the province of Québec is a vast landscape, at times rural, at times rugged, dotted with many charming small towns whose inhabitants are by and large French speaking, and where hockey and Catholicism are still the predominant religions.

Depending on how much time you have, you may want to escape Montréal and explore its surrounding regions. A jaunt into the hills of the countryside can be especially magical from late September to mid-October, when the leaves change colors. Ditto for anytime it snows, although the driving can be treacherous in heavy snowfall.

 Of course, the first place you want to check out after Montréal is Québec City (see Part IV of this book). And it's doable in a day. You may want to stay longer, though; Québec City is perfect for an overnight visit — very romantic. I strongly recommend fitting this historic capital into your travel itinerary, if at all possible. It's very different from Montréal.

In this chapter, I present three other trips you can do in a day. For each, I also provide lodging information, should you decide to stay overnight. All three trips are between an hour and two hours by highway from Montréal.

For the first day-trip to Ottawa, you can get there by bus, train, or airplane, but renting a car is probably the most practical route. You don't need a car, however, because taxis and an extensive bus system can get you around. For the other two more rural destinations, a car is also the best option — for mobility's sake.

# Ottawa, the Nation's Capital

Ottawa is so Canadian. After all, it's the nation's capital. But Ottawa, which is in the province of Ontario, is completely different from Montréal and more like the rest of Canada. The difference is palpable.

## Getting there

By car, Ottawa is about two hours, or 190 km (118 miles), away from Montréal. Be sure to get an early start, especially if you're visiting only for the day. From Montréal, travel west on Autoroute 40, which runs along the top of the Island of Montréal. Stay on the 40 until the 417, which goes to Hull and Ottawa.

When you're in Ottawa proper, take exit 119, Metcalfe Street, and follow it as it twists and turns to the downtown area. After several blocks, the street ends smack in front of **Parliament Hill,** Ottawa's crown jewel and the seat of Canada's legislature.

## Seeing the sights

Across from the Parliament Buildings is a tourist information center called the **Capital Infocentre,** 90 Wellington St. (☎ **800-465-1867;** www. canadascapital.gc.ca). It's open daily 8:30 a.m. to 9 p.m. from May to September, and 9 a.m. to 5 p.m. the rest of the year. The people at the center can help you round out the recommendations I provide here.

Because you're in Ottawa only for a short visit, don't feel pressured to see everything. In this section I include the best of the Canadian capital, which makes for a full day of sightseeing. Ottawa's downtown is small, compact, and ideal for walking around. And you may be surprised by how much of the city you can cover on foot.

Ottawa's main attraction is **Parliament Hill,** 1 Wellington St. (☎ **866-599-4999** or 613-239-5000; www.parl.gc.ca), set on a bluff overlooking the Ottawa River. It is mecca for civic-minded Canadians and an interesting window into the nation's inner workings.

You can take a free, half-hour guided tour, which runs throughout the day. For a self-guided tour, pick up the "Discovering the Hill" booklet. Take the elevator to the top of the Peace Tower for a 360-degree view of the city and the Ottawa River.

On the grounds during the summer, you find plenty going on. At 10 a.m., a **Changing of the Guard ceremony** with dapper and unflappable soldiers in fur hats is just like the ones in England! By night, you can watch free sound and light shows. To the left of the central Parliament Building and behind the library is a peculiar cat sanctuary. And when parliament is in session (about 137 days per year), you can attend question-and-answer periods in the public galleries of either the Senate or the House of Commons.

*Downtown Ottawa*

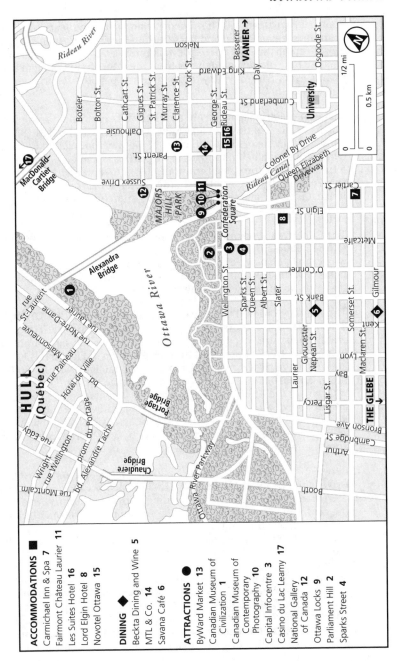

**ACCOMMODATIONS** ■
Carmichael Inn & Spa **7**
Fairmont Château Laurier **11**
Les Suites Hotel **16**
Lord Elgin Hotel **8**
Novotel Ottawa **15**

**DINING** ◆
Beckta Dining and Wine **5**
MTL & Co. **14**
Savana Café **6**

**ATTRACTIONS** ●
ByWard Market **13**
Canadian Museum of
  Civilization **1**
Canadian Museum of
  Contemporary
  Photography **10**
Capital Infocentre **3**
Casino du Lac Leamy **17**
National Gallery
  of Canada **12**
Ottawa Locks **9**
Parliament Hill **2**
Sparks Street **4**

**Sparks Street** (☎ 613-241-5353; www.ottawakiosk.com/panos/
sparks_street.html) runs parallel to Wellington Street and is a block
south of Parliament Hill. It's a pedestrian mall with plenty of shops,
boutiques, restaurants, and bars. During the summer, many Sparks
Street establishments open sidewalk terraces. If you feel so inclined, a
walking tour of the mall departs from the intersection of Elgin and
Sparks every Saturday May to October at 2 p.m. It lasts an hour and a
half and costs C$5.

Just east of Parliament Hill are the **Ottawa Locks,** which make up the
north entrance of the **Rideau Canal.** The waterway, built in 1827, starts
with eight flights of locks and runs all the way to Kingston on Lake
Ontario. Originally built for strategic purposes and employed mainly as
a trading route, the canal is now an 11-km (6¾-mile) parkland that runs
through the city like a ribbon. In the winter, it becomes the world's
longest ice rink, and office workers and students alike use it to skate to
work and class.

The **Canadian Museum of Contemporary Photography,** 1 Rideau Canal
(☎ 613-990-8257; cmcp.gallery.ca), housed in a reconstructed railway tunnel, displays photos from its large permanent collection and also
hosts traveling exhibitions. The museum's own collection spans from
the 1960s to the present. Admission is free.

The striking **National Gallery of Canada,** 380 Sussex Dr. (☎ 800-319-
2787 or 613-990-1985; www.gallery.ca), opened in 1988. The glass and
granite structure was designed by Moshe Safdie, the same architect
behind Montréal's Habitat '67 and the Museum of Fine Arts. Light shafts
and reflective panels make the most of natural light, which floods into
the galleries, but in a way that doesn't damage the art. The long, inclined
walkway to the Grand Hall, an impressive landmark on its own, provides
a dramatic view of the Parliament Buildings above the churning Ottawa
River. The gallery has the country's most extensive collection of Canadian
art, but it also features important works by artists from other countries
and from periods throughout the ages.

Between Parliament Hill and the National Gallery and to the east of Sussex
Drive is the **ByWard Market** (☎ 613-562-3325; www.byward-market.
com) area. A two-story market building, formerly a farmers' market, is at
the center of this neighborhood. The surrounding streets of 19th-century
brick-and-stone buildings are filled with trendy shops, restaurants, pubs,
and bars. During the summer, vendors at all kinds of outdoor stalls hawk
their wares, while street performers do their thing.

Across the Alexandra Bridge — that is, over the Ottawa River and back
in Québec province — is the **Canadian Museum of Civilization,** 100
rue Laurier (☎ 800-555-5621 or 819-776-7000; www.civilization.ca),
housed in a futuristic, riverfront building. The permanent exhibits celebrate Canada's aboriginal people and the evolution of this young country. Extensive artifacts are on display from native Canadian cultures; of

special note is the Grand Hall, which features 43 authentic totem poles from the West Coast. Other exhibits document various aspects of Canada's history, culture, and development. Also on the premises are an IMAX theater and a children's museum with "hands-on" displays.

For something completely different, you can try your luck at the **Casino du Lac Leamy,** 1 bd. du Casino (☎ 800-665-2274; www.casino-du-lac-leamy.com). Also in Québec province, it's open daily from 9 a.m. to 4 a.m. To get there from downtown Ottawa, take the Macdonald-Cartier Bridge, which becomes Highway 5, and get off at Exit 3.

## Where to stay

You may decide to have dinner in Ottawa, and dinner may turn into drinks. Suddenly, staying the night seems like a clever idea. Here are my choices for accommodations. All are centrally located, close to the places you're touring.

The **Fairmont Château Laurier,** 1 Rideau St. (☎ 800-441-1414 or 613-241-1414; www.fairmont.com), adjacent to the Rideau Canal and steps away from Parliament Hill, is the city's grandest hotel, in the same tradition as the Château Frontenac in Québec City and the Queen Elizabeth in Montréal. The **Lord Elgin Hotel,** 100 Elgin St. (☎ 800-267-4298 or 613-235-3333; www.lordelginhotel.ca), overlooks Confederation Park in downtown Ottawa, which is home to many seasonal events such as the Jazz Festival. **Les Suites Hotel,** 130 Besserer St. (☎ 800-267-1989 or 613-232-2000; www.les-suites.com), offers a few more amenities than the average hotel room and is adjacent to Rideau Centre's 180 shops as well as the restaurants of the ByWard Market area. The **Carmichael Inn & Spa,** 46 Cartier St. (☎ 613-236-4667; www.carmichaelinn.com), is a heritage home in a quiet neighborhood, but it's still close to the action and offers spa treatments. Lastly, **Novotel Ottawa,** 33 Nicholas St. (☎ 800-668-6835 or 613-230-3033; www.novotelottawa.com), is a sure bet. This outpost of the French hotel chain is centrally located. In the typical European tradition, the rooms are efficient and compact but appointed for its business-traveler clientele.

## Where to dine

If you're looking for a place to eat, here's the insider track. In 2003, **Beckta Dining and Wine,** 226 Nepean St. (☎ 613-238-7063), ranked as the fourth-best new restaurant in Canada in a biannual survey by *EnRoute* magazine. It's the first Ottawa restaurant to break the top ten. Beckta serves seasonal cuisine in a modern and intimate setting. **MTL & Co.,** 47–49 William St. (☎ 613-241-6314), seems like a fitting recommendation, given that MTL is short for Montréal, and true to its name the restaurant becomes a lively club after dinner. On the menu are reasonably priced fusion dishes. **Savana Café,** 431 Gilmour St. (☎ 613-233-9159), serves dishes inspired by the traditional ingredients of the Caribbean and the Pacific Rim.

# *The Laurentian Mountains*

For the quickest and easiest day-trip around Montréal, drive 45 minutes north to the Laurentian Mountains. These are rolling hills, not breathtaking peaks, but the Laurentians are impressive all the same.

## *Getting there*

The Laurentian Highway, or Autoroute 15, takes you directly to the Laurentians and gives you the scenic route to boot. You can reach Autoroute 15 by driving north from downtown Montréal (along boulevard St-Laurent is fine) and catching Autoroute 40 West (you drive about ten minutes until the Autoroute 15 interchange). Then follow signs to St-Jérôme. Autoroute 15 takes you through some urban sprawl for about 15 minutes, but the scenery is pretty after that.

If you have a little extra time, exit at St-Jérôme and pick up old Route 117. St-Jérôme is a small town with a quaint main street, a couple of pubs, and some gift and craft shops. It's remarkable more so for its charm than its substance. This takes you to the village of **Ste-Agathe des Monts** and through some typical older towns of the region along the way.

A good visitor information center covering the Laurentians area is Mirabel: **La Maison du Tourisme des Laurentides,** La Porte du Nort Rest Area, Exit 51 on Autoroute 15 (☎ **800-561-6673** or 450-436-5309; www.laurentides.com). The tourist office is in a red-roofed stone cottage. It's open daily in the summer from 8:30 a.m. to 8:30 p.m., and from 9 a.m. to 5 p.m. during the rest of the year.

**Orléans Express** buses leave regularly from Montréal's **Central Bus Station,** 505 bd. de Maisonneuve (☎ **888-999-3977** or 514-842-2281), with stops at Ste-Agathe, Ste-Adèle, St-Jovite, and Mont-Tremblant. For schedules, call the bus station or visit www.orleansexpress.com. The express bus to Ste-Adèle takes about an hour and a half; the trip to St-Jovite and Mont-Tremblant takes about two hours.

## *Seeing the sights*

The Laurentians boast a number of interesting villages; each one can be a day-trip in itself, depending on what you want to do and how much time you want to spend doing it. Driving from Montréal, your first stop is **St-Sauveur-des-Monts,** a popular ski resort town with lots of restaurants and street activity. In summer, the water park, **Parc Aquatique du Mont-St-Sauveur,** 350 rue St-Denis (☎ **514-871-0101** or 450-227-4671; www.parcaquatique.com), is a popular attraction because of its wave pool and mountain water slide.

Next stop is **Ste-Adèle** (Exit 67 off Route 117), a pretty village whose main street, **rue Valiquette,** is lined with cafes, galleries, and bakeries. The popular **Chantecler** ski resort here has 22 trails. For information, call the town's **Centre Municipale** at ☎ **450-227-3417.** For more

## The Laurentian Mountains

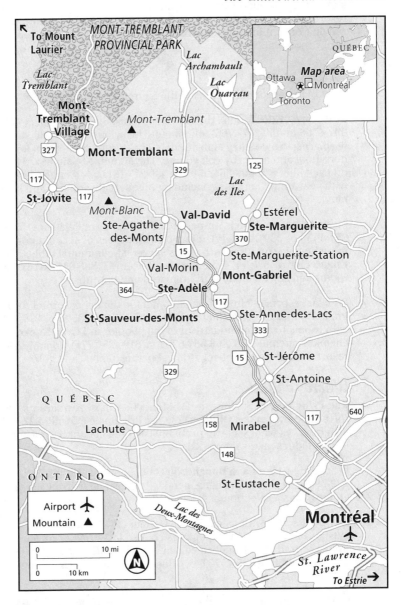

downhill skiing, continue along Route 117, and then take Route 327 to **Mont-Tremblant,** the highest peak in the Laurentians and an hour-and-a-half drive from Montréal. The commercial center that serves the area is

St-Jovite, whose main street, **rue Ouimet,** is lined with cafes and shops. For information on skiing and summer activities in this popular resort area, contact the **Bureau Touristique de Mont-Tremblant** on rue du Couvent in Mont-Tremblant (☎ **819-425-2434;** www.tourisme monttremblant.com).

## Where to stay

Most of the accommodations in the Laurentians are resorts.

In St-Sauveur-des-Monts, the **Relais St-Denis,** 61 rue St-Denis (☎ **888-997-4766** or 450-227-4766), offers quite luxurious rooms and suites, with fireplaces, in a country club atmosphere — complete with a heated outdoor pool and a nearby golf course. The **Manoir St-Sauveur,** 246 chemin du Lac-Millet (☎ **800-361-0505** or 450-227-1811), is a large resort hotel with year-round activities, including racquetball, squash, and in-house movies.

In Ste-Adèle, the **Hotel Alpine,** 1440 chemin Pierre Péladeau (☎ **877-257-4630** or 450-229-1545), offers different types of accommodations in rustic log structures with meals served at communal tables. The **Chantecler** resort, 1474 chemin Chantecler (☎ **888-916-1616**), has rooms and suites, many with fireplaces and hot tubs.

Popular resorts in Mont-Tremblant include the deluxe motel **Auberge La Porte Rouge,** 1874 chemin Principale (☎ **800-665-3505** or 819-425-3505), with rooms to accommodate up to ten people, and **Gray Rocks,** 525 chemin Principale (☎ **800-567-6767** or 819-425-2771), a family-friendly resort that offers horseback riding, boating, tennis, and golf.

## Where to dine

**Rue Principale** in St-Sauveur-des-Monts has many restaurants. One of the best known is **Les Oliviers,** 239 rue Principale (☎ **450-227-2110**), which serves what you can probably call French country cuisine, including beef, duck, and salmon dishes.

In Ste-Adèle, **L'Eau à la Bouche,** 3003 bd. Ste-Adèle (Route 117) (☎ **450-229-2991**), serves a changing menu with seasonal fish, meats, and vegetables, plus a selection of Québec cheeses.

In St-Jovite, try **Antipasto,** 855 rue Ouimet (☎ **819-425-7580**), for Italian cuisine, including individual pizzas cooked in a brick oven. For carefully prepared traditional Québec cuisine, try **La Table Enchantée,** 600 Rte. 117 Nord (☎ **819-425-7113**), considered one of the best dining spots in the Laurentians area.

In Mont-Tremblant, **Aux Truffes,** 3035 rue Principale (☎ **819-681-4544**), serves upscale contemporary French cuisine.

# The Eastern Townships

The **Eastern Townships** are one of Québec's best-kept tourism secrets. A beautiful landscape of rolling hills, mountains, farms, and small villages, the area has several quaint villages that are frequented mainly by Québec tourists. Much of the townships were originally settled by British loyalists who fled to the region during the Revolutionary War, and although 90 percent of the people speak French as their first language, you can see traces of English presence everywhere. Many towns and villages have English names or names that combine the original English name with that of a Catholic saint (given by the French-speakers who later moved into the region).

For tourist information about the Eastern Townships, contact **Tourism Cantons-de-l'Est,** 20 rue Don-Bosco Sud in Sherbrooke (☎ **800-355-5755;** www.cantonsdelest.com).

## Getting there

To head to the townships, count on two hours of driving. I suggest visiting either the small city of **Magog** (Lac Memphrémagog) or the quaint village of **North Hatley** (Lac Massawippi), which is about half an hour from Magog. Leave Montréal on the Champlain Bridge, which becomes Autoroute 10. Then follow directions toward Sherbrooke. Autoroute 10 goes directly to Magog. If you want to get there along a more scenic country road, leave the Autoroute 10 at Exit 37 and follow Route 112 East. To get to North Hatley, take Autoroute 108 east from Magog for about 20 minutes.

Buses for Magog and Sherbrooke leave Montréal's **Central Bus Station,** 505 bd. de Maisonneuve (☎ **888-999-3977** or 514-842-2281), roughly every two hours during the week. Call for daily schedules.

## Seeing the sights

Small and mainly industrial, the city of Magog is not where you want to spend a lot of time. Head straight to the waterfront area on **Lac Memphrémagog,** with its cafes and bars. You can take a **lake cruise** aboard the **Aventure** cruise ships. Call ☎ **819-843-8068** for information or contact the **Bureau d'Information Touristique Memphrémagog** at 55 rue Cabana in Magog (☎ **800-267-2744** or 819-843-2744). Near Magog, visit the popular provincial **Parc National du Mont Orford,** which offers a golf course and 48 km (30 miles) of skiing and hiking trails. To get there, take Exit 115 north off the Autoroute 10. For information, call ☎ **819-843-9855.** Admission is C$3.50 for adults, and C$1.50 for children 6 to 17 years old.

## The Eastern Townships

**North Hatley** is a tiny, beautiful village on the shore of Lac Massawippi. A former resort town for rich Americans, it is now the place well-to-do Québeckers come to relax and buy paintings in the village's many art galleries. The village's main street, **rue Principale,** is also full of cute cafes, restaurants, and boutiques selling crafts and clothing. Not many tourist attractions exist here per se. Instead, people come here for the exceptional atmosphere, beautiful lakefront scenery, and all-'round New England feel. The **Galerie Jeannine Blais,** 102 rue Principale (☎ 819-842-2784), has lovely, fanciful folk art, and **Au Grenier de Gife,** 330 chemin de la Rivière (☎ 819-842-4440), sells painted furniture and works by local artists.

## Where to stay

Lodging in Magog is neither plentiful nor very nice. If you want to stay the night, I suggest the **Relais de l'Abbaye,** 2705 chemin Gendreau (☎ 819-847-3721), a luxurious mansion-style guesthouse with elegant rooms.

But you'll probably be happier staying in North Hatley. **Le Tricorne,** 50 chemin Gosselin (☎ 819-842-4522), is an impeccably decorated, 125-year-old guesthouse. Rooms start at about C$125, and some include hot tubs. **Serendipity,** 340 chemin de la Rivière (☎ 819-842-2970), is a reasonably priced B&B with nice views.

## Where to dine

The **Auberge Ripplecove,** 700 chemin Ripplecove (☎ 800-668-4296), has a reputation for serving creative dishes based on local delicacies such as caribou. For less expensive but still tasty food, **Pilsen,** 55 rue Principale (☎ 819-842-2971), has a publike atmosphere and serves such quick food as nachos, burgers, and pasta. This is a great place to indulge in a large selection of locally brewed beers. Another good choice is the **Café Massawippi,** 3050 chemin Capelton (☎ 819-842-4528), for inventive but reasonably priced meals.

# Chapter 15

# Living It Up after Dark: Montréal Nightlife

- - - - - - - - - - - - - - - - - - - - - - - - - - - - - - - - - - - - - - - - -

## In This Chapter

▶ Watching performing arts for a dose of culture

▶ Figuring out where the beautiful people go at night

▶ Dancing the night away

▶ Hitting the right bars and clubs in the right order

- - - - - - - - - - - - - - - - - - - - - - - - - - - - - - - - - - - - - - - - -

*I*n this chapter, I open the curtains on Montréal's vibrant performing arts scene, which tends to be on the edgy and daring side. I organize the nightlife scene by category, giving you my top choices for each type of nightlife pursuit, regardless of where they're located.

## Applauding the Cultural Scene

Besides the many festivals, Montréal has a bevy of performing arts troupes that put on shows during their annual seasons, which usually run from the beginning of fall into the late spring. There's *cirque*, theater, symphony, and opera, just to name a few of the most popular. Really, these are only the tip of Montréal's cultural iceberg.

### Getting the inside scoop

The *Montréal Gazette,* the city's only English daily newspaper, as well as the *Hour* and the *Mirror,* two free English weeklies, cover the city's cultural calendar. These publications list films, art venues, events, music shows, and more. The weekly publications come out on Thursday mornings and preview the coming week. You can find them in the entranceways of many boutiques, cafes, restaurants, and bars in Montréal's neighborhoods. Attending the performing arts these days is a surprisingly casual affair. People seem to go in all sorts of dress — whatever makes them most comfortable. You should, too, although you won't be out of place if you dress up for the occasion.

Although much of Montréal's cultural scene is conducted in French, you can find plenty in English; besides, music and dance need little translation. Check the free weekly newspapers for listings.

## Raising the curtain on the performing arts

Deserving special mention, partly because it defies quick and easy categorization, is Québec's own **Cirque du Soleil** (www.cirquedusoleil.com), a performance spectacle under a big top but eons and galaxies beyond the corny entertainment that people sometimes associate with a circus. Founded in Québec and now an international entertainment empire, a Cirque du Soleil performance is a human zoo of acrobats, contortionists, singers, dancers, and musicians all taking part in an elaborate fantasy. Although the show tours the world, a troupe usually returns home to Montréal every year or so in the spring. All the Cirque du Soleil's new shows premier in Montréal.

### Theater

Most of Canada's English-language television and film productions, as well as the Broadway musical performances, happen in Toronto. This leaves Montréal's *Anglophone* (English-speaking) actors to fill the roles of the city's small-scale, short-run stage productions. But this situation can be a recipe for excellent theater. Before *Mambo Italiano* was a moderately successful movie, it was a hit play in Montréal, written by a local playwright.

Some of the best venues for Montréal theater today are:

- ✔ **Centaur Theatre Company,** 453 rue St-François-Xavier, Vieux-Montréal (☎ 514-288-3161), occupies a 1903 building, once the city's first stock exchange. Over the course of a season (end of Sept–end of May), Montréal's premier English-language theater company presents several plays on its two stages, including productions of modern classics, works of contemporary Canadian playwrights, and foreign adaptations. Métro: Place-d'Armes.

- ✔ **Geordie Theatre Productions** (☎ 514-845-9810), a professional children's theater company, stages a season's worth of kids' classics. Intended for grade- and high-school audiences, the company's main stage is the **D.B. Clarke Theatre,** 1455 bd. de Maisonneuve Ouest, on Concordia University's downtown campus. Métro: Guy-Concordia.

- ✔ **Saidye Bronfman Centre for the Arts,** 5170 Côte Ste-Catherine, West Montréal (☎ 514-739-2301), has a full season of plays that runs from late fall to early summer. This multidisciplinary arts center, which includes a gallery and fine-arts school, presents dramatic works from around the world, both contemporary and modern. Métro: Côte-Ste-Catherine.

### Dance

Following is a selection of Montréal's best dance offerings:

✔ **L'Agora de la Danse,** 840 rue Cherrier, Plateau (☎ 514-525-1500), is a part of the Department of Dance at the Université de Québec à Montréal (University of Québec at Montréal). **Le Studio,** its 256-seat venue, is the center of Canada's modern-dance community. Métro: Sherbrooke.

✔ **Les Grands Ballets Canadiens de Montréal,** 4816 rue Rivard (☎ 514-849-8681), produces four shows throughout its season and welcomes several visiting companies. The company adds fresh choreography to this classic ballet. Métro: Laurier.

✔ **Tangante,** 840 rue Cherrier (☎ 514-525-5584), bills itself as intimate laboratory theater. Dedicated to contemporary dance and experimental performance art, Tangante attempts upward of 90 performance projects during its September-to-June season. Métro: Sherbrooke.

### Classical music and opera

Classical music and opera are the pinnacle of highbrow cultural consumption. For some, the challenge is to stay awake; for the true connoisseurs, it's a waking dream. Consider the following options:

✔ **L'Opera de Montréal,** 260 bd. de Maisonneuve Ouest, Downtown (☎ 514-985-2258), marries music, singing, plot, costumes, and set design in six elaborate productions per season. Métro: Place-des-Arts.

✔ **L'Orchestre Symphonique de Montréal (OSM),** 260 bd. de Maisonneuve Ouest, Downtown (☎ 514-842-9951), one of Canada's major orchestras, performs in the Salle Wilfrid-Pelletier of the Place-des-Arts. The OSM performs regularly at New York's Carnegie Hall. Métro: Place-des-Arts.

# Hitting the Clubs and Bars

Whether you prefer a quiet cocktail at a jazz club or a night on the town flitting from one hot spot to the next, Montréal delivers an awesome nightlife — you can paint the town whatever color you choose. Activities peak between Thursday and Sunday, but something's always going down.

It all begins at quitting time on Thursday with the *cinq à sept* (the hours from 5–7 p.m.), the unofficial opening ceremonies of the weekend, when Montréal's office workers flock to their favorite watering holes to drink and snack, commiserate and socialize, and, of course, see and be seen. The party then carries on in the bars, cafes, pubs, restaurants, live-music venues, and dance clubs well into the night. Saturday is definitely the pinnacle of Montréal's frenzied nightlife activities. If it's a long weekend (a Mon holiday), concerts and all-night dance parties continue on Sunday, too.

True to its Latin spirit, Montréal's nocturnal activities start later and end later than other cities in North America. Last call is at 3 a.m., so don't be surprised if the pace doesn't really pick up until after 11 p.m. — many people are just finishing dinner at that hour — and peak around 1 a.m. Québec's legal drinking age is 18.

So where are the city's hot spots? Great spots are everywhere, but many can be found on rue Crescent and boulevard St-Laurent, the city's two main nightlife strips. You don't need to be excessively concerned about safety in these neighborhoods. Montréal's streets are relatively safe at night, partly because so many people are out. Everyone's very friendly, as people tend to be after a drink or two.

The cost of a night out can vary greatly. Many bars and clubs charge a cover, which ranges from C$5 to C$25. Drinks can cost anywhere from C$5 to C$8, depending on how snazzy the bar deems itself to be.

With four university campuses scattered around the downtown core, students rule the night and set the tone. Everywhere you go, all night, you're bound to see packs of students staggering about. Don't worry, though. Few bars in Montréal cater exclusively to students, so you don't risk stumbling into a scene from *Animal House.*

In fact, stepping out in Montréal requires a touch of class. No one in Montréal really dresses up at night, but people are still pretty chic as a whole. You won't see any baseball caps, fraternity sweatshirts, or running shoes. Some places even enforce a dress code. If you're not sure what to wear, just don black.

In terms of music, rock is almost dead and DJs rule the city. But you can find great live music if you like funk, jazz, world beat, Latin, bluegrass, blues, or punk. A number of venues host big-name acts passing through on the northeastern legs of their North American tours. The free weeklies are the best place to find out about who's playing where and when. Heck, you can spend the night as a groupie.

*NightLife,* a free glossy magazine with articles in both English and French, is also a good source. Each issue includes an exhaustive nightlife directory for the entire city, with a series of icons describing each establishment.

Also keep your eyes open for the events and acts advertised via guerilla marketing techniques: flyers and posters littering the downtown core, left on windshields, taped to poles, or pasted to the plywood barriers surrounding a construction site. For environmental reasons, I don't sanction them. But when you're looking for the latest nightlife happenings, they're hard to beat.

## Downtown Montréal Nightlife

Métro
Infotouriste Office
Underground City

Brutopia **7**
Centaur Theatre Company **16**
Club 1234 **8**
Club 737 **12**
Club Soda **20**
Comedy Nest **1**
Comedyworks **5**
D.B. Clarke Theatre **4**
Ecole de Danse Swing Cat's Corner **14**

## Plateau, Mile End, and Gay Village Nightlife

Baldwin Barmacie **3**

Barfly **17**

Barraca Rhumerie & Tapas **13**

Bily Kun **9**

Blizzarts **20**

Brasserie Dieu Du Ciel! **4**

Cabaret à Mado **28**

Cactus **11**

Cafe Saint Laurent Frappe **21**

Cafeteria **24**

Casa Del Popolo **5**

Edgar Hypertavern **12**

Else's **22**

Go Go Lounge **23**

Jello Bar **26**

La Sala Rosa **6**

Laika **18**

Le Cabaret **25**

Le Divan Orange **16**

Le Quai des Brumes **10**

Le Reservoir **19**

Les Grands Ballets Canadiens de Montréal **7**

Le Studio **27**

Mile End Bar **1**

Mocha Dance **2**

Salon Daome **8**

Sky Complex **30**

Sofa **15**

Tango Libre **14**

Unity II **29**

## *Shaking your groove thing: The best dance clubs*

The following sections list venues where the dance floor is the main attraction.

### *The hottest clubs*

DJs rule the night at these clubs, where the bold and beautiful clientele dance the night away. So go ahead: Strut your stuff and make the scene.

- ✔ **Blizzarts,** 3956-A bd. St-Laurent, Plateau (☎ **514-843-4860**), is a long, narrow spot that feels like a cafe and oozes with street-cred. Each night of the week, local DJs play a different sound: dance hall, reggae, drum'n'bass, and so on. Open: Daily 9 p.m. to 3a.m. Cover: Wednesday to Saturday C$3 to C$5. Métro: Sherbrooke.

- ✔ **Club 1234,** 1234 rue de la Montagne, Downtown (☎ **514-395-1111**), pronounced *twelve thirty-four,* located in a beautiful Victorian mansion, is something of a phenomenon as of late. The main-room dance floor is packed and sweaty. The drinks are expensive and the bouncers rude — yet no one seems to mind. In front, there's a lineup several people deep and it's impossible to make sense of the chaos after 11 p.m. Forget it! You're not getting in. To see the mayhem unfold on the inside, arrive before 10:30 p.m. The clientele seem to enjoy pitching stacks of napkins in the air like confetti — how festive. By the end of the night, everyone's wading through them, almost ankle-deep. Open: Thursday to Saturday 10 p.m. to 3 a.m. Cover: C$10 to C$20. Métro: Peel.

- ✔ At **Funkytown,** 1454 rue Peel, Downtown (☎ **514-282-8387**), an older clientele gathers to reminisce to a medley of remixed disco classics. When a '70s anthem plays, everyone rushes to the dance floor, where they sing along at the top of their lungs. Open: Friday to Saturday 8 p.m. to 3.a.m. Cover: C$8. Métro: Peel.

- ✔ **Mile End Bar,** 5322 bd. St-Laurent, Mile End (☎ **514-279-0200**), north of the main St-Laurent strip, has become a fixture of Thursday's *cinq à sept* landscape. Droves of flirting office workers, fresh from a hard day on the job, jam the bar downstairs. The action later moves to the nightclub upstairs, where there's a lofted seating area and a suspended catwalk. Open: Thursday to Friday 5 p.m. to 3 a.m., Saturday 7 p.m. to 3 a.m. Cover: Usually C$5 Friday to Saturday. Métro: Laurier.

- ✔ **Salon Daome,** 141 av. Mont Royal Est, Plateau (☎ **514-982-7070**), is an upstairs hideaway for lovers of funky and soulful music. The second-floor loft space feels more like an apartment than a nightclub, but it gets packed nonetheless. Tuesdays are a happening tech-house night, if you're looking for somewhere to go at the beginning of the week. Wednesdays are salsa. Thursdays through Saturdays a DJ spins funk, rare groove, and Afro-Latin-influenced sounds. Occasionally someone beats on a *djembe* as accompaniment. Open: Tuesday to Sunday 8 p.m. to 3 a.m. Cover: C$5 to C$10. Métro: Mont-Royal.

✔ **Society of Art and Technology (SAT),** 1195 bd. St-Laurent, Quartier Latin (☎ 514-844-2033), is the leader of the underground music scene. Its main room features video projections that play along with the music. The SAT often hosts parties in association with new media, and also hosts music, festivals, and events, which makes nights here varied and eclectic, as is the clientele. The schedule is erratic, but something is usually going on — call or check the Web site (www.sat.qc.ca). Métro: St-Laurent.

✔ **Time Supper Club,** 997 rue St-Jacques, Downtown (☎ 514-392-9292), is wildly popular after dinner, when the chairs are cleared from the main floor and everybody gets up to dance. The party carries on at a feverish pace, as people crowd the bar, mingle in the walkways, and take turns dancing on the island in the middle of the dining room. Open: Thursday to Saturday 7 p.m. to 3 a.m. Cover: C$20. Métro: Bonaventure.

✔ **Zoobizarre,** 6388 St-Hubert, Rosemont (☎ 514-270-9331), is a recent addition to Montréal's nightlife map in the northern reaches of the city. If you're into a kitsch brand of cool, it's worth the trek for electro clash and synth punk sounds. On the second floor, above some stores, is a stone-walled room with arched ceilings. It feels like a wine cellar or a dungeon and makes for an offbeat setting. It's actually the reincarnation of a bar in Bordeaux, France. Open: Thursday to Saturday 9 p.m. to 3 a.m.; schedule varies during the rest of the week. Cover: C$5 to C$10. Métro: Jean-Talon.

### Salsa, swing, and tango

Ever since disco bottomed out in the '80s, there's been a growing nostalgia for couples dancing, in Montréal as everywhere else. These days, swing is not the only dance in town. Salsa and tango are also extremely popular. Whichever style you opt for, couples dancing makes for a great night out. You can dance, watch, or learn — I hope a bit of each.

Most of the following places give free lessons or crash courses earlier in the evening, before the real party starts. So you can walk in a complete beginner and tango home like a pro. Well, sort of. Call to find out when the sessions are on.

✔ **Cactus,** 4461 rue St-Denis, Plateau (☎ 514-849-0349), Montréal's other salsa hot spot, is on two floors of a town house just around the corner from the Mont-Royal Métro station. It's a little less intimidating than La Salsatheque, perhaps because the setting is more intimate. Beginners try out their moves on the upstairs dance floor, while the regulars tear it up front and center. Open: Thursday 9 p.m. to 3 a.m., Friday to Saturday 10 p.m. to 3 a.m., Sunday 4 to 8 p.m. Cover: C$3 to C$5. Métro: Mont-Royal.

✔ **Ecole de Danse Swing Cat's Corner,** 486 rue Ste-Catherine Ouest, Suite 303, Downtown (☎ 514-874-9846), hosts the biggest swing night in Montréal on Fridays, with a crash course from 8:30 to

9:30 p.m. and then dancing until whatever hour. Open: Fridays 8:30 p.m. to 1 a.m. Cover: C$7. Métro: Place-des-Arts.

✔ **La Salsatheque,** 1220 rue Peel, Downtown (☎ **514-875-0016**), is Montréal's oldest Latin club. The décor is somewhat dated, but no one seems to mind. The action's on the steel dance floor as couples shimmy and spin to a variety of Latin rhythms, predominantly salsa, merengue, and bachata. Open: Thursday to Sunday 10 p.m. to 3 a.m. Cover: Friday to Saturday C$7. Métro: Peel.

✔ **Mocha Dance,** 5175-A av. du Parc, Mile End (☎ **514-277-5575**), is a dance studio with a bar and cafe, serving drinks and a light menu. Throughout the week, the space hosts evenings of tango (Tues, Fri, Sun) and salsa (Thurs, Sat). Open: Tuesday and Thursday 9 p.m. to 1 a.m., Wednesday 5 p.m. to 1 a.m., Friday 10 p.m. to 3 a.m., Saturday 9 p.m. to 3 a.m., Sunday 3 to 8 p.m. Cover: C$5 to C$8. Métro: Laurier.

✔ **Tango Libre,** 1650 rue Marie-Anne Est, Plateau (☎ **514-527-5197**), an intimate dance floor tucked away on a mainly residential street, has tango evenings beginning at 9:30 p.m. Friday and Saturday (Cover: C$7). Supervised practice sessions are Thursday and Sunday (Cover: C$6). In summertime, this tango studio organizes Sunday-evening dances at parks around the city. Métro: Mont-Royal.

## Grooving to live music

DJs may rule the city, but you can still find plenty of live, local music in the bars and clubs around town. And the summer festivals supercharge Montréal's concert schedule, drawing top talent and delighted crowds to city venues.

### Intimate settings

Do you feel like live music for a change? This doesn't necessarily mean rocking out at a concert in a stadium. Instead, here are several spots around town where live music is the main draw — where you can hear up-and-coming talent or an offbeat sound.

✔ **Barfly,** 4062-A bd. St-Laurent, Plateau (☎ **514-284-6665**), is a tiny spot on one of the city's main nightlife strips with a pool table and a stage. An eclectic mix of local talent plays lively and boisterous sets of folk music. Some nights are more brooding, when speakers and poets take the stage. Open: Daily 4 p.m. to 3 a.m. Cover: Friday to Saturday C$3 to C$5. Métro: Sherbrooke.

✔ **Casa Del Popolo,** 4873 bd. St-Laurent, Plateau (☎ **514-284 3804**), bills itself as a vegetarian hot spot. During the day it's a cafe; by night, it's an intimate bar and live-music venue. Along with the musical acts, the owners book a variety of performances, which can be broadly categorized as urban folk and include DJ nights, traveling video road shows, and spoken word. Casa also runs La Sala Rosa, a space across the street at 4848 bd. St-Laurent, which is for larger happenings. Open: Daily noon to 3 a.m. Cover: Occasional, C$5 to C$10. Métro: Laurier.

✔ **La Maison du Jazz,** 2060 rue Aylmer, Downtown (☎ 514-842-8656), formerly called Biddle's, was the haunt of late Montréal jazzman Charlie Biddle. Live jazz is played nightly on a small stage, with several tiers of seating in an Art Nouveau setting. Dinner is available and includes La Maison's famous ribs. The lounge and bar are just far enough removed to allow for quiet conversation. Open: Sun 6 p.m. to midnight, Monday to Wednesday noon to midnight, Thursday noon to 1 a.m., Friday noon to 2:30 a.m., Saturday 6 p.m. to 2:30 a.m. Cover: C$5 added to your bill. Métro: McGill.

✔ **Le Divan Orange,** 4234 bd. St-Laurent, Plateau (☎ 514-840-9090), is the latest bar to open on St-Laurent that features a vibrant live-music scene. It's a resto-cafe-showbar that has comfortable, cozy couches at the front; a long bar down the left-hand side; and a stage at the back. The vibe is laid back, deconstructed, and convivial. Open: Tuesday to Sunday 11 a.m. to 3a.m. Cover: Occasional, C$3 to C$5. Métro: Sherbrooke.

✔ **Le Quai des Brumes,** 4481 rue St-Denis, Plateau (☎ 514-499-0467), is a dark and smoky bar frequented by an older, mainly French-speaking clientele. The brick walls and wood paneling give it a warm ambience. Jazz, blues, or rock bands play on a small stage in the back every Wednesday and Saturday. Open: Daily noon to 3 a.m. Cover: Depending on the talent, cover can vary from C$3 to C$8. Métro: Mont-Royal.

✔ **Les Pierrots Boite à Chansons,** 104 rue St-Paul Est, Vieux-Montréal (☎ 514-861-1270), is the premier spot to hear traditional Québec folk music, from Thursday through Saturday, when the place is usually rockin'. If you don't speak French you won't be able to sing along, but you can still clap. For most of the crowd, the night is highly sentimental and emotionally charged as they sing along to the ballads they learned growing up. It's a memorable night out. Open: Daily 9 p.m. to 3 a.m. Cover: C$5 to C$6. Métro: Champ-de-Mars.

✔ **Sofa,** 451 rue Rachel Est, Plateau (☎ 514-285-1011), a lounge with a cigar humidor and many bottles of port, has live acts Thursday through Sunday — usually of the funk, soul, or R&B varieties. The bar is an island in the middle of the establishment. In front of it, a narrow space creates a sort of gauntlet for mingling 25- to 35-year-olds. Behind, groups of friends chill in the large alcoves with booths. Open: 4 p.m. to 3 a.m. Cover: C$4 to C$9. Métro: Mont-Royal.

✔ **Upstairs,** 1254 rue Mackay, Downtown (☎ 514-931-6808), also offers jazz nightly, but in a more intimate setting. The stage seems no more than a windowsill, as ensembles of up to six musicians jam together in close quarters. Mondays and Tuesdays are "Fresh Jazz" nights, featuring the latest talent among McGill University's music students. Shows start at 9 p.m. Dining available. Open: Monday to Friday 12:30 p.m. to 3 a.m., Saturday to Sunday 5 p.m. to 3 a.m. Cover: Friday to Saturday C$15 to C$20, Sunday C$10. Métro: Guy-Concordia.

### Concert venues

The clubs, or show bars, discussed in this section net a surprising amount of top talent on tour. They open only when there's a show, but that seems to be most nights. So, who's playing while you're in town? Find out by browsing Montréal's free weeklies, calling the box offices, or visiting the clubs' Web sites. You can also book your tickets in person, by phone, or on the Web. Be sure to check out the following:

- ✔ **Club Soda,** 1225 bd. St-Laurent, Quartier Latin (☎ **514-286-1010;** www.clubsoda.ca; Métro: St-Laurent)

- ✔ **Le Cabaret,** 111 bd. St-Laurent, Quartier Latin (☎ **514-845-2014;** Métro: St-Laurent)

- ✔ **Metropolis,** 59 rue Ste-Catherine Est, Quartier Latin (☎ **514-844-3500;** www.metropolismontreal.ca; Métro: St-Laurent)

## Hopping between hot spots: Montréal's cafes and bars

Montréal's nightlife begins early, carries on at a torrid pace, and ends late. Seasoned denizens look to hit at least two or three spots over the course of an evening. Choreographing the perfect night out is all about timing, variety, and keeping your options open.

Montréalers like to mix-and-match. The city's cafes and bars are perfect for this: meeting friends before a night of dancing or sharing impressions after a live show. Rather than clubs and concerts, where music is the main draw — and usually too loud for sustained conversation — the city's cafes and bars are definitely more social. This is also the best place to meet and mingle with the locals.

The expression in French is *M'as tu vu?* (pronounced *mah too voo,* and literally meaning "Have you seen me?"). The following places are very *M'as tu vu*:

- ✔ **Baldwin Barmacie,** 115 av. Laurier Ouest, Outremont (☎ **514-276-4282**), serves up concoctions to a loud and flirtatious crowd seeking strong antidotes for its angst. The hallway entrance is like a catwalk due to its several large windows that open onto the bar. The long layout of the two rooms, one down a half-flight of stairs, is somewhat disconcerting. If you want to order a drink from the upper level, you must hail the bartenders who are several feet below where you are. Makes for an interesting conversation starter. Open: Monday to Friday 5 p.m. to 3 a.m., Saturday to Sunday 8 p.m. to 3 a.m. Cover: None. Métro: Laurier.

- ✔ **Cafeteria,** 3581 bd. St-Laurent, Plateau (☎ **514-849-3855**), is really a restaurant. However, it is increasingly becoming a destination for drinks among the young and fashionable set. True to its name, the tables of the dining room are packed together, allowing for plenty of social mingling. Others mill around the bar. It's quite a scene that goes late into the night. Open: Daily 8 a.m. to 3 a.m. Cover: None. Métro: Sherbrooke or St-Laurent.

✔ **Club 737,** 1 Place Ville-Marie, Downtown (☎ 514-397-0737), atop Montréal's tallest skyscraper, is easy to locate: Just find the source of the spotlights that stretch across the night's sky. On the ground floor, patrons line up for an elevator to shuttle them to the club on the 42nd and 43rd floors. Undeniably, the vistas of Montréal by night are spectacular! The experience is even better during the summer months, when the club allows patrons out onto one of the observation decks. I think the view is the main attraction here; otherwise, the two floors are dark, hot, and sweaty. Open: Friday to Saturday 10 p.m. to 3 a.m. Cover: C$10 to C$20. Métro: Bonaventure.

✔ **Edgar Hypertavern,** 1562 av. Mont-Royal Est (☎ 514-521-4661), is several blocks east of St-Denis, in the heart of the Plateau. It's a popular destination for an attractive crowd of 20- and 30-somethings, dressed casually, yet at the height of fashion. The cramped quarters make the mingling rather intense. Large sculptures of sailfish trophies with hooks dangling from their bodies evoke thoughts of hunting and fishing, and perhaps set the tone of the evening. Open: Daily 3 p.m. to 3 a.m. Cover: None. Métro: Mont-Royal.

✔ **Newtown,** 1476 rue Crescent, Downtown (☎ 514-284-6555), bears the nickname of its owner, former Formula 1 driver Jacques Villeneuve. It is a literal translation of his last name and what his pals called him on the F1 circuit. The three floors of his establishment include a restaurant and terrace upstairs and a club in the basement. The main-floor bar draws an older clientele than most other places on rue Crescent. The décor is sleek and sophisticated. Open: Daily noon to 3 a.m. Cover: Friday to Saturday C$10. Métro: Guy-Concordia.

✔ **Versus,** 106 rue St-Paul Ouest, Vieux-Montréal (☎ 514-788-2040), is the bar of the Hotel Nelligan. It's particularly popular for after-work drinks among slick professionals working in the area. Plus, Hotel Nelligan seems to be the boutique hotel of choice among visiting A-list celebrities, which adds further mystique to the contemporary, yet warm, décor. Open: Daily 11 a.m. to 1 a.m. Cover: None. Métro: Place-d'Armes.

## Lounging like lizards

Sipping cosmopolitan martinis and other candy-colored concoctions — this has been "in" for a terribly long time. In the mid-1990s, even before the lounge scene became a widespread trend in North American urban centers, Montréal had already started opening places with comfy seating, retro décor, and long drink lists of elaborate cocktails with fancy names, all served in martini glasses.

✔ **Go Go Lounge,** 3682 bd. St-Laurent, Plateau (☎ 514-286-0882), is mayhem. At times it's so crowded that girls resort to dancing on the bar. Some of the staff are "in character" — with decked-out wigs and disco fashions, their get-ups are inspired by Go Go's full-on retro décor. There's no cover, but the line out front is notoriously slow; get there early or prepare to be patient. Open: Monday to Friday 5 p.m. to 3 a.m., Saturday to Sunday 7 p.m. to 3 a.m. Cover: None. Métro: Sherbrooke.

✔ **Jello Bar,** 151 rue Ontario Est, Quartier Latin (☎ 514-285-2621), was one of the forerunners of Montréal's martini movement. Its success in re-creating a '70s lounge environment coincided with the public's sudden and insatiable appetite for all things retro and a newfound and considerable thirst for sophisticated-looking drinks. DJs and live bands enhance the ambience in the form of jazz, Latin, funk, soul, R&B, and other lounge-friendly musical tangents. Open: Tuesday to Friday 5 p.m. to 3 a.m., Saturday 9 p.m. to 3 a.m. Cover: C$5 to C$8. Métro: St-Laurent.

✔ **Laika,** 4040 bd. St-Laurent, Plateau (☎ 514-842-8088), is centrally located, so it's an ideal place for friends to meet throughout the day, and particularly popular in the evening. A different local DJ of some repute spins sets throughout for the denizens bobbing their heads and chatting away, sitting at the cocktail tables in the front. At the back the space narrows, leaving room only for a long, wooden bar. Large windows open onto boulevard St-Laurent, and poorly disguised rubbernecking from both sides of the pane is common practice. Open: Daily 9 a.m. to 3 a.m. Cover: None. Métro: Sherbrooke.

✔ **Pub Quartier Latin,** 318 rue Ontario Est, Quartier Latin (☎ 514-845-3301), located just off St-Denis. Its inconspicuous location makes it hard to just happen upon. They play funk and rare groove, supposedly the variety of stuff you'd find pressed on 45 rpm records. A central bar anchors the first room surrounded by intimate banquettes along the wall. The second room is somewhat larger. An elevated area at the back is a makeshift stage for the funk and world music bands that play there. Open: Daily 3 p.m. to 3 a.m. Cover: None. Métro: Sherbrooke, Berri-UQAM.

## Dropping in to neighborhood bars

At the establishments in this section, you'll find plenty of locals and not many tourists. But don't be shy: Belly up to the bar, order a drink, and strike up a conversation with a regular.

✔ **Barraca Rhumerie & Tapas,** 1134 av. Mont-Royal Est, Plateau (☎ 514-525-7741), offers up a potentially volatile mix of booze and food, an extensive menu of aged rums, and a shorter list of tasty appetizers. Rich tones of stained wood, wrought-iron accents, and parchment lampshades contribute to the boudoirlike atmosphere. The long and narrow space is often crowded, making it extremely difficult to reach the small terrace in the back. Open: Daily 3 p.m. to 3 a.m. Cover: None. Métro: Mont-Royal.

✔ **Bily Kun,** 354 av. Mont-Royal Est, Plateau (☎ 514-845-5392), is a dimly lit and somewhat cavernous room, finished with bold lines, a beautiful tile floor, and ostrich-head trophies on the walls. It is a modern-day pub that attracts a hip but unpretentious clientele in their mid-20s and up. Order your drinks from the waiter; ask the busboy about the menu of light snacks. Open: Daily 3 p.m. to 3 a.m. Cover: None. Métro: Mont-Royal.

✔ **Else's,** 156 rue Roy Est, Plateau (☎ **514-286-6689**), is a comfortable, intimate spot that seems like a well-kept secret, with its inconspicuous location, soft lighting, and the constant murmur of conversation. Actually, it is quite popular. The bar's liquor license is such that you have to buy a token snack with your alcohol. On tap is an interesting selection of beer from Québec's microbreweries, as well as cider. Open: Daily 8 a.m. to 3 a.m. Cover: None. Métro: Sherbrooke.

✔ **Le Ste-Elisabeth,** 1412 rue Ste-Elizabeth, Quartier Latin (☎ **514-286-4302**), is hidden away, just off a seedy stretch of rue Ste-Catherine. But, put any apprehension aside and persevere, and you will be rewarded. It's a real gem on a summer night: an intimate outdoor terrace with tables and chairs on two levels, surrounded by ivy-covered walls, several stories high. In addition, it's right between the downtown's two festival sites, Place des Arts and rue St-Denis. Monday, all year around, the bar has a special: C$3 for pints of Boreal beer. Open: Daily 3 p.m. to 3 a.m. Cover: None. Métro: Berri-UQAM.

## What's brewing in Montréal?

If you take your obligations as a tourist seriously, you should try as many of the locally brewed beers as possible. Not only are there a wide variety of suds brewed by the province's microbreweries, but several brewpubs also craft their own beer, which is not available anywhere else. My recommendations are:

✔ **Brasserie Dieu Du Ciel!,** 9 av. Laurier Ouest, Mile End (☎ **514-490-9555**), features over 30 house recipes brewed on-site. The bar is dark and cozy, ideal for a quiet time on a cold night. A window allows patrons to peer down into the basement to see where the beer's made. Open: Daily 3 p.m. to 3 a.m. Cover: None. Métro: Laurier.

✔ **Brutopia,** 1219 rue Crescent, Downtown (☎ **514-868-9916**), consists of three bars and several rooms spread over three floors. By the main bar, there's a small stage for the nightly, live music. Sundays are a popular open-mic. During the warmer months, the brewery offers seating outside, both in back and out front. Brutopia brews its house beers in large brass barrels in the room behind the bar; try Indian Pale Ale, Raspberry Blonde, or Apricot Wheat. Open: Daily 3 p.m. to 3 a.m. Cover: None. Métro: Guy-Concordia.

✔ **Le Cheval Blanc,** 809 rue Ontario Est, Quartier Latin (☎ **514-522-0211**), was the first brewpub in Montréal and is responsible for launching this segment of bars, which has now matured into all-the-rage. The unpretentious crowd is a mixed bag. Serious beer aficionados come for the ales on tap, neighborhood-types are drawn in by the red glow of the Asian lanterns. Open: Monday to

Saturday3 p.m. to 3 a.m., Sunday 5 p.m. to 3 a.m. Cover: None. Métro: Berri-UQUAM.

✔ **Le Reservoir,** 9 av. Duluth Est, Plateau (☎ **514-849-7779**), has a window on its brewing operation to the right of the bar. Groups of friends and couples chat, seated at tables with votive candles. During the summer, the main-floor windows open onto the street, and the second-floor terrace is in full swing. Open: Monday to Friday noon to 3 a.m., Saturday to Sunday 10:30 a.m. to 3 a.m. Cover: None. Métro: Sherbrooke.

## Racking it up in a pool hall

You don't have to be a shark or a rounder to frequent a pool hall these days. In Montréal, they're practically chic. You can play for rounds of drinks, but be sure to size up your competition before making such a suggestion — lest you get fleeced. Two of the more popular places to play pool are:

✔ **Cafe Saint Laurent Frappe,** 3900 bd. St-Laurent, Plateau (☎ **514-289-9462**). Open: Daily noon to 3 a.m. Métro: Sherbrooke.

✔ **Sharx,** 1606 rue Ste-Catherine Ouest, Downtown (☎ **514-934-3105**). Open: Daily 11 a.m. to 3 a.m. Métro: Guy-Concordia.

## Yucking it up at comedy clubs

As the annual **Just For Laughs Festival** continues to grow, Montréal is increasingly a mecca for stand-up and improv comedians. They say it's the hardest profession in the world. Two places to try are:

✔ **Comedy Nest,** 2313 rue Ste-Catherine Ouest, Downtown (☎ **514-932-6378**). Open: Thursday to Saturday, shows at 8:30 p.m. and 10:30 p.m. Métro: Atwater.

✔ **Comedyworks,** 1238 rue Bishop, Downtown (☎ **514-398-9661**). Open: Monday to Friday 4 p.m. to 3 a.m., Saturday to Sunday 7 p.m. to 3 a.m. Métro: Guy-Concordia.

## Being out and proud in Gay Village

Montréal is quickly becoming the hottest gay destination in North America, and the city's gay community has a thriving nightlife scene. Gay Pride and the Black and Blue weekends are annual highlights on the city's nightlife calendar. Rue Ste-Catherine, east of rue St-Hubert, is packed with innumerable restaurants, cafes, bars, and clubs that are always hopping throughout the year. Some of the hottest spots are:

✔ **Cabaret à Mado,** 1115 rue Ste-Catherine Est, Gay Village (☎ **514-525-7566**), has drag queens strutting in cabaret shows on some nights. The rest of the time they emcee for karaoke, stand-up comedy, and theme parties. Open: Daily 11 a.m. to 3 a.m. Cover: C$5 to C$8. Métro: Beaudry.

- **Sky Complex,** 1474 rue Ste-Catherine Est, Gay Village (☎ 514-529-6969), is a pub, restaurant, cabaret, male strip club, mega-dance club, and rooftop terrace in one. For gay men, it's a sort of one-stop shop. Open: Monday to Tuesday 2 p.m. to 1 a.m., Wednesday to Sunday 2 p.m. to 3 a.m. Cover: Friday to Saturday C$4. Métro: Papineau.

- **Unity II,** 1171 rue Ste-Catherine Est, Gay Village (☎ 514-523-2777), is a mega-club in the Village spread over three floors and topped by a terrace on the roof. Take advantage of the two-for-one specials every day from 4 to 8 p.m. Open: Friday to Saturday 10 p.m. to 3 a.m. Cover: C$5 to C$10. Métro: Beaudry.

# Part IV
# Settling Into and Exploring Québec City

The 5<sup>th</sup> Wave                    By Rich Tennant

Great curb appeal.

Château Frontenac

# In this part . . .

A couple of hours downriver from Montréal is Québec City, an enchanted place that makes you feel as though you've stepped into another age. In this part, I explain where to go and what to do to get the most out of your visit. I tell you where to find the best hotels, restaurants, and attractions. I even give you a handy historical tour of Québec's Old City, so that you can see all the highlights in one afternoon.

# Chapter 16

# Arriving and Getting Oriented in Québec City

- - - - - - - - - - - - - - - - - - - - - - - - - - - - - - - - - - - - - - -

*In This Chapter*

▶ Getting to Québec City
▶ Figuring out the city's neighborhoods
▶ Traveling around the city

- - - - - - - - - - - - - - - - - - - - - - - - - - - - - - - - - - - - - - -

*Y*ou're likely to spend almost all your time in Québec City in the Old City, which is divided into a fortified **Haute-Ville** (Upper City), built behind walls on a cliff overlooking the St. Lawrence River, and a **Basse-Ville** (Lower City), at the foot of the cliff running along the riverfront, to the south and east. You can easily get lost in the winding cobblestone streets in either neighborhood, but don't worry if you do. The entire point of Québec City is strolling around and soaking up the unbelievable atmosphere. This chapter explains how to get to Québec City and how to get around after you arrive.

 No matter how you get to Canada from abroad, you have to pass through Customs. See Chapter 8 for details on what to expect from the stern-faced Customs agents you encounter at the border.

## Making Your Way to Your Hotel

Whatever you may have thought of your trip so far, get ready, Québec City will charm you. Getting to your hotel will feel like traveling back in time: from the suburban outskirts littered with modern-looking malls to the historic, walled city. You'll feel the centuries peeling away. The setting seems to appeal to the long-lost romantic in everyone.

### If you arrive by plane

If you arrive in Québec City by air, you will land at the small **Jean Lesage International Airport,** 500 rue Principale in the suburb of Sainte-Foy (☎ 418-640-2700; www.aeroportdequebec.com). Unfortunately, no shuttles or public transportation are available to downtown Québec

City. So you have two choices, renting a car or flagging a taxi or a limo. Walking is out of the question.

A taxi ride is a fixed rate of C$30. If you'd like to pay more to travel in style, a limo costs C$74. **Taxi Co-op** (☎ **418-525-5191;** www.taxicoop-quebec. com) is one of the companies operating to and from the airport. In terms of limo services, **Aristo Car** (☎ **418-660-5055;** www.aristo-car.com) and **Limousine Robert Boucher** (☎ **418-654-8884;** www.quebecairlimo. com) are two of the limo services with cars stationed at the airport.

If you want to rent a car, a few of the major agencies have desks at the Jean Lesage airport.

- ✔ **Avis:** ☎ **800-879-2847** or 418-872-2861
- ✔ **Enterprise:** ☎ **800-261-7331 or** 418-861-8820
- ✔ **Hertz Canada:** ☎ **800-654-3131** or 418-871-1571
- ✔ **National/Alamo:** ☎ **800-227-7368** or 418-877-9822

You may land at the province's main international airport, which is actually in Montréal: **Trudeau International Airport** (☎ **800-465-1213** or 514-394-7377; www.admtl.com). See Chapter 8 for more details about arriving here and traveling by land between Montréal and Québec City.

## If you arrive by car

From **New York City,** follow I-87 to Highway 15 to Montréal, and then pick up Autoroute 20 to Québec City. To get into the city, take Autoroute 73 Nord (Highway 73 North) across the Pierre-Laporte Bridge (Pont Pierre-Laporte) and exit on boulevard Laurier (going east). Follow it straight until it turns into Grande-Allée and then into rue St-Louis, and into the Old City through the St-Louis Gate.

From **Boston,** take I-89 to I-93 in Montpelier, Vermont, which connects with Highway 55 in Québec to link up with Autoroute 20. Follow the preceding directions.

From **Montréal,** you can take either Autoroute 20, which follows the south shore of the St. Lawrence River, or the more scenic, less-trafficked Autoroute 40, which follows the north shore. Either way, the trip takes about two and a half hours.

## If you arrive by train or bus

Trains pull into Québec City train station, **Gare du Palais,** 450 rue Gare-du-Palais. **Via Rail** (☎ **888-842-7245** or 418-832-0784; www.viarail.ca) is the company that handles passenger train travel.

Adjacent to the train station is the bus station, **Terminus Gare du Palais,** 320 rue Abraham-Martin. **L'Orléans Express** (☎ **418-525-3000;** www.

orleansexpress.com) is the bus company that takes passengers back
and forth to Montréal. Several different lines serve the surrounding
region, but for Québec City they all stop here.

# Figuring Out Québec City's Neighborhoods

Québec's Old City is really quite small, but it's so dense and packed with
interesting sites, shops, museums, cafes, restaurants, and other attractions that you can spend a lot of time wandering its winding streets and
still be surprised by new sites and curiosities. Some neighborhoods
you'll likely want to visit outside the Old City include St-Roch, Grande-
Allée, avenue Cartier, and boulevard René-Lévesque.

### Haute-Ville (Upper City)

This is the biggest part of the Old City, a neighborhood entirely surrounded by thick ramparts. Most of Québec City's main attractions can
be found here, including the **Château Frontenac,** the **Place d'Armes,** the
**Basilique Notre-Dame,** the **Québec seminary and museum,** and the **terrasse Dufferin** (a long promenade with a view of the St. Lawrence River
below). Most of the buildings are at least 100 years old, some much
older. The city was not built on a grid, so it can be disorienting, but don't
worry — sooner or later you'll arrive at a landmark and you'll be able to
figure out where you are on a map.

### Basse-Ville (Lower City)

Historically, this part of the city was reserved mainly for poor families
that worked in the docks. Now, it's pretty much a continuation of the
Haute-Ville. In the Basse-Ville, you find similar architecture, many restaurants, some small inns, and several major attractions, including the
spectacular *Musée de la Civilisation* **(Museum of Civilization).** Rue
St-Paul is a lovely strip with many art galleries and antiques stores and
some very cute accommodations.

Take the elevator or the stairs down from the terrasse Dufferin or Place
d'Armes, and you wind up on the delightful rue Petit Champlain, a
pedestrian alley full of shops of varying quality. Don't forget to stroll
along the port area. Recent development and an interest by the cruise
industry have made the area more attractive and festive. You'll be in awe
of the massive cruise ships from around the world that dock at the port.

### Grande-Allée

The Grande Allé, closest to the fortified Old City, is a long, wide street
running west of the St-Louis Gate that's lined with restaurants, boutiques, and bars. During the summer evenings, this street is hopping and
its terraces are packed with revelers.

## Québec City Orientation

ⓘ Information

QUÉBEC

Québec
Ottawa
Toronto ○  ★ Montréal
New York

Bassin Louise

rue Samson

rue de l'Arsenal

côte Dinan

PARC DE L'ARTILLERIE

BASSE–VILLE

rue McMahon

rue des Remparts

rue Charlevoix

côte du Palais

St-Jean

rue Couillard

rue Hamel

rue St-Paul

rue St-André

Dauphine

rue Ste-Angèle

rue St-Stanislas

Cook

rue St-Flavien

rue Ferland

côte de la Fabrique

rue Ste-Anne

rue Chauveau

rue Garneau

rue Ste-Famille

rue Ste-Ursule

VIEUX–QUÉBEC

des Jardins

Buade

rue Ste-Anne

Trésor

côte du Fort

rue de l'Université

Basilique Notre-Dame

rue Port-Dauphin

VIEUX–PORT

rue St-Louis

rue du Fort

PARC MONTMORENCY

du Sault-au-Matelot

rue St-Pierre

rue St-Jacques

Porte Prescott

côte de la Montagne

rue St-Antoine

rue Dalhousie

Promenade de la Pointe à Carcy

rue Haldimand

Château Frontenac

Escalier Cassé-Cou

Funicular

av. Ste- Geneviève

Mont-Carmel

rue Laporte

rue Notre-Dame

rue St-Pierre

rue Dalhousie

av. St-Denis

terrasse Dufferin

rue Sous-le-Fort

rue du Petit-Champlain

rue du Marché-Champlain

ES.GOUVERNEURS

CLIFFS

bd. Champlain

St. Lawrence River

0                    1/4 mi
0         0.25 km

### Avenue Cartier

From the Grande-Allée, keep heading west for about 15 minutes on foot and you'll reach avenue Cartier on your right — another lively street with many B&Bs, restaurants, shops, and bars.

### St-Roch

If you think everything about the Old City seems somewhat staged, perhaps it's time to escape to St-Roch (pronounced "Saint Rock") and the seemingly more authentic rue St-Joseph — Québec City's original downtown core. Its "hidden" location makes finding it feel like a rewarding discovery. (**Hint:** From the Lower City, go past the train station and under the concrete Autoroute Dufferin overpass.)

The recent urban renewal of this main street and the surrounding neighborhood is the most exciting thing that's happened to Québec City in, well, eons. Some of Québec City's best new restaurants have opened in this part of town, including **L'Utopie.** The large-scale toy store **Benjo** will give the kids a real charge. Along with several other destination boutiques, for the adults there's **Hugo Boss, Peak Performance,** and **Flirt,** an upscale lingerie boutique.

## Finding Information after You Arrive

Québec City has two good tourist information centers in handy locations. The main office is **Centre Infotouriste,** 12 rue Ste-Anne, just opposite the Chateau Frontenac at Place d'Armes (☎ **877-266-5687** or 418-692-2608). The office is well stocked with tons of brochures and is well staffed with bilingual employees who help you find information or book hotel rooms and tours. **Québec City Tourism,** 835 av. Laurier, near the Plains of Abraham and not too far from Grande-Allée (☎ **877-783-1608** or 418-641-6290), offers the same services but tends to be a little less busy.

## Getting Around Québec City

Québec City's small size makes it a snap to get around. By foot is best; however, at some point you have to contend with the steep hill between the Haute-Ville and Basse-Ville. This is when the *funiculaire* (elevator) comes in handy (yes, elevator — read on!).

### By foot

If you're in reasonably good shape and have comfortable walking shoes, you can probably dispense with all motorized transport while in Québec City, especially if your hotel is in the Old City. Walking is definitely the best way to travel; the only challenge on foot is getting between the

Upper and Lower cities. To do so, you have to climb the steep stairs that join côte de la Montagne (near the Petit-Champlain) to the Dufferin Terrace. If you want, you can take the *funiculaire* that leaves from the head of rue Petit-Champlain and also arrives on the Dufferin Terrace. In the north part of the Old City, near rue St-Jean, you can take advantage of a more gradual decline to get to the Basse-Ville by following rue côte-du-Palais down a gentle slope to rue St-Paul.

## By public transportation

I have only one exception to the rule of walking: if you're staying too far away from the Old City to make the trip in by foot. In that case, you can use several buses that run frequently into the Old City. Bus 7 runs up and down rue St-Jean; bus 11 runs along Grande-Allée and rue St-Louis. Both take you into the Old City, making stops all the way to Place d'Youville, just outside the walls on the north side of town. These buses pass about every ten minutes. Fares are C$2.30 of exact change, or you can purchase tickets at a reduced rate at a *dépanneur* (convenience store).

## By taxi

Taxis are plentiful in Québec City, and they're pretty easy to flag down around the big hotels and outside the gates of the Old City. Inside the Old City, you can find taxi stands at Place d'Armes and in front of the Hôtel-de-Ville (City Hall). The fares are the same as in Montréal, which can be a little expensive for short distances. The starting fare is C$3.15 and climbs at a rate of roughly C$2.50 per mile of driving, or C55¢ per minute of waiting in traffic. To call a taxi, try **Taxi Coop** (☎ 418-525-5191) or **Taxi Québec** (☎ 418-525-8123).

## By car

Trying to get around Québec City by car really makes no sense. You'll have great difficulty parking on the street in the Old City, which is so compact that you can easily walk everywhere. That said, if you arrive at your hotel by car, you can find plenty of places to leave it while you stroll about the city. Hotels either have parking lots or have worked out deals with parking lots nearby, and most will be able to direct you where to go to find a spot. For most parking lots, expect to pay around C$10 to C$12 per day. Some lots even allow you to come and go during the day at no extra charge.

## By bicycle

Given how hilly and dense the Old City is, cycling isn't a very attractive option. Still, you can rent bikes for the day at several locations. Try **Cyclo Service,** 160 rue St-André in the Basse-Ville (☎ 418-692-4052), or **Vélo Passe-Sport Plein Air,** 22 rue côte-du-Palais, near rue St-Jean (☎ 418-692-3643). The cost is around C$20 for 12 hours.

# Chapter 17

# Checking In at Québec City's Best Hotels

• • • • • • • • • • • • • • • • • • • • • • • • • • • • • • • • • • • • • •

## In This Chapter

▶ Finding the best accommodations in Québec City

▶ Knowing how much you'll pay

• • • • • • • • • • • • • • • • • • • • • • • • • • • • • • • • • • • • • •

*B*ecause Québec City is so small, accommodations can book up quickly for the high season (roughly May–Oct), so I suggest calling well in advance. If you're shopping around for a room before your trip, or if you need to find something at the last minute, check out my tips in Chapter 9 on how to get the best deal.

Each hotel listing in this chapter includes a $ symbol indicating the price range of the rooms. Prices included are the rack rates, the standard rate for a double room for one night before taxes. Table 17-1 fills you in on what the $ signs represent.

| **Table 17-1** | **Key to Hotel Dollar Signs** | |
|---|---|---|
| *Dollar Sign(s)* | *Price Range* | *What to Expect* |
| $ | Less than C$100 | Simple and inexpensive, these accommodations should offer all the basics: a room with a lock, a firm bed, and clean towels and sheets. A light continental breakfast may be included. Hotels offering rooms at these prices probably don't have an extensive catalog of services to cater to your every whim, but the front-desk clerks are usually delighted to point you in the right direction for whatever you want. |

| Dollar Sign(s) | Price Range | What to Expect |
|---|---|---|
| $$ | C$100–C$199 | Many of the rates offered by the chain hotels fall into this price range, as do the rates of the fancier independents. You can already expect the amenities to be better, such as bathrooms with hair dryers, coffeemakers with complimentary coffee, and Internet access. Some hotels in this category may have kitchens that provide late-night room service or a breakfast cart. Some even have swimming pools. |
| $$$ | C$200–C$299 | Along with the upper end of the chain hotels, boutique hotels and luxury hotels begin competing in this price bracket, with fine bed linens, feathery pillows, fluffy towels, and bathtubs built for two. The first-class hotels seem to differentiate themselves by striving for regal scale and elegance, while boutique hotels are strikingly modern. Expect high-speed Internet access in your room. |
| $$$$ | C$300 or above | At this price, you should want for nothing in terms of your stay. Expect a great view, an in-room hot tub, a CD player, thick terry cloth bathrobes, and even flowers. Highly deferential, personalized service is included, as well. |

# Québec City Hotels from A to Z

## Auberge du Quartier
### $$   Grande-Allée

If you want some peace and quiet, slightly off the beaten path, this charming inn is a good choice. A 15-minute walk from Vieux-Québec, the 15 rooms are colorful and compact — including several with exposed brick walls. Guest rooms are available with single, double, and queen beds, and are priced accordingly. The atmosphere is relaxing and friendly, complete with cozy armchairs in the living room/library. Rooms don't have TVs, but the living room has an available Internet connection, as well as piles of Québec literature to leaf through.

*170 Grande-Allée Ouest.* ☎ *800-782-9441 or 418-525-9726. Fax: 418-521-4891.* www. aubergeduquartier.com. *Parking: C$12. Rack rates: C$139–C$189. AE, MC, V.*

## Québec City Accommodations

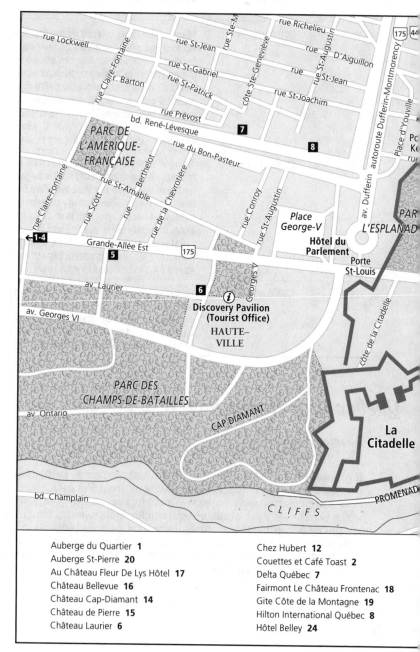

Auberge du Quartier **1**
Auberge St-Pierre **20**
Au Château Fleur De Lys Hôtel **17**
Château Bellevue **16**
Château Cap-Diamant **14**
Château de Pierre **15**
Château Laurier **6**

Chez Hubert **12**
Couettes et Café Toast **2**
Delta Québec **7**
Fairmont Le Château Frontenac **18**
Gite Côte de la Montagne **19**
Hilton International Québec **8**
Hôtel Belley **24**

Hôtel Clarendon **13**
Hôtel Dominion 1912 **21**
Hôtel du Vieux-Québec **10**
Hôtel Le St. Paul **23**
Hôtel Loew's Le Concorde **5**
Hôtel Royal William **25**

Le Krieghoff B&B **3**
Le Priori **22**
Maison Ste-Ursule **11**
Manoir Victoria **9**
Relais Charles-Alexandre **4**

### Auberge St-Pierre
**$$–$$$$** **Basse-Ville**

This new-ish hotel in the heart of the Basse-Ville does an almost magical job of looking and feeling antique, from the distressed painted furniture to deliberately scratched hardwood floors, high ceilings, exposed brick-and-stone walls, and old-fashioned hot-water radiators. But the rooms are utterly modern in term of amenities and convenience — the spacious bathrooms, for example, are generously equipped, right down to the built-in hair dryers. One luxurious suite has a hot tub and king-size bed.

*79 rue St-Pierre.* ☎ **888-268-1017** *or 418-694-7981. Fax: 418-694-0406.* www.auberge.qc.ca. *Parking: Valet C$18. Rack rates: C$189–C$249. AE, MC, V.*

### Au Château Fleur de Lys Hôtel
**$** **Haute-Ville**

The "Château" in the name may be a bit misleading; this quaint, family-run hotel occupies a stately, urban mansion built in 1876 on the uppermost part of the Haute-Ville. Perhaps its most castle-like feature is a gorgeous spiral staircase with a wooden banister leading to 18 rooms over three floors. Otherwise it tends toward run-down — in a romantic sense, more reminiscent of a European inn. The rooms themselves are basic, with comfortable beds and clean bathrooms. It's perhaps not the polish and pampering you were dreaming of, but the location and value of this Château are hard to beat.

*15 av. Ste-Geneviève (corner of rue de la Porte).* ☎ **877-691-1884** *or 418-694-1884. Fax: 418-694-1666.* www.quebecweb.com/cfl/. *Parking: C$12. Rack rates: C$100–C$150. AE, MC, V.*

### Château Bellevue
**$$–$$$** **Haute-Ville**

At first sight, you may mistake this small hotel for one of the oodles of B&Bs and guesthouses that surround it, all facing the peaceful Jardin des Gouverneurs park. Château Bellevue actually has 58 rooms, small (but not overly quaint), quiet, and equipped with basic amenities like phones and cable TV. Unlike many accommodations in the Old City, this place has an elevator, so you have no steep stairs to climb. The staff are very helpful. Some of the pricier rooms face the park, and in winter they have a view of the St. Lawrence River.

*16 rue Laporte.* ☎ **800-463-2617** *or 418-692-2573. Fax: 418-692-4876.* www.oldquebec.com/en/bellevue. *Parking: C$15. Rack rates: C$169–C$219. AE, DC, DISC, MC, V.*

### Château Cap-Diamant
**$$** **Haute-Ville**

The idyllic enclosed garden behind this Victorian guesthouse, with its crumbling rock walls, flower-filled porch, and fountain, is almost worth the price of a room itself. Each room in this quaint inn is different. All are decorated with antiques, and the place feels something like a work in progress. Bathrooms are tiny. Although most rooms are accessible by steep narrow stairs, there's a small elevator to lift luggage to the upper floors. Whew! Rooms have cable TV but no phones, and Internet access is available in the reception area. The owners are inviting and helpful. Ask for a room overlooking the rooftops of the Old City.

*39 av. Ste-Geneviève.* ☎ **418-694-0313.** *Fax: 418-692-1375.* www.hotelcapdiamant. com. *Parking: C$13. Rack rates: C$149–C$175. MC, V.*

### Château de Pierre
**$$   Haute-Ville**

A European-style inn on a quiet, elegant street packed with small B&B-style hotels, the Château de Pierre distinguishes itself in the details: polished banisters, pretty wallpaper, a chandelier in the reception area, and a small patio for summer lounging. The owners want you to take your time here, relax, and stay in bed late. All 15 rooms are nonsmoking, and most have bathtubs. The only drawback of this place is very steep staircases that you have to climb to get to most of the rooms.

*17 rue Ste-Geneviève.* ☎ **418-694-0429.** *Fax: 418-694-0153.* www.chateaude pierre.com. *Parking: C$15. Rack rates: C$135–C$155. AE, DC, MC, V.*

### Château Laurier
**$$–$$$$   Grande-Allée**

Facing the elegant Place George V, this recently renovated hotel keeps you in European-style comfort while putting you just a few minutes' walk from Vieux-Québec. The main reception area features a grand piano and sumptuous leather couches. Some rooms have working fireplaces, CD players, king beds, and Jacuzzis. Basic rooms are spacious and tastefully appointed. It's a family-owned establishment, but it feels like an upscale chain hotel. The hotel caters to tour groups, which yields a bustling atmosphere, but can also be a bit noisy. Ask for a room in the newer wing (they're bigger) and facing the park.

*1220 Place George V.* ☎ **800-463-4453** *or 418-522-8108. Fax: 418-524-8768.* www. hotelchateaulaurier.com. *Parking: Valet C$19. Rack rates: C$130–C$309 double and suite. AE, DC, DISC, MC, V.*

### Chez Hubert
**$   Haute-Ville**

This small B&B feels something like a nicely worn-in dollhouse, with its winding staircase and brightly painted, eclectic décor. It offers only three rooms, but each is large and handsomely renovated, with wood floors and lovely painted antique furniture. The three bathrooms are separate from the rooms. You'll find plenty of space for relaxing in the comfortable common living areas. Rooms have no TVs or telephones (both are available in the living room downstairs). Due to the presence of the family dog, no other animals are allowed. Call well ahead to reserve a room.

*66 rue Ste-Ursule.* ☎ *418-692-0958.* www.chezhubert.com. *Parking: Free. Rack rates: C$85. Rates include breakfast. No credit cards.*

### Couettes et Café Toast
**$    Avenue Cartier**

Located outside the walls of Vieux-Québec, this bed-and-breakfast is reputed as a linguistic guest home and encourages guests to immerse themselves in the French language and Québec culture. Breakfast, over a large, communal table, is a group affair and mostly in French. There's a reading room with lots of Francophone magazines and other media to flip through to round out your experience. The rooms are cozy and elegant. The neighborhood is a tucked-away commercial strip that has lots of charming boutiques and cafes — and it's really not that far away from the attractions in the historic district.

*1020 av. Cartier (near boulevard Rene-Levesque).* ☎ *8877-523-9365 or 418-523-9365. Fax: 418-523-6706.* www.toastandfrench.com. *Parking: Free. Rack rates: C$90–C$100. AE, MC, V.*

### Delta Québec
**$$–$$$    Boulevard Rene-Levesque**

This upscale, well-located hotel delivers comfortable rooms with all the trimmings — including a heated outdoor pool. Surprisingly easy to miss, it is actually connected to the Centre des Congrès, Québec City's convention center. The reception area is two floors up from the front entrance, and the maze of escalators and mezzanines is a little confusing, but you get the hang of it. Spacious, rustic-style rooms with pine furniture come with small desks equipped with ergonomic chairs and Internet connections. You're about a ten-minute walk from the Parliament Buildings and Vieux-Québec, making this a good choice for business or pleasure.

*690 bd. Rene-Levesque Est.* ☎ *888-884-7777 or 418-647-1717. Fax: 418-647-2146.* www.deltaquebec.com. *Parking: C$20. Rack rates: C$174–C$279 double and suite. AE, DC, DISC, MC, V. Wheelchair accessible.*

### Fairmont Le Château Frontenac
**$$$$    Haute-Ville**

A tourist attraction in itself, the 100-year-old Château Frontenac is definitely the place to stay if you want the full Vieux-Québec experience (and you pay for the privilege, of course). Perched on the *terrasse Dufferin,* it looks like a castle from the outside and feels like one on the inside — from the elaborate wood paneling of the reception area to the parking valets dressed in period costumes. The 618 rooms vary enormously, with everything from luxurious suites to standard, good-sized rooms that are actually a decent value for the money. Prices vary a lot depending on season and availability, and you get the best rates, by far, in package deals. There's plenty to keep kids amused, from the pool to kids' programs and a video arcade.

*1 rue des Carriéres.* ☎ ***800-828-7447*** *or 418-692-3861. Fax: 418-692-1751.* www. fairmont.com. *Parking: C$26, or valet C$32. Rack rates: C$549–C$749. Rates include breakfast. AE, DC, DISC, MC, V.*

### Gîte Côte de la Montagne
**$$   Basse-Ville**

Just three large rooms, one more like a loft, make up this bed-and-breakfast with spectacular views of the river and the Château Frontenac from a rooftop terrace. This intimate hideaway would be well suited for a romantic weekend. Best of all, you get to set the time when they serve breakfast. The nearly 300-year-old freestone building is halfway up the hill and backs onto the "Breakneck Stairs" for climbing up and down between the Haute- and Basse-Ville. The furnishings in the rooms are simple and rustic, but comfortable.

*54 côte de la Montagne (halfway up the hill).* ☎ ***888-794-4414*** *or 418-694-4414. Fax: 418-694-0889.* www.gitedelamontagne.com. *Parking: C$14. Rack rates: C$230–C$350. AE, MC, V.*

### Hilton International Québec
**$$–$$$   Boulevard Rene-Levesque**

In addition to all the comfort and pampering you expect from the name, Québec City's Hilton offers a simply amazing view of Vieux-Québec. In fact, you're probably better off staying here and looking at the stately Château Frontenac, than staying in the Frontenac itself. All the rooms are spacious and offer a view of the Old City. This Hilton is especially kid-friendly, with gifts, special kids' programs, and discount coupons for the hotel's restaurant — where, among other things, you can indulge in an all-you-can-eat lobster dinner. Added amenities include a health center with trainers, a heated outdoor pool open year-round, and high-speed Internet connections in every room. Plus, it's just a five-minute walk from the walls of Vieux-Québec and some 20 nearby gastronomic restaurants. Good rates are available off season.

*1100 bd. Rene-Levesque Est.* ☎ ***800-445-8667*** *or 514-647-2411. Fax: 418-647-6488.* www.hilton.com. *Parking: C$19, or valet C$21. Rack rates: C$109–C$425. AE, DC, DISC, MC, V. Some wheelchair-accessible rooms.*

### Hôtel Belley
**$–$$   Basse-Ville**

This is a fun and funky place to stay if you're looking for reasonably priced accommodations within walking distance of the art galleries and antiques stores along rue St-Paul. The Hôtel Belley has eight bright, if sparsely decorated, rooms, some with added touches such as exposed beams and brick walls and skylights. All rooms are nonsmoking. Bathrooms are extremely compact. Several rooms have extra pullout beds for kids, and one family-size room has a queen and two single beds. Light meals are available at all hours in the small tavern on the first floor of the hotel.

*249 rue St-Paul.* ☎ *888-692-1694 or 418-692-1694. Fax: 418-692-1696.* www.oricom. ca/belley. *Parking: Available nearby for C$8–C$11/day. Rack rates: C$100–C$140. AE, DC, MC, V.*

### Hôtel Clarendon
**$$–$$$ Haute-Ville**

This elegant, well-maintained Art Deco–style hotel is one of the oldest hotels in Vieux-Québec and has even maintained its original, wicket-style reception desk. Located in the heart of the Haute-Ville, it couldn't be better situated, and you'll definitely feel as though you've been transported back in time. Rooms are rather dark and claustrophobic, but bathrooms are modern. There's a lively pub, known for its jazz evenings, right off the reception area. The hotel's restaurant, Le Charles Baillargé, offers excellent French food. Facials, body scrubs, and massages are available on location.

*57 rue Ste-Anne.* ☎ *888-554-6001 or 418-692-4652. Fax: 418-692-4652.* www.hotel clarendon.com. *Parking: C$14 in public parking lot. Rack rates: C$169–C$279. AE, DC, DISC, MC, V.*

### Hôtel Dominion 1912
**$$–$$$ Basse-Ville**

Québec City's first skyscraper — a nine-story, 1912 structure — now houses an elegant, 60-room boutique hotel. Inside, the lobby's centerpiece is a black marble fireplace surrounded by plush, shabby-chic couches for guests to lounge on and sip complimentary coffee and hot chocolate. The décor throughout is decidedly modern, with a muted palette of black and grays. The high ceilings and large windows give many rooms on the upper floors spectacular views of the St. Lawrence River. The assured and competent staff are attentive and considerate and provide an elevated level of service. As is the case with boutique hotels, you can buy many of the items in the rooms.

*126 rue St-Pierre (near rue St-Paul).* ☎ *888-833-5253 or 418-692-2224. Fax: 418-692-4403.* www.hoteldominion.com. *Parking: C$16. Rack rates: C$205–C$305. AE, DC, MC, V. Rates include breakfast.*

### Hôtel du Vieux Québec
**$$–$$$ Haute-Ville**

Housed in a century-old brick manor, the Hôtel du Vieux Québec offers a cool, comfortable ambience, including spacious rooms and a cozy living room where you can rest after a busy day of sightseeing. This place is popular with families because many of the doubles have extra sofas. Kids stay for free in the winter, and significant rate reductions are available off season. The staff are friendly and helpful. The hotel is close to shopping, nightspots, and restaurants. Ask for one of the 24 recently renovated rooms.

*1190 rue St-Jean.* ☎ *800-361-7787 or 418-692-1850. Fax: 418-692-5637.* www. hvq.com. *Parking: C$13. Rack rates: C$134–C$244. AE, MC, V. Rates include complete breakfast.*

### Hôtel Le Saint-Paul
### $$   Basse-Ville

This 26-room hotel occupies a three-story, 19th-century town house in the Basse-Ville, along a street dotted with antiques shops and cafes. It may feel out of the way, but rue St-Paul, the hotel's namesake, is *the* place to be in this part of town. The rooms tend to be on the large side, with elegant Art Deco–inspired furnishings. The bathrooms are modern and some have large hot tubs. Throughout, the features of the old building add charm, but the amenities are completely up-to-date in the well-appointed rooms.

*229 rue St-Paul (near rue St-Vallier).* ☎ *877-778-8977 or 418-694-4414. Fax: 418-694-0889.* www.lesaintpaul.qc.ca. *Parking: C$12. Rack rates: C$189–C$309. AE, DC, MC, V. Rates include breakfast.*

### Hôtel Loew's Le Concorde
### $$$–$$$$   Grande-Allée

A large, upscale hotel, Loews is smack in the middle of the action on Grande-Allée and a ten-minute stroll through a lively neighborhood to the gates of Vieux-Québec. Rooms on the side of the hotel facing the Old City have a remarkable view. The lobby is a little worn, with threadbare furniture, but the rooms are spacious and classic feeling and include good-size bathrooms with marble counters. The hotel has a gym and a pool. A revolving restaurant at the top, L'Astral, serves excellent French food while offering a panoramic view of the city. Meanwhile, you're only an elevator ride away from cafes and restaurants galore down below on Grande-Allée. Special rates for kids.

*1225 place Montcalm.* ☎ *800-463-5256 or 418-647-2222. Fax: 418-647-4710.* www. loewshotels.com. *Parking: C$21 or valet C$23. Rack rates: C$159–C$299. AE, DC, DISC, MC, V.*

### Hôtel Royal William
### $$   St-Roch

Just a block away from the now bustling rue St-Joseph, the Royal William is in the up-and-coming district of St-Roch — somewhat removed from Old Québec and the concentration of the tourist attractions. However, when you discover this new commercial strip, you'll be glad your hotel is only a few steps away. The Royal William, named after the first steamship to cross the Atlantic Ocean, is a business-class hotel of 44 rooms with many amenities to satisfy this travel set.

*360 bd. Charest Est (between rues de la Courronne et Dorchester).* ☎ **888-541-0405** *or 418-521-4488. Fax: 418-521-6868.* www.royalwilliam.com. *Parking: Valet C$12. Rack rates: C$129–C$209. AE, MC, V.*

### Le Krieghoff B&B
**$   Avenue Cartier**

This clean and convenient B&B is perched above the boutiques, restaurants, and bars on lively avenue Cartier. The five rooms are surprisingly big and airy, although basic, and not all have bathrooms attached. A living area on the first floor has a microwave, a fridge for guests' use, telephone and TV, a big comfy couch, and a small balcony that looks over avenue Cartier. The only drawbacks include two flights of stairs to climb to the rooms and slightly indifferent service. Breakfast is served in the cafe downstairs, where decent food and coffee are served at reasonable prices all day.

*1091 av. Cartier.* ☎ **418-522-3711.** *Fax: 418-647-1429.* www.cafekrieghoff. qc.ca. *Parking: C$10. Rack rates: C$95–C$125. MC, V.*

### Le Priori
**$$   Basse-Ville**

Sleek and modern, this 26-room hotel, built inside an old building in the Basse-Ville, is a design buff's dream come true. It's reasonably priced and very conveniently located near the rue St-Paul strip of art galleries. Rooms are a little dark and on the small side, but the minimalist décor makes them seem spacious enough. All the comforts are there, including queen-size beds with down comforters. Suites have nice extras, including wood-burning fireplaces, kitchens, and Jacuzzis. The view is, unfortunately, restricted to neighboring rooftops.

*15 rue Sault-au-Matelot (corner rue St-Antoine).* ☎ **800-351-3992** *or 418-692-3992. Fax: 418-692-0883.* www.hotellepriori.com. *Parking: Public lot nearby for C$15. Rack rates: C$149–C$169. AE, DC, DISC, MC, V.*

### Maison Sainte-Ursule
**$   Haute-Ville**

This popular guesthouse has a distinct youth hostel feel to it, with its peeling wallpaper and slightly bohemian clientele, but it offers good accommodations at an excellent price in an even better location on a quiet street in Vieux-Québec. The second oldest house on the street, built in 1739, it boasts stone walls and a lovely, leafy sitting garden out back. Breakfast is not available in the hotel but is easy to find nearby. Several smoking rooms are available. Parking is not included but is available nearby.

*40 rue Ste-Ursule.* ☎ **418-694-9794.** *Fax: 418-694-0875.* www.quebecweb.com/ maisonste-ursule. *Rack rates: C$69–C$89. AE, DC, DISC, MC, V.*

## Manoir Victoria
$$–$$$$  **Haute-Ville**

The formal lobby of this small hotel, with its fireplaces, antique armchairs, and elegant dining room — done up in dark burgundy and blue — projects an old-world feel. The 145 rooms are classic in style, but modern and spacious, with two double beds. The hotel offers all the perks and services you'd expect in a larger hotel, including valet parking, an indoor pool, sauna and fitness center, Internet lounge, and even babysitting. This end of the Haute-Ville is convenient, with restaurants of all types for all budgets, and lots of shopping on nearby rue St-Jean. In the low season, it's popular among the corporate crowd.

*44 côte-du-Palais.* ☎ *418-692-1030. Fax: 418-692-5833.* www.manoir-victoria. com. *Parking: Valet C$18. Rack rates: C$159–C$279. AE, DC, DISC, MC, V.*

## Relais Charles-Alexandre
$$  **Grande-Allée**

A cool, peaceful, and meticulously kept inn close to the Plains of Abraham, this is one of the best deals along the Grand-Allée and a regular hangout for vacationing New Englanders — and it's just a ten-minute walk to the Old City. The 24 guest rooms are bright, spacious, and recently renovated, with polished wood floors and flowery, matching curtains and bedspreads. Rooms are equipped with small desks and TVs and have queen or twin beds; bathrooms have showers or baths. The staff are helpful and friendly.

*91 Grand-Allée Est.* ☎ *418-523-1220. Fax: 418-523-9556.* www.quebecweb.com/ rca. *Parking: C$9. Rack rates: C$124–C$134. AE, MC, V.*

# Chapter 18

# Dining and Snacking in Québec City

*F*rench, French, and more French. That's what you can expect to eat in the heart of historic New France — and, fortunately, Québec City has plenty of great French restaurants. But if you're not a fan of frogs' legs, don't worry: Québeckers are enthusiastic about all categories of culinary delights. You can find everything to satisfy your palate, from sushi to pizza and pasta.

You can find great places to eat all over the city, but in this chapter I give you the best choices in and around the Old City and Grande-Allée. I just figure that's where you'll probably be when you get hungry.

## Getting the Dish on the Local Scene

If you think locals avoid Québec City's touristy areas, think again. Many of the city's finest restaurants are in the Old City and on the Grande-Allée, and locals come here to indulge in a good meal.

### The Old City

Both the Upper and Lower cities are full of quaint and charming eating spots that serve some variation of French food, from cafe fare to bistro meals and formal dining. Most of these serve quite traditional cuisine — French onion soup; crepes; mussels and fries; steak frites; and lamb, pork, and fish dishes.

Prices at restaurants in the Old City aren't astronomically high, as you may have suspected, but you can save money by shopping around a little. Almost all restaurants in the Old City display menus in the window with prices. Check them out before you enter. Many offer a complete meal menu *(table d'hôte),* and they're usually a good deal. Many also offer a special lunch menu, and these are usually a *very* good deal.

### Grande-Allée

As you step outside the Porte St-Louis and head down Grande-Allée, the restaurants get a little more modern. In the summer, after just a five-minute walk outside the gate, you see a broad boulevard lined with rows of tables on each side. It looks like one huge terrace, but it's actually the combined effect of patios of dozens of different restaurants, crammed together for blocks.

You can find just about every type of food here, from fine French dining to traditional Québec cooking, plus Italian restaurants, burger joints, bagel and sandwich spots, sushi restaurants, pizzerias, and seafood and steak places. Stroll along and read the menus, which are usually displayed near the sidewalk. Or just cut to the chase and head to the places I recommend in this chapter.

## Québec City's Best Restaurants

In this section, you find my top choices for dining in Québec City.

The dollar-sign ratings represent the price of one dinner (appetizer, entree, and dessert), including drinks and tip, and correspond with the price ranges in Table 18-1.

| Table 18-1 | Key to Restaurant Dollar Signs |
|---|---|
| *Dollar Sign(s)* | *Price Range* |
| $ | Less than C$20 |
| $$ | C$20–C$39 |
| $$$ | C$40–C$59 |
| $$$$ | C$60 or above |

You can cut your dining costs in a variety of ways. I explain these techniques in Chapter 10, and a lot of them apply to Québec City as well.

In the heady tourist atmosphere of Québec City at high season, the best restaurants fill up quickly. Make your dinner reservations at least in the afternoon of the same day, and preferably the night before. In the off season (Oct–Apr) — when the tourist frenzy in Québec City cedes to an atmosphere of barely discernible activity in the streets — you can get a table in most establishments on the spot. And they'll be happy to see you.

## Québec City Dining and Snacking

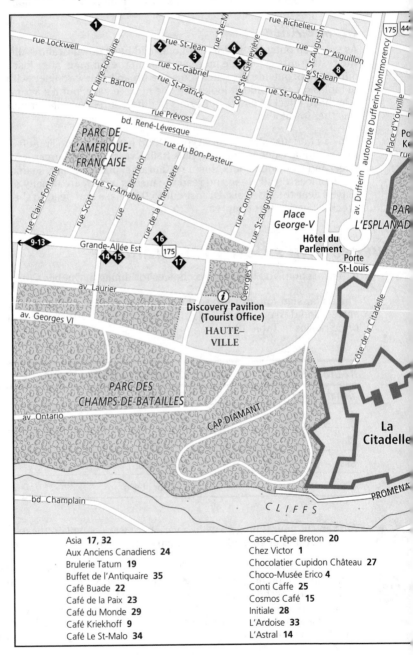

| | |
|---|---|
| Asia **17, 32** | Casse-Crêpe Breton **20** |
| Aux Anciens Canadiens **24** | Chez Victor **1** |
| Brulerie Tatum **19** | Chocolatier Cupidon Château **27** |
| Buffet de l'Antiquaire **35** | Choco-Musée Erico **4** |
| Café Buade **22** | Conti Caffe **25** |
| Café de la Paix **23** | Cosmos Café **15** |
| Café du Monde **29** | Initiale **28** |
| Café Kriekhoff **9** | L'Ardoise **33** |
| Café Le St-Malo **34** | L'Astral **14** |

### Asia
**$$–$$$    Grande-Allée    ASIAN**

This extremely popular restaurant is a great place to turn if you're getting tired of French food (not likely, but it happens). Asia offers a wide variety of dishes with Thai, Vietnamese, and Indochinese influences. Its specialty is grilled meats, but the restaurant also offers seafood plates, an excellent red curry chicken, and marinated shrimp and sautéed pork, plus Thai soup and pad thai. Asia has a second location in the Basse-Ville.

*585 Grande-Allée Est.* ☎ *418-522-0818. Basse-Ville location: 89 rue Sault-au-Matelot (☎ 418-692-3799). Reservations recommended. Table d'hôte: C$24–C$26. AE, MC, V. Open: Lunch Mon–Fri, dinner daily.*

### Aux Anciens Canadiens
**$$$    Haute-Ville    QUÉBEC**

This restaurant brings historic Québec all together. It's housed in the oldest private dwelling in the Haute-Ville, the Maison Jacquet, built in 1690. Aux Anciens Canadiens is named after one of its early owners' novels. It translates into Canadians of Old. The food is authentic Québec cuisine, from old standards like pork and beans, ham, *tourtière* (meat pie), caribou, and blueberry pie to more recently discovered delicacies, such as duck from the Eastern Townships (see Chapter 14). The servers are dressed in period costumes to complete the effect. If the price makes you hesitate, try it out at lunch, when the price of the *table d'hôte* is quite reasonable.

*34 rue St-Louis (corner of rue Haldimand).* ☎ *418-692-1627. Reservations recommended. Main courses: C$26–C$45. AE, DC, MC, V. Open: Lunch and dinner daily.*

### Buffet de l'Antiquaire
**$–$$    Basse-Ville    QUÉBEC**

Strolling by the antiques shops along rue St-Paul, you may not even notice this closet-sized restaurant at first. It's worth a stop, though. This is where locals go to eat hearty, authentic, and homemade Québec specialties such as *poutine* (fries with gravy and cheese curd) and *fèves au lard* (Québec's version of pork and beans: all lard, no meat). Meat dishes, such as *tourtière* and *pâté chinois,* or lighter meals, such as soup, sandwiches, and salads, are also on the menu. This place is definitely off the tourist track — yet right in the middle of the action — plus it's cheap.

*95 rue St-Paul (near rue Sault-au-Matelot).* ☎ *418-692-2661. Main courses: C$9–C$16. MC, V. Open: Lunch and dinner daily.*

### Café de la Paix
**$$$$    Haute-Ville    FRENCH**

It looks small and unpresuming from the street, but if you want high-quality, classic French cooking in a totally classic setting, this is the place. You'll find frogs' legs, as well as beef sirloin, chateaubriand, rabbit, scallops, steak tartare, lobster, duck, and (need I say it?) French onion soup.

The atmosphere is dark and cozy. Service is not genteel, but the career waiters — mostly surly older men — do know their stuff. You feel like you're in France.

*44 rue des Jardins (between Donnacona and rue St-Louis).* ☎ *418-692-1430. Reservations recommended. Main courses: C$15–C$50. AE, DC, DISC, MC, V. Open: Lunch Mon–Sat, dinner daily.*

### Café du Monde
**$$–$$$$    Basse-Ville    FRENCH BISTRO**

This legendary Québec City bistro recently moved from its small, Parisian-style digs on rue Dalhousie to a big, new, glamorous location in the *términal des croisières* (cruise liner terminal) facing the port. The two walls facing the river are made entirely of glass, so the river view is exceptional. And, I'm happy to say, the food is as good as ever. Famous for such brasserie fare as mussels, steak frites, sausage, and duck confit, Café du Monde also serves up sandwiches, salads, and seafood selections. Service is friendly, but waiters don't have time to linger at your table. Reservations are not taken for the terrace (with river views), so get there early if you want to eat outside.

*84 rue Dalhousie (near the cruise liner terminal on the Old Port).* ☎ *418-692-4455. Reservations required; not accepted for the terrace. Main courses: C$12–C$21. AE, DC, MC, V. Open: Lunch and dinner daily, brunch Sat–Sun.*

### Casse-Crêpe Breton
**$–$$    Haute-Ville    CRÊPES**

This little place on rue St-Jean is extremely popular — with both locals and tourists — and you almost always encounter a line at lunchtime. It's worth the short wait. The crepes are perfect and very filling, and you can have them as a main course, dessert, or both. A long list of potential main course fillings includes ham, cheese, mushrooms, asparagus, eggs, and more, and dessert options range from chocolate to fruit to plain sugar. You can watch them being prepared in the open kitchen. Service is friendly, but don't dawdle: Other people are waiting for your seat!

*1136 rue St-Jean (near rue Garneau).* ☎ *418-692-0438. Reservations not accepted. Main courses: C$5–C$9. MC, V. Open: Daily for breakfast, lunch, and dinner.*

### Conti Caffe
**$$–$$$    Haute-Ville    ITALIAN**

With its stone walls and fashionable modern décor, this new Italian bistro definitely stands out among the more traditional eateries on rue St-Louis. It's a great spot for lunch — you can have a three-course meal here with coffee for C$10. At night, the menu gets a little more sophisticated, with such additions as veal medallions, beef sirloin, and even escargot to the pasta and pizza selections. Pizza is of the thin-crust variety, with imaginative toppings.

*26 rue St-Louis (next to its owner, Le Continental Restaurant, which has the same address).* ☎ *418-692-4191. Main courses: C$17–C$34. AE, MC, V. Open: Lunch and dinner daily.*

### Initiale
**$$$$** **Basse-Ville** **FRENCH**

This is *the* place to go in Québec City for fine French cuisine in an elegant, rather formal setting. Located in a former bank building, its décor is classical and modern, with high ceilings and decorative moldings. Like most skilled, up-to-the-minute chefs these days, Yvan Lebrun focuses on local, seasonal ingredients. Plates range from French classics, such as grilled salmon, lamb, lobster, and filet mignon, to slightly more adventuresome dishes such as foie gras and pigeon. Give the Québec cheeses a try between your main course and dessert. Expect service to be attentive and none too quick. And the point here is savoring, not saving.

*54 rue St-Pierre (corner of Côte de la Montagne).* ☎ *418-694-1818. Reservations recommended. Main courses: C$40–C$45. AE, DC, MC, V. Open: Lunch Tues–Fri, dinner Tues–Sat daily.*

### L'Ardoise
**$$–$$$** **Basse-Ville** **FRENCH BISTRO**

The dishes served in French bistros are what the French consider comfort food. That's what you'll get at L'Ardoise, which caters equally to locals and tourists with its welcoming casual atmosphere and hearty dishes. Specialties include mussels and fries — with seconds of mussels for free — grilled blood sausage, veal liver, rib steak, and fish selections. Fish lovers with an appetite should try the Royale de la mer (Royal Sea) dish of salmon, shrimp, mussels, and scallops in a rich sauce. This is a nice place to hang out and sip an after-dinner espresso.

*71 rue St-Paul (near rue des Navigateurs).* ☎ *418-694-0213. Reservations recommended for dinner. Main courses: C$15–C$30. AE, DC, MC, V. Open: Lunch Mon–Sat, dinner daily, brunch Sun.*

### Largo
**$$$–$$$$** **St-Roch** **MEDITERRANEAN**

If Québec City on the whole feels somewhat sedate, this hidden-away restaurant and jazz bar brims with brio. Jazz ensembles Wednesday through Saturday and a Mediterranean menu make it a hopping destination for dinner among a smartly dressed, middle-aged clientele. Despite the hushed tones and refined textures of the dining room's décor, the din of conversation indicates that everyone is delighted to be a part of the urbane atmosphere. A crush of patrons mingle at the bar, often having to wait for a table. "In the zone," waiters ferry large plates with inventive presentations of favorites from Provence and beyond: bowls of bouillabaisse and dishes of lamb, veal, fish, and pasta.

*643 rue St-Joseph Est (between rues de la Chapelle and Du Pont).* ☎ *418-529-3111. Main courses: C$16–C$31. AE, DC, DISC, MC, V. Open: Lunch and dinner daily.*

## L'Astral
**$$$–$$$$**  **Grande-Allée**  **FRENCH**

With capacity for a thousand guests, this rotating restaurant on top of the Loew's hotel on the Grande-Allée is obviously not the place to come for intimacy. But the view is as good as it gets, stretching dozens of miles across the Plains of Abraham and the Old City all the way to the Laurentian Mountains. For such a huge place, the food is, surprisingly, very good — a mix of mainly French-based plates with Asian and Cajun touches. Prices are reasonable, and, if you calculate the view, the entire experience is pretty easy on your wallet. Sunday brunches here are quite lavish. Just make sure the weather is clear before you go.

*1225 cours du Général-de-Montcalm (corner Grande-Allée).* ☎ *418-647-2222. Reservations recommended. Main courses: C$21–C$45. AE, DC, DISC, MC, V. Open: Lunch Mon–Sat, dinner daily, brunch Sun.*

## Laurie Raphaël
**$$$$**  **Basse-Ville**  **CONTEMPORARY FRENCH**

Daniel Vézina is Québec City's premier chef and hosts one of the province's TV cooking shows. His restaurant is one of the city's *grand tables,* a category of restaurant meaning *the* best. A native of the Île d'Orleans, a fertile island of farming communities just downriver, his market cuisine reflects his intimate knowledge of the region's seasonal *terroir* ingredients. Jean-Pierre Viau, a renowned Montréal designer, was behind the sharp lines, muted tones, and rich materials of the establishment's C$1 million makeover, including a large "peek-a-boo" window looking right into the kitchen. You can also sign up for a cooking course or visit the boutique showcasing the work of local producers and artisans.

*117 rue Dalhousie (near rue St-André).* ☎ *418-692-4555. Reservations required. Main courses: C$32–C$45. AE, DC, MC, V. Open: Dinner Tues–Sat.*

## L'Echaudé
**$$–$$$**  **Basse-Ville**  **FRENCH BISTRO**

This is one of the slicker French bistros in the Basse-Ville, with its checker-tiled floor, zinc bar, and Art Deco décor. The food, however, is very good and reasonably priced. Specialties include grilled meats, bouillabaisse seafood stew, fish selections, steak and salmon tartare, steak frites, and ravioli. Drinkswise, L'Echaudé distinguishes itself by carrying 24 brands of beer and 125 different wines, including ten wines by the glass.

*73 rue du Sault-au-Matelot (near rue St-Paul).* ☎ *418-692-1299. Reservations recommended. Main courses: C$18–C$42. AE, MC, V. Open: Lunch Mon–Fri and Sun, dinner daily.*

### Le Continental
**$$$$   Haute-Ville   CONTINENTAL**

One of the oldest restaurants in Québec City, Le Continental has been a hangout for Québec's political class for the last five decades. Don't expect any great surprises, and you won't be disappointed — you get a classic menu with an atmosphere to match. Plates range from crab in hollandaise sauce to steak tartare and duck à l'orange. Waiters are attentive, courteous, and discreet — as they should be when they spend their days inadvertently listening in on gossip among Québec's political elite.

*26 rue St-Louis.* ☎ **418-694-9995.** *Reservations recommended. Main courses: C$24–C$37. AE, DC, MC, V. Open: Daily lunch and dinner.*

### Le Momento
**$$–$$$$   Grande-Allée   CONTEMPORARY ITALIAN**

This modern-feeling restaurant has a trattoria feel and offers sophisticated Italian cooking with an emphasis on fresh ingredients — definitely not one of those places serving huge portions of pasta with stick-to-your-ribs meat sauce. Instead, you choose from eight California-style thin-crust pizzas with such dressings as marinated chicken and sun-dried tomatoes; pasta selections with savory and interesting sauces; and heartier plates such as *osso buco* and lamb dishes.

*1144 av. Cartier (corner rue Aberdeen).* ☎ **418-647-1313.** *Reservations recommended for dinner. Main courses: C$15–C$30. AE, DC, MC, V. Open: Lunch Mon–Fri, dinner daily. Wheelchair accessible.*

### Le Paris-Brest
**$$$–$$$$   Grande-Allée   CONTEMPORARY FRENCH**

Considered one of the best tables in Québec City, this fashionable restaurant offers French food with modern flair. The menu includes fancy items such as Dijon rib of beef and milk veal with Brie cheese, but it also includes such high-brow French classics as lamb cutlets, scallops, steak tartare, and sweetbreads. Lighter selections include pasta dishes with seafood. Atmosphere is fairly informal, but neat.

*590 Grande-Allée Est (corner of rue de la Chevrotière).* ☎ **418-529-2243.** *Reservations recommended. Main courses: C$15–C$28. AE, DC, MC, V. Open: Lunch Mon–Fri, dinner daily.*

### Le Saint-Amour
**$$$$   Haute-Ville   CONTEMPORARY FRENCH**

Tucked in among the many B&Bs along rue Ste-Ursule, Le Saint-Amour offers a truly gastronomic experience. The décor is elegant and romantic, with lace curtains, flickering candles, and a glass roof for star-gazing lovers. Award-winning Chef Jean-Luc Boulay presents delicacies with a regional flavor, such as lobster from Québec's Gaspé area, caribou steak, and duck from the Eastern Townships (discussed in Chapter 14), and tops it off with such selections as foie gras, served with fig compote and caviar. Expect the meal to move slowly — the waiters assume you want to take your time. If you're in a hurry, let them know.

_48 rue Ste-Ursule._ ☎ **418-694-0667.** _Reservations recommended. Main courses: C$38–C$52. AE, MC, V. Open: Lunch Mon–Fri, dinner daily._

### Les Frères de la Côte
**$$–$$$   Haute-Ville   ITALIAN**

This lively pizzeria–cafe on rue St-Jean is a favorite of locals and a great place to bring kids. With 17 kinds of pizza — cooked in wood-burning ovens — plus pasta dishes and platters of meat and fish brochettes, you're sure to find something for even the pickiest pint-sized eater. The music is loud practically all the time, but the high spirits that reign here are infectious. Also open for Sunday brunch.

_1190 rue St-Jean._ ☎ **418-692-5445.** _Reservations recommended. Main courses: C$14–C$23. AE, DC, MC, V. Open: Lunch and dinner daily, brunch Sun._

### L'Utopie
**$$$$   St-Roch   FUSION**

When many guests leave here, their heads are slightly woozy thinking of superlatives to describe their experience. Smack in the middle of the rue St-Joseph renaissance, this is one of the destinations that's driving the action to this long overlooked and recently remodeled section of town. Monthly, the kitchen devises a special four-course menu around a particular ingredient, which appears in each dish. There's also another set menu of five-courses, each paired with a different glass of wine. All of the dishes are contemporary and ambitious, with a main course including selections of beef, duck, game, and several kinds of fish. Their wine list has several exclusive importations and an alarming number of choices by the glass.

_226½ rue St-Joseph (near rue Carron)._ ☎ **418-523-7878.** _Reservations recommended. Main courses: C$25–C$29. AE, MC, V. Open: Lunch Tues–Fri, dinner Tues–Sun._

### Poisson d'Avril
**$$–$$$   Basse-Ville   SEAFOOD**

One of the few seafood restaurants in Québec City, the décor is straight out of Cape Cod: nautical motifs, hanging model ships, and marine prints. The expansive menu includes starters of mussels, crab, and smoked salmon, escargot, oysters, and fish soup. Main courses include combo plates with scallops and seasonal fish. The restaurant also serves mussels and shrimp; straightforward salmon, cod, and tuna plates; southern

French bouillabaisse; and, of course, lobster. Prices are probably comparable to what you'd pay in Cape Cod, too: not cheap, but not outrageous.

*115 quai St-André (in the Old Port, near rue St-Thomas).* ☎ **418-692-1010.** *Reservations
recommended. Main courses: C$30–C$45. AE, DC, DISC, MC, V. Open: Dinner daily.*

### Sushi Taxi
**$$–$$$   Grande-Allée   SUSHI**

Québec City is not exactly a sushi town, but this small chain has garnered
a loyal following of locals for its good, reasonably priced offerings. The
avenue Cartier restaurant recently expanded to add some atmosphere to
the menu with 30 tables (30 more on the terrace in the summer) in a Zen-
like décor. If you're unfamiliar with the art of eating raw fish, Sushi Taxi
has a Discovery Plate with a bit of maki, nigiri, temaki, and sashimi.

*813 av. Cartier.* ☎ **418-529-0068.** *Table d'hôte: Lunch C$18, dinner C$25. AE, MC, V.
Open: Lunch Mon–Fri, dinner daily.*

### Voodoo Grill
**$$$–$$$$   Grande-Allée   ASIAN/FRENCH**

Quite a hot spot on Grande-Allée, this restaurant adds a bar atmosphere
to its lounge look, which results in a restaurant with a post-modern Middle
Eastern décor with African and designer influences. The menu is as vari-
ously inspired, with everything from Singapore chicken and Bangkok soup
to volcano steak, with plenty of grilled fish selections and some sushi
tossed in for good measure. Although the concept may sound a little un-
focused, the food is surprisingly good, well prepared, and beautifully pre-
sented. Just be ready for some entertainment of dubious quality and
mysterious origin, such as belly dancers, and count on loud music. Servers
were evidently hired more for looks than skill, but they do the job.

*575 Grande-Allée Est.* ☎ **418-647-2000.** *Reservations recommended. Main courses:
C$15–C$50. AE, DC, MC, V. Open: Lunch and dinner daily.*

### Yuzu Sushi
**$$$–$$$$   St-Roch   FUSION**

If you've grown tired of the traditional Japanese restaurant experience,
Yuzu is the place to refresh your palate. Modern, daring, and unusual, the
dishes on the menu are in the same vein as the dining room's décor. The
name refers to a Japanese citrus flavor — a widely used, secret ingredient
of sorts in a variety of Japanese sauces. Besides the standard sashimi (raw
fish), nigiri (raw fish on a rice ball), and maki (raw fish — or cooked shell-
fish — and rice rolled in seaweed or soy paper), sushi, the menu boasts a
section of Yuzu maki, original combinations devised by the chef. The main
courses are fusion and they combine ingredients from East and West.
Several other options exist as well: oyster shooters, dishes for sharing, or
a five- or seven-course "Discovery menu."

*438 rue de l'Église (near rue St-Joseph).* ☎ **418-521-7253.** *Reservations recom-
mended. Main courses: C$11–C$36. AE, DC, MC, V. Open: Lunch Mon–Fri, dinner daily.*

# Québec City's Best Snacks

As a tourist town, Québec City is loaded with eating opportunities of all types and qualities. You're more likely to feel anxiety over the abundance rather than the lack of eating options packed into this small area. The following sections list snacks and light food and should help you narrow the field when you want to grab a coffee, a sweet, or a bite to eat.

## Cafes for coffee and more

Cafes aren't just for coffee, although you can usually get an excellent cup of joe at the following recommended places. You can often get light meals at these cafes, too, including soups, salads, and sandwiches.

- **Brulerie Tatum,** 1084 rue St-Jean (☎ 418-692-3900), specializes in its own roasts of coffee and serves such tasty snacks as *croque monsieurs* (a toasted roll with ham, tomato, and cheese).

- **Café Buade,** 31 rue de Buade (☎ 418-692-3909), serves coffee and lighter meals, such as pizza and pasta, in a classic French cafe atmosphere.

- **Café Krieghoff,** 1091 av. Cartier (☎ 418-522-3711), serves light tasty meals including salads, quiche, and soup in a down-to-earth, French-style cafe. In summer, a covered terrace offers pleasant street views.

- **Café Le St-Malo,** 75 rue St-Paul (☎ 418-692-2004), with its charming sidewalk terrace and nautical décor, is a great place for a drink and a light bite.

- **La brûlerie de café de Québec,** 75 rue St-Jean (☎ 418-529-4769), promises a good cup of joe from the moment you step inside. Wafts of roasting coffee greet customers at the door.

- **Le Hobbit,** 700 rue St-Jean (☎ 418-647-2677), has a cafe on the first floor that serves coffee, while meals are served on the second floor.

- **Les Cafes du Soleil,** 143 rue St-Paul (☎ 418-692-1147), is another roaster, but in Basse-Ville. This tucked-away place will feel like a find. There's a light menu and a strong base of regulars dropping in and out.

- **Pub Java,** 1112 av. Cartier (☎ 418-522-5282), is a fun place for coffee or snacks, such as panini or burgers and fries.

## Pizza and burgers

Québec is even less of a burger town than Montréal, so I have only two good burger joints to recommend, but they really are great, despite being members of a rare species. If you're looking for a quick meal, you'll find more choices in the pizza category.

- **Chez Victor,** 143 rue St-Jean (☎ 418-529-7702), **tops in the city,** comes up with new and imaginative types of burgers every day.

- **Cosmos Café,** 575 Grande-Allée Est (☎ 418-640-0606), right in the thick of the Grande-Allée action, serves respectable burgers and very good breakfasts.

- **La Piazzetta,** 707 rue St-Jean (☎ 418-529-7489), a Québec chain, was one of the forerunners in the local trend toward European-style pizza. Pizzas have interesting toppings and very thin crusts.

- **Pain, Pizza & Dolce Vita,** 519 rue St-Jean (☎ 418-653-2741), has a wide variety of fresh-baked goods in the Italian tradition: pizza, panini, and foccacia to name but a few. Nothing too fancy — square slices, delicious foccacia, and panini on homemade bread.

- **Pizzédélic,** 1145 av. Cartier (☎ 418-525-5981), puts a psychedelic spin on the thin-pizza concept, offering one-serving pizzas with original toppings. Salads are great.

- **Pizza Mag,** 363 rue St-Paul (☎ 418-692-1910), offers 20 different types of more traditional, thick-crust pizza, some with unusual toppings such as leek, escargots, and smoked fish.

- **La Pointe des Amériques,** 964 rue St-Jean (☎ 418-694-1199), serves gourmet pizza, with all the combinations of toppings you can imagine.

## For chocolate lovers

If you have a hankering for something tastier than the convenience-store quality of your favorite brown substance, you have two excellent places to go for chocolate in the Old City. You can find French, Belgian, and Swiss varieties at **Chocolatier Cupidon Château,** 1 rue des Carrières, behind the Château Frontenac (☎ 418-692-3340). At **Choco-Musée Erico,** 634 rue St-Jean (☎ 418-524-2122), high-quality chocolate comes in some very interesting forms.

## All crêpes, all the time

It's hard to imagine visiting Québec City without eating crepes at least once. They're a great option for lunch, because they're cheap and relatively quick. And no worries — you can really fill up on them, especially if you order them for your main course and dessert. I give you my top choices in this section, but honestly, crepes are pretty hard to screw up (unless you order them in a place that doesn't specialize in them). They're just stuffed pancakes, after all.

My first choice is the **Casse-Crêpe Breton,** 1136 rue St-Jean (☎ 418-692-0438), for both its bustling atmosphere and delicious fresh dishes. In the shadows of the Château Frontenac sits **Le Petit Château,** 5 rue St-Louis (☎ 418-694-1616), yet another good bet with a wide selection of sweet and savory crepes.

## *A vegetarian outpost*

Vegetarians are not exactly in the Promised Land in this town of blood sausage and veal scallops. Really, only one restaurant in the Old City caters exclusively to vegetarians. **Le Commensal,** 860 rue St-Jean (☎ **418-647-3733**), serves excellent buffet-style vegetarian food that is sold by weight. Otherwise, much to the dismay of hardcore foodies, such as Anthony Bourdain, and French-trained chefs, more and more restaurants are catering to their vegetarian clientele. Vegetarian visitors in Québec City would be hard pressed to find a restaurant without one or two satisfying veggie items.

# Chapter 19

# Exploring Québec City

∙∙∙∙∙∙∙∙∙∙∙∙∙∙∙∙∙∙∙∙∙∙∙∙∙∙∙∙∙∙∙∙∙∙∙∙∙∙∙∙∙∙∙∙∙∙

## In This Chapter
▶ Exploring Québec City's best attractions
▶ Seeing the city by guided tour
▶ Discovering Québec City's historical highlights

∙∙∙∙∙∙∙∙∙∙∙∙∙∙∙∙∙∙∙∙∙∙∙∙∙∙∙∙∙∙∙∙∙∙∙∙∙∙∙∙∙∙∙∙∙∙

*Q*uébec City's most interesting attractions are conveniently packed together in an area that you could probably cross by foot in half an hour if you walked straight without stopping. Of course, you have many, many reasons to stop, so you're likely to linger a bit longer than 30 minutes. Half a day will give you a good overall impression, but several days still won't be enough to see absolutely everything. In this chapter, you find the top sights you want to try to hit.

## Exploring Québec City's Top Sights from A to Z

There's plenty to do in Québec City. The past comes alive here because many of the attractions recount the history of this fortified city — the only one in North America.

### Basilique Notre-Dame de Québec (Notre-Dame de Québec Basilica)
**Haute-Ville**

The site of the oldest Christian parish north of Mexico, Québec City's founder Samuel de Champlain originally chose this spot for a chapel back in 1633. Over the centuries, the Basilique Notre-Dame was built, torn down, burned, and expanded into roughly its present, neo-baroque style in the 1920s. The light inside is quite inspiring, combining the effects of candlelight and two floors of stained-glass windows depicting scenes of evangelists, arch angels, saints, and the Virgin Mary. Opinions are mixed about *Feux Sacrés (Sacred Fire)*, a 30-minute light and sound show on five centuries of Québec history that plays outside the basilica during the summer. Some say it's impressive; others say it's tacky. You be the judge.

*16 rue Buade (corner Côte de la Fabrique).* ☎ *418-692-2533. Admission: Free; guided tours C$1. Open: Daily 8:30 a.m.–4 p.m. Guided tours: Daily May–Nov, Sat during winter season, or by reservation.*

### Chapelle/Musée des Ursulines (Ursuline Convent and Museum)
Haute-Ville

The French nun Marie de l'Incarnation founded the Ursulines order in Québec when she arrived in 1630; the convent was built in 1642. The chapel came much later, in 1902, but much of what you see in the interior dates to 1732. The museum and chapel interior are packed with artifacts, including Louis XIII furniture, a painting that was removed from Paris during the French Revolution, and altar cloths and church robes that the Ursuline nuns wove with gold thread. General Montcalm, who led the French troops when they lost Québec to the English in 1759, was originally buried here.

*12 rue Donnacona (corner rue des Jardins).* ☎ *418-694-0694. Admission: Chapel free; museum adults C$5, seniors C$4, students and children 12–16 C$3.50, children under 12 free. Open: May–Sept, Tues–Sat 10 a.m. to noon and 1–5 p.m., Sun 1–5 p.m.; Oct–Apr Tues–Sun 1–4:30 p.m.*

### Château Frontenac
Haute-Ville

If one piece of architecture symbolizes Québec City, this is it. In Chapter 17, I recommend that you stay at this castlelike hotel, but in case you can't afford to actually spend the night, take a few minutes to wander inside. You really can't miss it. Just look for the pointy, green copper roof rising above the cliff overlooking the St. Lawrence River. The chateau was built by the Canadian Pacific Railway in the early 1890s, and although it was inspired by the chateaux of the Loire Valley in France, it was designed by an American architect, Bruce Price. The inside is truly regal, with wood paneling, imposing antiques, and dainty boutiques surrounding the reception area. Guided 50-minute tours are given from May to October.

*1 rue des Carrières (facing the terrasse Dufferin).* ☎ *418-691-2166.* www.tours chateau.ca. *Admission: Free for a peek; tours adults C$8.50, seniors C$7.75, children 6–16 C$6, children 5 and under free. Open: Tours May to mid-Oct daily, on the hour 10 a.m.–6 p.m. Mid-Oct to Apr Sat and Sun hourly, noon–5 p.m.*

### La Citadelle
Grande-Allée

Much of Québec City's history is dominated by the battles various empires waged to get control of this prime trading port on the St. Lawrence River. La Citadelle gives you a taste of the stormy military past — even though it was never actually used during a war. Still, you get an idea of the stakes of a possible enemy attack when you visit this star-shaped fortress comprising 25 separate buildings. First built by the French in the late 1700s, then rebuilt by the English in the 1830s, La Citadelle now houses a French Canadian regiment of the Canadian army. Notable features include a powder house and a prison. The guided tour is a little dry and perhaps better suited to military-history buffs, but the changing of the guards, usually once a day, is pretty cool.

## Québec City Attractions

Assemblée nationale du Québec **5**
Basilique Nôtre-Dame-de-Québec **10**
Chapelle/Musée des Ursulines **9**
Château Frontenac **13**
Ferry Ride **14**
Fortifications de Québec **6**
La Citadelle **7**

Marché du Vieux-Port **19**
Musée de l'Amérique Française **11**
Musée de la Civilisation **16**
Musée du Fort **12**
Musée national des beaux-arts du Québec **1**
Musée Naval de Québec **18**

Observatoire de la capitale **3**
Parc Aquarium du Québec **2**
Place de l'Artillerie **8**
Parc des Champs-de-Bataille **4**
Place-Royale **15**
Promenade de la Pointe à Carcy **17**

*1 côte de la Citadelle (enter off rue St-Louis, leaving the St-Louis Gate in the direction of Grande-Allée).* ☎ *418-694-2815.* www.lacitadelle.qc.ca. *Admission: Families C$22, adults C$10, seniors C$9, children 7–17 C$5.50, free for persons with disabilities and children 6 and under. Open: July–Labour Day daily 9 a.m.–6 p.m.; off-season hours vary. Guided tours leave on the hour.*

## Marché du Vieux-Port
**Basse-Ville**

See what's *terroir* — locally grown or raised fruits, vegetables, meats, poultry, and dairy products. Québec farmers are very proud of what comes from their land. Built on the original site of Québec City's first marketplace, the farmers from the particularly fertile surrounding regions, such as L'Île d'Orléans, still come here to sell their wares. Québeckers are quite proud of their fruits, vegetables, meats, and poultry products. It's much more interesting than going to a grocery store: you can haggle over prices and speak with the folks in their stalls behind the mounds of produce. There's always one or two places handing out samples, so it's fun to poke around for those.

*160 Quai St-André.* ☎ *418-692-2517.* www.marchevieuxport.com. *Admission: Free. Open: May–Dec daily 9 a.m.–5 p.m. Jan–Apr Thurs–Sun 9:30 a.m.–5 p.m.*

## Musée de la Civilisation (Museum of Civilization)
**Basse-Ville**

If you have time for only one major museum outing, this is the place. It won't teach you the most about the specific history of Québec City, but the permanent exhibits on daily life in the history of the province of Québec (called *Memoires,* or Memories) and on Canada's First Nations (called *Nous, les Premiéres Nations*) are captivating. Though light on written explanations, the exhibits have objects displayed beautifully and sensibly. They draw in visitors and satisfy all their senses (except maybe smell), while doing a good job of illustrating two distinct cultures. Plan on spending about two hours here. An added bonus: On the second floor, there's a lovely, bright, and modern visitors' lounge with computers where you can check your e-mail for free.

*85 rue Dalhousie (corner rue St-Antoine).* ☎ *418-643-2158.* www.mcq.org/en/mcq. *Admission: Adults C$10, seniors C$9, students 17 and over C$7, children 12–17 C$4, free for children 11 and under. Open: Late June–Labour Day daily 9:30 a.m.–6:30 p.m.; Sept–June Tues–Sun 10 a.m.–5 p.m.*

## Musée de l'Amérique Française (Museum of French America)
**Haute-Ville**

Housed in a former seminary built in 1663, this museum is an excellent place to get a French perspective on history. The museum is dedicated to showing the evolution of French culture and civilization in North America through the history of all seven French communities in the New World. The five floors of the museum contain 450,000 artifacts in all — everything from silverware and scientific instruments to paintings, engravings, parchments, old and rare books, and even the first Egyptian mummy to be brought to North America. Descriptions are in both English and French.

*2 côte de la Fabrique.* ☎ *418-692-2843.* www.mcq.org/en/maf. *Admission: Adults C$6, seniors C$5, students 17 and over C$3.50, children 12–16 C$2, free for children 11 and under. Open: Late June–Labour Day daily 9:30 a.m.–5 p.m.; Sept to mid-June, daily 10 a.m.–5 p.m. Guided tours available; call for information.*

## Musée National des Beaux-Arts du Québec (Québec National Museum of Fine Art)
### Grande-Allée

Not too far from the Parc des Champs-de-Bataille, this museum houses the largest collection of Québec art in North America, including over 23,000 pieces dating from the 18th century to the present. Eight galleries are spread over three buildings. The Great Hall has a reception area and attached auditorium. The Gérard Morrisset Pavilion houses permanent exhibits, including works from the early colonial period, African masks and carvings, and musical instruments. The Baillargé Pavilion, a former prison built in 1867, holds temporary exhibits.

*1 av. Wolfe-Montcalm (near Place George V).* ☎ *418-643-2150.* www.mnba.qc.ca. *Admission: Permanent collection free; special exhibitions adults C$15, seniors C$12, students C$7, children 12–16 C$4 (US$3.50), children 11 and under free. Open: June–Labour Day daily 10 a.m.–6 p.m., Wed till 9 p.m.; Sept–May Tues–Sun 10 a.m.–5 p.m., Wed till 9 p.m.*

## Parc des Champs-de-Bataille (The Battlefields Park)
### Grande-Allée

If the Château Frontenac stands as a symbol of Québec City, this park is the symbol of tension between Canada's English and French populations. Québec's Battlefield Park is where General Montcalm led the French against General Wolfe and the English in the famous battle of the Plains of Abraham in 1759 (the English won; both generals died). Although it's famous for a battle, the 108-hectare (267-acre) park is actually a rather idyllic place to stroll (with some 5,000 trees), not too far from the Grande-Allée. Locals like to cross-country ski here in the winter and inline skate and bike in the summer. Summer also brings theater and musical performances. The park's **Maison de la Découverte (Discovery Pavilion)** explains the significance of the Plains of Abraham to Québec.

*Discovery Pavilion, 835 av. Laurier.* ☎ *418-648-4071.* www.ccbn-nbc.gc.ca. *Admission: Free. Open: Park 24 hours; Discovery Pavilion May–Sept daily 10 a.m.–5:30 p.m., Oct–May Tues–Sun 10 a.m.–5 p.m.*

## Place-Royale
### Basse-Ville

This quaint cobblestone square, located on the spot where Champlain founded Québec in 1608, feels like a microcosm of Vieux-Québec. Right at the bottom of the Breakneck stairs, Place-Royale is dominated by the Notre-Dame-des-Victoires church, the oldest church in Canada; built in 1688, it's small and rather plain but contains some lovely paintings and a large model boat suspended from the ceiling. This was a town marketplace during the 17th and 18th centuries. Now you can see a bust of French King Louis XIV, a copy of the original bust erected in 1686. All the buildings around the square have been restored, and you can souvenir shop to your heart's content in this part of the Basse-Ville. The **Centre d'Interpretation de Place-Royale (Interpretation Center)** explains the history of the square.

*Centre d'Interpretation de Place-Royale, 27 rue Notre-Dame (walk down the Breakneck stairs and take côte de la Montagne to rue Notre-Dame).* ☎ *866-710-8031 or 418-646-3167.* www.mcq.org/en/cipr. *Admission: Adults C$5, seniors C$4.50, students 17 and over C$3.50, children 12–16 C$2, children 11 and under free. Open: Sept–June daily 9:30 a.m.–5 p.m.; Late June–Sept Tues–Sat 10 a.m.–5 p.m.*

# Finding More Cool Things to See and Do

In this section, you find suggestions for following a specific interest, whether you want to keep the kids entertained; get your fill of wars, battles, and armory; make your teenagers happy; stroll some lovely streets; or take a tour.

## Kid-pleasing places

Kids are sure to be enchanted by Québec City, whether it's the fairy-tale-castle effect of the Château Frontenac or the real (but not in use!) cannons and armory scattered around the city. The best museum for kids is the **Musée de la Civilisation,** which has great exhibits plus loads of room to run around. Following are a few other suggestions for entertaining children.

### Ferry Ride
**Old Port**

Not very expensive, but usually a thrill for the little ones, you can cross the river from Québec City over to Lévis in about ten minutes. The view of Québec City from the river is quite spectacular, especially at night. There's not much to do in Lévis, but take a stroll around anyway. The ferry leaves close to Place-Royale. Buy tickets at the Société des Traversiers du Québec building, right on the port.

*Société des Traversiers du Québec, 10 rue des Traversiers.* ☎ *418-644-3704.* www.traversiers.gouv.qc.ca. *Tickets: Adults C$2.65, seniors C$2.40, children 5–11 C$1.85, children 4 and under free. Departures three or four times per hour.*

### Observatoire de la Capitale (Observation Deck)
**Grande Allée**

Kids go dizzy with vertigo on this observation deck, which is Québec City's highest point. By modern-day, skyscraper standards this government building is an unimpressive 31 floors, but the views of this historic city and the St. Lawrence River are really worthwhile. The otherwise large-looming Château Frontenac doesn't seem that big from here. It's the river that's so impressive.

*1037 rue de la Chevrotière.* ☎ *888-497-4322 or 418-644-9841.* www.observatoire capitale.org. *Admission: Adults C$5, seniors and students C$4 seniors and students, free for children 12 and under. Open: Mid-June to mid-Oct daily 10 a.m.–5 p.m.; mid-Oct to mid-June Tues–Sat 10 a.m.–5 p.m.*

### Parc Aquarium du Québec (Québec Aquarium)
**Ste. Foy**

All kids leave this place wanting to be marine biologists, which is probably a good thing. Various-windowed tanks and glassed tunnels lead visitors through several underwater ecosystems. Polar bears, penguins, and seals cavort as a scuba diver in the deep-sea tank show visitors, up close, some examples of the over 650 different species.

*1675 av. des Hôtels (15 minutes from Vieux-Québec; bus 13).* ☎ *418-659-5264.* www.sepaq.com/paq/en. *Admission: Adults C$16, seniors C$15, students 13–17 C$13, children 6–12 C$11, children 3–5 C$5.50, children 2 and under free. Open: Daily 10 a.m.–5 p.m.; Oct–Apr until 4 p.m.*

### Parc de la Chute-Montmorency
**Outside Québec City**

A labyrinth of paths and wooden staircases leads to a suspended bridge for daredevils to cross the frothy mouth of this 272-foot waterfall — significantly higher than Niagara Falls. Summer or winter it's a dramatic outdoor adventure. At the top are spectacular views of the river and surrounding area. The Manoir Montmorency, an enormous English country house with a well-regarded kitchen, serves regional cuisine with local, or *terroir,* ingredients. It's a touch of civilization in an otherwise rugged place. Those who don't feel like making the climb can take a cable car to the top.

*2490 av. Royale.* ☎ *800-665-6527 or 418-663-3330.* www.sepaq.com/ct/pcm/en. *Admission: Round-trip on the cable car adults C$8.25, children 6–16 C$4, children 5 and under free. Parking: C$9. Open: Hours vary seasonally.*

### Terrasse Dufferin
**Haute-Ville**

Head straight to this square looking out onto the St. Lawrence River for a kind of one-stop children's entertainment package. Within a short walking distance (even shorter running distance), you have **coin-operated telescopes** for a look across the river. In the summer, **street entertainers** abound, from living "statues" to mimes to musicians playing wine glasses. If you want to burn off some serious steam, try tackling the Breakneck stairs, leading down to the Basse-Ville. For a real thrill, take the kids to nearby Place d'Armes and pick up a **horse-drawn carriage ride** (C$80 for a 35-minute ride).

## For military and history buffs

Kids aren't the only ones fascinated by epic battles. If you like stories about warfare, this section gives you few places to find them.

### Assemblée Nationale du Québec (Québec Legislature)
**Grande Allée**

Heckle the politicians from the gallery in Québec's legislature. Just kidding — don't. Instead, watch democracy in action and brush up on your knowledge of parliamentary procedure. Most of the law-making is done in French so it can be rather opaque, but not understanding somehow adds to the spectacle. You can take a free guided tour in English of this imposing 18th-century building inspired by the Louvre in Paris, or eat breakfast or lunch in the restaurant among Québec's political elite. Access can vary depending on the official events of the day.

*45 rue des Parlementaires (just outside the walls of the Haute-Ville).* ☎ *418-643-7239.* www.assnat.qc.ca. *Admission: Free. Open: Year-round Mon–Fri 9 a.m.–4:30 p.m.; June–Sept Sat–Sun 10 a.m.–4:30 p.m.*

### Fortifications-de-Québec (Fortifications of Québec)
**Haute-Ville**

If the wall around Québec City — built to protect the city from marauding invaders — is still standing, it's because it was restored and remains a protected site. You can walk the complete 3-mile circuit starting at the kiosk of terrasse Dufferin, or take a 90-minute tour and discover the wall's history.

*Tour tickets available at kiosk at terrasse Dufferin.* ☎ *418-648-7016.* www.pc.gc.ca/fortifications. *Tour: Adults C$10, seniors C$7.50, children 6–16 C$5, children 5 and under free. Open: May–Sept daily 10 a.m.–5 p.m. Oct–Apr open upon reservation.*

### Musée du Fort
**Haute-Ville**

For explanations of sieges and battles fought in Québec City, this small museum just off Place d'Armes is hard to beat. Battles are retold using sound and light, in both English and French.

*10 rue Ste-Anne.* ☎ *418-692-1275.* www.museedufort.com. *Admission: Adults C$7.50, seniors C$6, students C$5. Open: Apr–Oct daily 10 a.m.–5 p.m.; Oct–Apr Thurs–Sun 11 a.m.–4 p.m.*

### Musée Naval de Québec (Naval Museum of Québec)
**Basse-Ville**

The flow of the mighty St. Lawrence River is a constant reminder of Québec's naval history — both military and merchant. Did you know that there were German U-boats in the St. Lawrence River during World War II?

This new museum's unique collection of over 1,000 objects reveals the different boating eras over the last century, but it focuses on the Battle of the St. Lawrence during WWII. It features several recovered items from torpedoed boats that sank nearby. The museum looks at the historical, social, and even environmental consequences that were at stake.

*170 rue Dalhousie (near Promenade de la Pointe-à-Carcy).* ☎ **418-694-5387.** www. mnq-nmq.org. *Admission: Free. Open: May–Sept daily 10 a.m.–5:30 p.m.; Oct–Apr Tues–Sun 1–4 p.m.*

### Parc de l'Artillerie (Artillery Park)
**Haute-Ville**

Near the Porte St-Jean, this enormous military installation was the French military headquarters starting in 1747. Later, it housed the British garrison, and then became a munitions factory, which was in use until 1964. Now it serves as an interpretive center. Don't miss the scale model of Québec City, showing what the city looked like in the 1800s.

*2 rue d'Auteuil (near St-Jean Gate).* ☎ **418-648-4205.** *Admission: Adults C$4, seniors C$3.50, children 6–16 C$2, children 5 and under free. Open: May–Sept daily 10 a.m.– 5 p.m.; Oct–Apr open upon reservation.*

## Teen-tempting areas

Québec City is a popular destination for school trips, especially for the early teen demographic. If you happen to find yourself accompanied by members of that select group, this section tells you where you can take them.

### Rue St-Jean

This street has shops galore. The busy commercial street on the north end of the Haute-Ville has souvenir boutiques, clothes stores, inexpensive cafes, bookstores and CD shops, and plenty of action to keep your teenagers engrossed for hours.

### Place-Royale

Perhaps your teenagers aren't that interested in the history of early French colonialism. Not a problem. This little area has plenty of distractions for them, including cute boutiques and even cuter cafes. They'll go nuts. Just make sure each kid has a map.

## The best strolling streets

There's really no such thing as just "strolling around" Québec City. Vieux-Québec is so packed with things to see and do, you're sure to get sidetracked. But whether you have some specific purchases in mind or you just want to stretch your legs, the walking suggestions in this section should do the trick.

### Le Petit Champlain
**Basse-Ville**

This narrow pedestrian alley tucked into the base of the cliffs right below the Château Frontenac gets A's for atmosphere. One of the oldest streets in Québec City, opened in 1685, Le Petit Champlain originally housed artists, and then became the home of poor Irish immigrants in the 1800s. These days, it's packed with quaint, mostly high-quality souvenir shops, cafes, and restaurants. It's a good place to pick up items such as jewelry made by Québec designers, unique toys, clothing, and French kitchen implements. Take the Breakneck stairs, and then keep following côte de la Montagne down the hill. You hit another set of stairs, and Le Petit Champlain starts at the bottom of them.

### Promenade de la Pointe à Carcy
**Old Port**

The cruise-ship business in Québec City's port has really taken off over the last decade, and the port area has benefited from the increased activity. Unlike in Montréal, though, no commercial street runs along Québec City's port (rue Dalhousie is the closest one). Instead, city authorities have transformed this area into a kind of urban park, with a bike trail, fountains, and scrupulous security guards who make sure tourists don't get too close to the edge. It's a great place to park on a bench and read or just wander around gazing at the river traffic.

### Rue du Trésor
**Haute-Ville**

This little street runs between rue St-Louis and rue de Buade and is a veritable outdoor art market, with artists lined up the whole length of the street selling paintings, sketches, and engravings of various styles and qualities. More for shopping than walking, it's still worth checking out, just for the atmosphere. Head here if you want your caricature drawn.

### Rue St-Joseph
**St-Roch**

This is by far the most happening part of Québec City, and, unlike the rest, this strip is only a few years old. It already features several destination boutiques, some of the city's hottest restaurants, and a handful of nightlife options. The street was always there, but recently became the target of an urban renewal scheme. It feels trendy but not touristy, which could be a welcomed relief after a day of seeing the sights.

### Rue St-Paul
**Basse-Ville**

Slightly off the beaten track — off the beaten *tourist* track, anyway — this street running parallel to the Bassin Louise has an authentic port feel to it. It's also packed with antiques shops, has a number of good art galleries, and boasts quiet little eateries where you can have a leisurely drink or coffee.

Take côte du Palais (just off rue St-Jean) and walk down past the city wall and down rue des Vaisseaux-du-Roi and you'll hit rue St-Paul. Turn right.

## Seeing Québec City by guided tour

If you're short on time, a guided tour is a good option for seeing a lot of Québec City with minimum effort. Walking is my first choice and should be yours (as long as you're able), but you can also get around by bus tours, horse-drawn carriages, or even river cruises. This section gives you my recommendations.

### Walking tours

Walking is the best way to see the many nooks and crannies of Québec City. With a walking tour, you get history, hear insider info, and have areas of interest pointed out to you that you probably wouldn't normally notice on your own. Most walking tours leave from the terrasse Dufferin. The best idea is to see what's being offered at the nearby **Centre Infotouriste** at 12 rue Ste-Anne, just opposite the Château Frontenac at Place d'Armes (☎ 877-266-5687). Or call the **Association des Guides Touristiques de Québec** (☎ 418-683-2140), which provides guides for any length of time, on foot, or in your car or theirs.

Two other good tour companies are:

✔ **La Compagnie des Six Associés** (☎ 418-692-3033) also offers thematic tours. "Vice and Drunkenness," explaining the underbelly of the history of Québec, is a popular one. Book your tour at the main tourist office opposite Place d'Armes. Tours cost C$16 per person.

✔ A new initiative, **Québec Trail,** is a series of over 40 stops on an audio tour. For around C$15 travelers can buy a set of headphones at tourist offices as well as some stores, hotels, and restaurants around town. They come with a special adapter that allows you to plug in to the recording at each stop. It gives you the ultimate flexibility in seeing the sites — you can pick up on another day or just at random whenever you happen upon a listening post. Best of all, you get to keep the earphones when you're done.

### Bus tours

If you're not up to walking, or if it's extremely hot (or cold) and you want to escape the elements (while not missing the sights), bus tours are a good solution. Two good companies offer tours year-round:

✔ **Les Tours du Vieux-Québec** (☎ 800-267-8687 or 418-664-0460; www.oldquebectours.com) offers guided tours in small comfortable buses, both inside the city and in surrounding areas like Île d'Orléans. Québec City tours last about two hours and cost C$30 per person.

✔ **Les Tours Dupont** (☎ 888-558-7668 or 418-694-9226; www.tourdupont.com) offers more-luxurious tours in bigger buses, both of the city and the surrounding area. Tours last about two hours and cost C$30 per person.

### Horse-drawn carriage tours

Get a tour of Québec City the old-fashioned way and experience not only the sights and sounds but also the smells of yesteryear. You can visit Vieux-Québec by *calèche* all year round. Rides cost C$80 for 40 minutes. You can pick one up on the fly at **Place d'Armes** or call **Calèches du Vieux-Québec** (☎ 418-683-9222) or **Les Calèches de la Nouvelle France** (☎ 418-684-0068).

### River cruises

You won't get the most out of seeing Québec City by boat, but, if you like cruises, try **Croisières AML** (☎ 800-563-4643 or 418-692-1159), which offers 90-minute cruises aboard a renovated 1930s ferry, departing three times daily from Quai Chouinard, 10 rue Dalhousie, near Place-Royale in the Lower Town. The show comes with bilingual guides, and full dining facilities and a bar are right on the boat. Evening cruises last two and a half hours, with dining and dancing included. Prices for day cruises start at C$32 for adults, C$30 for seniors, and C$18 for kids, and go up in the evening. You can buy tickets at the kiosk on terrasse Dufferin.

# Hitting the Historical Highlights of Vieux-Québec

Québec City *is* history. Step through any gate leading in to the Old City, and you see that for yourself. The walking tour in this section stops at some of the top historical sites and shows you some other nice things to see (and eat) along the way. You can wander along the itinerary at your own leisure or do the entire thing backward, if you like. Some sights are bound to interest you more than others, so pick and choose as you go along.

Start by entering Vieux-Québec at the **Porte St-Louis,** which you reach either by walking along the Grande-Allée or by turning left onto rue St-Louis from avenue Honoré-Mercier. The gate was designed to bring to mind medieval castles and horsemen, but it's actually Victorian — the work of an Irish architect that was completed in 1878.

A few steps inside the gate, on your left, is the **Fortifications of Québec National Historical Site,** where you can learn about the history of the wall that surrounds the Old City. The wall, originally wooden, was first erected by the French in 1693. The same French started working on the stone wall in 1745, but they had to hand the job over to the English when the Brits conquered the city in 1759.

Continue along rue St-Louis until your reach rue du Parloir, turn left, and you'll see the **museum and the monastery of the Ursulines,** the first order of French nuns to set up shop in Québec, around 1630.

At the end of rue du Parloir, turn right on rue Donnacona, and then left on rue des Jardins. Follow this street to rue Ste-Anne. On your left, you'll

## Historical Highlights of Vieux-Québec

1 Fortifications of Quebec National Historical Site
2 Chapelle/Musée des Ursulines
3 Hôtel Clarendon
4 City Hall (Hôtel-de-Ville)
5 Café Buade
6 Basilique Notre-Dame
7 Musée de l'Amérique Française
8 Centre Infotouriste
9 Place d'Armes
10 Chateau Frontenac
11 Place-Royale

see the **Hotel Clarendon,** the oldest hotel still operating in Québec City, built in 1870. Wander in and check out the Art Deco entrance. If all this history is exhausting you, the **L'Emprise** cafe/bar inside the hotel is a great place to stop for a coffee or beer.

Continue along rue des Jardins, and you'll see Québec City's old **Hôtel-de Ville (City Hall),** built in 1895. If you're interested in knowing more about the history of urban planning in Québec, the **Centre d'Interprétation de la Vie Urbaine de la Ville de Québec (City Hall Interpretation Center)** is in the basement.

Continue along rue des Jardins to the end of the Place de l'Hôtel-de-Ville turn right on Côte de la Fabrique, and you'll see the **Basilique Notre-Dame,** first built in 1647, and then destroyed and built again about five times over until it took its final form around the end of the 1700s. (Well, actually, they were still putting finishing touches on it in 1959.) On the same street, you'll see the **Musée de l'Amérique Française (Museum of French America),** where you can get a thorough history of French colonization in the New World, in Québec, and beyond.

Time for another coffee break? Or maybe some lunch or a light snack? You're not too far from rue de Buade, where the **Café Buade,** 31 rue Buade (☎ 418-692-3909) offers pizzas, sandwiches, coffee, and the like at a reasonable price.

Keep going along rue de Buade until you reach **rue du Trésor.** The name (which means "treasury") dates from the French regime, when colonists used to pass along this street on their way to pay their taxes. Now it's a great little walkway where artists hang their paintings, sketching, etchings, and more.

Rue du Trésor takes you to rue Ste-Anne right in front of Place d'Armes. Turn left, and you'll see the **Infotouriste Center.** Cross Place d'Armes, and you'll be standing in front of the majestic, castlelike **Château Frontenac,** built in 1893 by the Canadian Pacific Railway Company.

If want to see the Basse-Ville from here, walk to the lookout area in front of the Château Frontenac. On your left are the **Breakneck stairs,** there since 1682. Take the stairs down to côte de la Montagne, and then keep going down on this street until you reach the next set of stairs. These take you to **Le Petit Champlain,** one of the oldest streets in the city, where the houses date to the 17th and 18th centuries — a shopper's delight, to boot.

Your last stop should be the **Place-Royale,** down the hill from Le Petit Champlain (toward the river). This is where it all started. It's the spot where the French explorer Samuel de Champlain founded New France in 1608.

# Chapter 20

# Shopping the Québec City Stores

• • • • • • • • • • • • • • • • • • • • • • • • • • • • • • • • • • • • • • • •

### In This Chapter

▶ Checking out shopping opportunities in Québec City

▶ Finding the big-name stores

▶ Discovering Québec City's best malls and shopping neighborhoods

• • • • • • • • • • • • • • • • • • • • • • • • • • • • • • • • • • • • • • • •

*O*n the whole, people in Québec City like things a little classy. Of course, given that tourism is a mainstay industry here, not-so-classy trinket boutiques abound, especially in the Old City. But don't be fooled by the trashy souvenir shops. Unique, high-quality items are available throughout Québec City, from Inuit art to antiques and clothing. Just don't go looking for bargains — you're likely to be disappointed.

## Surveying the Scene

Souvenir stores aside, Québec City is probably best known as a place to buy antiques, art, and crafts. The antiques stores keep their tourist clientele in mind and tend to specialize in smaller, more portable items such as lamps, china, and bedside tables and stools. Prices for antiques are reasonable, partly because Québeckers, as a whole, are not especially drawn to antiques (leaving plenty left over for you).

For a small city, Québec has a lot of art galleries. They run the full gamut of price and style, offering both traditional and abstract works done by new and established artists at both steep and affordable prices. Most — but not all — of the works for sale are from Québec artists. If you don't feel up to investing in art, the city has plenty of stores featuring less expensive crafts and creations from local artisans.

If shopping for clothes, books, or CDs is more your style, you'll find plenty of ways to spend your cash — believe me. Québec City residents are known for stylish dressing, and while you won't find the quantity of local designers available in Montréal, the clothing selection here reflects

Québeckers' flair. Most books for sale in the city are French, but plenty of English books are available, as well. The city has a decent selection of music, but if you're looking in particular for French music you'll find the selection is excellent.

Outside of the Old City, store hours in Québec City are similar to those throughout Canada. Most stores open at 9 or 10 a.m. and close at 5 or 6 p.m., Mondays through Wednesdays and Saturdays. Thursdays and Fridays, stores usually stay open until 9 p.m. Many stores open Sunday from around noon until 5 p.m. In the Old City, however, hours are very seasonal. During the high season, you're likely to find shops open long hours, pretty much every day.

Remember to keep track of your purchases. You have to come clean at the border and fork over the details of your purchases to Customs agents before you leave. If you stay in Canada more than two days, you can bring back US$800 in goods without paying duty. This includes 200 cigarettes, 100 cigars, and 1 liter of an alcoholic beverage. If you stay less than two days, your limit drops to US$200. If you buy more than this, no one will throw you in jail — you'll just have to pay a tax that's a small percentage of the amount that surpasses your limit. Check out Chapter 12 for more details.

Before you commence your Québec City shopping frenzy, don't forget the Canadian tax man (or tax woman). You must pay taxes adding up to roughly 13 percent of your purchases.

## Checking Out the Big Names

Downtown Québec City has only one big-name store, and that's **Simons** at 20 côte de la Fabrique (☎ **418-692-3630**). This slightly upscale department store, which opened in 1840, offers a good selection of clothing and accessories for men, women, and children, plus fine bed linens. This is the place to come if you unexpectedly find yourself in the middle of a cold spell and need a hat, scarf, and gloves — not a likely event until at least mid-October, but you never know.

The other big department store you find in Québec City is **La Baie** (The Bay, short for the Hudson's Bay Company), but you have to leave the confines of the downtown area and head out to the shopping malls in the 'burbs. You can find La Baie stores at **Galeries de la Capitale, Place Fleur de Lys,** and **Place Laurier.**

## Going to Shopping Malls

People really like to shop here, and for a small city Québec has an impressive roster of shopping malls. Maybe the winter weather drives Québeckers into these indoor havens of consumption.

You have two shopping mall options within walking distance of the Old City:

- ✔ **Les Promenades du Vieux-Québec,** 43 rue de Buade (☎ 418-692-6000): This small complex is just a few steps away from the Château Frontenac and has 12 upscale boutiques where you can find jewelry, furs, perfumes, gifts, candies, fine art, arts and crafts, and more.

- ✔ **Place Québec,** 900 bd. René-Lévesque Est (☎ 418-529-0551): A multilevel shopping complex attached to the Hilton Hotel, this mall has 30 boutiques and is a ten-minute walk from the Old City.

Trouble is (for visitors, anyway), the biggest and best of the malls are a fair distance from the Old City. But if mall crawling is what you want (not a bad alternative when the weather works against you), catch a cab and take off to one of the following:

- ✔ **Galeries de la Capitale,** 5401 bd. des Galeries (☎ 418-627-5800): A 20-minute drive from the Old City, this mall has 250 shops and a small amusement park with games, rides, an IMAX theater, 12 movie theaters, and assorted restaurants.

- ✔ **Place Fleur de Lys,** 552 bd. Wilfrid-Hamel (☎ 418-529-8128): Winner of the Canadian Maple Leaf Award for the most beautiful shopping interior design, Place Fleur de Lys is a five-minute drive from downtown Québec City and has 250 boutiques plus major chains.

- ✔ **Place Laurier,** 2700 bd. Laurier (☎ 800-322-1828): A good 20-minute drive from the Old City, this is the mother of all shopping centers. It's the largest shopping center in Eastern Canada with some 350 stores.

- ✔ **Place Sainte-Foy,** 2450 bd. Laurier (☎ 418-653-4184): This is a fashionable mall, featuring 130 stores and boutiques; it's a 20-minute drive from the Old City.

# Discovering the Best Shopping Neighborhoods

You can find loads of great shopping in Québec. I assume you want to spend most of your time in the Old City, or not too far from it, maybe venturing out, at most, to Grande-Allée for a change of scenery. So, for your shopping ease and pleasure, I break the city down into six shopping areas, discussed in the following six sections. Like almost everything else I recommend in the Québec City part of this book, all these areas are within walking distance of each other.

For antiques and art, you can't beat the **rue St-Paul** area in the Basse-Ville. For less touristy types of shops, **rue St-Jean** is the place to go, with its books, CD, and clothes stores (and plenty of cafes and restaurants to rest between your shopping sprints). For souvenirs, arts and crafts, and even clothes, I recommend the area around **Le Petit-Champlain** in the Basse-Ville, including Place-Royale and the area around the **Château Frontenac** in the Haute-Ville. Finally, if you really want a break from the Vieux-Québec experience, I recommend strolling down Grande-Allée to **avenue Cartier,** where you find a small concentration of shops with items like clothes, outdoor items, and home décor. Yet, **rue St-Joseph** is perhaps the most exciting shopping street of them all. It is away from Vieux-Québec, somewhat, but here's where you'll see a more authentic version of the city.

## Rue St-Paul

You can get to rue St-Paul in the Basse-Ville by following rue St-Pierre from Place-Royale. Or, you can start at the other end of the street. On rue St-Jean, take côte du Palais. You pass through the city walls, and then walk down to the Basse-Ville via rue des Vaisseaux-du-Roi.

This is where you find the biggest concentration of antiques stores in the city. But these aren't the kind of dusty, cluttered antiques stores you find on rue Notre-Dame in Montréal (see Chapter 12). Instead, most are neat places that specialize in a certain type of antiques. There's definitely something for everyone. This section lists a few places to visit on your stroll down rue St-Paul.

For old and rare books, check out **Argus Livres Anciens,** 160 rue St-Paul (☎ 418-694-2122). If Victorian and Edwardian furniture, silver, porcelain, and paintings are your thing, stop by **Boutique aux Memoires Antiquités,** 105 rue St-Paul (☎ 418-692-2180). For authentic Québec pine furniture, I recommend **Gérard Bourguet Antiquaire,** 97 rue St-Paul (☎ 418-694-0896). The store offers many 18th- and 19th-century pieces, but you can expect to pay a fair penny for them. **L'Héritage Antiquité,** 109 rue St-Paul (☎ 418-692-1681), also specializes in Québec furniture and sells clocks, oil lamps, and ceramics.

Rue St-Paul's other specialty is art galleries, although you'd be wise to wander off along some of the neighboring streets, such as rue Sault-au-Matelot or rue St-Pierre, to get the full experience. **Galerie Madeleine Lacerte,** 1 côte Dinan (☎ 418-692-1566), is one of the best-known galleries of the neighborhood. It sells contemporary paintings and sculpture. **Galerie d'art Alain Lacaze,** 131 rue St-Paul (☎ 418-692-4381), sells oils and watercolors.

Other noteworthy boutiques along rue St-Paul fall outside of the art and antiques category. **Vitrine,** 329 rue St-Paul (☎ 418-694-7384), specializes in furniture and other objects made by local designers. For one of the best selections of fur coats in the Old City, visit **Les Fourrures du Vieux-Port,** 55 rue St-Pierre (☎ 418-692-6686).

## Rue St-Jean

Rue St-Jean is probably the least quaint, yet most practical, of the shopping areas in the Old City. A busy commercial street, here you find a number of Québec chain stores. It's also a good place to head if you want specialty food items, books, CDs, clothes, or a comfortable pair of walking shoes. I include rue de la Fabrique in this area, which is a continuation of rue St-Jean uphill toward the Hôtel-de-Ville. The same bustling commercial spirit reigns on both streets.

This is the destination for clothes. For comfortable but elegant men's and women's fashions, Québec chain **America,** 1147 rue St-Jean (☎ 418-692-5254), is a good place to start. **Bedo,** 1161 rue St-Jean (☎ 418-692-0623), another chain, carries edgier, urban women's and men's fashions. **Louis Laflamme,** 1192 rue St-Jean (☎ 418-692-3774), carries stylish menswear. A little more into the "interesting" category of clothes, **Artisans du Bas-Canada,** 30 côte de la Fabrique (☎ 888-339-2109 or 418-692-2109), offers a wide selection of outdoor garments, gifts, and collectibles.

Food-wise, if you're a chocolate fanatic, you'll love **Choco-Musée Érico,** 634 rue St-Jean (☎ 418-524-2122), where, with two days' notice, *chocolatier* Éric Normand sculpts whatever you like out of chocolate. You can get good ice cream here, too. For maple products and Québec wines and beers, visit the **Marché Je-An-Dré,** 1097 rue St-Jean (☎ 418-692-3647).

You can find plenty of bookstores along rue St-Jean. Although many are principally *Francophone* (French-speaking), you can find English books and magazines at **Archambault,** 1095 rue St-Jean (☎ 418-694-2088), and at the **Maison de la Presse Internationale,** 1050 rue St-Jean (☎ 418-694-1511).

For gifts, souvenirs, and jewelry, check out **Abaca,** 54 côte de la Fabrique (☎ 418-694-9761).

## Le Petit-Champlain/Place-Royale

Although extremely touristy, Place-Royale and Le Petit-Champlain are still your best bets for souvenirs. Although cheap trinkets abound, most stores offer high-quality items, and many specialize in handmade and Québec-made clothing and jewelry. Plus, a number of reputable art galleries are located here.

If you're in the market for one of those striped French nautical shirts, you can find it at the nautical store **Le Capitaine d'à Bord,** 63 Petit-Champlain (☎ 418-694-0624). Into leather? **Peau sur Peau,** 85 Petit-Champlain (☎ 418-694-1921), offers leather clothing, shoes, luggage, and accessories from Québec and international designers. **Ibiza,** 57 Petit-Champlain (☎ 418-692-2103), also carries leather goods by Québec designers.

**Zazou,** 31 Petit-Champlain (☎ 418-694-9990), sells clothes made by Québec designers.

Maple products, a true Québec specialty, abound at the **Petit Cabane à Sucre,** 94 Petit-Champlain (☎ 418-692-5875). **Le Jardin de l'argile,** 51 Petit-Champlain (☎ 418-692-4870), carries Québec-made porcelain, pottery, bronze works, and more.

## Château Frontenac

Most of the nicer boutiques in and around the Château Frontenac in the Haute-Ville carry objects best qualified as "upscale souvenir."

Among these, don't miss the boutiques that sell Inuit art. **Aux Multiples Collections,** 69 rue Ste-Anne (☎ 418-692-1230), offers a wide selection of Native Canadian carvings in stone, bone, and tusk. You can also find a great choice of Inuit carving at **Brousseau et Brousseau,** 35 rue St-Louis (☎ 418-694-1828). **Kulik Art Inuit,** just inside the Château Frontenac at 1 rue des Carrières (☎ 418-692-6174), has a wide range of Inuit prints and sculptures.

Two other boutiques worth checking out in this area include the highly specialized **Boutique de Noël de Québec** (Québec Christmas Boutique), 47 rue de Buade (☎ 418-692-2457), which is open all year long. It's definitely a good spot to pick up a souvenir for that somebody who has everything. **La Maison Darlington,** 7 rue de Buade (☎ 418-692-2268), specializes in imported woolen garments including merino and cashmere sweaters, caps, ties, scarves, and gloves for children and adults.

If you want to bring back some locally made beer or Québec liqueurs made out of blueberry or maple syrup, the **SAQ Signature** spirits boutique has them. It's located just inside the Château Frontenac at 1 rue des Carrières (☎ 418-692-1182).

## Avenue Cartier

As nice as the Old City is, its intensely touristy and cramped shops can make you feel claustrophobic. Avenue Cartier is a great place to go for a little breathing space. Leave the Old City from the St-Louis Gate and walk along rue St-Louis until it turns into Grande-Allée. Continue walking west for ten minutes and until you reach avenue Cartier on your right.

Avenue Cartier, with its many boutiques, feels like a pedestrian promenade even though cars are allowed to drive through. It's a nice place to stroll about and has plenty of interesting cafes and restaurants where you can take a break. **Paris Cartier,** 1180 av. Cartier (☎ 418-529-6083), has elegant clothes for women. For home décor items check out **Zone,** 999 av. Cartier (☎ 418-522-7373), a great store that's loaded with extremely tempting stuff for the kitchen, bathroom, or living room.

**Azimut,** 1194 av. Cartier (☎ 418-688-7788), is an excellent outdoors store that sells tents, sleeping bags, and hiking boots. A good spot for CDs is **Sillons le Disquaire,** 1149 av. Cartier (☎ 418-524-8352).

## Rue St-Joseph

Rue St-Joseph is a brand-new Main Street for Québec City's residents. It's somewhat removed from the tourist sites. You'd never cross it just wandering around unless a local steers you straight. It's not far at all, just hidden away to some extent.

Rue St-Joseph may seem like an odd place for an upscale shopping district filled with "destination boutiques." This is mainly due to the fact that, as a visitor, your perception of the city, with the Château Frontenac in the middle, is somewhat skewed.

At the end of the 20th century Québec City was a doughnut, meaning that most of the population lived in the surrounding areas, leaving the middle empty. And, admittedly, Vieux-Québec can feel deserted at times.

In recent years, municipal authorities have taken it upon themselves to reverse this demographic trend, and the once dingy rue St-Joseph is now at the heart of a major urban renewal project. It's rapidly becoming a glitzy strip filled with shops, restaurants, cafes, and bars attractive to both tourists and residents alike.

The buildings are larger in scale than in Vieux-Québec, the town-house architecture more recent; still, most of it dates from the late 19th century. Yet, rue St-Joseph feels light years away from the colonial smarminess of the historic district. It's a more day-to-day reflection of contemporary Québec City, hip and tuned in to global culture.

Rue St-Joseph's recent makeover is far from complete. Yet already there's plenty of buzz and momentum. It's definitely the most exciting place to go in Québec City outside the traditional tourist agenda.

So, what do large European fashion houses think about the potential of this street? Well in November 2005, **Hugo Boss,** 505 rue St-Joseph Est (☎ 418-522-4444), opened its first "all-brand" store in North America. Unlike other Hugo Boss outlets on the continent, this one promises to carry every line made by the German designer. Swedish athletic outfitters **Peak Performance,** 565 rue St-Joseph Est (☎ 418-525-5003), chose to open its first North American store just down the street.

Other stylish boutiques include **Flirt,** 525 rue St-Joseph Est (☎ 418-529-5241), for lingerie, sexy undergarments, and boudoir apparel. Québec City is such a romantic place that you'll want to get into the act. They carry different lines imported from Europe, some on an exclusive basis.

Don't be shy: The store prides itself on offering a selection that flatters many different silhouettes.

Next door, **Mademoiselle B,** 541 rue St-Joseph Est (☎ **418-522-0455**), has unique jewelry designs from New York and Paris. **De Nîmes,** 557 rue St-Joseph Est (☎ **418-523-4848**), carries a tight selection of European fashion lines for both men and women, such as Nolita and Rare.

The hills surrounding Québec City are alive with all sorts of outdoor possibilities. Gear up at **Mountain Equipment Co-op,** 405 rue St-Joseph Est (☎ **418-522-1200**), a one-stop-shop for such stuff as hiking boots and rock climbing harnesses to kayaks and bicycles, and almost everything in between.

If you're looking for more-refined pleasures, try **Plaisirs de Provence,** 529 rue St-Joseph Est (☎ **418-524-4114**), a store packed with imports from France, fine tableware, and small decorative items. Or, **Villa,** 600 rue St-Joseph Est (☎ **418-524-2666**), sells larger imports, luxury furniture for your chalet or vacation home — supposedly. **Baltazar,** 461 rue St-Joseph Est (☎ **418-524-1991**), has an inventory of more contemporary and urban *objets.*

**Benjo,** 543 St-Joseph Est (☎ **418-640-0001**), must be the largest toy store closest to the North Pole. And everyone knows what that means! Yes, this is where Santa shops. Kids get preferential treatment at the glassed entrance with small central doors covered by an elegant awning. Big people, please use the regular doors on the sides. The scale of the store is such that there's even a small train helping young, gleeful shoppers on their commute between the stuffed animals and superhero action figures.

Although most of these stores are new kids on the block, **Mode Laliberté,** 595 rue St-Joseph Est (☎ **418-525-4841**), has been in this neighborhood through thick and thin. It is a longstanding, local, family-run department store. It's not as high fashion as the rest of the boutiques on the street, but, for affordable furs, it is a good place to look.

Tons of food outlets are on rue St-Joseph — and not all of them are sit-down and formal. **De Blanchet,** 435 rue St-Joseph Est (☎ **418-525-9779**), is a brightly lit bakery and gourmet shop that stands out for its modern décor and long display case of cheese. This is an excellent place to pick up a sampler of Québec's different varieties. The smaller **La Boîte à Pain,** 289 rue St-Joseph (☎ **418-647-3666**), is an artisan bakery with long lines spilling out the door. It makes innumerable kinds of bread, some of which are available only on Fridays and Saturdays (so that's the time to go). **Camellia Sinensis,** 624 rue St-Joseph Est (☎ **418-525-0247**), named after the scientific name for tea, has an astounding variety of leaves from around the world. A small sitting area is used for tastings, and the knowledgeable staff can help you make an intriguing choice.

Rue St-Joseph used to have a roof covering the entire street. The easternmost portion still does. Passing through the doors, you enter what amounts to a gloomy and run-down mall. Actually, this is what the entire strip used to be like before the city demolished most of the roof to initiate the neighborhood's renewal. Still, chocolate lovers who venture into this less scenic part will be glad they did when they eventually find **Champagne Le Maitre Confiseur,** 783 rue St-Joseph Est (☎ **418-652-0708**). It's on the right. This candy factory makes all sorts of chocolate and treats. Empty boxes are waiting to be filled with truffles from the display case. For something out of the ordinary, try the *larme du diable* ("the devil's tear"), a chocolate with zing, made with hot peppers. Peek through the door into the large kitchen in the back — it's a scene straight out of *Charlie and the Chocolate Factory.*

# Chapter 21

# Living It Up after Dark:
# Québec City Nightlife

. . . . . . . . . . . . . . . . . . . . . . . . . . . . . . . . . . . . . . . . . . . . . .

## In This Chapter

▶ Hitting Québec City's best dance floors
▶ Hearing live music acts throughout the city
▶ Finding neighborhood spots filled with locals

. . . . . . . . . . . . . . . . . . . . . . . . . . . . . . . . . . . . . . . . . . . . . .

*I*n the end, Québec City is quite a small town, and staunchly French. This limits the cultural opportunities, to a large extent, for English-speaking visitors. Mimicking Montréal, there's a yearlong festival schedule with diverse programming; I cover the main highlights in Chapter 3. Québec City also lacks a homegrown performing arts scene, in part because the most talented artists move to big-time Montréal, the province's largest city. Culture vultures would be wise to follow this migration to satisfy cravings such as opera, ballet, symphony, *cirque*, theater, as well as other forms of performance and spectacle. See Chapter 15 for my recommendations after you get there.

However, for a place its size, Québec City has a booming nightlife. Inside the walls of the **Haute-Ville,** the scene has a resortlike feel, like a misplaced Yesterdayland from a Disney theme park. Numerous watering holes line the maze of main streets within the walls. The majority of them are small, dimly lit, and intimate places, often with acoustic acts and flickering candles, exposed stone walls, and wooden beams. Folk music of all sorts suits the setting and is, indeed, the norm.

The **Grande-Allée** is Québec City's most popular nightlife strip, with clubs and bars on a larger scale. Many occupy more than one floor of the converted town houses where they often dwell, which seem to sway to the music spilling out of their windows. Most places offer a DJ and dance floor, but a few showcase live music.

**Basse-Ville** offers lots of action, but it's spread out, extending to the west beyond the underpass and along the cliffside. Because the rents are cheaper, it's where many of Québec City's edgier, more interesting bars have popped up — away from the colonial razzle-dazzle of the tourist areas.

Nearby, rue St-Joseph, in **St-Roch,** is the site of a major urban renewal project, which already boasts several essential destinations.

In this chapter, I tell you about Québec City's most popular nightlife destinations; some lesser known but equally great spots; and some places frequented only by locals. Some are outside the main tourist districts but are definitely worth checking out. Of course, I do point out the best spots in the Upper and Lower cities, as well as along the Grande-Allée.

On the whole, you spend less money going out in Québec City than in Montréal. Drinks are cheaper, distances between hot spots shorter, and cover charges less frequent. Last call is at 3 a.m., most places don't get going until 11 p.m., and the night peaks at 1 a.m. The legal drinking age is 18. Because of Québec City's quaint size, the dress code is less cosmopolitan than in Montréal. Lots of clubbers dress in jeans and comfy sweaters, but don't let that stop you from looking your best. Ideally, you want to wear something that gets you through a variety of settings, from a cozy pub to a swinging dance club.

# Finding Out What's Going On

Unfortunately, Québec City's free nightlife listings magazines are in French. But you don't really need to know French to decipher event listings, so if you want to find something in particular go ahead and take a look. **Le Soleil** and the **Journal du Québec** are the two French dailies, and their Arts and Entertainment sections may prove helpful. **Le Guide Québec Scope** is a free cultural magazine, partially in English, with restaurant reviews, neighborhood profiles, theater, shopping, and nightlife features, as well as event and show listings. Québec City also has an edition of **Voir,** a free weekly that comes out on Thursdays and has probably the most comprehensive coverage of the city's cultural calendar.

When deciphering French listings, know that they appear, more often than not, in the 24-hour-clock notation. An easy technique is to subtract 12 if the number is over 12h (noon). So 8h30 is 8:30 a.m., but 20h30 is 8:30 p.m. Also, the days of the week are listed in French. They are:

- ✔ *dimanche* (Sun)
- ✔ *lundi* (Mon)
- ✔ *mardi* (Tues)
- ✔ *mercredi* (Wed)
- ✔ *jeudi* (Thurs)
- ✔ *vendredi* (Fri)
- ✔ *samedi* (Sat)

# Checking Out the Scene

"No coats; no cover" sums up the action in the winter. Shivering teens scurry between the city's nightlife destinations, dressed merely in scant club-wear and no coats. Many of the bars and clubs have no cover charge, so many of these brazen partygoers opt to leave their warmer gear behind, despite the sub-zero temperatures. This way, they avoid the hassle of coat check at the front door and can head straight to the dance floor or the bar and bop between as many places as they choose. Other spots around town offer a more authentic and less rowdy experience, such as neighborhood spots where clamorous patrons talk and laugh over the music and pints of locally brewed draft beer.

Musically speaking, you hear more songs played by live bands than dance music tracks spun by DJs. You're likely to hear lots of live blues, rock, Celtic, and French folk music. In the city's popular *boîtes a chanson* (literally, singing boxes), you hear Québec folk songs in the *chansonier* (or folk) tradition.

For each place in this chapter, if you have to pay a cover charge I tell you how much, but these clubs are few and far between. I also include the opening nights for an establishment, if they're not open all week.

# Dancing the Night Away: Québec City's Best Clubs

Although your choices may be limited, most clubs play a mix of Top 40, hip-hop, R&B, techno, and all the requisite anthems from the '70s and '80s. My top picks to get you moving are:

✔ **Boudoir,** 441 rue de l'Église (☎ 418-524-2777), is, hands down, the city's hottest nightlife destination. Other places are somewhat quaint, but Boudoir feels jet-set and plugged in to global culture. During the summer months there's a sprawling terrace out front with heavy mingling action. The main room offers the sharply dressed and smart-looking clientele several seating arrangements in warmly lit, Zen décor, with Buddhist and Far East influences. The downstairs dance-club portion features a vibrating floor. Open: Daily 11:30 a.m. to 3 a.m. Monday to Friday, Saturday to Sunday 4 p.m. to 3 a.m. Cover: Occasionally C$5.

✔ **Chez Dagobert,** 600 Grande-Allée Est (☎ 418-522-0393), is Québec City's most famous nightclub and always a good bet. Le Dag has a stage on the main floor for live performances. Upstairs, an immense steel dance floor is enveloped by pounding bass, blinding lasers, and swiveling, colored spotlights. The entire setup is really quite elaborate. Open: Daily 9 p.m. to 3 a.m. Cover: None.

- ✔ **Chez Maurice Night Club,** 575 Grande-Allée Est (☎ 418-640-0711), has a main room with several bars that surround a dance floor packed with a dapper clientele that's between 18 and 30 years old. During the summer there's plenty of action on the front terrace, which is right on the Grande-Allée. Open: Daily 8 p.m. to 3 a.m. Cover: C$5.

- ✔ **Le Beaugarte,** 2600 bd. Laurier (☎ 418-659-2442), in Ste-Foy, is a cab ride away from Québec City's historic downtown in the suburb of Ste-Foy. If you're looking for that frenzied disco feel with a more mature crowd, it's worth the trip. This is the city's mega-club for 30-somethings and up. Open: Tuesday to Friday 11:30 a.m. to 3 a.m., Saturday to Sunday 5 p.m. to 3 a.m. Cover: None.

- ✔ **Le Soñar,** 1147 av. Cartier (☎ 418-640-7333), a basement tapas bar with a small dance floor, is an intimate but decidedly modern lounge. The bar glows like a white cube and is the centerpiece in an otherwise dark setting; the DJ spins a variety of electronic beats, ranging from ambient to deep house. Le Soñar is a refreshing change from the otherwise large spaces, indistinguishable décor, and music of Québec City's other dance clubs. Open: Daily 5 p.m. to 3 a.m. Cover: Occasionally Friday and Saturday, about C$5 to C$10.

- ✔ **Quartier de la Lune,** 799 av. Cartier (☎ 418-523-4011), attracts a 30-plus crowd, who cut loose and rock out to retro-classics. Everyone gets down without any pretense or even a second thought. Attitude? Who needs it? Sunday evenings are a popular blues night. Open: Daily 2 p.m. to 3 a.m. Cover (includes coat check): Friday to Saturday C$2; blues evenings C$7.

## Grooving to Live Music: Where to Catch Québec City's Best Acts

Live music seems to be Québec City's *raison d'être* in terms of nightlife, especially within the confines of the Haute-Ville. The scale and mood of the establishments seem best fit for lone balladeers and their guitars or small acoustic acts. On most nights, you can find rock, blues, and folk, but not much jazz.

- ✔ **Scanner Bistro Multimédia,** 291 rue St-Vallier Est (☎ 418-523-1916), is a bar with oodles of street cred and plenty of urban edge. Local indie-rock acts play on a small stage up front and a central bar divides the room. At the back, you'll find a pool table and a computer terminal with free Internet access. Upstairs has more seating and pool tables. Open: Monday to Friday 11:30 a.m. to 3 a.m. Saturday to Sunday 3 p.m. to 3 a.m. Cover: Friday to Saturday C$5.

- ✔ **Charlotte Lounge,** 575 Grande-Allée Est (☎ 418-640-0711), above the main room of Chez Maurice Night Club, has live music most

## Québec City Nightlife

nights. Wednesday, Friday, and Sunday feature a Latin band. On Thursday, it's a '70s rock cover band. But on Saturday, a DJ takes to the decks. Open: Tuesday to Sunday 8:30 p.m. to 3 a.m. Cover: C$5.

✔ **Le Chantauteuil,** 1001 rue St-Jean (☎ 418-692-2030), has been a venue for traditional folk singers and pub-theater since 1968. This low-key spot attracts an artsy clientele of writers, musicians, painters, poets, and photographers, who gather to commiserate over pints of beer. Open: Daily 11 a.m. to 3 a.m. Cover: None.

✔ **Le Pape Georges,** 8 rue du Cul-de-Sac (☎ 418-692-1320), is a small place with a tiny terrace in the Basse-Ville, serving a menu that features many reds and whites by the glass, cheeses, and cold-cuts. Thursdays through Saturdays blues, cabaret, and folk performers play late into the night. Open: Daily noon to 3 a.m. Cover: Thursday to Saturday C$1.

✔ **Les Voûtes Napoléon,** 680 Grande-Allée Est (☎ 418-640-9388), this *boîte à chansons,* set in a downstairs cellar, is very popular for its warm and friendly atmosphere and entertainers who get the crowd singing along. Open: Daily 8:30 p.m. to 3 a.m. Cover: None.

# Drinking In the Local Flavor: Québec City's Neighborhood Bars and Pubs

The following are the neighborhood watering holes where you're likely to find Québeckers — lots of local flavor and character, but not many tourists:

✔ **La Barbarie,** 310 rue St-Roch (☎ 418-522-4373), a brewpub operated as a co-op, makes its own beers. You can get a sampler of eight fine brews, each glass held in a special slot of a wooden carousel. It is a small, cozy pub, with dangling Christmas lights around the bar. Open: Daily noon to 3 a.m. Cover: None.

✔ **Le Sacrilège,** 447 rue St-Jean (☎ 418-649-1985), is a neighborhood bar along rue St-Jean but outside the gates, to the west of the walled Haute-Ville. It is a long and narrow establishment with a beautiful and verdant back terrace during the summer. It's crowded — groups of friends sit down wherever there's space. Sometimes, this means joining another table and meeting new people. No worries, though; everyone is very friendly. Open: Daily noon to 3 a.m. Cover: None.

✔ **Les Salons Edgar,** 263 rue St-Vallier Est (☎ 418-523-7811), is larger than a typical neighborhood bar, frequented by a young and hip clientele. It has two rooms with extremely high ceilings. The front room has different seating options, along with a long deconstructed bar where patrons mill about. The back room has five pool tables, which you can rent on an hourly basis. Open: Wednesday to Sunday 4:30 p.m. to 3 a.m. Cover: None.

- ✔ **L'Inox,** 37 quai St-André (☎ **418-692-2877**), is a Québec City brew-pub that makes about a dozen beers. Plenty of seating can be found in the bar and outside on the terrace May through September. This establishment enjoys a steady flow of regular patrons and hard-core beer lovers. Open: Daily noon to 3 a.m. Cover: None.

- ✔ **Mo Taverne Urbaine,** 810 bd. Charest Est (☎ **418-266-0221**), is a good spot for after-work drinks among a crowd of young urban pro-fessionals relaxing in this updated tavern décor. In an interesting twist, beer taps are found at each table. Patrons serve themselves and pay by the ounce. There's a tapas menu which offers small snacks to accompany your drinks. Open: Monday to Saturday 11 a.m. to 3 a.m. Cover: None.

- ✔ **Pub St-Patrick,** 45 rue Couillard (☎ **418-694-0618**), a former muni-tions store during the French colonial period, has a warm atmos-phere, made so by the stone hearth and Celtic musicians who almost sit among the clientele as they play. This pub has more than a dozen varieties of beer on tap. If you're feeling homesick, this may be a good place to hear some slurred English. Ah, that's better. Open: Daily 11:30 a.m. to 3 a.m. Cover: None.

- ✔ **Taverne Jos Dion,** 86 rue St-Joseph Ouest (☎ **418-525-0710**), located in working-class St-Roch, is the oldest tavern in the city. You know you're in deep Québec by the bright fluorescent lighting, the moose-head trophy above the bar, other dated memorabilia, and the stern-faced regulars. Currently, this place is enjoying a revival in popularity among the younger crowd, as the rest of the neighborhood becomes an increasingly hip nightlife destination. Open: Daily 8 a.m. to 3 a.m. Cover: None.

## *Being Out and Proud in Québec City*

The first few blocks of rue St-Jean, to the west of the walled city just after crossing côte d'Abraham, is Québec City's Gay Village. Along with gay-run cafes, restaurants, and shops, you also find a growing number of nightlife establishments that cater to a gay clientele. One of the best is **Le Drague,** 804 rue St-Joachim (☎ **418-649-7212**), Québec City's largest gay club — with two stories, a drag show, and a dance floor from Thursdays to Sundays. Something for everyone, really. Men cram into the main bar to take in the performances, featuring lip-syncing transves-tites. Those who can't squeeze in can watch the proceedings on closed-circuit TV monitors in the establishment's other rooms. Open: Daily 10 a.m. to 3 a.m. Cover: Friday to Sunday around C$3.

# Part V
# The Part of Tens

# In this part . . .

*I*t's just *le fun* to end with Top Ten lists. *Le fun* — a cute mix of French and English meaning "good times" — is a popular expression in Québec. Go ahead, try it in a sentence and drop it on a local. They'll know exactly what you mean. This part lists some essential items that are *le fun* to seek out during your visit.

# Chapter 22

# Ten *Terroir* Ingredients and Local Specialties to Put on Your Plate

*Q*uébec is passionate about its food. This mania probably comes from the province's French roots. By now, numerous other immigrant communities have also made their mark on the culinary landscape, evidenced by the dazzling array of restaurants in both cities and the large inventory of exotic ingredients available from Montréal's independent grocers.

However, Québec produces many delicacies of its own, from cheeses and berries to seafood and game. This bountiful land is filled with different specialty ingredients that you'll want to fill up on during your stay — if you're adventurous.

Instead of having to trek out into the woods and fetch dinner yourself (the way it was done around here until not so long ago), you can experience Québec's increasing number of restaurants specializing in cooking with local ingredients. Some of them call this type of menu "market cuisine." Going to the markets yourself is another way to get your hands on, and mouth around, Québec's *terroir*. Buying locally is an often-overlooked part of eating organic and "slow-food" activism.

# Maple Syrup

Although many in Québec don't care much for the maple leaf on the Canadian flag as a national symbol, this province is the world capital of maple syrup production. Ironic, eh? During the great spring thaw, sap flows in the maple trees, which sugar bush farmers tap and boil down into this liquid gold. Sugar bushes are found all over Québec, but the maples are thickest in the region of Montérégie, southeast of Montréal. In March and April, packs of urbanites trek to sugar shacks for a traditional maple-syrup-bathed feast. It's a rite of spring known as "sugaring off."

# Unpasteurized Cheese

Part of what makes Québec distinct from the rest of Canada is the province's laissez-faire attitude. This is a good thing when it comes to cheese — and Martha Stewart would agree. Québec has an outstanding variety of local, specialty cheeses. Many of the best are made from unpasteurized milk, giving them extra flavor and richness. This encourages small dairy farmers to make new varieties from the milk of a single herd — a practice taboo in the rest of Canada because of food-safety concerns. So, *vive la difference!* Some of Québec's more notable unpasteurized varieties include Pied de Vent, from the Îles de la Madeleine, and Chateau Mailloux, from Charlevoix. *Riopelle* cheese from Île-aux-Grues, named after the late contemporary Québec artist who was most often compared to Jackson Pollock, is the most recent variety to create a buzz among foodies here.

# Microbrewery Beer

Although Molson and Labatt are the two major Canadian beer companies, locals in Montréal and Québec City often opt for microbrewery products instead. A number of these beers exist in the province of Québec, available on tap in bars and in bottles from stores. Unibroue makes several popular kinds, including Blanche de Chambly and Fin du monde. The latter has a high alcohol volume of 9 percent. Its name means, "The end of the world." McAuslan brews Griffon, St-Ambroise, and also an Apricot Wheat Ale. The Brasseurs du Nord make Boreal, which is probably the most popular microbrew province-wide.

# Cidre de Glace

Unable to match icewine from Ontario, Québec's beverage industry recently answered by producing "ice cider" from apples. This remarkably similar golden and syrupy alcoholic beverage is also meant to accompany cheese or dessert. It's gaining in popularity, mainly as a cheaper alternative to ice wine. Québec's harsh climate makes it a hostile land for vineyards and producing a palatable wine. Most of the ice cider comes from the Montérégie, a region rich with orchards.

# Duck from Lac Brôme

Lake Brôme ducks are shipped around the world. The lakefront duck farm is the oldest in the country. Started in 1912, it remains one of the largest employers in the region. They breed Peking ducks, which have delicious meat. In Montréal a large number of restaurants have duck, usually a *confit de canard* or a *magret de canard*. If Lac Brôme is not mentioned on the menu, ask the waiter where the kitchen gets its ducks.

# Lamb

Québec has two regions renowned for their lamb. On Île-Verte, in the lower St. Lawrence River, the lambs are "presalted," because they graze on marshes flooded by brackish water. This makes their meat extra tasty. In Charlevoix, the government granted the lamb producers of this region a special designation for their meat. It is the first agricultural product in the province to be protected in such a way. For producers to be able to label their lamb as *de Charlevoix,* they must abide by strict rules for raising their small herds.

# Blueberries from Lac St-Jean

After maple syrup, blueberries from Lac St-Jean are perhaps the second most famous agricultural crop in Québec. Blueberries are loaded with antioxidants and make excellent pies. They're in season in August. You'll see two kinds in Québec's markets: wild and farmed. The most worthwhile are the smaller, wild blueberries, intense and flavorful. The people from this region are renowned for their warm hospitality — the region is seen as the province's heartland of sorts.

# Strawberries from Île d'Orléans

The St. Lawrence River widens beyond Québec City. Just downriver lies the Île d'Orléans, an island filled with fields, wooded glades, and rural farming communities. It's said to be the birthplace of French America, because it's where the explorers first settled. The island is also referred to as "Québec City's garden," because it supplies the capital with much of its seasonal fruits and vegetables. Visitors can go fruit picking all summer long; many come in mid-July for the strawberries, which are particularly delicious.

# Tourtière

Nutmeg, clove, allspice, and pepper are the four essential seasonings for this traditional meat pie, a recipe that dates back to 17th-century France. The name refers to a special pot with legs used for baking the pie over the embers of an open fire. As many different versions of *tourtière* exist as there are willing cooks in Québec. A lively province-wide debate rages on between entire regions and extended families about whose *tourtière* is best.

## *Poutine*

Two cities in Québec, Drummondville and Victoriaville, claim to be the birthplace of *poutine*. This local fast-food delicacy, consisting of French fries, brown gravy, and cheese curds, is a favorite at snack bars across the province. Fancier restaurants make upscale versions, with seared foie gras and the like.

# Chapter 23

# Ten (or So) T-Shirts with Tons of Montréal Street-Cred

*I*t seems that in many venues nowadays you can get dressed up merely by wearing your best T-shirt. As a fashion item the tee is often about making a statement, which shows that the wearer is somehow hip and in the know.

So, if you're looking to take souvenirs back home but want to do better than a T-shirt from the Hard Rock Cafe (ho-hum) or something generic from a souvenir shop on rue Ste-Catherine (blah), this chapter offers some creative suggestions.

These tees are locally designed or inspired, and they're all the rage on Montréal's busy streets. They're the T-shirts that stand out if you look at the streaming crowds long enough. For different reasons, each has attained a level of cult status and street cred among locals.

## J'♥ CISM

Echoing the iconic New York City tee, local University of Montréal radio station CISM 89.3 has paraphrased and translated the famous motto on a T-shirt for its rabid fandom. Given the abysmal state of Montréal's radio airwaves, CISM listeners can be righteous about their choice — its eclectic programming is a brilliant showcase of the different local music scenes, including the latest bands breaking into Montréal's vibrant indie-rock scene. The T-shirt is the local equivalent of the Apple Computer "Think

Different" bumper stickers popular on some cars. Available directly from the radio station on the University of Montréal campus.

## Nordiques/Expos

For local sports fans, a ton of nostalgia is wrapped up in wearing T-shirts or other memorabilia from Québec's now defunct professional sports teams: hockey's Québec Nordiques and baseball's Montréal Expos. (For those *not* keeping score, these sports franchises are now the Colorado Avalanche in the National Hockey League and the Washington Nationals of Major League Baseball.)

Baseball fans are rabid for any Expos shirt with 27 on it — it was the number worn by star player Vladimir Guerrero. A Québec Nordiques equivalent would be Joe Sakic's number 19.

## McGill/Concordia

A T-shirt from one of Montréal's two English universities also makes for an out-of-the-ordinary souvenir. It's the red and white of the McGill Redmen versus the burgundy and gold of the Concordia Stingers. A wide selection of styles is available in the bookstore of each university on their centrally located downtown campuses. An increasing number of U.S. students are enrolling in these schools, due in part to their low tuition fees. McGill also has quite a reputation: In 2005, it cracked *Playboy* magazine's list of the top ten party schools.

## Piknic Electronik

Every Sunday from May to September there's an outdoor dance party on Île Ste-Hélène in Parc Jean-Drapeau featuring some of Montréal's most innovative electronic music producers and DJs. They play under a gargantuan statue — *Man,* by Alexander Calder — with stunning views of the city's skyline. It's an idyllic setting that draws a mixed crowd in various states of leisure: from bouncing revelers to groups of friends lounging in the grass to young families. There's a T-shirt for the event, and some revelers have such a good time that they feel compelled to buy one. You can spot an increasing number of people wearing them about town — testament to the event's growing popularity.

## Bily Kun

This bar at the main crossroads of the Plateau is emblematic of this neighborhood's signature brand of cool. An evening here will immediately expose you to a variety of shabby-chic characters who like to drop by this lively den. The name means "White Horse" in Czech, after the local microbrewery they seem to favor on tap. They also serve absinthe, imported direct from Prague. It's a special place. The T-shirt is for its most ardent fans.

# St-Viateur Bagels

Fresh, steaming bagels usually get devoured in seconds. They just don't last as long as a T-shirt. Perhaps you'll want to remember the experience of eating one of these fresh-from-the-oven bagels with a T-shirt from this Mile End bakery. Although the other tees on this list intend to be fashionable, one from St-Viateur bagel is completely unselfconscious, retro without meaning to be, pure kitsch.

# Onetop.ca

Onetop.ca is an annual design competition for Québec illustrators, graphic designers, and other visual-media artists. A jury selects 40 winners from among the submissions, and the designs show on T-shirts in a gallery for two months during the summer (June to July-ish). They're slightly more expensive than something store-bought, but a good cut of the price goes to the artists. So, you can look good in a new T-shirt and feel comfortable that you've done your share in supporting the local arts scene.

# Montrealite.com

The people behind Montrealite.com have really taken the T-shirt-as-a-blank-canvas idea to heart. This site is the source of many of the cool images you see on tees around town, inspired by different peculiarities including the well known Métro/Retro design, which is an apt parody of the symbol for the '70s-looking subway system.

# Three Monkeys

At this street-couture boutique, located in Cours Mont-Royal, the souvenir T-shirt and the fashion tee become one. Three Monkeys commissions Montréal artists to design graphics for their "local series." The T-shirts feature landmarks and icons from the city's streets and skyline, such as Habitat '67; the rooftop, milk-bottle, water tank somewhere downtown; the sign above the Five Roses flour mill; and the Biosphere. All of these urban snapshots are indeed a part of Montréalers' collective imagination.

# Quick Concierge

• • • • • • • • • • • • • • • • • • • • • • • • • • • • • • • • • • • •

## *Fast Facts*

### AAA

Canada's affiliate is the CAA. In Montréal their office is downtown at 1180 rue Drummond (☎ 514-861-5111; www.caa quebec.com). It's open Monday through Friday, 9 a.m. to 6 p.m., Thursdays until 8 p.m. The toll-free, emergency road service number for members is ☎ 800-222-4357. While it's free for members, non-members can call as well but there is a charge for the service.

Québec City's branch of the CAA is located at 444 rue Bouvier (☎ 418-624-8222). Business hours are Monday through Wednesday 9 a.m. to 5:30 p.m., Thursday and Friday 9 a.m. to 8 p.m., and Saturday 10 a.m. to 4 p.m. The emergency road service number for Québec City is ☎ 800-222-4357.

If you're a member of AAA, you can pick up maps, tour books, and traveler's checks at these offices at no extra charge; you can also make travel arrangements here.

### Area Code

The area code on the Island of Montréal for downtown Montréal is **514**. For suburbs around Montréal, the area code is **450**.

The area code for Québec City and Ste-Foy is **418**.

### ATMs

Automated teller machines, bank machines, or *guichets (guee-shea)* in French, are ubiquitous throughout the province of Québec. You can find ATMs in the heart of downtown and throughout the suburban areas. The Bank of Montréal, Banque Nationale, Royal Bank, and Scotiabank use the Cirrus network. The Caisse populaire, Royal Bank, TD Canada Trust, and CIBC use the Plus network. For further information, the toll-free numbers for these major banking networks are ☎ 800-424-7787 (Cirrus) and ☎ 800-336-8472 (PLUS). For a list of ATMs that accept MasterCard or Visa, ask your bank or go to www.mastercard.com or www.visa.com.

### Baby Sitters

Most major hotels have someone on staff who can look after your children or can make arrangements for child care if you need it. Be sure to advise them of your child's special needs well in advance.

Montréal YMCA, downtown on rue Stanley (☎ 514-849-8393, ext 777; www.ymca.ca), offers educational day care for kids 18 months to 5 years.

### Business Hours

Similar to elsewhere in North America, stores generally open at 9 or 10 a.m. and close at 5 or 6 p.m., Monday through Wednesday and Saturday. Thursdays and Fridays, most stores open at the same time but stay open until 9 p.m. Most stores are also open on Sundays from noon to 5 p.m.

Montréal banks are usually open Monday through Friday, from 8 or 9 a.m. to 4 p.m.

In Québec City, banks are usually open from 10 a.m. to 3 p.m. Monday through Friday, but may also have evening hours on Thursday and Friday.

### Camera Repair

In downtown Montréal, AFC Camera Service, 1015 Beaver Hall (☎ 514-397-9505), repairs cameras, as does Camera Technic Company, 1218 Union (☎ 514-866-2223).

In Québec City, Service Camera Pro, 2042 bd. Père-Lelievre (☎ 418-527-0880), repairs every kind of camera on-site: film, digital, and camcorders. Also try Camera Test, 51 bd. René-Levesque (☎ 418-529-2803).

### Car Rentals

See Chapter 7 for information on car rentals in Montréal and Québec City.

### Convention Centers

Montréal's Palais des Congrès, near Vieux-Montréal and Chinatown, sits between rue Viger and rue St-Antoine and runs west for several blocks starting at the corner of rue Jeanne Mance until rue McGill (☎ 800-268-8122 or 514-871-3170). Métro: Place-d'Armes or Square-Victoria, Place-des-Arts.

Montréal's Place Bonaventure (☎ 514-397-2222) also hosts its share of major conventions and trade shows. The main entrance is at 800 rue de la Gauchetière Ouest. Métro: Bonaventure.

Québec City's Centre des Congrès is located at 1000 bd. René-Levesque Est, just outside the walls of Vieux-Québec and to the right of the Hôtel du Parlement (☎ 888-679-4000 or 418-644-4000).

### Credit Cards

To report lost or stolen credits cards, contact the following: American Express (☎ 800-268-9824); Diners Club (☎ 800-363-3333); Discover (☎ 800-347-2683); MasterCard (☎ 800-826-2181); or Visa (☎ 800-336-8472).

### Currency Exchanges

Banks and *bureaux de change* (exchange offices) almost always offer better exchange rates than hotels, restaurants, and shops — which you should use only in emergencies. You'll also find windows where you can exchange currency at airports and train stations.

In Montréal, the majority of currency exchange offices are Downtown or in Vieux-Montréal. There's one in the Infotouriste office on Dorchester Square, 1001 Square Dorchester, and several others nearby. One of them is Calforex, 1250 rue Peel (☎ 514-392-9100). In Vieux-Montréal, look for Notre-Dame Bureau de Change, 55 rue Notre-Dame Ouest (☎ 514-282-9442).

In Québec City, a *bureau de change* office is in the tourist information office near the Château Frontenac at 12 rue Ste-Anne (☎ 418-694-1014). There's another at the bottom of the steps in Basse-Ville at 46 rue du Petit Champlain (☎ 418-694-0011).

### Customs

Canada Border Services Agency has a toll-free line called the Border Information Service (☎ 800-461-9999). The number for the U.S. Customs and Border Protection office in Montréal is ☎ 514-636-3875.

### Dentists

In case of a dental emergency, during regular, weekday business hours travelers can call the Ordre des Dentistes du Québec for assistance in finding a nearby dentist's office (☎ 800 361-4887 or 514-875-8511).

Or you can consult the "Find a Dentist" page on their website, www.ordredesdentist esduquebec.qc.ca. If you enter the first three digits of the postal code of where you are located, the search engine kicks out a list of the closest dentist offices (however, there is no way to tell if they are open 24 hours).

Here are the number for two dental offices open 'round the clock: ☎ 514-288-8888 and ☎ 514-342-4444.

In Québec City, try ☎ 418-653-5412 or ☎ 418-691-5214.

Failing any of this, the next best thing is to head to the emergency ward of a nearby hospital. Please see the section on hospitals, below.

## Doctors

All major hotels should have a doctor on call or be able to call one for you. Embassies and consulates maintain lists of physicians with good reputations. See "Embassies and Consulates," later in this section.

Also, in the province of Québec there's a 24-hour Info Santé/Health Line staffed by registered nurses that you can call any time for help and referrals. In Montréal, call ☎ 514-521-2100. In Québec City, try ☎ 418-648-2626.

## Driving Rules

See Chapter 8.

## Electricity

Canada uses the same electricity (110 volts, 60 Hz) as the United States and Mexico, with the same flat-prong plugs and sockets.

## Embassies and Consulates

All embassies are in Ottawa.

In Montréal, the American Consulate General is located at 1155 rue St-Alexandre (☎ 514-398-9695, or, for after-hours emergencies, ☎ 514-981-5059). The United Kingdom has a Consulate General at 1000 rue de la Gauchetière Ouest, Suite 4200 (☎ 514-866-5863).

In Québec City, the U.S. Consulate is located near the Château Frontenac, facing Jardin des Gouverneurs, at 2 terrasse Dufferin (☎ 418-692-2095, or, for after-hours emergencies, ☎ 418-692-2096).

## Emergencies

Dial **911** for the police, firefighters, or an ambulance.

## Holidays

Québec celebrates the following public holidays: New Year's Day (Jan 1); Easter Monday (the Mon following Easter); Victoria Day or *Journée des Patriotes* (May 24); St-Jean-Baptiste Day (June 24); Canada Day (July 1); Labour Day (first Mon in Sept); Thanksgiving (second Mon in Oct); Remembrance Day (Nov 11); Christmas Day (Dec 25); Boxing Day (Dec 26). Banks and shops are likely to be closed on these days, although museums and restaurants usually stay open. The exceptions to this rule-of-thumb are Christmas Day and Jan 1.

## Hospitals

The following downtown Montréal hospitals have emergency rooms: Montréal General Hospital, 1650 rue Cedar (☎ 514-934-1934 or ☎ 514-398-6644); the Royal Victoria Hospital, 687 av. des Pins Ouest (☎ 514-934-1934); the Hôtel Dieux, 3840 rue St-Urbain (☎ 514-890-8000); and the Hôspital Notre-Dame, 1560 rue Sherbrooke Est (☎ 514-890-8000).

In Québec City, the centrally located Hôtel Dieu is at 11 Côte du Palais (☎ 418-525-4444).

## Hot Lines

In Montréal: Alcoholics Anonymous (☎ 514-376-9230); Depressed Anonymous (☎ 514-278-2130); Gay Line (☎ 888-505-1010 or ☎ 514-866-5090); Gambling Help and Referral (☎ 514-527-0140); Info-Sante/Health-Line (☎ 514-521-2100); Kids-Help, for children in crisis (☎ 800-668-6868 or 514-273-7007); Parents Line (☎ 800-361-5085 or ☎ 514-288-5555); Sexual Assault Line for Victims (☎ 514-934-4504); SOS Spousal Abuse (☎ 514-873-9010); Suicide Action Montréal (☎ 514-723-4000); Tel-Jeunes, for children or teenagers in crisis (☎ 514-939-2621); Youth Protection (☎ 514-527-7211); Gas Odor Detection (☎ 514-598-3111).

In Québec City: Alcoholics Anonymous (☎ 418-529-0015); Health Info (☎ 418-648-2626); Tel-Aide, for emotional distress (☎ 418-686-2433).

## Information

Montréal's Infotouriste Centre (☎ 877-266-5687 or ☎ 514-873-2015; www.bonjourquebec.com) is located at 1001 Dorchester Square St., 1 block south of rue Ste-Catherine Ouest, between rue Peel and rue Metcalf. June through early September, the center is open daily 8:30 a.m. to 7:30 p.m. Mid-September through May, it operates daily 9 a.m. to 6 p.m.

Québec City's main Tourist Information Centre is located at 12 rue Ste-Anne, just opposite the Château Frontenac at Place d'Armes (☎ 877-266-5687). It's open June through Labor Day 8:30 a.m. to 7:30 p.m., and Labor Day through June 9 a.m. to 5 p.m.

## Internet Access and Cybercafes

Most large hotels have in-room Internet access for your computer, via a high-speed cable. And an increasing number offer hot spots for wireless laptops either throughout the establishment or in the main lobby area.

There is a free Wi-Fi Internet signal in many parts of the city. Go to www.ilesansfil.org to find out where these hot spots are; the access points are usually located in a cafe or other laptop-friendly commerce site. If you don't feel like buying anything, you can always squat on their connection from a bench outside. Would-be surfers have to register and log in with Ile Sans Fil prior to surfing at will.

You can find cybercafes throughout Montréal. One good, centrally located option is Virus Café at 3672 bd. St-Laurent (☎ 514-842-1726). In Chinatown, there's Café SinoNet, 71A rue de la Gauchetière Ouest (☎ 514-878-0572). And Netopia, 1737 av. St-Denis (☎ 514-286-5446), is open 24 hours in the Quartier Latin.

In Québec City, Cybar-Café is at 353 rue St-Joseph and is open 24/7 (☎ 418-529-5301). Across the street, Bibliothèque Gabrielle-Roy, 350 rue St-Joseph Est (☎ 418-641-6789), has free Internet but is not open as late. Also, the Musée de la Civilisation, 85 rue Dalhousie (☎ 418-643-2158), has computers with free Internet access in its new cafe.

## Language

Québec's official language is French, which is spoken by 85 percent of the population. In Québec City this average holds. However, in Montréal native French speakers, or Francophones, are closer to 60 percent of the population.

Either way, in the service and hospitality industries employees serving the general public speak at least both French and English.

**Liquor Laws**

You must be 18 or over to legally drink in Québec. Beer and wine are sold in restaurants, bars, lounges, and taverns. You can also purchase alcohol at the government-controlled Société des alcools du Québec (SAQ). There are two convenient downtown locations in Montréal: 677 rue Ste-Catherine Ouest between rue Université and McGill-College (☎ 514-282-9445), and 440 bd. de Maisonneuve Ouest (☎ 514-873-2274). Also downtown, at 1250 rue Ste-Catherine Est, there's an SAQ "Express," which has a smaller selection but is always open until 10 p.m. (☎ 514-521-0184).

Québec City also offers two central locations: in the concourse of the Château Frontenac, 1 rue des Carriéres (☎ 418-692-1182), and near the train station at 400 bd. Jean-Lesage (☎ 418-643-4339).

Throughout Québec, beer and a limited selection of wine are available in grocery and convenience stores until 11 p.m.

**Mail**

Postage for mailing letters within Canada costs C52¢. Letters to the U.S. cost C93¢, and letters overseas cost C$1.55.

Montréal's main post office (bureau de poste), at 800 bd. René-Levesque Ouest, near rue Université (☎ 514-846-5401), is open Monday through Friday 8 a.m. to 6 p.m. In Vieux-Montréal, the post office is at 157 rue St-Antoine Ouest, between rues Jeanne-Mance and de Bleury (☎ 514-393-1664). The hours there are weekdays 8:30 a.m. to 5:30 p.m.

Some neighborhood convenience or drugstores throughout the city have small

post office outlets located at the back of their stores. Look for the red and white Postes Canada logo in the window, or check out the "Find a Post Office" feature on www.canadapost.ca.

Québec City's most central post office, near the Château Frontenac at 5 rue du Fort (☎ 418-694-6102), is open from 8 a.m. to 5:45 p.m.

**Maps**

City maps are available for free from city tourist offices, in the Yellow Pages, and perhaps at the front desk of your hotel. To find out where specific buildings or sites are located, you can also use Canada's online directory assistance, www.canada411.com, which provides small maps of locations along with the usual listing information.

In Montréal, the Infotouriste office is at Dorchester Square (see "Information," earlier in this section). You can also find maps at bookstores like Chapters, 1171 rue Ste-Catherine Ouest (☎ 514-849-8825); Indigo, 1500 av. McGill-College (☎ 514-281-5549); or Paragraphe Bookstore, 2220 av. McGill-College (☎ 514-845-5811). If you want a very thorough street map of Montréal, look for the large yellow books published by MapArt Publishing, widely available in bookstores and convenience stores across the city.

In Québec City, you can pick up free city maps at the Tourist Information office, 12 rue Ste-Anne, just opposite the Château Frontenac at Place-d'Armes. You can also find maps at Archambault, 1095 rue St-Jean (☎ 418-694-2088), and at the Maison de la Presse Internationale, 1050 rue St-Jean (☎ 418-694-1511).

**Newspapers/Magazines**

Montréal's English-language daily paper is the Montréal Gazette, which provides good coverage of city news and arts and entertainment listings, as well as some world news. Canada has two national newspapers, the *Globe and Mail* and the *National Post,* which cover Canadian and world news. You can find these papers at convenience stores throughout the downtown area. English-language papers are harder to find outside the downtown area.

For arts and entertainment coverage exclusively, pick up one of Montréal's weekly alternative publications: the *Hour* or the *Mirror.* Both are available in convenience stores and at the entrance of bars, cafes, and some restaurants downtown, in the Plateau neighborhood, and throughout the city.

In Québec City, major Canadian and American English-language newspapers and magazines are sold in the newsstands of the large hotels, at vending machines on tourist corners in Vieux-Québec, and at Maison de la Presse Internationale, 1050 rue St-Jean (☎ 418-694-1511). For events listings, look for the free-press publications *Québec Scope,* a monthly magazine, and *Voir,* a weekly paper. (Both are in French.)

## Pharmacies

Québec's major drugstore chain is Pharmacie Jean Coutu, which has a downtown Montréal location in the Ailes de la Mode complex, 677 rue Ste-Catherine Ouest (☎ 514-289-0800), and another big store at 974 rue Ste-Catherine Ouest (☎ 514-866-7791). The other big chain is Pharmaprix, which has a big store at 450 rue Ste-Catherine Ouest (☎ 514-875-7070), open 24 hours.

In Québec City, the Louis Philippe et Jacques Royer pharmacy is located in the Basse-Ville at 57 rue Dalhousie (☎ 418-694-1262).

## Police

Dial **911** for emergencies. Québec has three types of officers: the municipal police, the Sûreté du Québec (comparable to state police or highway patrol), and the RCMP (like the FBI), which handles cases involving federal laws. RCMP officers are required to speak English. The Montréal and Québec City police provide service in English.

To reach the Sûreté du Québec in Montréal, dial ☎ 514-310-4141. In Québec City, call ☎ 800-461-2131.

## Radio Stations

CISM (89.3 FM) is the University of Montréal's radio station, while CKUT (90.3) is McGill University's. The two offer a wide variety of community-based programming and are great sources for hearing about upcoming events in the immediate future.

CJAD (AM 800), an English-language talk-radio station, covers news, sports, weather, and traffic. Canada's National Public Radio equivalent is the CBC (Canadian Broadcasting Corporation). Their Radio One (88.5 FM) is mainly news, while CBC Radio Two (93.5 FM) plays classical music and has various shows on arts, news, and current events. For popular music, try Mix 96 at 95.9 FM, or CKOI at 96.9 FM.

## Restrooms

You can find clean restrooms in hotel lobbies, museums, and shopping malls.

In Montréal, including Centre Eaton, 705 rue Ste-Catherine Ouest; Cours Mont-Royal, 1455 rue Peel; Les Promenades de la Cathédrale, corner of rue Université and rue Ste-Catherine Ouest; and Les Ailes de la Mode, 677 rue Ste-Catherine Ouest. There are public washrooms at La Baie department store, 585 rue Ste-Catherine Ouest.

In Québec City, the Tourist Information Centre, 12 rue Ste-Anne, has clean and spacious washrooms in the basement.

### Safety

Montréal is much safer than many U.S. cities of the same size. However, it does have its seedy parts, like around the red-light district on rue Ste-Catherine Est, between boulevard St-Laurent and rue St-Denis. It doesn't mean you can't go there, just stay alert to your surroundings and use the usual urban precautions that are part of city life.

Québec City, still under a million people, is a small town by comparison. The main guideline here is to avoid leaving valuable possessions in full view in your car. They're best "out-of-sight-out-of-mind" in a trunk.

### Smoking

As of May 31, 2006, smoking indoors in public places became illegal throughout Québec. Now, smokers have to go outside.

### Taxes

Canada's Goods and Services Tax (*Taxe de produits et services* or TPS in Québec) is 5 percent and applies to everything but alcoholic beverages. Québec's *Provincial Sales Tax* (TVQ) is 7.5 percent, calculated on the price plus the GST.

### Taxis

In Montréal, you'll find taxis lined up in front of downtown hotels and busy street corners. At all times, you can hail one passing by. You can also call a taxi company directly and usually have a ride within five to ten minutes. Two major companies are Taxi Co-op (☎ 514-725-9885) and Taxi Diamond (☎ 514-273-6331).

In Québec City, hailing a cab is somewhat more difficult; however, most businesses will be happy to call one for you. If you need to do so yourself, Québec City's two main taxi companies are Taxi Coop (☎ 418-525-5191) and Taxi Québec (☎ 418-525-8123).

### Telephone

Bell Canada operates the phone system in Québec. To get the operator, dial 0 (the operator will answer in both French and English). For information or directory assistance, call 411.

Pay phones require C50¢ for a local call, and you can use any combination of coins (except pennies). Pay phones are usually located in glass telephone booths on busy streets, in grocery stores, or in hotel lobbies. Shopping centers usually have pay phones near the restrooms.

### Time Zone

Montréal, Québec City, and the day-trip destinations mentioned in Chapter 14 are all in the eastern time zone. Daylight saving time is observed from late April through late October.

### Tipping

The standard for waiters is 15 percent. Cabbies seem to expect 10 percent, even if you don't have any luggage. For bellhops, tip C$1 or C$2 per bag. For hotel housekeeping, count C$1 per person per day. For valet parking, tip C$1 or C$2.

### Transit Information

In Montréal, call the STM (*Société de Transport de Montréal)* (☎ 514-786-4636) for information about the Métro, city buses, or parabuses for disabled passengers. For airport transportation, call L'Aérobus (☎ 514-842-2281).

Québec's transit authority is the RTC (☎ 418-627-2511).

# Toll-Free Numbers and Web Sites

## Airlines flying into Montréal

**Air Algérie**
☎ 888-905-0148
www.airalgerie.dz

**Air Canada**
☎ 888-247-2262
www.aircanada.ca

**Air France**
☎ 800-667-2747
www.airfrance.com

**American Airlines**
☎ 800-433-7300
www.aa.com

**British Airways**
☎ 800-247-9297
www.british-airways.com

**Continental**
☎ 800-231-0856
www.continental.com

**Czech Airlines**
☎ 800-561-5171
www.csa.cz

**Delta**
☎ 800-361-1970
www.delta.com

**KLM**
☎ 800-345-7458
www.klm.com

**Lufthansa**
☎ 800-345-7458
www.lufthansa.com

**Mexicana**
☎ 800-531-7923
www.mexicana.com

**Northwest**
☎ 800-345-7458
www.nwa.com

**Olympic Airlines**
☎ 514-878-9691
www.olympicairlines.com

**Royal Jordanian**
☎ 800-363-0711
www.rja.com/jo

**Royal Maroc Airlines**
☎ 800-361-7508
www.royalairmaroc.com

**Swiss International Air Lines**
☎ 877-359-7947
www.swiss.com

**Transaero**
☎ 514-284-4400
www.transaero.ru

**United**
☎ 800-241-6522
www.united.com

**US Airways**
☎ 800-432-9768
www.usairways.com

**WestJet**
☎ 888-937-8538
www.westjet.com

## Airlines flying into Québec City

**Air Canada**
☎ 888-247-2262
www.aircanada.ca

**Continental**
☎ 800-231-0856
www.continental.com

**Northwest**
☎ 800-345-7458
www.nwa.com

## Major hotel and motel chains

**Best Western International**
☎ 800-528-1234
www.bestwestern.com

**Clarion Hotels**
☎ 800-CLARION
www.clarionhotel.com

**Comfort Inns**
☎ 800-228-5150
www.hotelchoice.com

**Days Inn**
☎ 800-325-2525
www.daysinn.com

**Delta Hotels**
☎ 877-814-7706
www.deltahotels.com

**Econolodge**
☎ 877-424-6423
www.hotelchoice.com

**Fairmont Hotels**
☎ 800-257-7544
www.fairmont.com

**Gouverneur Hotels**
☎ 888-910-1111
www.gouverneur.com

**Hilton Hotels**
☎ 800-HILTONS
www.hilton.com

**Holiday Inn**
☎ 800-HOLIDAY
www.basshotels.com

**Howard Johnson**
☎ 800-654-2000
www.hojo.com

**Hyatt Hotels & Resorts**
☎ 800-228-9000
www.hyatt.com

**Marriott Hotels**
☎ 800-932-2198
www.marriott.com

**Novotel**
☎ 800-359-6279
www.novotel.com

**Radisson Hotels**
☎ 800-333-3333
www.radisson.com

**Ramada Inns**
☎ 800-2-RAMADA
www.ramada.com

**Sheraton**
☎ 800-325-3535
www.sheraton.com

**Travelodge**
☎ 800-255-3050
www.travelodge.com

**Wyndham Hotels and Resorts**
☎ 800-822-4200
www.wyndham.com

## Major car-rental agencies

**Avis**
☎ 800-831-2874
☎ 800-TRY-AVIS in Canada
www.avis.com

**Budget**
☎ 800-527-0700
www.budgetrentacar.com

**Discount**
☎ 800-263-2355
www.discountcar.com

**Dollar**
☎ 800-800-3665
www.dollar.com

**Hertz**
☎ 800-654-3131
www.hertz.com

**Sauvageau**
☎ 800-463-8800
www.sauvageau.qc.ca

**Thrifty**
☎ 800-847-4389
www.thrifty.com

# Where to Get More Information

## Local tourist information offices

I mention Montréal's and Québec City's main tourism offices throughout this book, but for a quick reference, I include them here as well: **Centre Infotouriste Montréal**, 1001 Square Dorchester (☎ 877-266-5687 or 514-873-2015; www.bonjourquebec.com); **Tourist Information Centre of Old Montréal**, 174 rue Notre-Dame Est (www.tourisme-montreal.org); **Centre Infotouriste Québec City**, 12 rue Ste-Anne (☎ 877-266-5687; www.bonjourquebec.com); **Greater Québec Area Tourism and Convention Bureau** (Québec City), 835 av. Laurier (☎ 418-649-2608; www.quebecregion.com). Also for the **Québec City's 400th**, there's www.monquebec2008.com.

## Newspapers and magazines

You can find up-to-the-minute listings of shows, exhibitions, and concerts by visiting the free Web sites of the following English-language publications in Montréal: the *Hour* (www.hour.ca), the *Mirror* (www.montreal mirror.com), and the *Montréal Gazette* (www.montrealgazette.com). *Nightlife Magazine* is a bilingual publication with articles photos and a nightlife agenda (www.nightlifemagazine.ca).

## Other sources of information

Several Internet sites list shows, restaurants, and hotels and offer travel information. My favorites include **Made in MTL** (www.madeinmontreal.ca), **Martini Boys** (www.martiniboys.com), **MontréalPlus.ca** (english.montrealplus.ca), **Montréal Info** (www.montrealinfo.com), **Ville de Montréal** (www.ville.montreal.qc.ca), **Design Montréal** (www.commercedesignmontreal.qc.ca), **QuébecPlus.ca** (www.quebecplus.ca), and **QuébecWeb** (www.quebecweb.com/tourisme).

To find the address or phone number of an establishment not listed in this book, try www.canada411.com, the online version of the phone books.

If you need to check transit information before you leave home, you can find it by visiting the following Web sites: **Access to Travel** (www.accesstotravel.gc.ca), **Montréal transit** (www.stm.info), **Québec City transit** (www.rtcquebec.ca), **Jean Lesage International Airport in Québec City** (www.aeroportdequebec.com), and **Montréal-Trudeau Airport** (www.admtl.com). Weather information sources are **Environment Canada** (www.ec.gc.ca) or **The Weather Network** (www.theweathernetwork.com).

# Index

See also separate Accommodations and Restaurant indexes at the end of this index.

### • O •

### • P •

## *Restaurant Index, Québec City*

## SPORTS, FITNESS, PARENTING, RELIGION & SPIRITUALITY

0-7645-5146-9

0-7645-5418-2

**Also available:**
- The Bible For Dummies
  0-7645-5296-1
- Buddhism For Dummies
  0-7645-5359-3
- Catholicism For Dummies
  0-7645-5391-7
- Curling For Dummies
  1-894413-30-X
- Pilates For Dummies
  0-7645-5397-6
- Rugby For Dummies
  0-470-83405-6
- Teaching Kids to Read For
  Dummies 0-7645-4043-2
- Weight Training For Dumm
  0-7645-5168-X

## TRAVEL

0-470-83398-X

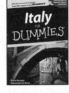

0-7645-5453-0

**Also available:**
- Alaska For Dummies
  0-7645-1761-9
- Cancun and the Yucatan For
  Dummies 0-7645-2437-2
- Cruise Vacations For Dummies
  0-7645-6941-4
- Europe For Dummies
  0-7645-5456-5
- Ireland For Dummies
  0-7645-5455-7
- Las Vegas For Dummies
  0-7645-5448-4
- London For Dummies
  0-7645-4277-X
- New York City For Dummie
  0-7645-6945-7
- Paris For Dummies
  0-7645-5494-8
- Walt Disney World & Orlan
  For Dummies 0-7645-6943

## NETWORKING, SECURITY, PROGRAMMING & DATABASES

0-7645-3910-8

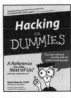

0-7645-5784-X

**Also available:**
- A+ Certification For Dummies
  0-7645-4187-0
- Access 2003 All-in-One Desk
  Reference For Dummies
  0-7645-3988-4
- Beginning Programming For
  Dummies 0-7645-4997-9
- C++ For Dummies
  0-7645-6852-3
- C For Dummies 0-7645-7068-4
- Firewalls For Dummies
  0-7645-4048-3
- Home Networking For
  Dummies 0-7645-4279-6
- Network Security For
  Dummies 0-7645-1679-5
- Networking For Dummies
  0-7645-1677-9
- TCP/IP For Dummies
  0-7645-1760-0
- VBA For Dummies
  0-7645-3989-2
- Wireless All-in-One Desk
  Reference For Dummies
  0-7645-7496-5

## HEALTH & SELF-HELP

0-470-83370-X

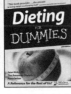

0-7645-4149-8

**Also available:**
- Alzheimer's For Dummies
  0-7645-3899-3
- Asthma For Dummies
  0-7645-4233-8
- Controlling Cholesterol For
  Dummies 0-7645-5440-9
- Depression For Dummies
  0-7645-3900-0
- Fertility For Dummies
  0-7645-2549-2
- Fibromyalgia For Dummies
  0-7645-5441-7
- Improving Your Memory Fe
  Dummies 0-7645-5435-2
- Pregnancy For Dummies
  0-7645-4483-7
- Quitting Smoking For
  Dummies 0-7645-2629-4
- Relationships For Dummie
  0-7645-5384-4
- Thyroid For Dummies
  0-7645-5385-2

## EDUCATION, HISTORY & REFERENCE

0-470-83656-3

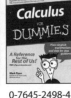

0-7645-2498-4

**Also available:**
- Algebra For Dummies
  0-7645-5325-9
- British History For Dummies
  0-7645-7021-8
- English Grammar For
  Dummies 0-7645-5322-4
- Forensics For Dummies
  0-7645-5580-4
- Italian For Dummies
  0-7645-5196-5
- Latin For Dummies
  0-7645-5431-X
- Science Fair Projects For
  Dummies 0-7645-5460-3
- Spanish For Dummies
  0-7645-5194-9
- U.S. History For Dummies
  0-7645-5249-X